BUSINESS STATISTICS

Dr. P.K. Mathur
(M.Phil., Ph.D., PGDBM)
Surya School of Planning Mgt. Tech., Lucknow.

Ashutosh Bajpal
(M.B.A., Ph.D.)
IISE, Lucknow.

M.P. Singh
(M.Phil., M.B.A., Ph.D.)
TMITM, Moradabad.

Himalaya Publishing House
ISO 9001:2008 CERTIFIED

First Edition : 2011
Reprint : 2017

Published by : Mrs. Meena Pandey for **Himalaya Publishing House Pvt. Ltd.,**
"Ramdoot", Dr. Bhalerao Marg, Girgaon, Mumbai - 400 004.
Phone: 022-23860170, 23863863; **Fax:** 022-23877178
E-mail: himpub@vsnl.com; **Website:** www.himpub.com

Branch Offices :

New Delhi : "Pooja Apartments", 4-B, Murari Lal Street, Ansari Road, Darya Ganj, New Delhi - 110 002. Phone: 011-23270392, 23278631; Fax: 011-23256286

Nagpur : Kundanlal Chandak Industrial Estate, Ghat Road, Nagpur - 440 018. Phone: 0712-2738731, 3296733; Telefax: 0712-2721216

Bengaluru : Plot No. 91-33, 2nd Main Road Seshadripuram, Behind Nataraja Theatre, Bengaluru - 560 020. Phone: 080-41138821; Mobile: 09379847017, 09379847005

Hyderabad : No. 3-4-184, Lingampally, Beside Raghavendra Swamy Matham, Kachiguda, Hyderabad - 500 027. Phone: 040-27560041, 27550139

Chennai : New No. 48/2, Old No. 28/2, Ground Floor, Sarangapani Street, T. Nagar, Chennai - 600 012. Mobile: 09380460419

Pune : First Floor, "Laksha" Apartments, No. 527, Mehunpura, Shaniwarpeth (Near Prabhat Theatre), Pune - 411 030. Phone: 020-24496323, 24496333; Mobile: 09370579333

Lucknow : House No. 731, Shekhupura Colony, Near B.D. Convent School, Aliganj, Lucknow - 226 022. Phone: 0522-4012353; Mobile: 09307501549

Ahmedabad : 114, "SHAIL", 1st Floor, Opp. Madhu Sudan House, C.G. Road, Navrang Pura, Ahmedabad - 380 009. Phone: 079-26560126; Mobile: 09377088847

Ernakulam : 39/176 (New No. 60/251), 1st Floor, Karikkamuri Road, Ernakulam, Kochi - 682 011. Phone: 0484-2378012, 2378016; Mobile: 09387122121

Bhubaneswar : 5, Station Square, Bhubaneswar - 751 001 (Odisha). Phone: 0674-2532129; Mobile: 09338746007

Kolkata : 108/4, Beliaghata Main Road, Near ID Hospital, Opp. SBI Bank, Kolkata - 700 010. Phone: 033-32449649; Mobile: 07439040301

Printed by : Shri Krishna Offset Press, Delhi. On behalf of HPH.

Dedicated
to
Our Parents

PREFACE

The Book "Business Statistics" has been written to meet the requirement of the students of M.B.A., B.B.A., B.M.S., B.Com, P.G. D.B.M. and other courses.

With great pleasure we wish to express our sincere regards and deep sense of gratitude to **Prof. B.LBajpai**, Ex-Head, Department of Business Administration, Faculty of Commerce, Lucknow University and **Prof. A. Chatterji**, Head, Department of Commerce, Lucknow University, for their kind patronage and help. We also owe debt of gratitude to **Prof. Niraj Kumar,** Ex-Head, Department of Business Administration, Lucknow University, for his kind and invaluable help and inspiration throughout the completion of the book.

We are specially indebted to Prof. Yaesesh Singh Director (SSPEM, Lucknow) and Shri Aproova Verma, Chairman IISE, Lucknow, who has always been a source of encouragement to us and Dr. S.B. Mishra (Head, Deptt. of Maths, M.L.K.P.G. College, Balrampur).

The authors also wish to express their thanks to Shri M.C. Pandey and Shri Bacchan Ji & Kaushal Yadav as well as all the Himalaya Publishing House Team

Finally we are grateful to Almighty God.

Authors

ACKNOWLEDGMENT

List of Professors, Recommended This Book

Prof. Sanjay Medhavi,	Lucknow University
Prof. J.K.Sharma,	Lucknow University
Prof. Ajay Kumar,	Lucknow University
Prof. Ajay Prakash (Director)	IILM, Lucknow
Dr. A.K. Garg (Director)	TMIMT, Moradabad
Dr. Manjula Jain (Director)	IFTM, Moradabad
Dr. Suvigya Awashthi (Director)	MIT-CM, Moradabad
Dr. Mohd. Hussain (Director)	Azad Institute, Lucknow
Prof. Mukul Gupta (Director)	SITM, Unnao
Prof. (Dr.) Haider (Director)	GITM, Lucknow
Dr. Rajeev Sharma (Director)	RBS, Agra
Dr. (Prof.) R.P.Dubey (Director)	DCET Business School, Lucknow
Dr. Anurag Srivastava,	DCET Business School, Lucknow
Dr. Y.P.Singh,	IISE, Lucknow
Prof. Ajay Kumar Gupta,	DCET Business School, Lucknow
Prof. Avishkar Gupta,	Head,DCET Business School, Lucknow
Prof. Sanjay Shukla,	DCET Business School, Lucknow
Mr. Kshitiz Banarjee,	IISC, Lucknow
Prof. Naveen Upreti,	IISE, Lucknow
Prof. Satendra,	IISE, Lucknow
Prof. Vikas Prasad,	IISE, Lucknow
Prof. Manoj Kumar,	IISE, Lucknow
Dr. Surjit Victor,	SSPEM, Lucknow
Prof. Ashok Dhal	SSPEM, Lucknow
Prof. Vinay,	SITM, Unnao
Dr. Pavanesh,	IILM, Lucknow
Prof. K.K.Mishra,	SITM, Barabanki
Dr. Ajay,	SRIMT, Lucknow
Dr. Shishir Srivastava,	GITM, Lucknow
Dr. Dharmendra singh,	SMS, Lucknow
Dr. Praveen Srivastava,	BIET Jhanshi
Dr. Suman Yadav,	BIET Jhanshi
Prof. Anil Singh,	GLA, mathura

Prof. S.K.Malhotra,	Lucknow
Prof. Bobby Lyall	SRCEM,
Prof. Rakesh Yadav	AIM, Ghaziabad
Dr. N.Y.Khan,	AIM, Ghaziabad
Dr. M.K.Rastogi,	NIEC, Lucknow
Dr. Purushottam Tripathi,	KCNIT, Banda
Prof. Bhagwan Singh,	RSMVT, Varanasi
Prof. Aman,	RSMVT, Varanasi
Prof. Amit,	Jaunpur
Prof. Laxamn,	IET, Sitapur
Prof. Vivekanand Pandey,	SCM, Lucknow
Prof. (Dr.)Anjani Kumar,	KRS, Gonda
Prof. Sunil Agrahari,	KRS, Gonda
Prof. Pankaj Sinha,	JBS, Faizabad
Prof. Ekta Singh,	JBS, Faizabad
Prof. (Dr.) Abhishek Srivastava,	DDITM, Kanpur
Prof. (Dr.) Anshuman Mishra,	Gorakhpur
Dr. Mushir Ahmad,	NIEC, Lucknow
Dr. Sushil Pandey,	NIEC, Lucknow
Mr. C.L. Tiwari,	MVIVT, Kaushambhi
Prof. Rajesh Srivastava	Sherwood, Barabanki
Dr. Dharmendra Vashney	Saroj ITM, Lucknow
Dr. Himanshu Rashtogi	Amity, University, Lucknow
Dr. Nimesh Singh	RITM, Lucknow
Dr. Vivek Mishra	RITM, Lucknow
Dr. Ranchay Bhateja	KIET, Ghaziabad
Ms. Mani Tyagi	KIET, Ghaziabad
Dr. Prabhat Pandey	MIET, Meerut
Prof. Rajeev Mishra	MPEC, Lucknow
Dr. Mohit Saxena	Lucknow
Prof. R.K. Prajapati	ICCMRT, Lucknow
Mr. Santosh Pathak	AXIS, Kanpur
Dr. Dipti Pandey	DBS, Lucknow
Mr. Sunil Kumar	BNCET, Lucknow
Dr. R.K. Pandey	NIEC, Lucknow
Dr. A.K. Dwivedi	NIEC, Lucknow
Dr. A.K. Srivastava	NIEC, Lucknow

CONTENTS

1 INTRODUCTION

1.1 Introduction

Statistics is a set of decision making techniques which helps businessmen in making suitable policies from the available data. In fact, every businessman needs a sound background of statistics as well as of mathematics. The purpose of statistics and mathematics is to manipulate, summarize and investigate data so that the useful decision making results can be executed. The term 'statistics' has been derived from the Latin word *'status'*, Italian word *'statista'* or German word *'statistik'*. All these words mean 'Political state'. In ancient days, the states were required to collect statistical data mainly for the number of youngmen so that they can be recruited in the Army. Also to calculate the total amount of land revenue that can be collected. Due to this reason, statistics is also called 'Political Arithmetic'.

Meaning of statistics

According to Bowley, "Statistics are numerical statements of facts in any department of enquiry placed in relation to each other."

According to Yule and Kendall,

"By statistics, we mean quantitative data affected to a marked extend by multiplicity of causes."

According to Horace Secrist,

"By statistics, we mean aggregate of facts affected to a marked extent by multiplicity of causes, numerically expressed, enumerated or estimated according to reasonable standards of accuracy, collected in a systematic manner for a pre-determined purpose and placed in relation to each other."

According to Croxton and Cowden

Statistics may be defined as the collection, presentation, analysis and interpretation of numerical data."

Uses of statistics and mathematics in business decision making :

(*a*) Uses of statistics in business **(M.B.A. Dec. 2003)**

The following are the main uses of statistics in various business activities:

(*i*) With the help of statistical methods, a quantitative information about production, sale, purchase, finance etc.; can be obtained. This type of information helps the businessmen in formulating suitable policies.

(*ii*) By using the techniques of time series analysis which are based on statistical methods, the businessman can predict the effect of a large number of variables with a fair degree of accuracy.

(*iii*) In business decision theory, most of the statistics techniques are used in taking a business decision which helps us in doing the business without uncertainty.

(*iv*) Now a days, a large part of modern business is being organised around systems of statistical analysis and control.

(*v*) By using 'Bayesian Decision Theory', the businessmen can select the optimal decisions for the direct evaluation of the payoff for each alternative course of action.

(*b*) Uses of mathematics for decision making : (M.B.A. June 2003)

(*i*) The number of defects in a roll of paper, bale of cloth, sheet of photographic film can be judged by means of Control Chart based on Normal distribution.

(*iii*) In statistical quality control, we analyse the data which are based on the principles involved in Normal curve.

(*c*) Uses of statistics in economics: Statistics is the basis of economics. The consumer's maximum satisfaction can be determined on the basis of data pertaining to income and expenditure. The various laws of demand depend on the data concerning price and quantity. The price of a commodity is well determined on the basis of data relating to its buyers, sellers etc.

Importance of statistics: Statistics in today life has become an essential part of various business activities which is clear from the following points:

(*a*) Importance of statistics in Business and Industry.

(M.B.A. May 2004, 2006)

In past days, decisions regarding business were made only on personal Judgments. However, these days, they are based on several mathematical and statistical techniques and the best decision is arrived by using all these techniques. For example, by using the testing hypothesis, we can reject or accept the null hypothesis which are based upon the assumption made from the population or universe.

By using 'Bayesian Decision Theory', or 'Decision Theory', we can select the optimal decisions for the direct evaluation of the payoff for each alternative course of action. Mathematics and statistics have become ingredients of various decisions problems which is clear from the following:

(*i*) **In selecting alternative course of action:** The process of business-decisions involve the selection of a single action among some set of alternative actions. When there are two or more than two alternative courses of action, and we need only one course of action, statistical decisions theory helps us in selecting the required course of action by applying Bayesian decision theory and thus saves lot of time.

(*ii*) **In removing uncertainty:** In decision making problems, uncertainty is very common in a situation, when the course of action is not known to us. When there are many possible outcomes of an event, we cannot predict with certainty that what will happen. By applying the concept of joint and conditional probability, the uncertainty about the event can be removed very easily.

(*iii*) **In calculating E.O.L, C.O.L. etc.:** In business, the opportunity loss is very often, which can be defined as the difference between the highest possible profit for an event and the actual profit obtained for the actual action taken. The expected opportunity loss

(E.O.L.) and conditional opportunity loss (C.O.L.) can be easily calculated by using the concept of maximum and minimum criteria of pay-off.

(*b*) Importance in the field of science and research: Statistics has great significance in the field of physical and natural sciences. It is widely used in verifying scientific laws and phenomenon. For example, to formulate standards of body temperature, pulse rate, blood pressure, etc. Success of modern computers depends on the conclusions drawn on the basis of statistics.

(*c*) Importance in the field of banking: In banking industry, the bankers have to relate demand deposits, time deposits, credit etc. It is on the basis of data relating to demand and time deposits that the bankers determine the credit policies. The credit policies are based on theory of probability.

1.2 History of Statistics

The science of statistics has assumed great importance in recent years. Today it has become an all-important science, without which no other science can progress. Modern age is the age of statistics and it can be correctly said that the extent of economic development of a country can be best known by finding out the extent to which statistical organization has developed there.

In India, the importance of statistics increased considerably after independence, with the start of the era of economic planning. In fact, economic planning cannot be imagined in the absence of statistical data.

Today, 'statistics' is a very commonly used word but surprisingly enough, it is understood by different people in different senses. To some, the word statistics connotes just a set of figures like the number of children born in India, in various months of a particular year and their sex. Some people think of statistics as something used to reinforce a qualitative statement. Thus, when someone says that the economic condition of the Indian masses has improved during the last five years, and gives the figures of rising per capita income during this period, he is using statistics to support a qualitative statement. To many others statistics means the representation of a phenomenon with the help of figures, charts, diagrams and pictograms, etc. There are many who think of statistics as a complex set of relationships between a number of variables and also as a technique by which they can reduce the element of uncertainty in their decision process. It is seen by many as a device to achieve a degree of precision in the concept and theories of social sciences which by nature are inexact.

However, if we analyze the way the word statistics is looked at, we find that broadly speaking there are two categories – one, in which the word refers to a set of figures and other in which it refers to a set of techniques and methods.

Therefore, in common parlance, the word statistics denotes some sort of numerical data. If, for example, somebody says that he has studied the statistics of man-hours lost by the Indian cotton mills due to strikes in the year 2002, or that he has seen the statistics of automobile accidents in the USA, he refers to the numerical figures or data relating to these phenomena. In this sense, statistics are numerical descriptions of the quantitative aspects of things. They take the form of counts or measurements. Statistics about the membership of a certain hostel, for example, include a count of the number of members of various kinds, as postgraduate or undergraduate or over and under 21 years of age. They might include such measurements as the weights and heights of the members, etc., or the ratio between weights and heights. *The use of the word statistics in this sense is always in plural.* However, any figure or set of figures cannot be called statistics irrespective of any other consideration. Many things have to be taken into account before using the word statistics for any group of figures. However, instead of using the word statistics in the above sense for indicating numerical facts, data is a more appropriate term.

The second sense in which the word statistics is used refers to the techniques and methods used in the collection, analysis and interpretation of data. In this sense, the word is used in singular.

Thus Statistics are numerical facts, but Statistics is also a body of methods for making decisions when there is uncertainty arising from the incompleteness or the instability of the information available. The decisions may be required to be taken either for the practical purpose of selecting a course of action or for the scientific purpose of gaining knowledge.

1.3 Definition of Statistics

The term statistics has been defined differently by different authors. Some authors have defined the word as used in the first sense (numerical data) while others have defined it as used in the second sense (the science).

Of the first type of definitions, the one given by Horace Secrist is the most exhaustive:

By statistics we mean aggregates of facts affected to a marked extent by multiplicity of causes numerically expressed, enumerated or estimated according to reasonable standards of accuracy, collected in a systematic manner for a pre-determined purpose and placed in relation to each other.

The above definition makes it clear that statistics (as numerical data) should possess the following characteristics:

(*i*) They should be aggregates of facts.
(*ii*) They should be affected to a marked extent by multiplicity of causes.
(*iii*) They should be numerically expressed.
(*iv*) They should be enumerated or estimated according to reasonable standards of accuracy.
(*v*) They should be collected in a systematic manner.
(*vi*) They should be collected for a predetermined purpose.
(*vii*) They should be placed in relation to each other.

Another definition of statistics states:

"Statistics are the classified facts representing the conditions of the people in a State ... specially those facts which can be stated in numbers or in tables of numbers or in any tabular or classified arrangement."

This definition is rather narrow, but it gives an idea about the origin of the term 'statistics.'

Of the second type of definitions of the term statistics (as statistical methods or the science of statistics), the one given by Seligman is very short and simple and yet quite comprehensive:

"Statistics is the science which deals with the methods of collecting, classifying, presenting, comparing and interpreting numerical data collected to throw some light on any sphere of enquiry."

According to Wallis and Roberts:

Statistics is a body of methods for making decisions in the face of uncertainty.

On the basis of the above definitions, we may evolve a comprehensive definition of statistics on our own:

Statistics (as used in the sense of data) are numerical statements of facts capable of analysis and interpretation and the science of statistics is a study of the principles and methods used in the collection, presentation, analysis and interpretation of numerical data in any sphere of enquiry.

1.4 Role of Statistics

Statistical methods are applicable to a very large number of fields. They are used in social sciences like economics, anthropology, sociology and psychology. Even professional disciplines like medicine, engineering and business rely heavily on statistical methods. Statistical methods are applied, to a limited extent, even in the realm of physical sciences which are by nature exact and experimental in character. In fact, statistical methods provide a set of tools that can be profitably used by professionals in different disciplines in the manner in which they deem fit.

Statistics is related to various other sciences and disciplines such as economics, mathematics, astronomy, biology, meteorology, etc. in fact the science of statistics is associated with all the other important sciences – both physical as well as social. Bowley has rightly said, "A knowledge of statistics is like a knowledge of a foreign language ... it may prove of use at any time under any circumstances."

Statistics finds use in economics, planning, commerce, business management, matters of governance, research, war, etc. It is useful for bankers, brokers and insurance companies also.

1.5 Application of Inferential Statistics in Managerial Decision-Making

Inferential Statistics: Inferential statistics is concerned with making inferences from samples about the populations from which they have been drawn. In other words, if we find a difference between two samples, we would like to know, is this a "real" difference (that is, is it present in the population) or just a "chance" difference (that is, it could just be the result of random sampling error). That's what tests of statistical significance are all about. Any inferred conclusion from a sample data to the population from which the sample is drawn must be expressed in a probabilistic term. Probability is the language and a measuring tool for uncertainty in our statistical conclusions.

Decision-making implies selecting the best alternative from among those available. Statistics can play a major role in analyzing the information available, on whose basis the various alternatives have to be compared. In order to bring about uniformity and consistency in their decisions, organizations need to remove subjectivity and introduce objectivity in the process of decision-making. Quantitative techniques in general, and among them, statistics can help in accomplishing this.

Since the complexity of business environment makes the process of decision-making difficult, the decision-maker cannot rely entirely upon his observation, experience or evaluation to make decision. Decisions have to be based upon data which show relationship, indicate trends, and show rates of change in various relevant variables. The field of statistics provides methods for collecting, presenting, analyzing and meaningfully interpreting data. Thus, the statistical methodology in collection, analysis and interpretation of data for better decision-making is a *sine qua non* for managerial decision-making and research in both physical and social sciences, particularly in business and economics.

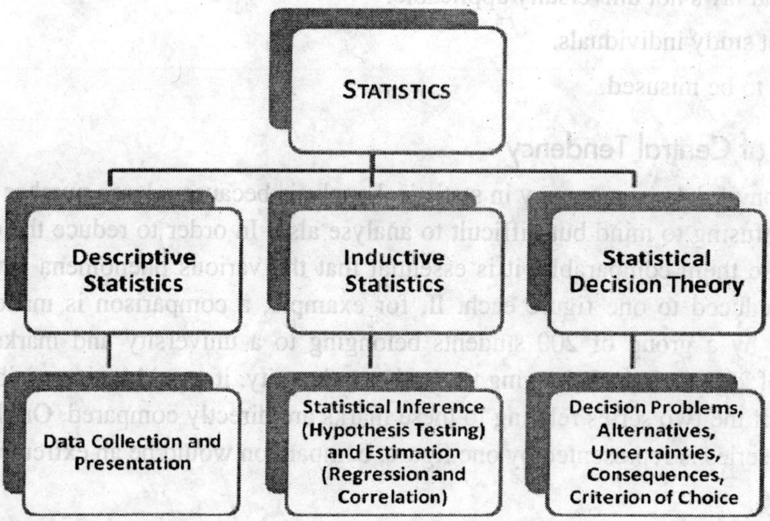

Statistical data constitute the basic raw material of statistical methods. These data are either readily available or collected by the analyst. The manager may face four types of situations:

(*i*) When data need to be presented in a form which helps in easy grasping;

(*ii*) Where no specific action is contemplated but it is intended to test some hypotheses and draw inferences;

(*iii*) When some unknown quantities have to be estimated or relationships established through observed data; and (*iv*) When a decision has to be made under uncertainty regarding a course of action to be followed.

While the first situation falls in the realm of descriptive statistics, second and third situations fall in the area of inductive statistics, and the last situation is dealt by statistical decision theory. Thus, descriptive statistics refers to the analysis and synthesis of data. Statistical decision theory concerns itself with establishment of rules and procedures for choosing one course from the alternative courses of action under situations of uncertainty.

Inductive statistics is concerned with the development of scientific criteria so that values of a group may be meaningfully estimated by examining only a small portion of that group. The group is known as 'population' or universe and the portion is known as 'sample.' Further, values in the sample are known as statistics and values in the population are known as parameters. Thus, inductive statistics is concerned with estimating universe parameters from the sample statistics. The term inductive statistics is derived from the inductive process which tries to arrive at information about the general (the universe) from the knowledge of the particular (the sample).

Limitations of Statistics

1. Does not study qualitative phenomena.
2. Does not reveal the entire story.
3. Statistical laws not universally applicable.
4. Does not study individuals.
5. Is liable to be misused.

1.6 Measures of Central Tendency

Condensation of data is necessary in statistical analysis because a large number of big figures are not only confusing to mind but difficult to analyse also. In order to reduce the complexity of data and to make them comparable, it is essential that the various phenomena which are being compared are reduced to one figure each. If, for example, a comparison is made between the marks obtained by a group of 200 students belonging to a university and marks obtained by another group of 200 students belonging to another university, it would be impossible to arrive at any conclusion if the two series relating to these marks are directly compared. On the other hand, if each of these series is represented by one figure, comparison would be an extremely easy affair.

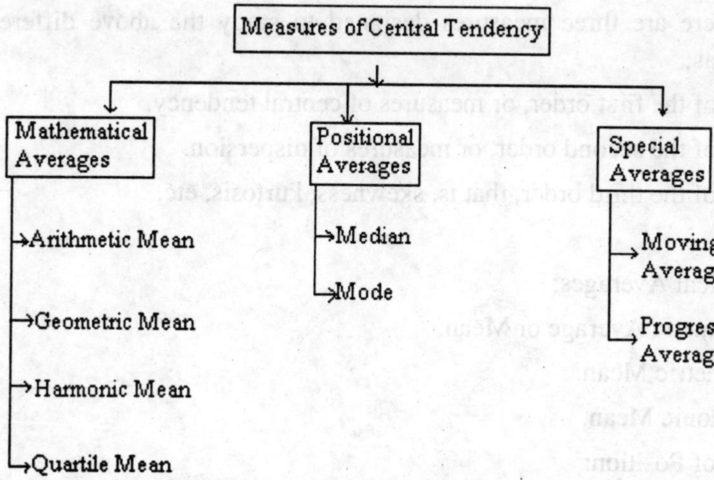

It is obvious that a figure which is used to represent a whole series should neither have the lowest value in the series nor the highest value but a value somewhere between these two limits, possibly in the centre, where most of the items of the series cluster. Such figures are called the measures of central tendency or averages. The average represents a whole series and as such, its value always lies between the minimum and maximum values and generally it is located near the centre or middle of the distribution.

The word average or the term measure of central tendency can be defined as a typical value around which other figures congregate.

Objectives of Averaging

(*i*) To get a single value which is representative of the characteristics of the entire mass of data.

(*ii*) To facilitate comparison.

Characteristics of a Good Average

(*i*) It should be rigidly defined.

(*ii*) It should be based on all the observations of the series.

(*iii*) It should be capable of further algebraic treatment.

(*iv*) It should be easy to calculate and simple to follow.

(*v*) It should not be affected by fluctuations of sampling.

Measures of Various Orders

Statistical series may differ from each other in the following three ways:

(*i*) They may differ in the values of the variable around which most of the items cluster.

(*ii*) They may differ in the extent to which items are dispersed around the central value.

(*iii*) They may differ in the extent of departure from a normal distribution.

Accordingly, there are three measures designed to study the above differences. They are respectively known as:

(*i*) Measures of the first order, or measures of central tendency.

(*ii*) Measures of the second order, or measures of dispersion.

(*iii*) Measures of the third order, that is, skewness, kurtosis, etc.

Types of Averages

(*a*) Mathematical Averages:

1. Arithmetic Average or Mean.
2. Geometric Mean.
3. Harmonic Mean.

(*b*) Averages of Position:

1. Median.
2. Mode.

Besides these there are some less important averages like the quadratic mean. There are also some averages which are mostly calculated by using the technique of the arithmetic average in a modified form. Examples of such averages are weighted average, moving average and progressive average. These find use in the analysis of commercial statistics and the utility of moving average is very great in the analysis of time series.

Of the above, mean, median and mode are the most popular ones, and we shall limit our discussion to these only.

1.7 Mean (Arithmetic Average)

Arithmetic average or mean of a series is the figure obtained by dividing the total values of the various items by their number.

Calculation of Mean in a Series of Individual Observations:

Direct Method:

$$\bar{X} = \frac{\Sigma X}{N}$$

Where

X = arithmetic average,

X = values of the variable,

$\sum$ = summation or total,

N = number of items.

Short-cut Method:

$$\bar{X} = A + \frac{\sum dx}{N}$$

Where

A = assumed mean,

$\sum dx$ = sum of deviations from assumed mean.

Calculation of Mean in a Discrete Series

Direct Method:

$$\bar{X} = \frac{\Sigma fX}{N} = \frac{\Sigma fX}{\Sigma f}$$

Where

$\sum fX$ = sum of products of X and corresponding frequencies

$\sum f$ = sum of frequencies

Short-cut Method:

$$\bar{X} = A + \frac{\sum fd_x}{N}$$

Where

$\sum fdx$ = sum of product of deviations from assumed mean and respective frequencies.

Step-Deviation Method:

$$\bar{X} = A + \frac{\sum fd_x}{N} \cdot \times i$$

Where

dx = deviations from assumed mean divided by a common factor,

i = the common factor.

Calculation of Mean in a Continuous Series

The process is the same as in case of a discrete series. The same formulae can be used after finding the mid-values of various classes. The method remains the same for both the exclusive as well as inclusive classes. Mean can also be calculated if class intervals are unequal. However, mean cannot be calculated in case of open-ended classes. (In such a situation, mean may be calculated by assuming the missing class limits.)

Direct method

$$\bar{X} = \frac{\sum_{i=1}^{N} f_i x_i}{\sum_{i=1}^{N} f_i} \qquad (\because N = \Sigma f)$$

Shortcut method:

$$\bar{X} = A + \frac{\Sigma fd_x}{N}$$

Step-deviation method:

$$\bar{X} = A + \frac{\Sigma fd_x}{N} \cdot \times i$$

Mathematical Properties of Mean

(*i*) The sum of the deviations of the items from the mean is always equal to zero.

(*ii*) The sum of squared deviations of the items from the mean is less than the sum of squared deviations of items from any other value.

(*iii*) If the mean values of two or more series are known individually, then the mean of the combined series formed by taking the observations of all these series together can be easily expressed in terms of the weighted average of the means of the component series.

(*iv*) The mean of all the sums (or differences) of corresponding observations in two series (with equal number of observations) is equal to the sum (or difference) of the means of the two series.

Merits of Mean

(*i*) It is rigidly defined.

(*ii*) It is based on all the observations of the series.

(*iii*) It is capable of further algebraic treatment.

(*iv*) It is simple to follow, and, arguably, it is also easy to calculate.

(*v*) It is least affected by fluctuations of sampling.

Drawbacks of Mean

(*i*) Sometimes abnormal items may considerably affect the value of mean.

(*ii*) It cannot be calculated if the exact values of all the observations are not known.

(*iii*) It is more difficult to calculate than median and mode.

(*iv*) It can have a value that does not even exist in the series.

(*v*) As a corollary to the above point, mean may sometimes give results that appear absurd. For instance, we may find that the average number of children in the families of a certain region is 3.4!

(*vi*) It may give fallacious conclusions. In such situations, measures of the second and third order may be needed to be calculated.

(*vii*) Mean has an upward bias, that is, it gives more importance to greater items of a series and less importance to smaller items.

Example 1:

(i) X : 10 15 12 9 6 8

X	$dX = X - A$
10	0
15	5
12	2
9	-1
6	-4
8	-2
	$\sum dx = 0$

$$A = 10$$

$$dX = X - A$$

$$\bar{X} = A + \frac{\sum dx}{N} = 10 + \frac{0}{6} = 10$$

(ii) Step deviation method $\bar{X} = A + \frac{\sum dx}{N} \times i$ A = Assumed mean

dx = deviation from $X, dx' = \frac{dx}{i}$

i = class interval

Example 2: X : 150 120 140 190 170

X	$dx = X - A$	$dx' = dx/10$
150	10	1
120	-20	- 2
140	0	0
190	50	5
170	30	3
		$\sum dx' = 7$

Say A = 140, i = 10

$$\bar{X} = A + \frac{\sum Dx'}{N} \times i = 140 + \frac{7}{5} \times 10 = 140 + 14 = 154$$

Discrete/Continuous Series

Direct methods:

If $x_1, x_2 ......x_n$ occur with respective frequencies $f_1, f_2, f_3 ......f_n$, the Arithmetic Mean

$$\bar{X} = \frac{\sum_{i=1}^{n} f_i x_i}{\sum_{i=1}^{n} f_i}$$

where $\bar{X}$ = Arithmetic mean

f_i = frequencies

$x_i \rightarrow$ variable or mid points of class interval frequency

N = Total Number of frequencies in the series.

Example 3:

X	20	30	40	50	60	70
No. of students	8	12	20	10	6	4

X	*dx = X - A*	*dx' = dx/10*
20	8	160
30	12	360
40	20	800
50	10	500
60	6	360
70	4	280
	$N = 60$	$\sum fx = 2460$

$$\bar{X} = \frac{2460}{60} = 41.$$

Short Cut Method

$$\bar{X} = A + \frac{\sum fd}{N}$$

where X = Arithmetic mean

d = Deviations as (X- A).

$\sum fd$ = Sum of product of d with their respective frequencies

N = Number of frequencies in the series

A = Assumed mean.

Example 4: *Calculate mean under short-cut method and step deviation method of the above statement.*

Solution:

x	*f*	*dx*	*fdx*	*dx'=dx/10*	*fdx'*
20	8	-30	-240	-3	-24
30	12	-20	-240	-2	-24
40	20	-10	-200	-1	-20
50	10	0	0	0	0
60	6	10	60	1	6
70	4	20	80	7	8
	$N = 60$		$\sum fdx = -540$		$\sum fdx' = 54$

$$A = 50, \bar{X} = \frac{\sum dx}{N} = 50 + \frac{-540}{60} = 50 - 9 = 41.$$

$$\bar{X} = A + \frac{\sum dx'}{N} \times i$$

A = Assumed mean, dx = deviation from X

dx' = dx/i, i where = class interval

$$\bar{X} = 50 + \frac{-54}{50} \times 10 = 50 - 9 = 41$$

Example 5: *Calculate the mean using different methods*

x :	0-10	10-20	20-30	30-40	40-50	50-60
f :	5	10	25	30	20	10

Solution:

x	f	m	fm	dx	$dx' = dx/10$	fdx	fdx'
0-10	5	5	25	-20	-2	-100	-10
10-20	10	15	150	-10	-1	-100	-10
20-30	25	25	625	0	0	0	0
30-40	30	35	1050	10	1	300	30
40-50	20	45	900	20	2	400	40
50-60	10	55	550	30	3	300	30
	$N = 100$		3300			800	80

(*i*) $\bar{X}$ under direct method

$$\bar{X} = \frac{3300}{100} = 33$$

(*ii*) $\bar{X}$ short-cut method

$$\bar{X} = 25 + \frac{800}{100} 25 + 8 = 33$$

(*iii*) $\bar{X}$ under step deviation method

$$\bar{X} = 25 + \frac{80}{100} \times 10 = 25 + 8 = 33.$$

Example 6: *Find mean of the following data.*

Marks	below 10	10-30	30-60	60-100	100-150	above 150
No. of Students	4	7	10	16	8	2

Solution: In the above statement, the difference between two variables are differ by 10, 20, the last difference between two variables is 60 because the previous difference is 50.

x	f	m	ds	dx'	fdx'
0-10	4	5	-40	-8	-32
10-30	7	20	-25	-5	-35
30-60	10	45	0	0	0
60-100	16	80	35	7	112
100-150	8	125	80	16	128
150-210	2	180	135	27	54
	$N = 100$				$\Sigma fdx = 227$

$$\bar{X} = A + \frac{\Sigma fdx'}{N} \times i$$

$$= 45 + \frac{227}{47} \times 5 = 69.149$$

Note: It is regarded essential to convert all other types of series into exclusive type, otherwise we will proceed to a wrong result.

Example 7:

Class Interval	4-6	7-9	10-12	13-15	16-18	19-21	22-24
Frequency	1	3	7	15	11	3	2

Solution:

x	3.5-6.5	6.5-9.5	9.5-12.5	12.5-15.5	15.5-18.5	18.5-21.5	21.5-24.5	Total
f	1	3	7	15	11	3	2	42
m	5	8	11	14	17	20	23	
fm	5	24	77	210	187	60	46	609

$$\bar{X} = \frac{\Sigma fm}{N} = \frac{609}{42} = 14.5$$

Note: 'm' is mid-point of class interval and treated as '*x*'.

Example 8:

X	*F*
0-2	1
2-5	2
5-6	6
6-8	2
8-10	3
10-20	6
20-21	1
21-25	4

Solution: First, calculate the class intervals equal, the class intervals must be minimum 5 and maximum 12 or 13.

So now,

x	*f*	*m*	*fm*
0-5	3	2.5	7.5
5-10	11	7.5	82.5
10-15	3	12.5	37.5
15-20	3	17.5	52.5
20-25	5	22.5	112.5
	25		292.5

$$\bar{X} = \frac{\Sigma fm}{N} = \frac{292.5}{25}$$

$= 11.7$

Example 9: *Calculate average income from the following data:*

Class interval	0	1	2	3	4-7	8-11	12-16	17-19	20-27	28-37	38-47
Frequency	10	23	28	24	20	50	30	20	9	8	3

Solution:

As no common factor can be taken, direct method will be applied.

Class	*Mid-points X*		*F*
0	0	10	0
1	1	23	23
2	2	28	56
3	3	24	72
4-7	5.5	20	110
8-11	9.5	50	475
12-16	14	30	420
17-19	18	20	360
20-27	23.5	9	211.5
28-37	32.5	8	260
38-47	42.5	3	127.5
		N = 225	$\Sigma fx = 2115$

First, calculate the class intervals equal, the class intervals must be minimum 5 and maximum 12 or 13.

$$\bar{X} = \frac{\sum fm}{\sum f} = \frac{2115}{225} = 9.4$$

Example 10:

Less than X	50	60	70	80	90	100
F	3	11	34	59	72	80

Find means.

Solution:

The difference between two variables in class interval that is 10, so now

X	*F*	*m*	$d_m = n - 65$	*dm'*	*fdm'*
40-50	3	45	-20	-2	-6
50-60	8	55	-10	-1	-8
60-70	23	65	0	0	0
70-80	25	75	10	1	25
80-90	13	85	20	2	26
90-100	8	95	30	3	24
	N = 80				$\sum dm' = 61$

$$\bar{X} = A + \frac{\sum fm'}{N} \times i$$

$$= 65 + \frac{61}{80} \times 10 = 72.625$$

Example 11:

X	Above 40	50	60	70	80	90
F	80	77	69	46	21	8

Solution:

X	*F*	*m*	$d_m = n - 65$	*dm'*	*fdm'*
40-50	3	45	-20	-2	-6
50-60	8	55	-10	-1	-8
60-70	23	65	0	0	0
70-80	25	75	10	1	25
80-90	13	85	20	2	26
90-100	8	95	30	3	24
	N = 80				61

$$\bar{X} = A + \frac{\sum fdm'}{N} \times i \qquad 65 + \frac{61}{80} \times 10 = 72.625$$

Example 12: *From the following distribution of marks obtained by 50 students in quantitative methods. Calculate Arithmetic Mean:*

Marks	More than 10	20	30	40	50	60
No. of Students	50	46	40	20	10	03

Solution: The data is in cumulative form. Let us first convert it into simple frequency distribution. It is given that 50 students have marks over 10 and 46 over 20, the number of students having marks between 10-20 is 50 – 46 = 4. In the same manner, frequencies of 20 – 30, 30-40 can be computed.

Marks (x)	*f*	*m*	*dx*	*dx'*	*fdx'*
10-20	4	15	-20	-2	-8
20-30	6	25	-10	-1	-6
30-40	20	35	0	0	0
40-50	10	45	10	1	10
50-60	7	55	20	2	14
60-700	3	65	30	3	09
	$\sum f = 50$				$\sum fdx' = 19$

$$\bar{X} = A + \frac{\sum fdx'}{N} \times C.$$

$$= 35 + \frac{19}{50} \times 10$$

$$= 35 + 3.8 = 38.8$$

Example 13: *The mean wages of 100 workers per day was found to be Rs. 80, but later on it was found that the wages of two labourers, Rs. 93, were misread as Rs. 39 and Rs. 95, respectively. Find the correct mean wage per day.* **(U.P.T.U.)**

Solution: $N = 100, \bar{X} = 80$, Correct items = 93, 59 Incorrect items = 39,95

Now, $\Sigma X = N.\bar{X} = 100(80) = 8000$

Correct ΣX = Incorrect ΣX - wrong items + correct items

$= 8000 - (39 + 95) + (93 + 59)$

$= 8000 - 134 + 152 = 8018$

Correct $\bar{X} = \frac{\text{Correct } \bar{X}}{N} = \frac{8018}{100} = 80.18.$

Example 14: *The arithmetic mean of 50 terms was calculated as 30.2, but later on it was known that without increasing the number of terms, one term with a value of 36 was included twice. Find the correct mean.*

Solution:

Incorrect total $(\Sigma x) = 50 \times 30.2 = 1510$

Correct, $\Sigma x = 1510 - 36$ (Included twice) = 1474

Now, $\bar{X} = \frac{1474}{50} = 29.48$

Example 15: *The following table shows the frequency distribution of marks obtained by students in Economics.*

Marks	5-10	10-15	15-20	20-25	25-30	30-35	35-40
Frequency	1	8	18	36	20	10	7

On scrutiny, the following mistakes in calculation were revealed.

Students	A	B	C	D	E	F
Correct marks	41	23	36	16	33	21
Marks entered	36	28	34	6	17	26

Revise the frequency table and calculate the mean.

Solution:

Marks	*Frequency*	*Adjust +ve*	*Adjust-ve frequency*	*Adjusted*	*M*	*dx*	*dx'*	*fdx'*
5-10	1		1	0	7.5	-20	-4	0
10-15	8			8	12.5	-15	-3	-24
15-20	18	1	1	18	17.5	-10	-2	-36
20-25	36	1+1		38	22.5	-5	-1	-38
24-30	20		1+1	18	27.5	0	0	0
30-35	10	1	1	10	32.5	5	1	10
35-40	7	1	1	7	37.5	10	2	14
40-45	0	1		1	42.5	15	3	3
	N = 100	6	6	N = 100			$\sum fdx' = -71$	

$$\overline{X} = A + \frac{\sum fdx'}{N} \times i$$

$$= 27.5 + \frac{-71}{100} \times 5$$

$$= 23.95$$

Example 16: $\overline{X}$ *of* 40 *terms is* 30 *but two terms* 13 *and* 24 *were misread as* 22 *and* 48. *Find correct* $\overline{X}$ *if:*

(*a*) it is an individual series

(*b*) it is continuous series as:

(*i*) 10-15, 15-20, 20-25 ....

(*ii*) 10-20, 20-30, 30-40 ....

Solution:

$\overline{X}$ of 40 terms = 30

Total of 40 terms ($\sum X$) = 40 × 30 = 1200

(*a*) and (*b*) : it is an individual or discrete series case

(Incorrect) total = 12000

$$\text{Correct } \overline{X} = \frac{1167}{40} = 29.175$$

(*b*) If it is continuous series

(*i*) With class intervals 10-15, 15-20, 20-25

Incorrect			Correct		
Value	Class Interval	Middle value	Value	Class Interval	Middle Value
22	20-25	25	13	10-20	15
48	45-50	45	14	20-30	25

Correct total = 1200 + 15 + 25 – 25 – 45 = 110

$$\text{Correct } \overline{X} = \frac{1170}{40} = 29.25$$

Example 17: *Hundred students took a test. The result of those who secured less than 60% marks is given as:*

Marks	0-20	20-40	40-60
Students	16	24	40

If the average marks of the students were 50, find out the average marks for those who secured 6% or more marks. **(U.P.T.U.)**

Solution: Let N denote the students who secured less than 60% and N_2 the students who secured 60% or more marks.

Marks (*x*)	*f*	*m*	*fm*
0-20	16	10	160
20-40	24	30	720
40-60	40	50	2000
	N = 80		$\Sigma fm = 2880$

$$\overline{X}_1 = \frac{\Sigma fm}{N}$$

$$= \frac{2880}{80} = 36 \text{ marks}$$

Also, combined average $\overline{X}_{12} = 50$ marks

Total number of students = $N_1 + N_2 = 100$

∴ Number of students N_2 who got 60% or more marks = 20

Let average marks of those who secured 60% or more marks be $\overline{X}_2$

$$\overline{X}_{12} = \frac{N_1.\overline{X}_1 + N_2.\overline{X}_2}{N_1 + \overline{X}_2}$$

$$50 = \frac{80 \times 36 + 20N_1.\overline{X}_2}{80 + 20}$$

$$50(100) = 2880 + 20\overline{X}_2$$

$$20\overline{X}_2 = 5000 - 2880$$

$$\overline{X}_2 = \frac{2120}{20} = 106$$

∴ Mean marks of students who secured or more than 60% marks = 106.

Example 18: *Calculate missing frequency if* $\overline{X}$ = 28 *and assumed mean* = 25 *from the following data.*

x	0-10	10-20	20-30	30-40	40-50	50-60
F	12	18	27	4	17	6-

Solution:

x	*F*	*m*	*dx*	*dx'*	*fdx'*
0-10	12	5	-20	-2	-24
10-20	18	15	-10	-1	-18
20-30	27	25	0	0	0
30-40	A	35	10	1	A
40-50	17	45	20	2	34
50-60	6	55	30	3	18
	N = 80 + A				10 + A

$$\overline{X} = A + \frac{\Sigma fdx'}{N} \times i$$

$$28 = 25 + \frac{10 + A}{80 + A} \times 10$$

$$28 - 25 = \frac{100 + 10A}{80 + A}$$

$$240 + 3A = 100 + 10A$$

$$A = 20$$

Example 19: *The mean of the following series is 30.5, find missing figure.*

Marks	10	20	*x*	40	50
Students	8	10	20	15	7

Solution: We denote missing figure as x

Marks (x)	Students (f)	fx
10	8	80
20	10	200
x	20	20x
40	15	600
50	7	350
	N= 60	$\sum fx$ =1230 + 20x

$$A=\frac{\sum fx}{N}$$

$$30.5=\frac{1230+20x}{60}$$

$$1830=1230+20x \Rightarrow 20x=600 \Rightarrow x=30$$

Example 20: *Calculate the class interval if mean = 30 and assumed mean = 35.*

dx'	2	1	0	-1	-2	-3
f	10	20	30	25	10	5

Solution:

dx'	*f*	*fdx'*
2	10	20
1	20	20
0	30	0
-1	35	-25
-2	10	-20
-3	5	-15
	N= 100	$\sum fdx' = -20$

$$\bar{X}=\frac{\sum fdx'}{N}\times i$$

$$33=35+\frac{-20}{100}\times 10$$

$$dx=dx^{i=10}\times 10$$

$= 2 \times 10, 1 \times 10, 0 \times 10....$

$= 20, 10, 0, ...$

I[st] class intervals 5 – 5 to 5 + 5 = 0-10

IInd class intervals 15 – 5 to 15 + 5 = 10-20

IIIrd class intervals 25 – 5 to 25 + 5 = 20-30

IVth class intervals 35 – 5 to 35 + 5 = 30-40

V[th] class intervals 55 – 5 to 5 + 5 = 50-60

Example 21: *A train runs 25 km at a speed of 30 km per hr and another 50 km at a speed of 40 km per hr. Due to repairs of the track, it travels at a speed 10 kmh for 6 minutes, and finally covers the remaining distance of 24 km at a speed of 24 kmph. What is the average speed in kmph?*

Solution: Time taken in covering 25 km at a speed of 30 kmph = 50 minutes and so on. Therefore, taking the time taken as weights.

Speed in kmph (X)	Time taken n minutes (W)	WX
30	50	1500
40	75	3000
10	6	60
24	60	1440
	$\sum W = 191$	$\sum WX = 6000$

$$\text{Average Speed} = \frac{\sum wx}{\sum w} = \frac{6000}{191} = 31.41 \text{ kmph.}$$

Example 22: *From the results of the colleges X and Y, state which of them is better and why.*

	College A		College B	
Name of Exam.	**Appeared**	**Passed**	**Appeared**	**Passed**
M.A.	300	250	1000	800
M.Com	500	450	1200	950
B.A.	2000	1500	1000	700
B.Com.	1200	750	800	500
Total	4000	2950	4000	2950

(Q. Bank, U.P.T.U.)

Solution: Weighted Average Mean for College A.

Name of Exam.	Appeared W_1	Pass % age x_1	$W_1 X_1$
M.A.	300	$250/300 \times 100 = 83.3$	24990
M.Com.	500	$450/500 \times 100 = 90$	45000
B.A.	2000	$1500/2000 \times 100 = 75$	150000
B.Com.	1200	$750/1200 \times 100 = 62.5$	75000
	$\sum W_1 = 4000$		$\sum W_1 Z_1 = 294990$

Weighted average mean of College *A*

$$\bar{X}w = \frac{\sum W_1 X_1}{\sum W_1} = \frac{294990}{4000} = 73.78$$

Weighted average mean of College *B*

Name of Exam.	Appeared W_2	Pass % age (x_2)	$W_2 X_2$
M.A.	1000	$80/1000 \times 100 = 80$	80000
M.Com.	1200	$950/1200 \times 100 = 79.17$	95004
B.A.	1000	$700/1000 \times 100 = 70$	70000
B.Com.	800	$500/800 \times 100 = 62.5$	50000
	$\sum W_2 = 4000$		$\sum W_2 Z_2 = 295004$

$$\text{Weighted average mean of College } B = \frac{\sum W_2 X_2}{\sum W_2} = \frac{295004}{4000} = 73.751$$

Average pass percentage of college *B* > college *A*, so

College *B* is better.

Example 23: *A firm buys machinery worth Rs.* 2,00,000 *every year and writes off depreciation as given below :*

Types of machines	Cost Rs.	Depreciation on (Rate)
I	1200000	8%
II	600000	6%
III	200000	5%

Find the average depreciation rate per year.

Solution:

Now, arranging the data for 3 parts, we find

Types of machines	Cost (Rs.) (W)	Rate of Dep (X)	*Product WX*
I	1200000	8%	9600000
II	600000	6%	3600000
III	200000	5%	1000000
	$\Sigma W = 2000000$		$\Sigma WX = 14200000$

Calculation average depreciation rate:

$$\bar{X}w = \frac{\Sigma WX}{\Sigma W} = \frac{14200000}{2000000} = 7.1\%$$

Example 24: *The number* 3.2, 5.8, 7.9 *and* 4.5 *have frequencies x,* (x+2), (x – 3) *and* (x + 6), *respectively, if* 4.8%, *find the value of* x.

Solution:

x	f	fx	
3.2	x	$x\,(3.2)$	$= 3.2x$
5.8	$x + 2$	$5.8\,(x + 2)$	$= 5.8x + 11.6$
7.9	$x + 3$	$7.9\,(x - 3)$	$= 7.9x - 23.7$
4.5	$x + 6$	$4.5\,(x + 6)$	$= 4.5x + 27$
	$N = 4x + 5$		$\Sigma fx = 21.4x + 14.9$

As, $\quad \bar{X} = \dfrac{\Sigma fx}{N}$

$\therefore \quad 4.876 = \dfrac{21.4x + 14.9}{4x + 5}$

or, $\quad 4.876(4x + 5) = 21.4x + 14.9$

$$19.504x + 24.38 = 21.4x + 14.9$$

$$1.896x = 9.48$$

$$\bar{X} = \frac{9.480}{1.896} \Rightarrow X = 5.$$

Example 25: *The average salary of male employees in a firm was Rs. 520 and that of female was Rs. 420; the mean salary of all the employees was Rs. 500. Find the percentage of male and female employees.*

Solution: We represent by N_1 and N_2 the number of male and female employees in the concern and X_1 and X_2 represent, respectively, their average salary. We denote X_{12} as the average salary of all the workers in the firm.

$$\bar{X}_1 = 520, \bar{X}_2 = 420, \bar{X}_{12} = 500$$

$$\bar{X}_{12} = \frac{N_1\bar{X}_1 + N_2\bar{X}_2}{N_1 + N_2}$$

Putting the all value, we get

$$500 = \frac{520N_1 + 420N_2}{N_1 + N_2}$$

$$500N_1 - 520N_1 = 420N_2 - 500N_2$$

$$-20N_1 = -80N_2$$

$$\frac{N_1}{N_2} = \frac{80}{20} = \frac{4}{1}$$

$$N_1 : N_2 :: 4:1$$

Thus, the percentage of male employees in the firm is

$$\frac{4}{4+1} \times 100 = \frac{4}{5} \times 100 = 80\%$$

percentage of female = 100% - percentage of male

100% - 80% = 20%.

Example 26: *The pass result of* 40 *students who took up a class test is given below:*

Marks	4	5	6	7	8	9
No. of Students	8	10	9	6	4	3

If the average marks for all 50 *student were* 5, 16, *find out the average marks of the students who failed.*

Solution: Here,

Marks obtained by 40 students who passed:

Marks (x)	Frequency (f)	fx
4	8	32
5	10	50
6	9	54
7	6	42
8	4	32
9	3	27
	$N = 40$	$\sum fx = 237$

Total marks of all 50 students = 50 × 5.16 = 258

Total marks of 40 students who passed = 237

∴ Marks of the remaining 10 students = 258 – 237 = 21

Hence, the average marks of 10 students

$$\text{who failed} = \frac{21}{10} = 2.1 \text{ Marks.}$$

Example 27: *Marks obtained by a class of 20 students is as following. Find X using:*

(i) *class intervals*

(ii) *Whole data.*

Marks	0	1	2	3	4	5	6	7	8	9	Total
0-9	–	–	–	–	–	1	–	–	–	1	2
10-19	–	2	–	1	–	2	–	–	–	–	5
20-29	3	–	–	–	4	–	–	–	2	–	9
30-39	–	–	–	2	–	–	–	1	–	–	3
40-49	–	–	–	–	–	–	1	–	–	–	1

Solution:

(i) Using class intervals

Marks	m.p.(x)	f	dx'	fdx'
0-9	4.5	2	–2	–4
10-19	14.5	5	–1	–5
20-29	24.5	9	0	0
30-39	34.5	3	1	3
40-49	44.5	1	2	2
		$N = 20$		$\Sigma fdx' = -4$

Assumed mean = 24.5, *i.* = 10 because - .5 to 9.5 difference is 10

$$\bar{X} = A + \frac{\Sigma fdx'}{N} \times i$$

$$\bar{X} = 24.5 + \frac{-4}{20} \times 10 = 24.5 - 2 = 22.5$$

(ii) Using whole data

$$(0+5)\times 1 + (0+9)\times 1 + (10+1)\times 2 + (10+3)\times 1 + (10+5)\times 2 + (20+2)\times 3 +$$

$$\sum x = \frac{(20+5)\times 4+(20+8)\times 2+(30+3)\times 2+(30+7)\times 1+(40+6)\times 1}{20}$$

$$= \frac{5+9+22+13+30+66+100+56+66+37+46}{20} = \frac{450}{20} = 22.5$$

1.8 Median

Median is the value of the middle item of a series arranged in ascending or descending order of magnitude. As opposed to mean which is the mathematical average, median is the positional average. It divides the series into two equal parts, one containing items smaller than the median value and the other containing items greater than it. The value of the median is given by the value of the middle item, irrespective of all other values.

Calculation of Median

The calculation of median involves two steps:

(*i*) Finding the location of the middle item; and

(*ii*) Finding the value of this middle item.

The middle item in a series of individual observations and also in a discrete series is $\left(\frac{n+1}{2}\right)^{th}$ item, where n is the total number of observations. In case of a continuous series $\left(\frac{n}{2}\right)^{th}$ item is the middle term of the series.

Once the middle item is located, its value has to be found out. In a series of individual observations, if the total number of items is an odd figure, the value of the middle item is the median value. On the other hand, if the number of items is even, the median value is the average of the two items in the centre of the distribution.

Calculation of Median in a Series of Individual Observations/Discrete Series:

(*i*) Arrange the values in ascending or descending order of magnitude.

(*ii*) M = value of $\left(\frac{n+1}{2}\right)^{th}$ item

Calculation of Median in a Continuous Series:

(*i*) Arrange the values in ascending or descending order of magnitude.

(*ii*) Find the value of $\left(\frac{n}{2}\right)$ to identify the median class.

(*iii*) $M = L_1 + \frac{\frac{n}{2} - cf}{f} \times i$

where

M = median,

L_1 = lower class limit of median class,

L_2 = upper class limit of median class,

N = total number of observations,

cf = cumulative frequency of the class preceding the median class,

f = frequency of the median class,

i = class interval of the median class.

Merits of Median

(*i*) It is rigidly defined.

(*ii*) It is easily calculated (sometimes it can be located by mere visual inspection) and understood.

(*iii*) It is not affected by the values of the extreme items.

(*iv*) Even if all values are not known, median can be calculated.

(*v*) It gives best results in a study of those phenomena which are incapable of direct quantitative measurement, for example, intelligence.

Drawbacks of Median

(*i*) It may not be representative of the series in certain cases. This is specially so when there are wide variations between the values of different items.

(*ii*) It is not suitable for further algebraic treatment.

(*iii*) In case of continuous series, calculation of median requires interpolation which assumes that all the values of a class are evenly spread over the values in that particular class. (However, this drawback is also present in case of mean and mode.)

(*iv*) Median does not consider the values of all the items. Even if the values of some of the items are changed, the median may remain unchanged. (This is a drawback of mode also.)

(*v*) It is more likely to be affected by the fluctuations of sampling.

(*vi*) It cannot be calculated without rearranging the data in ascending or descending order.

Example 1: *Find the medium of following data:*

391, 384, 591, 407, 672, 522, 777, 753, 1490

Solution: First arrange in ascending order:

$$X = 384, 391, 407, 522, 591, 672, 753, 777, 1490$$

$$\text{Median} = \frac{(N+1)^{\text{th}}}{2} \text{ item}$$

$$= \frac{9+1}{2} = 5^{\text{th}} \text{ item}$$

So, Median = 591.

If even number, like number of items are 10

Then, $\frac{N=1}{2}=\frac{10+1}{2}=5.5 \text{ term}=\frac{5^{th}+6^{th}}{2}$

Example 2: *Find the median from the following data:*

Income	100	150	80	200	250	180
No. of Persons	12	13	8	10	3	15

Solution:

x	f	cf
80	8	8
100	12	20
150	13	33
180	15	48
200	10	58
250	3	61

Median $=\frac{N+1^{th}}{2}$ item $=\frac{61+1}{2}=3^{th}$

Just greater than 31 is 33, and corresponding variable is 150

Therefore, Median = 150

Example 3: *Find the value of median of following data:*

X	0-10	10-20	20-30	30-40	40-50
F	3	5	2	6	4

Solution:

x	f	cf
0-10	3	3
10-20	5	8
20-30	2	10
30-40	6	16
40-50	4	20

Median = $N/2$ = 20/2 = 10 lies 20-30

$$\text{Median} = 20 + \frac{10-8}{2} \times 10 \quad \text{item} = \frac{61+1}{2} = 3^{\text{th}}$$

$$= 20 + 10 = 30.$$

Example 4: *Calculate median from following data:*

Income (Rs.)	0-100	0-200	0-300	0-400	0-500	0-800	0-1200
No. of Workers	10	45	108	260	370	448	500

(U.P.T.U.)

Solution: Here, we will convert is first into exclusive form to get proper class-intervals and then proceed.

Given *C.I.*	*C.I.* (Exclusive from)	*f*	*cf*
0-100	0-100	10	10
0-200	100-200	45-10 = 35	45
0-300	200-300	108-45 = 63	108
0-400	300-400	260-108 = 152	260
0-500	400-500	370-260 = 110	370
0-800	500-800	448-370 = 78	448
0-1200	800-1200	500-448 = 52	500

$$N = \frac{500}{2} = 250, \text{ size } 300\text{-}400$$

$$L = 300; f = 152$$

$$cf = 108; i = 100$$

$$M = 300 + \frac{250-108}{152} \times 100$$

$$= 300 + \frac{14200}{152} = 300 + 93.42 = 393.42$$

Example 5: *Calculate the median for the following frequency distribution:*

Marks	No. of Students	Marks	No. of Students
45-50	10	20-25	31
40-45	15	15-20	24
35-40	26	10-15	15
30-35	30	5-10	7
25-30	42		

Solution: First, arrange the data in ascending order and then find out median.

Calculation of median

Marks (x)	f	Cf	Marks	f	Cf
5-10	7	07	35-50	25	175
10-15	15	22	40-45	15	190
15-20	24	46	45-50	10	200
20-25	31	77			
25-30	42	119		-	
30-35	30	149			

$$\text{Median} = \text{Size of } \frac{N^{th}}{2} \text{ item} = \frac{200}{2} = 100^{th} \text{ term}$$

Median lies in the class 25-30

$$\text{Median} = L_1 + \frac{\frac{N}{2} - cf}{f} \times i$$

$$L = 25, N/2 = 100 Cf = 77, f = 42, i = 5$$

$$\text{Median} = 25 + \frac{100 - 77}{42} \times 5$$

$$= 25 + 2.74 = 27.74$$

Example 6: *The following is the table which gives you the distribution of marks secured by source students in the examination:*

Marks	0-20	21-30	31-40	41-50	51-60	61-80	71-80
No. of Students	42	38	120	84	48	36	31

(U.P.T.V)/L.U.)

Find (i) Median marks (ii) The percentage of failure if the minimum for a pass is 35 marks.

Solution: We are to make the class-boundaries from the class-limits given and then to find the cumulative frequency.

Class Boundaries	f	cf
0.5-20.5	42	42
20.5-30.5	38	80
30.5-40.5	120	200
40.5-50.5	84	284
50.5-60.5	48	382
60.5-70.5	36	368
70.5-80.5	31	399
	$N = 399$	

Median = Value of $N/2^{th}$ item

Example 7: *Calculate the median from the following data:*

Value	*Frequency*	*Value*	*Frequency*
Less than 10	04	Less than 50	86
Less than 20	16	Less than 60	112
Less than 30	40	Less than 70	120
Less than 40	76	Less than 80	125

Solution: Since cumulative frequencies are given, first find the frequencies.

Value	*Frequency*	*cf*	*Value*	*Frequency*	*cf*
0-10	4	4	40-50	20	96
10-20	12	16	50-60	16	112
20-30	24	40	60-70	8	120
30-40	36	76	70-80	5	125

Median = Size of $N/2^{th}$ item = Size of 125/2 = 62.5^{th} item

Hence, median lies in the class 30-40

$$\text{Median} = L + \frac{\frac{N}{2} - Cf}{f} \times i$$

where $L = 3\text{–}, N/2 = 62.5, f = 36, cf = 40, i = 10$

$$\text{Median} = 30 + \frac{62.5 - 40}{36} \times 10 = 30 + 6.25 = 36.25$$

Missing Frequency

Example 8:

Median = 25, $N = 20$, find missing value **(L.U.)**

x	0-10	10-20	20-30	30-40	40-50	Total
f	3	x	5	y	2	20

Solution:

x	f	cf
0-10	3	3
10-20	x	$3 + x$
20-30	5	$8 + x$
30-40	y	$8 + x + y$
40-50	2	$10 + x + y$
	$N = 20$	

The given median is 25, it lies between 20 and 30

Now,

$$\text{Median} = L_1 + \frac{N/2 - cf}{F} \times i$$

$$25 = 20 + \frac{10-(3+x)}{5} \times 10$$

$$5 = \frac{7-x}{5} \times 10 \Rightarrow 5 = \frac{70-10x}{5} 5$$

$$25 = 70 - 10x$$

$$25 - 70 = 10x$$

$$-45 = -10x$$

$$x = 4.5$$

$$20 = 10 + x + y$$

$$10 = x + y$$

$$y = 10 - 4.5 = 5.5$$

$$x = 4.5$$

$y = 5.5$ Answer.

Example 9: *Compute median from the following data:*

Mid-value	Frequency	Mid-value	Frequency
115	6	165	60
125	25	175	38
135	48	185	22
145	72	195	03
155	116		

Solution: Since we are given the mid-values, we should find out the upper and lower limits of the various classes.

Class group	*f*	*cf*	Class group	*f*	*cf*
110-120	6	6	160-170	60	327
120-130	25	31	170-180	38	365
130-140	48	79	180-190	22	387
140-150	72	151	190-200	03	390
150-160	116	267			

Median = Size of $N/2$th item = size of 390/2 = 195th item.

Median lies in the class 150-160

$$\text{Median} = L + \frac{\frac{N}{2} - cf}{f} \times i$$

where, $L = 150$, $N/2 = 195$, $f = 116$, $cf = 151$, $i = 10$

$$\text{Median} = 150 + \frac{195 - 151}{116} \times 10 = 150 + 3.79 = 153.79$$

Example 10: *10% of the workers in a firm employing a total of 1,000 workers earn less than Rs. 5 per day, 200 earn between Rs. 5 and 9.99, 30% between Rs. 5 and 9.99, 30% between 10 and 14.99, 250 workers between 15 and 19.99 the rest Rs. 20 and the above.*

What is the median wages?

Solution: First, convert the given figure in a frequency distribution as follows :

Wages (Rs.)	No. of Workers (f)	cf
Below 5	1000 × 10/100 = 100	100
5-9.99	200	300
10-14.99	1000 × 30/100 = 300	600
15-19.99	250	850
20 and above	150	1000
	$N = 1000$	

$$\text{Median} = \text{Size of } \frac{N}{2} \text{ the item} = \text{Size of } \frac{1000}{2} = 500^{th} \text{ item.}$$

Median lies the class interval 10-14.99 but the real limit of this class 9.995-14.995

$$\text{Median} = L + \frac{\frac{N}{2} - cf}{f} \times i$$

where, $L = 9.995$, $N/2 = 500$, $cf = 300$, $f = 300$, $i = 5$

$$\text{Median} = 9.995 + \frac{50 - 300}{300} \times 5 = 9.995 + 3.333 = 13.328$$

Example 11: *The following table shows the age distribution.* **(U.P.T.U.)**

Age	Below 10	20	30	40	50	60	70	70 and above
No. of Persons	2	5		12	14	15	15.5	15.6

Find: (a) median (b) why is the median a more suitable measure of central tendency than the mean in the case?

Solution: Firstly, the series is converted into continuous series,

x	f	cf
0-10	2	2
10-20	3	5
20-30	4	9
30-40	3	12
40-50	2	14
50-60	1	15
60-70	0.5	15.5
70-80	0.1	15.6
	$N = 15.6$	

$$M_e = L_1 \frac{\frac{N}{2} - cf}{f} \times i$$

$$\text{Median} = 20 + \frac{7.8 - 5}{4} \times 10 = 20 + \frac{28}{4} = 27$$

1.9 Partition Value (Quartiles, Deciles, Percentiles)

Just as median is appositional average and **partitions** the series into two equal parts, similarly there are other positional values which divide a series into different number of equal parts. The most common of these partition or positional values (fractiles) are quartiles, deciles and percentiles.

Quartiles

The values which divide the given data into four equal parts are known as quartiles. Obviously, there will be three such values. The first quartile, which is also called the lower quartile and is represented by Q_1, covers the first 25% items of the series so that 75% of the items are greater than it. It divides the first half of the series into two equal parts. Similarly, the second quartile (Q_2) covers the first 50% items of the series and divides it into two equal parts (It is the same as median). The third quartile, also called the upper quartile (Q_3) covers the first 75% of the items of the series and divides the second half of the series into two equal parts. Before calculation of quartiles, as in the case of median, the series has to be arranged in ascending or descending order.

$$\boxed{Q_1 < Q_2 < Q_3}$$

$$Q_n = L_1 + \frac{\frac{nN}{4} - cf}{f} . i \qquad (n = 1, 2, 3)$$

Where

Q_n = n^{th} quartile,

cf = cumulative frequency of the class preceding n^{th} quartile class,

f = frequency of the nth quartile class,

i = class interval of the nth quartile class.

Deciles

The values which divide the given data into ten equal parts are known as deciles. There are nine deciles denoted by D_1, D_2, D_3, D_4, D_5, D_6, D_7, D_8, and D_9. The fifth decile (D_5)is equal to the median.

$$P_n = L_1 + \frac{\frac{nN}{100} - cf}{f} x i \qquad (n = 1,2,3,4,5,6,7,8,9)$$

Where

D_n = n^{th} decile,

cf = cumulative frequency of the class preceding n^{th} decile class,

f = frequency of the nth decile class,

i = class interval of the nth decile class.

Percentiles

The values that divide the given data into hundred equal parts are known as percentiles. There will therefore be ninety nine deciles denoted by P_1, P_2, P_3 ... P_{99}. The fiftieth percentile (P_{50}) is equal to the median.

$$P_n = L_1 + \frac{\frac{nN}{100} - cf}{f} x i \qquad (n = 1 - - - - 99)$$

Where

P_n = n^{th} percentile,

cf = cumulative frequency of the class preceding n^{th} percentile class,

f = frequency of the nth percentile class,

i = class interval of the nth percentile class.

Thus,

$$M = Q_2 = D_5 = P_{50}$$

$$Q_1 = P_{25}$$

$$Q_3 = P_{75}$$

Ogive (Locating Median Graphically)

Median, quartiles, deciles, percentiles, etc., can be obtained graphically in any one of the following two ways:

First Method:

(*i*) Draw an ogive (cumulative frequency curve) by 'less than' method.

(*ii*) Plot the values of the variable on the x-axis and the cumulated values (less than) on the y-axis.

(*iii*) Determine the position of the median value by the formula $\frac{N}{2}$.

(*iv*) Locate this value on y-axis and from this draw a line parallel to the base cutting the curve at a point. From this point of intersection draw a line parallel to the y-axis and the point where it cuts the x-axis or the base line is the median value.

The values of quartiles, deciles and percentiles, etc., can also be located in the same manner.

Second Method:

(*i*) Draw two ogives (one 'less than' and the other 'more than') from the data given.

(*ii*) From the point of intersection of these ogives draw a line parallel to y-axis. It would be a perpendicular on x-axis. The point where this perpendicular touches the x-axis or the base line gives the value of the median.

	Quartile k = 1, 3	**Deciles** k = 1, 2, ...9	**Percentile** k = 1, 2, 3, ...99
Individual Series	$Q_k = \frac{k(N+1)^{th}}{4}$	$D_k = \frac{k(N+1)^{th}}{10}$	$P_k = \frac{k(N+1)^{th}}{100}$
Discrete Series	$Q_k = \frac{k(N+1)^{th}}{4}$	$D_k = \frac{k(N+1)^{th}}{10}$	$P_k = \frac{k(N+1)^{th}}{100}$
Continuous Series	$Q_k = l + \frac{\frac{kN}{4} - cf}{f} \times i$	$Q_k = l + \frac{\frac{kN}{10} - cf}{f} \times i$	$P_k = l + \frac{\frac{kN}{100} - cf}{f} \times i$

Example 1: *Calculate the lower and upper Quartile, third Deciles and Percentile from the following data :*

Central Value	2.5	7.5	12.5	17.5	22.5
Frequency	7	18	25	30	20

Solution: Since we are given mid-point, we will first find the lower and upper limits of the various classes. The method for finding out these limits is to take the difference between the two central values, divide it by 2, deduct the values so obtained from lower limits and add it to upper limits in the given case. The first class shall be 0.5, 5-10 and so on.

Class group	*f*	*cf*
0-5	7	7
5-10	18	25
10-15	25	50
15-20	30	80
20-25	20	100

Q_1 = size of $N/4^{th}$ item = 100/4 = 25th item

Q_1 = lies in the class 5-10

$$\boxed{Q_1 = L_1 + \frac{N/4 - c.f}{f} \times i}$$

where $L_1 = 5, N/4 = 25, c.f = 7, f = 18, i = 5$

$$Q_1 5 + \frac{25-7}{18} \times 5 = 5 + 10$$

Q_1 = 15-20

∴ $$\boxed{Q_3 = L_1 + \frac{3N/4 - c.f}{f} \times i}$$ where, $3N/4 = 75$, $cf = 50$

$$Q_3 = 15 + \frac{75-50}{30} \times 5 = 15 + 4.16 = 19.16$$

$$D_3 = \text{size of } \frac{3N}{10} th \text{ item} = \frac{3 \times 100}{10} = 30^{th} \text{ item}$$

D_3 lies in class

$$D_3 = L_1 + \frac{\frac{30N}{10} - cf}{f} \times i$$

where $L_1 = 10$, $3N/10 = 30$, $c.f. = 25, f = 25, i = 5$

$$D_3 = 10 + \frac{30-25}{25} \times 5 = 10 + 1 = 11$$

$$P_{20} = \text{Size of } 20\ N/100^{th} \text{ item} = \frac{20}{100} \times 100 = 20^{th} \text{ item}$$

$$= 5 + 3.61 = 8.61$$

Example 2: *Find percentage of the students of a class getting marks (i) above* 46 *(ii) between* 26 *and* 66 *(iii) if* 60% *students pass this test, find minimum marks prescribed to pass the test.*

Marks	0-10	10-20	20-30	30-40	40-50	50-60	60-70	70-80
No. of Students	20	45	85	160	70	55	35	30

Solution:

x	*f*	*cf*
0-10	20	20
10-20	45	65
20-30	85	150
30-40	160	310
40-50	70	380
50-60	55	435
60-70	35	470
70-80	30	500
	500	

(i) No. of students above 46 marks =

$$= 28 + 55 + 35 + 30 = 148$$

(*ii*) In this case, minimum marks to pass the test are X, then (100-160) = 40% students get marks below X. So, if we find P_{40}, it should be equal to *x*.

Now, N_1 for $P_{40}(N/100) =$

$$P_{40} = L_1 + \frac{N_1 - cf}{f} \times 1$$

$$= 30 + \frac{200-150}{160} \times 1 = 33.31 \text{ or } 33$$

The minimum marks to pass the test are 33.

Example 3: *Following is the distribution of marks obtained by 50 students in percentile law.*

Marks	More than 0	10	20	30	40	50
No. of Students	50	46	40	20	10	8

Calculate the median marks, if 60% of the students pass their test, find the minimum marks obtained by a pass candidate.

Solution: The above data can be written in the following form:

Marks	f	cf
0-10	4	4
10-20	6	10
20-30	20	30
30-40	10	40
40-50	7	47
50-60	3	50
	$N = 50$	

Since, $N/2 = 50/2 = 25$, the median class is 20 – 30.

Therefore, Median $= L_1 + \frac{N/2 - cf}{f} \times i$

$$= 20 + \frac{25-10}{20} \times 10 = 20 + \frac{150}{20} = 27.5 =$$

If 60% students pass, in order to find out the minimum marks obtained by a pass candidate, we have to calculate 40th percentile of the above distribution.

Since $40\left(\frac{N}{100} = 40 \times \frac{50}{100} = 20, P_{40}\right)$ lies in the class 20-30

Hence $P_{40} = L_1 + \frac{40N - cf}{} f \times i$

$$= 20 + \frac{20-10}{20} \times 10$$

$$= 20 + \frac{100}{20} = 20 + 5 = 25$$

Hence, minimum marks obtained by a pass candidate is 25.

1.10 Mode

Mode is the most typical or fashionable value of the series. It is the most common item of a series. It is generally the value which occurs the largest number of times in a series, that is, the value with the highest frequency. The mode of a distribution is the value at the point around which the items tend to be most heavily concentrated. At times, therefore, mode may not necessarily be the value which occurs the largest number of times in a series, as, in some cases, the point of maximum concentration may be around some other value. In some cases there may be more than one points of concentration of values and the series may be bi-modal or multi-modal.

Calculation of Mode in a Series of Individual Observations

A series of individual observations has to be converted into a discrete or continuous series for computation of mode.

Calculation of Mode in a Discrete Series

(*i*) Visual Inspection: The value with highest frequency is the mode.

(*ii*) Grouping Method: This method is adopted when a series is either bi-modal or multi-modal, or if high frequencies are concentrated around more than one item. This method helps in identifying the point of maximum concentration.

a. Arrange the values in ascending (or descending) order.

b. Add frequencies in two's.

- *i.* Add frequencies of item numbers 1 and 2, 3 and 4, ...
- *ii.* Add frequencies of item numbers 2 and 3, 4 and 5, ...

c. Add frequencies in three's.

- i. Add frequencies of item numbers 1, 2 and 3, 4, 5 and 6, ...
- ii. Add frequencies of item numbers 2, 3 and 4, 5, 6 and 7, ...
- iii. Add frequencies of item numbers 3, 4 and 5, 6, 7 and 8, ...

d. If necessary, add frequencies in four's and five's also.

e. The size of items containing the maximum frequencies in each case are noted down.

f. The item that has the maximum frequency the largest number of times is called the mode.

N.B.: In case of continuous series, grouping helps in identifying the modal class.

Calculation of Mode in a Continuous Series

$$Z = L_1 + \frac{f_1 - f_0}{2f_1 - f_0 - f_2} \times i$$

$$Z = L_2 + \frac{f_1 - f_0}{2f_1 - f_0 - f_2} \times i$$

Where

Z = mode,

L_1 = lower limit of modal class,

L_2 = upper limit of modal class,

f_0 = frequency of the class preceding modal class,

f_1 = frequency of the modal class,

f_2 = frequency of the class succeeding modal class,

i = class interval.

Histograms (Locating Mode Graphically)

The value of mode can be graphically determined in a frequency distribution. For this, the series has to be first represented by a histogram. After this, two lines are drawn diagonally inside the modal class in such a manner that they touch the upper corner of the modal bar and the upper corner of the adjacent bar. Then a perpendicular is drawn from the intersection of these lines to the x-axis. The point at which the perpendicular touches the x-axis gives the modal value.

Merits of Mode

(*i*) It is a very simple measure of central tendency. Often it can be calculated by mere visual inspection of the data.

(*ii*) It is commonly understood.

(*iii*) The values of mean and median can sometimes be not even be present in the series. But mode will always be present in the series.

(*iv*) Mode is normally not affected by extreme values.

(*v*) For determination of mode, it is not even necessary to know the values of all the items of the series.

Drawbacks of Mode

(*i*) It is ill-defined, indeterminate, indefinite.

(*ii*) It is not based on all the observations of the series.

(*iii*) It is not capable of further mathematical treatment.

(*iv*) It may be unrepresentative in many cases.

(*v*) In many cases, it may be impossible to get a definite value of mode.

Empirical Relationship between Mean, Median and Mode

In a symmetrical distribution, mean, median and mode are identical, that is, they have the same value. However, in actual life, most distributions are not symmetrical – they are skewed. In case of moderately skewed (or moderately asymmetrical) distributions, the value of the mean, median and mode have the following empirical relationship (given by Karl Pearson):

Mode = 3Median – 2 Mean

$$or\ Z = X - 3(X - M)\ i.e.$$

$$Z = 3M - 2X$$

Thus

$$X - M = \frac{1}{3}(X - Z)$$

We can see that the difference between mean and mode is three times the difference between mean and median. In other words, in moderately skewed distributions, median is closer to mean than mode. If we plot any frequency distribution in the form of a curve, mode (Z) touches the peak of the curve indicating maximum frequency, median (M) divides the area of the curve into two equal halves, and mean ($\bar{x}$) is the centre of gravity.

This relationship between the values of mean, median and mode is of great value. In cases where mode is ill-defined, or the series is bi-modal and mode cannot be calculated through the formula, this relationship can give us an empirical value of the mode.

Implications of Mean, Median and Mode

Mean: Arithmetic average or mean of a series is the figure obtained by dividing the total values of the various items by their number.

Median: As the name itself suggests, median is the value of the middle item of a series. It divides the series into two equal groups, one containing values less than the median and the other part containing values greater than it. It is a positional average.

Mode: It is the most fashionable value, or, more accurately, the value around which there is maximum concentration of items.

Example 1: *Discreet series (Direct method)*

y	2	4	6	8	10	12
f	3		8	1	3	2

Solution: The highest frequency is 8 therefore, the corresponding value 6 is the value of mode.

Continuous series (Direct method)

The formula of this series is

$$Z = L + \frac{f_1 - f_0}{2f_1 - f_0 - f_2} \times i$$

L_1 = lower value of class limit

f_1 = highest value of frequency

f_0 = preceding the value of highest frequency

f_2 = succeeding the value of highest frequency

i = difference between two variables

calculated in special circumstances when $2f_1 - f_0 - f_2 = 0$. Under such cases the above formula with all the symbols used as explained can be determined as:

$$\text{Mode} = L_1 + \frac{\Delta_1}{\Delta_1 + \Delta_2} \times i$$

where $\Delta_1 = |f_1 - f_0|$

$\Delta_2 = |f_1 - f_2|$

Example 2: *Find the value of mode of the following data:*

x	0-8	8-16	16-24	24-32	32-40
y	5	1	10	2	4

Find the value of mode

Solution:

x	f	cf
0-8	5	
8-16	1	f_0
16-24	10	f_1
24-32	2	f_2
32-40	4	

The highest value of frequency is 10 therefore mode lies between 16-24

$$Z = L_1 + \frac{f_1 - f_0}{2f_1 - f_0 - f_2}$$

$$Z = 16 + \frac{10-1}{2\times10-1-2}\times 8$$

$$= 16 + \frac{72}{17} = 20.24$$

Example 3: *Calculate the mode for the following distribution:*

Gross profit as % of sale	0-7	7-14	14-21	21-28	28-35	35-42	42-49
No. of co's	19	25	36	72	51	43	28

Solution: Here, the largest frequency is 72. It lies in the class 21-28, so the model class is 21-28 and the lower limit of the model class is 21. Thus

x	f	cf
0-7	19	
7-14	25	
14-21	36	f_0
21-28	72	f_1
28-35	51	f_2
35-42	43	
42-49	28	

$$\text{Mode} = L_1 + \frac{f_1 - f_0}{2f_1 - f_0 - f_2} \times i = 21 + \frac{722 - 36}{2 \times 72 - 36 - 51} \times 7$$

$$= 21 + 4.2 = 25.2$$

Example 4: *Grouping Method in Discrete series. (When question is silent)*

x	f
2	1
4	5
6	2
8	10
10	9
12	1
14	3
16	2

Find the value of mode.

Solution: In the question, the highest value of frequency is 10 and the succeeding value of that frequency is 9; if the difference is ≤ 3 then we apply grouping method.

x	f	(1+2) (II)	(2+3) (III)	(1+2+3) (IV	(2+3+4) (V)	(3+4+5) (VI)
2	1					
		6		8		
4	5		7		17	
6	2					
		12				21
8	10		19	20		
10	9				13	
		10				6
12	1		4			
14	3					
		5				
16	2					

Analysis table

X→	2	4	6	8	10	12	14	16
I				1				
II				1				
III			1	1				
IV				1	1			
V		1	1	1	1	1		
VI			1	1				
					1			
		1	3	6	3	1		

There highest frequency repeated is 6. Therefore, corresponding value 8 is mode.

Note: If value s more than one time, highest values are repeated then it means, that is a biomodel series, the formula of bi-model series is

Mode = 3 Median – 2 Mean

This is called *Empirical formula*

Example 5: *Calculate the median and mode (by grouping method) from the following data:*

Central size	15	25	35	45	55	65	75	83
Frequency	5	9	13	21	20	15	8	3

Solution: Firstly, central size (mid-point) converted into C.I.

Class groups	f	*m.p.*	$d = m - 55/10$	*fd*	*cf*
10-20	5	15	–4	–20	5
20-30	9	25	–3	–27	14
30-40	13	35	–2	–26	27
40-50	21	45	–1	–21	48
50-60	20	55	0	0	68
60-70	15	65	1	15	83
70-80	8	75	2	16	19
80-90	3	85	3	9	94
	$N = 94$			$\sum fd = -54$	

$$\text{Median} = \text{size of } \frac{N}{2} \text{th item } \frac{94}{2} = 47^{\text{th}} \text{ item}$$

Median lies in the class 40-50

$$\text{Median} = L + \frac{N - c.f}{f} \times i = 40 + \frac{47-27}{21} \times 10 = 40 + 9.524 = 49.524$$

Class groups	f	(1+2)	(2+3)	(1+2+3)	(2+3+4)	(3+4+5)
10-20	5	14		27		
20-30	9		22		43	
30-40	13	34				54
40-50	21		41			
50-60	20	35		56		
60-70	15		23		43	26
70-80	5	11				
80-90	8					

Analysis table

Group	Class interval	10-20	20-30	30-40	40-50	50-60	60-70	70-80	80-90
I					1				
II						1	1		

III					1	1	1		
IV					1	1			
V			1	1	1	1	1	1	
VI				1	1	1			
Total			1	3	5	5	3	1	

This series is bi-model series and hence we shall determine the mode by the indirect method

Mode = 3 Me – 2 Mean

$$\text{Mean} = A + \frac{\sum fx'}{N} \times i = 55 - \frac{54}{94} \times 10 = 55 - 5.745 = 49.255$$

Mode = 3(49.524) – 2 (49.55)

= 148.572 – 98.51 = 50.062

Example 6: *Find the value of mode of the following data:*

Weight	100-110	110-120	120-130	130-140	140-150	150-160	160-170	170-180
No. of Persons	4	6	20	32	33	17	8	2

Solution:

Weights	*No. of Persons*	**Col: 2 (1+2)**	**Col: 3 (2+3)**	**Col: 4 (1+2+3)**	**Col: 5 (2+3+4)**	**Col: 6 (3+4+5)**
100-110	4					
110-120	5	10		30		
120-130	20		26		58	
130-140	32	52				85
140-150	33		65	82		
150-160	17	50				
160-170	8	25			58	
170-180	2	10				

Analysis table

Weight	**100-110**	**110-120**	**120-130**	**130-140**	**140-150**	**150-160**	**160-170**	**170-180**
I					√			
II			√	√				
III				√	√			
IV				√	√	√		

V		√	√	√	√	√	√	
VI		`	√	√	√			
Total		1	3	5	5	2	1	

According to the above table, this is abi-model series hence, mode has to be determined by applying the formula: Mode = 3 median – 2 mean

Weights (1 hs) in	*M*	No. of Persons	*c.f*	*d=(m-135)*	*d'=(d/10)*	*fd'*
100-110	105	4	4	-30	-3	-12
110-120	115	6	10	-20	-2	-12
120-130	125	20	30	-10	-1	-20
130-140	135	32	62	0	0	0
140-150	145	33	95	0	1	33
150-160	155	17	112	10	2	34
160-170	165	8	120	30	3	24
170-180	175	2	122	40	4	8
Total		*N* = 122				$\sum fd' = 55$

$$\overline{X} = A + \frac{\sum fd}{N} \times i$$

where $A = 55, \sum fd' = 55, N = 122, i = 10$

$$\overline{X} = 135 + \frac{55}{122} \times 10$$

$$\overline{X} = 135 + 4.51 = 139.51$$

Median = Size of *N*/2th items = size of $\frac{122}{2} = 61^{st}$ item

Hence, median lies in the class 130-140

$$\text{Median} = L + \frac{N/2 - c.f}{f} \times i$$

Where $L = 130, N/2 = 61, c.f. = 30, f = 32, i = 10$

$$\text{Median} = 130 + \frac{61-30}{32} \times 10 = 130 + \frac{310}{32} = 139.69$$

Mode = 3 median – 2 mean

Median = (3 × 139.69) – (2 × 139.51) = 419.07 – 279.02

= 140.05

Hence, model weight 140.05 1bs.

Example 7: *Calculate the value of mode by usual formula.*

Class Interval	10-20	20-30	30-40	40-50	50-60	60-70	70-80	80-90	90-100	100-110
No. of Persons	4	6	5	10	20	22	24	6	2	1

Solution:

Class Interval	f	Col: 2 (1+2)	Col: 3 (2+3)	Col: 4 (1+2+3)	Col: 5 (2+3+4)	Col: 6 (3+4+5)
10-20	4	10		15		
20-30	6		11		21	35
30-40	5	15				
40-50	10		30	(52)		
50-60	$20 = f_0$	(42)			(66)	(52)
60-70	$22 = f_1$		(46)			
70-80	(24) $= f_2$	30		32	09	
90-100			8			
	6					
100-110		3				
	2					
	1					

Analysis table

Class Interval	10-20	20-30	30-40	40-50	50-60	60-70	70-80	80-90	90-100	100-110
C_1							√			
C_2					√	√				
C_3						√	√			
C_4						√				
C_5				√	√	√	√			
C_6					√	√	√	√		
Total				1	3	5	4	1		

Thus, mode lies between 60-70

$$\text{Mode} = L + \frac{\Delta_1}{\Delta_1 + \Delta_2}$$

where $\Delta_1 = | f_1 - f_0 | \Rightarrow | 22 - 20 | = 2$

and, $\Delta_2 = | f_1 - f_0 | \Rightarrow | 22 - 24 | = 2$

$$\text{Mode} = 60 + \frac{2}{2+2} \times 10$$

$$= 60 + 5 = 65$$

Note: It may be noted that in the above question the formula

$$Z = L_1 + \frac{f_1 - f_0}{2f_1 - f_0 - f_2} \times i \text{ fails because}$$

$$= 2f_1 - f_0 - f_2$$

$$= 2 \times 22 - 20 - 24 = 44 - 44 = 0$$

Example 8: *In the following wage distribution, the median and mode are Rs.* 33.5 *and Rs.* 34, *respectively, but three class frequencies are missing. Find out the missing frequency.* **(U.P.T.U.)**

Wages (Rs.)	0-10	10-20	20-30	30-40	40-50	50-60	60-70	Total
Frequency	4	16	–	–	–	6	4	230

Wages	f	cf
0-10	4	4
10-20	16	20
20-30	$x = f_0$	$20 + x$
30-40	$y = f_1$	$20 + x + y$
40-50	$z = f_2$	$20 + x + y + z$
50-60	6	$26 + x + y + z$
60-70	4	$30 + x + y + z$

Let the missing frequencies be *x, y, z* as recorded in the table.

Now, $N = x + y + z + 30 = 230$ (given)

$\therefore$ $x + y + z = 230\text{-}30 = 200$ ...(i)

Median is the value of $\frac{Nth}{2} = \frac{230th}{2} = 115^{\text{th}}$ item

$$\text{Median} = 33.5 \text{ (given)}$$

It lies in the class interval 30-40

Therefore, $$\text{median} = L_1 + \frac{\frac{N}{2} - c.f}{f} \times i$$

where, $L_1 = 30$, $N/2 = 115$, $c.f = 20 + x$, $f = y$, $i = 10$

$$33.5 = 30 + \frac{115 - (20 + x)}{y} \times 10$$

$$3.5 = \frac{95 - x}{y} \times 10$$

$$3.5y + 950 - 10x$$

or, $$3.5y + 10x = 950 \qquad \ldots\text{(ii)}$$

Now, mode is 34, lies between 30-40

$$\text{Mode} = L_1 + \frac{f_1 - f_0}{2f_1 - f_0 - f_2} \times i$$

where, Mode = 34, $L_1 = 30$, f_1 y, $f_0 = x$, $f_2 = z$, $i = 10$

$$x + y + z = 200$$

∴ $$z = 200 - x - y$$

$$34 = 30 + \frac{y - x}{2y - x - z} \times 10$$

$$34 - 30 = \frac{y - x}{2y - x - (200 - x - y)} \times 10$$

$$4 = \frac{10y - 10x}{2y - x - 200 + x + y}$$

$$12y - 800 = 10y - 10x$$

or, $$12y - 10y + 10x = 800$$

or, $$2y + 10x = 800$$

Subtracting eqn. (iii) from (ii), we get

$$1.5y = 150$$

$$y = 150/1.5 = 100$$

Putting the value of $y = 100$ in eqn. (ii), we get

$$3.5\ (100) + 10x = 950$$

$$350 + 10x = 950$$

$$10x = 950 - 350$$

$$10x = 950 - 350$$
$$10x = 600$$
$$x = 60$$

Putting the values of $y = 100$ and $x = 60$ in eqn. (i), we get

$$60 + 100 + z = 200$$
$$160 + z = 200$$
$$z = 200 - 160 = 40$$

Therefore, $x = 60, y = 100, z = 40$

1.11 Relationship among Mean, Median Mode

(L.U. & A.U.)

Mean, median and mode are the important measures of central tendency. There is a very close relationship between the three of them.

1. In a perfect mathematical distribution, the mean, median and mode will be the same. symbolically.

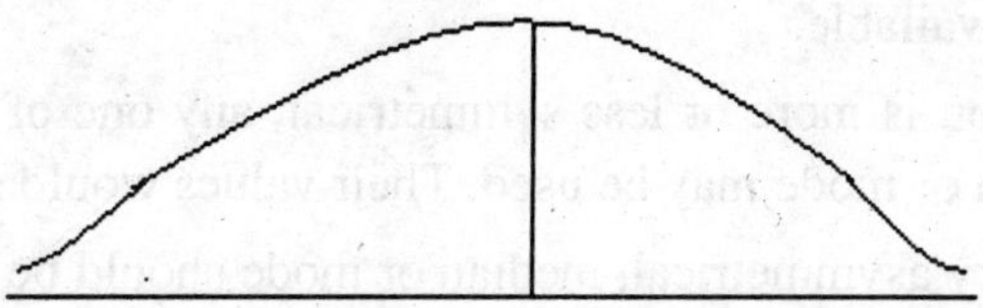

$\bar{X} = M = z$ Symmetrical

2. In a moderate distribution, the relationship between mean, median and mode can be shown through following points:

(i) The distribution is positively skewed when it shift to right.

Symbolically;

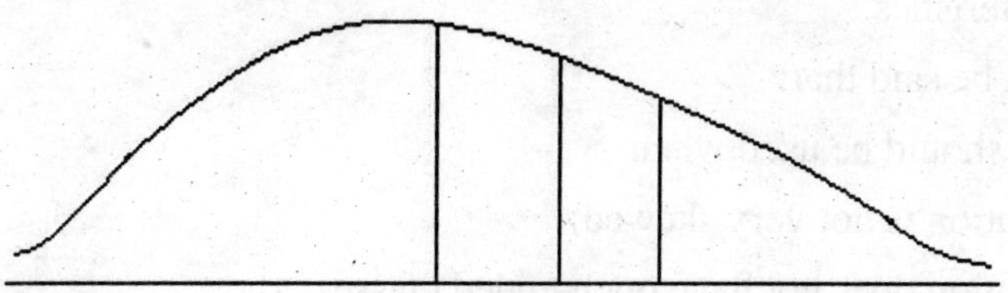

Positively skewed distribution

(ii) The distribution is negatively skewed when it shifts to left

Symbolically, $X < M < Z$

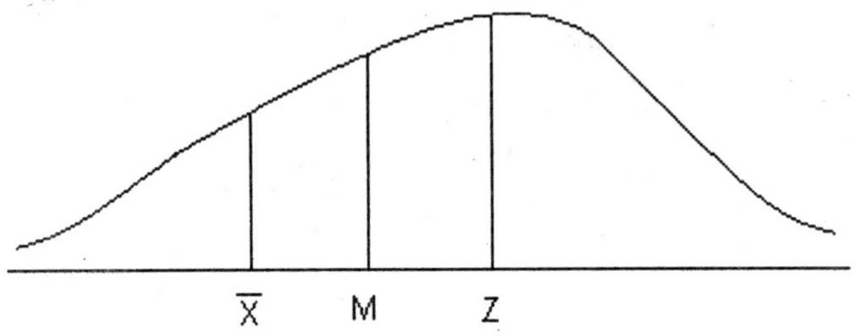

Negatively skewed distribution

1.12 Choice of an Average

The choice of an average should be made very cautiously, as, if a wrong average has been chosen, inaccurate conclusions are likely to follow. Selection of a particular average should be done after giving consideration to a number of points noted below:

(*i*) The object or purpose for which the average is being calculated.

(*ii*) Whether the average would be used for further statistical computations.

(*iii*) The nature of data available.

a. If the distribution is more or less symmetrical, any one of the three measures, that is, mean median or mode may be used. Their values would not differ much.

b. If the data is very asymmetrical, median or mode should be used instead of mean.

c. If the distribution has unequal class intervals, median should be used as it considers only the class interval of the median class. Mean can also be used in such cases. If it is necessary to calculate mode in such a situation, the series should be regrouped to get classes with equal intervals.

d. In case of any open ended classes, mean cannot be calculated, therefore median or mode should be used.

At times, it may be worthwhile to calculate more than one average and draw conclusions based on their characteristics.

To sum up, it can be said that:

Arithmetic Mean should be used when

(*a*) The distribution is not very skewed;

(*b*) The distribution does not have open-ended classes;

(*c*) When the distribution does not have very large and very small items.

Median should be used when we have open ended distribution and, more particularly, when plotted as a curve, the distribution is found to be of J-shape or reverse J-shape. In case of price or income distribution, median is the best average.

Mode should be used when we are dealing with qualitative data, and where we have to find the preferences of people. Consumer preferences are best studied with the help of mode. In some cases of discrete series like the average number of rooms in households or average size of shoe, mode is the only appropriate average.

Limitations of Averages

(1) Even the most judiciously chosen average will have its limitations. An average is a single figure representing a series, and no single figure can condense in itself all the properties of the items it represents. For instance, if the average height of a group of women is less than the average height of a group of men, it does not mean that no woman is taller than any man.

(2) An average may have a value which is not even present in the series.

(3) As a corollary to the above point, mean may sometimes give results that appear absurd. For instance, we may find that the average number of children in the families of a certain region is 3.4!

(4) Averages do not throw light on the formation of the series. The mean of 2, 3 and 55 is 20, and the mean of 19, 20 and 21 is also 20.

However, if wrong conclusions are drawn by the use of averages, it is not the fault of the averages. The fault lies with the person drawing the conclusions. The inherent limitations of averages should always be kept in mind and they should not be expected to reveal more than what they can.

1.13 Geometric Mean

Geometric mean is defined as the nth root of the product of *n* items. For example, if we have two items then we will take square root, if we take three items then we take cube root and so on. It can be calculated from following formula:

$$GM = \sqrt[n]{(X_1)\times(X_2)\times(X_3)\times.......X_n}$$

Where $x_1, x_2.....x_n$ = various items in a series

n = number of items

Properties of Geometric Mean

1. Geometric mean is defined as the nth root of the *n* items therefore the *n* the power of the GM is always equal to the product of all the *n* items.

Symbolically

$$GM = (X_1, X_2, X_3.....X_n)^{1/n}$$

$$G^n = X_1, X_2, X_3.....X_n$$

2. If the information of more than one group is given that is (GM_1 _ GM_2) and N_1, N_2 then we can calculate the combined geometric mean through following formula :

$$GM_{12} = \text{Antilog}\left(\frac{N_1 \log GM_1 + N_2 \log GM_2}{N_1 + N_2}\right)$$

3. If given number of items in more than two series are equal, then GM of the product of the corresponding items in the series is same as the product f GM of items.
4. The total of the deviations of the logs of the values from the log of the GM is always zero.
5. The geometric mean of the ratios of the corresponding items of two series with equal number of observation is equal to the ratio of geometric means.

In case of Individual Series

$$\log GM = \frac{\Sigma Log X}{N}$$

$$GM = \text{antilog } \frac{(\Sigma Log X)}{N}$$

Where CM = geometric mean.

$X_1, X_2, X_3.....X_n$ = various items of the series.

Example 1: *Calculate the Geometric Mean from the following data:*

x = 9 112 87 0.6 1.8 0.09 24.9

Solution:

Calculation of GM

x	Adjusted log x
9.0	0.9542
112.0	2.0492
87.0	1.9395
0.6	-0.2218
1.8	0.2553
0/09	- 1.0458
24.9	1.3962
	$\Sigma \log x = 5.3268$

$$GM = \text{anti log}\left[\frac{\Sigma \log x}{N}\right] = \text{anti log}\left[\frac{5.3268}{7}\right]$$

A.L [0.7609] = 5.766

(i) In case of Discrete Series

$$\text{Log GM} = \frac{\Sigma \log x}{N}$$

$$\text{GM} = \text{Antilog}\left[\frac{\Sigma f \log x}{N}\right]$$

where, GM = geometric mean.

Example 2: *Find the GM from the following data:*

x	3	6	12	12	15
y	7	8	9	6	5

Solution:

Calculation of GM

x	*f*	**log *x***	***f* log *x***
3	7	0.4771	3.3397
6	8	0.7782	6.2256
12	9	0.9594	8.6346
12	6	1.0792	6.4752
15	5	1.1761	5.8805

$$\text{GM} = \text{anti log.}\left[\frac{\Sigma f \log x}{\Sigma f}\right] = A.L.\left[\frac{30.5556}{35}\right]$$

Anti log. [0.8730] = 7.464

(ii) In case of Continuous Series

The following formula will be used in continuous series for calculation:

$$\text{GM} = \frac{\Sigma f \log x}{N}$$

or, $$\text{GM} = \text{antilog}\ \frac{\Sigma f \log m}{N}$$

where, GM = geometric mean.

m = mid-value of various class intervals

$\Sigma f \log$ m = sum of the product of the log m with their respective frequency.

n = No. of frequencies.

Combined Geometric Mean

Example 3: *Initially, the population of a town was 5,000. At first, it rose at the rate of 2% per annum for two years. What will be the population of the town after 5 years?*

Solution:

$$P_n = P_o\left[1+\frac{r}{100}\right]^n$$

$$P_n = 5000\left[1+\frac{2}{100}\right]^5$$

Taking log on both sides

$$\log x = \log 5000 + 5 \log 1.02$$

$$\log x = 3.6990 + 50\ (0.086)$$

$$x = \text{A.L. } [3.7420]$$

$$x = 5521.0$$

Example 4: *The population of a town was 10,000. At first, it increased at the rate of 3% per annum for the first population of the town after 5 years?*

Solution: We are given

$$P_0 = 10000, r = 0.03$$

$$r_0 = 0.02, n_1 = 3, n_2 = 2, P_n = ?$$

$$P_n = P_0(1+r_1^3 - (1-r_2)^2$$

$$P_n = 10000(1+0.03)^3(1-0.02)^2$$

$$P_n = 10000(1.03)^3(0.98)^2$$

$$P_n = 10000\times 1.0496 = 10496$$

Weighted G.M.

Example 5: *Find the weighted GM from the following data:*

x	7	8	9	10	11	12
y	3	1	5	4	6	2

Solution: Calculation of weighted GM:

x	*w*	**log *x***	***w* log *x***
7	3	0.8451	2.5353
8	1	0.9031	0.9031
9	5	0.9542	4.7710
10	4	1.0000	4.0000
11	6	1.0414	6.2484
12	2	1.0792	2.1584
	$\sum w = 21$		$\sum w \log = 20.6162$

$$\text{GM} = A.L.\left[\frac{\sum w \log x}{\sum w}\right] = A.L.\left[\frac{20.6162}{21}\right]$$

A.L. [0.9817] = 9.588

1.14 Harmonic Mean

Harmonic Mean (HM is defined as the reciprocal of the arithmetic average of the reciprocal of the value of various items. It can be solved through the following formula:

$$HM = \frac{N}{\frac{1}{X_1} + \frac{1}{X_2} + \ldots + \frac{1}{x_n}}$$

(i) In case of Individual Series

$$\text{HM reciprocal of} = \frac{\frac{1}{X_1} + \frac{1}{X_2} + \ldots + \frac{1}{x_n}}{N}$$

$$\therefore \quad HM = \frac{N}{\sum\left[\frac{1}{X}\right]}$$

Example 1: *Calculate the HM from the following data:*

x: 18 12 16 21 7 9

Solution: Calculation of HM:

x	Reciprocals $\left[\frac{1}{x}\right]$
18	0.0556
12	0.0833
6	0.1667
21	0.4762
7	0.1429
9	0.1111
	$\Sigma\left[\frac{1}{X}\right] = 1.0358$

$$HM = \frac{N}{\Sigma(1/x)} = \frac{6}{1.0358} = 5.7926$$

(ii) In case of Discrete Series

$$\text{HM} = \frac{N \text{ or } \Sigma f}{\Sigma\left(\frac{f}{x}\right)}$$

Example 2: *Calculate HM from the following data:*

Wages (x)	0-20	20-40	40-60	60-80	80-100
No. of Workers (f)	25	18	17	20	15

Solution:

Wages (x)	No. of Workers (f)	Mid-value (m)	f/x
0-20	25	10	2.5
20-40	18	30	0.6
40-60	17	50	0.34
60-80	20	70	0.29
80-100	15	90	0.17
	$\Sigma f = 95$		$\Sigma f/x = 3.9$

$$\text{H.M.} = \frac{\Sigma f}{\Sigma f} = \frac{95}{3.9} = 24.36$$

Comparative Study of Different Averages

Sl. No.	Particulars	Mean (A.M.)	Median	Mode	G.M.	H.M.
1.	Effect of extreme values	Badly affected	Unaffected	Unaffected	Slightly affected	Affected less than G.M.
2.	Algebraic treatment	Yes	No	No	Yes	Yes
3.	Relation	A.M. > G.M. > H.M.	Lies between Mean and Mode	No definite relation	A.M. > G.M. > H.M.	H.M. < G.M. < A.M.
4.	Inspection/Graphical estimation	No	Yes	Yes	No	No
5.	Sampling fluctuations	Least affected	Affected more than mean	Affected	Not much affected	Not affected very much
6.	Property	$\Sigma(x_i - \bar{x}) = 0$ $\Sigma(x_i - \bar{x})^2$ is minimum	$\Sigma(x_i - med.)$ minimum	-	$\Sigma(\log x_i - \log G.M.) = 0$	-
7.	Open-end classes	Indeterminate	Determinate	Determinate	Indeterminate	Indeterminate
8.	Calculation based on	All observations	Middle value (s)	Value with highest frequency	All observations	All observations
9.	Can be calculated and understood	Easily	Easily	With slight difficulty	With difficulty	With difficulty
10.	Rigidly defined	Yes	Yes	No	Yes	Yes
11.	Preference to data	All types	Where middle value is typical	Data of distinct central tendency	Ratios, rates percentages	Rates of reciprocal expression
12.	Qualitative measurements	No	Yes	Yes	–	–

1.15 Dispersion

(U.P.T.U.) (L.U.)

We have seen that the measures of central tendency have their own limitations. Often, they fail to reveal the entire story of a phenomenon. There may be a dozen series whose averages may be identical but which may differ from each other in several ways. Obviously, in such cases further statistical analysis of the data is necessary so that these differences between various series may also be studied.

Consider the following three series:

	Series A	Series B	Series C
	40	36	1
	40	37	9
	40	38	20
	40	39	30
	40	40	40
	40	41	50
	40	42	60
	40	43	70
	40	44	80
Total	360	360	360
Mean	40	40	40

In the first series, the mean is 40 and the values of all the items are identical. The items are not at all *scattered* and the mean fully discloses the characteristics of this distribution. In the second case, though the mean is again 40, yet all the items have different values. But the items are not very *scattered.* In this case also, the mean value is a good representative of the series. However, in the third series, although the mean is still 40, the values are *very widely scattered.* The mean is 40 times the smallest value and half of the maximum value. It therefore does not satisfactorily represent the individual items in this group. More importantly, no differentiation can be made between the above three series on the basis of mean alone. In order to have a deeper analysis of these three series, it is essential that we study something more than their central tendencies. We find that the *scatter* in the first case is nil, in the second case it is small, while in the third series the items are very *scattered.* It is evident from this example that a study of the extent of the *scatter* around an average should also be studied to throw more light on the composition of a series. The name given to this *scatter* is ***dispersion***.

Dispersion Defined

- Dispersion or spread is the degree of the scatter or variation of the variable about a central value.
- Measures of variability are usually used to indicate how tightly bunched the sample values are around the mean (or any other measure of central tendency).

Since for a precise study of dispersion we have to average deviations of the values of the various items, from their average, the various measures of dispersion are called ***averages of the second order***.

Dispersion or variation can be expressed either in terms of the original unit of a series or as an abstract figure like a ratio or percentage. These are known as ***absolute and relative dispersion*** respectively. In a comparison of variability of two or more series, relative dispersion should be taken into account.

Objects of Measuring Dispersion

(1) To judge the reliability of measures of central tendency.

(2) To make a comparative study of the variability of two series.

(3) To identify the causes of variability with a view to control it.

(4) To serve as a basis for further statistical analysis.

1.16 Measures of Dispersion

(U.P.T.U.) (L.U. & A.U.)

(1) Range;

(2) Inter Quartile Range;

(3) Semi-Inter Quartile Range (Quartile Deviation);

(4) Average Deviation (Mean Deviation);

(5) Standard Deviation or Root Mean Square (rms) Deviation;

(6) Lorenz Curve.

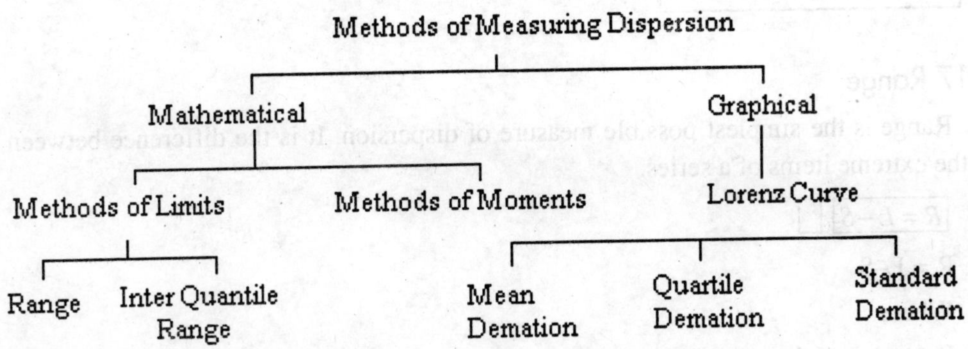

Of the above, the first three are positional measures. Fourth and fifth are algebraic measures or calculation measures. The last one is a graphic method. We shall limit our discussion to range, mean deviation and standard deviation.

Properties of a Good Measure of Dispersion

These are the same as the properties of a good measure of central tendency. These are:

(*i*) A good measure of dispersion should be rigidly defined.

(*ii*) It should be based on all the observations of the series.

(*iii*) It should be capable of further algebraic treatment.

(*iv*) It should be simple to calculate and easy to follow.

(*v*) It should not be affected by fluctuations of sampling.

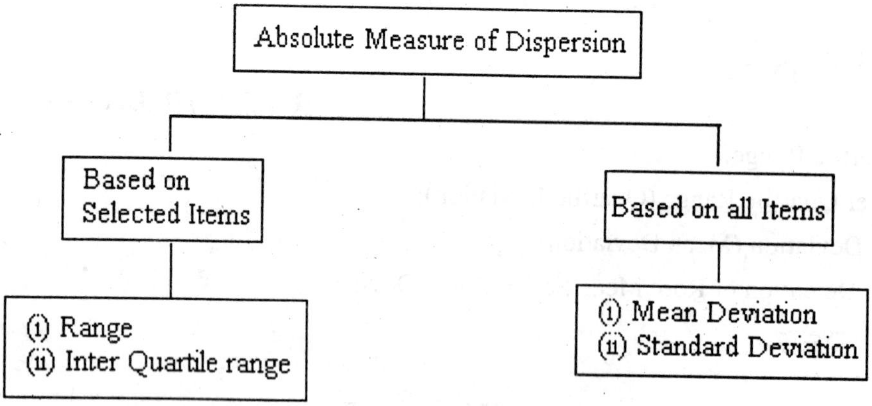

1.17 Range

Range is the simplest possible measure of dispersion. It is the difference between the values of the extreme items of a series.

$\boxed{R = L - S}$

R = L–S

Where

L = value of the greatest item of the series,

S = value of the lowest item of the series.

$$\text{Ratio of Range/Coefficient of Scatter} = \frac{L-S}{L+S}$$

In case of continuous series range is calculated by any one of the following two methods:

(*i*) By subtracting the lower limit of the lowest class from the upper limit of the highest class.

(*ii*) By subtracting the mid-value of the lowest class from mid-value of the highest class.

Merits

(*i*) It is rigidly defined.

(*ii*) It is easy to calculate and simple to follow.

Demerits

(*i*) It is greatly affected by the fluctuations of sampling.

(*ii*) It is not based on all the observations of the series.

(*iii*) It cannot be used in case of open-ended distributions.

Uses of Range

(*i*) Quality control.

(*ii*) Variation in money rates, share values, exchange rates and gold prices, etc.

(*iii*) Weather forecasting.

Example 1: *The marks obtained by* 6 *students were* 24, 12, 16, 11, 40 *and* 42. *Find range and co-efficient of range.*

Solution:

Here, maximum marks = 42

Minimum marks = 11

Range = 42 – 11 = 31 marks

$$\text{Co-efficient of range} = \frac{L-S}{L+S}$$

$$= \frac{41-11}{42+11} = \frac{31}{53} = 0.585$$

Discrete Series

In the discrete series, the frequencies are ignored and the importance is only of x-axis. In this series the value of range is also highest values minus lowest value.

Example 2: *Find the range and coefficient of range*

x	2	4	6	8	10	12	14
f	1	5	7	3	2	6	1

Solution: In the above series, the highest value is of x-axis and, is 14 and lowest value of x-axis is . But the frequencies are ignored.

$$\therefore \quad \text{Range} = L - S$$

$$= 14 - 2 = 12$$

$$\text{Co-efficient of range} = \frac{L-S}{L+S}$$

$$=\frac{14-2}{14+2}=\frac{12}{16}=0.75$$

Example 3: *Find the range and co-efficient of range.*

x	4	8	12	16	20	24	28
f	3	1	5	4	6	2	8

Solution: Going through the variable,

Highest value of $x = 28$

Lowest value of $x = 4$

$$\text{Range} = L - S$$

$$= 28 - 4 = 24$$

$$\text{Co-efficient of range} = \frac{L-S}{L+S}$$

$$=\frac{28-4}{28+4}=\frac{24}{32}=0.75$$

Example 4: *Compute range and coefficient of range*

x	2	4	6	8	10	12	14	16

Solution: In the above series the highest value is 8 and lowest value is -6.

Now,

$$\text{Range} = L - S$$

$$= 16 - 2 = 14$$

$$\text{Co-efficient of range} = \frac{L-S}{L+S}$$

$$=\frac{16-2}{16+2}=\frac{14}{18}=0.778$$

Example 5: *Find the range and coefficient of range from the following series:*

x	5-10	10-15	15-20	20-25	25-30
f	8	7	1	10	6

Solution: Here, highest value is 30 and lowest value is 5.

$$\text{Range} = L - S$$

$$= 30 - 5 = 25$$

$$\text{Co-efficient of range} = \frac{L-S}{L+S}$$

$$= \frac{30-5}{30+5} = \frac{25}{35} = 0.714$$

Example 6: *Find the range and co-efficient of range.*

x	1-6	6-10	10-15	15-20	20-30
f	10	6	2	9	8

Solution:

$$\text{Range} = L - S$$

$$= 30 - 1 = 29$$

$$\text{Co-efficient of range} = \frac{L-S}{L+S}$$

$$= \frac{30-1}{30+1} = \frac{29}{31} = 0.935$$

Example 7: *Following data compute inter-quartile range, quartile deviation and co-efficient f quartile deviation.* **(U.P.T.U.)**

x	23	6	10	8	16	2	19	13	3	21	26

Solution: Arranging the series in ascending order

x	2	3	6	8	10	13	16	19	21	23	26

Here, $N = 11$

$$Q_1 = \text{Size of} \left(\frac{N+1}{4}\right)^{th} \text{item} = \text{Size of} \left(\frac{14+1}{4}\right)^{th} \text{item}$$

$$= \text{Size of } 3^{rd} \text{ term} = 6$$

$$Q_1 = \text{Size of } 3\left(\frac{N+1}{4}\right)^{th} = 3\left(\frac{14+1}{4}\right)^{th} \text{item}$$

$$= \text{Size of } 9^{th} \text{ term} = 21$$

$$\text{Inter-quartile range} = Q_3 - Q_1 = 21 - 6 = 15$$

$$\text{Quartile deviation} = \frac{Q_3 = Q_1}{Q_3 + Q_1} = \frac{21-6}{21+6} = \frac{15}{27} = 0.556$$

Example 8: *Calculate standard deviation by actual mean and assumed mean method from the following series:*

Marks	40	44	54	60	62	64	70	80	90	96

and also find the co-efficient of SD.

Solution: Actual method:

Marks (X)	$x = X - \overline{X}$	$x^2 = (X - \overline{X})^2$
40	-26	676
44	-22	484
54	-12	144
60	-6	36
62	-4	16
64	-2	4
70	4	16
80	14	196
90	24	576
96	30	900
$\sum x = 660$	$\sum x = 0$	$\sum x^2 = 3048$

$$\overline{X} = \frac{\sum x}{N} = \frac{660}{10} = 66$$

Now, $$\sigma = \sqrt{\frac{\sum x^2}{N}} = \sqrt{\frac{3048}{10}} = \sqrt{304.8} = 17.4585$$

Co-efficient of SD $$= \frac{\sigma}{X} = \frac{17.4585}{66} = 0.2645$$

Assumed method:

x	$dx = x - 70$	dx^3
40	-30	900
44	-26	676
54	-16	256
60	-10	100
62	-8	64
64	-6	36
70	0	0

80	10	100
90	20	400
96	26	676
	$\sum dx = -40$	$\sum dx^2 = 3208$

The highest value is 96 and the lowest value is 40, the mid-point of these two figures for assumed mean.

$$\frac{96+40}{2} = \frac{136}{2} = 68$$

The near about value of 68 is 70, so assumed means is 70.

Now, $$\sigma = \sqrt{\frac{\sum dx^2}{N} - \left(\frac{\sum dx}{N}\right)^2} = \sqrt{\frac{3208}{10} - \left(\frac{-40}{10}\right)^2}$$

$$= \sqrt{320.8 - 16} =$$

$$= \sqrt{304.8} = 17.4585$$

Example 9: *Find the Standard deviation with direct method.*

$x = 5$ 1 4 3 21

Solution :

x	x^2
5	25
1	1
4	16
3	9
2	4
$\sum x = 15$	$\sum x^2 = 55$

$$\sigma = \sqrt{\frac{\sum x^2}{N} - \left(\frac{\sum x}{N}\right)^2} = \sqrt{\frac{55}{5} - \left(\frac{15}{5}\right)^2} = \sqrt{11-9} = 1.414$$

Discrete Series:

Example 10: *Find out standard deviation from the following data:*

Size of item	3.5	4.5	5.5	.5	7.5	8.5	9.5
Frequency	3	7	22	60	85	32	8

Solution:

x	f	$dx = x - 6.5$	fdx	fdx^2
3.5	3	-3	-9	
4.5	7	-2	-14	
5.5	22	-1	-22	
6.5	60	0	0	
7.5	85	1	85	
8.5	32	2	64	
9.5	8	3	24	
	$N = 217$		$\sum fdx = 128$	$\sum fdx^2 = 362$

$$\sigma = \sqrt{\frac{\sum fdx^2}{N} - \left(\frac{\sum fdx}{N}\right)^2} = \sqrt{\frac{362}{217} - \left(\frac{128}{217}\right)^2}$$

$$= \sqrt{1.668 - 0.348} = 1.149$$

Direct method

x	f	fx	fx^2
3.5	3	10.5	36.75
4.5	7	31.5	141.75
5.5	22	121.0	665.5
6.5	60	390.0	2535.0
7.5	85	637.5	4781.25
8.5	32	272.0	2312.0
9.5	8	76.0	722.0
	$N = 217$	1538.5	11,194.25

$$\sigma = \sqrt{\frac{\sum fx^2}{N} - \left(\frac{\sum fx}{N}\right)^2} = \sqrt{\frac{11{,}194.25}{217} - \left(\frac{1538.5}{217}\right)^2}$$

$$= \sqrt{51.59 - 50.27} = 1.15$$

Communication Series:

Example 11: *Find the standard deviation from the following data:*

Age urder	10	20	30	40	50	60	70	80
No. of persons dying	15	30	53	75	100	110	115	125

Solution:

Age (*x*)	*f*	*m*	*dx = m - 35*	*dx' = dx/10*	*fdx'*	*fdx*²
0-10	15	5	-30	-3	-45	135
10-20	15	15	-20	-2	-30	60
20-30	23	25	-10	-1	-23	23
30-40	22	35	0	0	0	0
40-50	25	45	10	1	25	25
50-60	10	55	20	2	20	40
60-70	5	65	30	3	15	45
70-80	10	75	40	4	40	160
	N = 125				2.	488

$$\sigma = \sqrt{\frac{\sum fdx'^2}{N} - \left(\frac{\sum fdx'}{N}\right)^2} \times i = \sqrt{\frac{488}{125} - \left(\frac{2}{125}\right)^2} \times 10$$

$$= \sqrt{3.904 - 0.0003} \times 10 = 1.976 \times 10$$

$$= 19.76$$

Example 12: *The following table gives heights of boys and girls studying in a college. Find (i) standard deviation, where heights are more variable.* **(L.U.)**

	Boys	*Girls*
Number	400	100
Average height	68"	65"
Variance	9	4

Solution:

$$\sigma_{12} = \sqrt{\frac{N_1\left(d_1^2 + \sigma_1^2\right) + N^2\left(d_2^2 + \sigma_2^2\right)}{N_1 + N_2}}$$

$$\bar{X}_{12} = \frac{\bar{X}_1 N_1 + \bar{X}_2 N_2}{N_1 + N_2}$$

$$N_1 = 400, N_2 = 100\bar{X} = 68, \bar{X}^2 = 65$$

$$\bar{X}_{12} = \frac{68 \times 400 + 65 \times 100}{}500$$

$$= \frac{27200 + 6500}{500} = \frac{33700}{500} = 67.4$$

$$d_1 = (\bar{X}_1 - \bar{X}_{12}) = (68 - 67.4) = 0.6$$

$$d_2 = (\bar{X}_2 - \bar{X}_{12}) = (65 - 67.4) = 2.4$$

$$\sigma_{12} = \sqrt{\frac{400(0.36+9) + 100(5.76+4)}{40+100}}$$

$$= \sqrt{\frac{3744 + 976}{500}} = \sqrt{\frac{4720}{500}} = \sqrt{9.44} = 3.07$$

(i) Boys

$$\text{C.V.} = \frac{\sigma}{X} \times 100$$

$$= \frac{3}{68} \times 100 = 4.41$$

(ii) Girls

$$\text{C.V.} = \frac{\sigma}{X} \times 100$$

$$= \frac{2}{65} \times 100 = 3.08$$

Hence, coefficient of variation is more for boys, the height of boys shows greater variation.

Example 13: *The number of workers employed, the mean wage (in Rs.) per month and standard (in Rs.) in each section of a factory are given below; calculate* x *and standard deviation of all workers taken together:*

Section	*No. of workers employed*	*Mean wage (in Rs.)*	*SD (in Rs.)*
A	50	1113	60
B	60	1120	79
C	90	1115	80

Solution:

$$\bar{X}_{123} = \frac{N_1\bar{X}_1 + N_2\bar{X}_2 + N_3\bar{X}_3}{N_1 + N_2 + N_3}$$

$$= \frac{(50 \times 1113) + (60 \times 1120) + (90 \times 1115)}{200}$$

$$= \frac{55650 + 67200 + 100350}{200} = \frac{223200}{200}$$

= Rs. 1116

Combined SD

$$\sigma_{12} = \sqrt{\frac{N_1(d_1^2 + \sigma_1^2) + N_2(d_2^2) + N_3(d_3^2 + \sigma_3^2}{N_1 + N_2}}$$

$$d_1 = \left(\bar{X}_1 - \bar{X}_{123}\right) = (1113 - 1116) = -3$$

$$d_2 = \left(\bar{X}_2 - \bar{X}_{123}\right) = (1120 - 1116) = 4$$

$$d_3 = \left(\bar{X}_3 - \bar{X}_{123}\right) = (1115 - 1116) = -1$$

$$\sigma_{123} = \sqrt{\frac{50(9 + 3600) + 60(16 + 4900) + 90(1 + 6400)}{50 + 60 + 90}}$$

$$= \sqrt{\frac{180450 + 294960 + 576090}{200}}$$

$$= \sqrt{\frac{1051500}{}200} = \sqrt{5257.5} = 72.51$$

Example 14: *Find missing figures from the following data:*

Section	*No. of workers employed*	*Mean wage (in Rs.)*	*SD (in Rs.)*
N	50	-	200
$\bar{X}$	113	-	116
SD	6	7	7.746

Solution:

$$N_1 = 50, N_2 = ?\, N_3 = 90, \text{ Total} = 200$$

$$X_1 = 113, X_2 = ?\, \bar{X}_3 = 115, \bar{X}_{123} = 116$$

$$\sigma_1 = 6, \sigma_2 = 7, \sigma_3 = ?, \sigma_{123} = 7.746$$

Now, as : $N_1 + N_2 + N_3 = 200$

50 + Nz + 90 = 200

∴ $N_2 = 60$

$$\bar{X}_{123} = \frac{\bar{X}_1 N_1 + \bar{X}_2 N_2 + \bar{X}_3 N_3}{N_1 + N_2 + N_3}$$

$$116 = \frac{50 \times 113 + 60 \times \bar{X}_2 + 90 \times 115}{200}$$

or, $$116(200) = 5650 \times 60\bar{X}_2 + 10350$$

$$60\bar{X}_2 = 23200 - 5650 - 10350$$

$$\bar{X}_2 = \frac{23200 - 16000}{60}$$

$$= \frac{7200}{60} = 120$$

$$d_1 = (\bar{X}_2 - \bar{X}_{123}) = (113 - 116) = -3$$

$$d_2 = (\bar{X}_2 - \bar{X}_{123}) = (120 - 116) = 4$$

$$d_3 = (\bar{X}_3 - \bar{X}_{123}) = (115 - 116) = -1$$

$$S_{123} = \sqrt{\frac{N_1\sigma_1^2 + N_2\sigma_2^2 + N_3\sigma_3^2 + N_1\sigma_1^2 + N_2\sigma_2^2 + N_3\sigma_3^2}{N_1 + N_2 + N_3}}$$

$$7.746 = \sqrt{\frac{(50)(6)^2 + (60)(7)^2 + (90)\sigma_3^2 + (50)(-3)^2 + (60)(4)^2 + (90)(-1)^2}{50 + 60 + 90}}$$

Squaring both side and adjusting the terms.

$$(200)\ (7.746)^2 = 50\ (36 + 9) + 60\ (49 + 16) + 90\ (\sigma_3^2 + 1)$$

$$(200)\ (60.000516) = 50\ (45) + 60\ (65) + 90\ \sigma_3^2 + 90$$

$$12000 = 2250 + 3900 + 90 + 90\sigma_3^2$$

$$\sigma_3^2 = \frac{5760}{90} + 64$$

$$\sigma_3 = 8$$

Example 15: *Mean of* 40 *terms is* 25 and SD is 4, *find sum and sum of square of all the terms.*

Solution:

$$\bar{X} = \frac{\Sigma X}{N}$$

$$25 = \frac{\sum X}{40} = \sum X = 40 \times 25 = 1000$$

and $$SD = \sqrt{\frac{\sum X^2}{40} - \left(\frac{\sum X}{40}\right)^2}$$

$$(4)^2 = \sqrt{\frac{\sum X}{40} - \left(\frac{1000}{40}\right)^2}$$

$$16 = \frac{\sum X^2}{40} - 625$$

$$\frac{\sum X^2}{40} = 625 + 16 = 641$$

$$\Rightarrow \quad \sum X^2 = 641 \times 40 = 25640$$

Correct Standard Deviation

Example 16: *Calculate the correct value of SD if SD = 5, $N = 100 \bar{X} = 10$ wrong item 15 and right item is* 17.

Solution:

As $$\bar{X} = \frac{\sum X}{N} = 10 = \frac{\sum X}{100} = \text{Incorrect} \sum X = 10 \times 100 = 1000$$

Correct $\sum X$ = Incorrect $\sum X$ – Wrong item + Right item

= 1000 – 15 + 17 = 1002

Correct $$\bar{X} = \frac{\text{Correct} \sum X}{N} = \frac{1002}{100} 10.02$$

$$\sigma = \sqrt{\frac{\sum X^2}{N} \left(\frac{\sum X}{N}\right)^2}$$

$$(5)^2 = \frac{\sum X^2}{100} - 100$$

$$25 = \frac{\sum X^2}{100} - 100$$

$$25 = \frac{\sum X^2 - 10000}{100}$$

$$2500 = \sum X^2 - 10000 = \sum X^2 = 2500 + 10000$$

Incorrect $\sum X^2 = 125000$

$$\text{Correct } \sum X^2 = \text{Incorrect } \sum X^2 = (\text{Wrong item})^2 + (\text{Right item})^2$$

$$= 12500 - (15)^2 + (17)^2$$

$$= 12500 - 225 + 289 = 12564$$

$$\text{Correct } \sigma = \sqrt{\frac{\text{Correct} \sum X^2}{B} - (\text{Correct } \bar{X})^2} = \sqrt{\frac{12564}{100} - (10.02)^2}$$

$$= \sqrt{125.64 - 100.40 = 5.024}$$

1.18 Mean Deviation

The range suffers from a major defect; that it is calculated by taking into account only two values of the series. This method of studying dispersion (by location of limits) is also called the ***method of limits***.

Because of the demerits of range, we shall now consider another two more measures of dispersion that take into account all the observations of a series, and is calculated in relation to a central value. This method of calculating dispersion is called the ***method of averaging*** deviations. The first among these two measures is mean deviation.

Mean deviation of a series is the arithmetic average of the deviations of various items from a measure of central tendency (mean, median or mode).

Theoretically, deviations can be taken from any of the three averages mentioned above, but in actual practice mean deviation is calculated either from mean or from median. Mode is usually not considered, as its value is very often not well-defined. Between mean and median, the latter is supposed to be better than the former because the sum of deviations from median is less than the sum of the deviations from mean. Therefore the value of mean deviation from median is always less than the value calculated from mean.

Since the purpose of a measure of dispersion is to study the variation of items from a central value, while aggregating deviations, the algebraic signs are not taken into account. This step of ignoring the signs renders mean deviation incapable of further algebraic treatment.

Mean deviation is also known as the ***first moment of dispersion***.

Mean Deviation from Mean

$$\delta\bar{X} = \frac{\Sigma |d\bar{X}|}{N}$$

Mean Deviation from Median

$$\delta M = \frac{\Sigma |dM|}{N}$$

Mean Deviation from Mode

$$\delta Z = \frac{\Sigma |dZ|}{N}$$

Mean Coefficient of Dispersion

From Mean

$$\frac{\delta \bar{X}}{\bar{X}}$$

From Median

$$\frac{\delta M}{M}$$

From Mode

$$\frac{\delta Z}{Z}$$

Calculation of Mean Deviation in a Series of Individual Observations

Direct Method:

The above-discussed formulae give the direct method of calculation of mean deviation (in a series of individual observations.

Short-cut Method:

Median (or mean, or mode) is calculated and the total of the values of the items below the median (or mean, or mode) and above it are found out. The former is subtracted from the latter and divided by the number of items. The resulting figure is the mean deviation from median (or mean, or mode).

Symbolically:

$$\delta M = \frac{1}{N}(M_y - M_x)$$

$$\delta \bar{X} = \frac{1}{N}(\bar{X}_y - \bar{X}_x)$$

$$\delta Z = \frac{1}{N}(Z_y - Z_x)$$

Calculation of Mean Deviation in a Discrete Series

Direct Method

(*i*) Calculate median (or mean, or mode).

(*ii*) Find the deviations from the median (or mean, or mode), ignoring sign.

(*iii*) Multiply these deviations with the respective frequencies and total these products.

(*iv*) Divide the total ($\sum fdM$ or $\sum fd\bar{x}$ or $\sum fdZ$) by the number of observations to get mean deviation.

Symbolically:

$$\delta M = \frac{\Sigma |fdM|}{N}$$

$$\delta \bar{X} = \frac{\Sigma |fd\bar{X}|}{N}$$

$$\delta Z = \frac{\Sigma |fdZ|}{N}$$

Short-cut Method

1. Deviations are taken from an assumed median (or mean, or mode), multiplied by their respective frequencies, and the products are totaled.
2. Number of items less than the actual median (or actual mean, or actual mode) are multiplied by the difference between the actual and assumed mean.
3. Similarly, the number of items greater than the actual median (or actual mean, or actual mode) are multiplied by the difference between the actual and assumed mean.
4. The latter (No. 3) is deducted from the former (No. 2) and the balance is added to the sum of the products of deviations from the assumed median (or mean, or mode) and their frequencies (No. 1).
5. To resulting figure when divided by the number of items gives the value of mean deviation.

Calculation of Mean Deviation in a Continuous Series

Direct Method

Same procedure as in case of discrete series.

Short-cut Method

A. If the actual and assumed median (or mean, or mode) lie in the same class, the procedure is the same as in case of discrete series.

B. If the actual and assumed median (or mean, or mode) lie in different classes, following adjustments are required:

   1. In such a situation, the frequency of the class in which the actual median (or actual mean, or actual mode) lies is treated separately. It is multiplied by the difference of the deviation of the mid-value from the actual and assumed medians (or mean, or mode).
   2. This product is subtracted from the total deviations from the assumed median (or mean, or mode).
   3. The rest of the procedure is the same as in the case of discrete series.

Merits of Mean Deviation

1. It is rigidly defined.
2. Its calculation is not very difficult.
3. It is readily understood.
4. It is based on all observations
5. It is not affected much by the values of the extreme items.

Demerits of Mean Deviation

1. It is not capable of further mathematical treatment.
2. At times, mean deviation may not be a very accurate measure of dispersion.
   (*a*) If it is calculated from mode, mode may be ill-defined.
   (*b*) If it is calculated from median, it may not be very reliable if the degree of variability is high in the series.
   (*c*) If it is calculated from mean, it is not very scientific because the sum of deviations from mean (ignoring the signs) is greater than the sum of deviations from median.

Utility of Mean Deviation

1. Finds favour with economists and businessmen due to simplicity in calculation.
2. Has an advantage over standard deviations which gives greater importance to the deviations of extreme values.
3. This method has been found to be more useful than others in forecasting business cycles.
4. It is useful for small sample studies where elaborate statistical analysis is not needed.

Example 17: *Find the mean Deviation and coefficient of mean deviation from mean.*

x	8	6	3	1	5	7

Solution:

x	$\lvert D\rvert = \lvert X - \bar{X}\rvert$
8	3
6	1
3	2
1	4
5	0
7	2
$\sum x = 30$	12

$$\bar{X} = \frac{\Sigma X}{N} = \frac{30}{6} = 5$$

$$= \frac{\Sigma |d|}{N} = \frac{12}{6} = 2$$

Co-efficient of MD $= \frac{M.D.}{\bar{X}} = \frac{2}{5} = 0.4$

Example 18: *Find the mean deviation and co-efficient of mean deviation from median and mode.*

x	21	18	15	12	3	6	9

Solution: Arrange the series in ascending order:

x	$\lvert D \rvert = \lvert X - Me \rvert$
3	9
6	6
9	3
12	0
15	3
18	6
21	9
	36

Median $= \frac{N+1}{2}$th item $= \frac{7+1}{2} = 4^{th}$ item

∴ Me = 12

$$MD = \frac{\Sigma |D|}{N} = \frac{36}{7} = 5.143$$

$$\text{Co-efficient of MD} = \frac{\text{MD}}{\text{Median}} = \frac{5.143}{12} = 0.429$$

Mean Deviation from Mode

In the above series the highest value is 21, therefore, the mode value is 21.

x	$\lvert D\rvert = \lvert X - Z\rvert$
21	0
18	3
15	6
12	9
3	18
6	15
9	12
	63

Mode, $Z = 21$

$$\text{MD} = \frac{\Sigma \lvert D\rvert}{N} = \frac{63}{7} = 9$$

$$\text{Co-efficient of MD} = \frac{9}{21} = 0.429$$

Discrete Series

Example 19: *Find the mean deviation from $\bar{x}$ and Median.* **(A.U.)**

Units	6	12	18	24	30	36	42
Frequency	4	7	10	18	12	7	2

Solution:

From $\bar{X}$

x	f	fx	$\lvert D\rvert = \lvert X - \bar{X}\rvert$	$f\lvert D\rvert$
6	4	24	17.6	70.4
12	7	84	11.6	81.2
18	10	180	5.6	56.0
24	18	432	0.4	7.2
30	12	360	6.4	76.8
36	7	252	12.4	86.8
42	2	84	18.4	36.8
	$N = 60$	$\sum fx = 1416$		$\sum f\lvert D\rvert = 415.2$

$$\overline{X} = \frac{\Sigma fx}{N} = \frac{1416}{60} = 23.6$$

$$\text{M.D.} = \frac{\Sigma f\,|D|}{N} = \frac{415.2}{60} = 6.92$$

$$\text{Co-efficient to M.D.} = \frac{M.D.}{\overline{X}} = \frac{6.92}{23.6} = 0.293$$

From Median:

x	f	cf	$\|D\| = \|X - Me\|$	$f'\|D\|$
6	4	4	12	48
12	7	11	6	42
18	10	21	0	0
24	18	39	6	108
30	12	51	12	144
36	7	58	18	126
42	2	60	24	48
	$N = 60$			516

$$\text{Me} = \frac{N+1}{N} = \frac{60+1}{2} = 15.25 \text{ lies } 21$$

Me = 18

$$\text{MD} = \frac{\Sigma f\,|D|}{N} = \frac{516}{60} = 8.6$$

$$\text{Coefficient of MD} = \frac{\text{MD}}{\text{Median}} = \frac{8.6}{18} = 0.478$$

Example 20: *Calculation mean deviation from the following series:* **(U.P.T.U.)**

x	5	10	15	20	25	Total
f	6	7	8	11	8	40

Also find the co-efficient of MD.

Solution:

x	f	cf	$\lvert D\rvert = \lvert X - Me\rvert$	$f\lvert D\rvert$
5	6	6	10	60
10	7	13	5	35
15	8	21	0	0
20	11	32	5	55
25	8	40	10	80
	$N = 40$			230

Note: If nothing mention, calculate MD from median.

$$\text{Me} = \frac{N+1}{2}\text{th term} = \frac{40+1}{2} = 20.5 \text{ lies } 21$$

$$\therefore \quad \text{Me} = 15$$

$$\text{MD} = \frac{\sum f\,|D|}{N} = \frac{230}{40} = 5.75$$

$$\text{Coefficient of MD} = \frac{\text{MD}}{\text{Median}} = \frac{5.75}{15} = 0.384$$

Example 21: *Calculate mean deviation of co-efficient of MD from Mode.*

x	5	10	15	20	25	30
f	3	4	8	12	7	2

Solution: The highest values of frequency is 12. Therefore, the value of mode is 20.

x	f	$\lvert D\rvert = \lvert X - M_0\rvert$	$f\lvert D\rvert$
5	3	15	45
10	4	10	40
15	8	5	40
20	12	0	0
25	7	5	35
30	2	10	20
	36		$\sum f\lvert D\rvert = 180$

Note: If nothing mention, calculate MD from median.

$$\text{MD} = \frac{\sum f\,|D|}{N} = \frac{180}{36} = 5$$

Coefficient of MD $= \frac{\text{MD}}{\text{Mode}} = \frac{5}{20} = 0.25$

Continuous Series:

Example 22: *The mean deviation from $\bar{X}$ and median.*

Divided Yield	0-6	6-12	12-18	18-24	24-30
No. of Companies	8	10	12	9	5

Also, calculate the value of co-effident mean deviation

Solution:

Divided yield	No. of Co's (*f*)	*m*	*dx*	*dx' = dx'/6*	*fdx'*	|D|=m -X	*f* | *D* |
0-6	8	3	-12	-2	-16	11.05	88.4
6-12	10	9	-6	-1	-10	5.05	50.5
12-18	12	15	0	0	0	0.95	11.4
18-24	9	21	6	1	9	6.95	62.55
24-30	5	27	12	2	10	12.5	62.5
	$N = 44$				-7		275.35

$$\bar{X} = A + \frac{\Sigma fdx'}{N} \times o = 15 + \frac{(-7)}{44} \times 6 = 15\frac{42}{44} = 14.05$$

$$\text{MD} = \frac{\Sigma f \mid D \mid}{N} = \frac{275.35}{44} = 6.258$$

$$\text{Co-efficient of MD} = \frac{MD}{\bar{X}14.} = \frac{6.258}{14.05} = 0.45$$

From Median:

Dividend Yield	No. of Co's (*f*)	*cf*	*m*	|*D*| = |*X* − *Me*|	*f* | *D* |
0-6	8	8	3	11	88
6-12	10	18	9	5	50
12-18	12	30	15	1	12
18-24	9	39	21	7	63
24-30	5	44	27	13	65
	$N = 44$				$\Sigma f \mid D \mid = 278$

Me = *N*/2 = 44/2 = 22 Lies 12-18

$$\text{Median} = 12 + \left(\frac{22-18}{12}\right) \times 6 = 14$$

$$\text{MD} = \frac{\sum f\,|D|}{N} = \frac{278}{44} = 6.32$$

$$\text{Co-efficient of MD} = \frac{MD}{Me} = \frac{6.32}{14} = 0.451$$

1.19 Standard Deviation

The concept of standard deviation was first used by Karl Pearson in 1893. It is the most commonly used measure of dispersion. It removes the drawback in the technique of the calculation of mean deviation, where algebraic signs are ignored. One of the easiest ways of doing away with algebraic signs is to square the figures, and this process is adopted in the calculation of standard deviation.

Standard deviation is the square root of the arithmetic average of the squares of the deviations measured from the mean. It is therefore also known as the root-mean-square (rms) deviation from mean. Some other terms like mean square error and error of mean square are also used to denote standard deviation.

Thus, in the calculation of standard deviation, first mean is calculated, and the deviations of various items from this mean value are squared. The squared items are totaled and the sum is divided by the number of items. The square root of the resulting figure is the standard deviation of the series.

Symbolically,

$$\sigma = \sqrt{\frac{\sum d^2}{N}}$$

Merits, Demerits and Uses of Standard Deviation

Merits:

(1) It is rigidly defined.

(2) It is based on all the observations.

(3) It is amenable to further algebraic treatment and possesses many mathematical properties.

(4) It is less affected by fluctuations of sampling than most other measures of dispersion.

(5) The squaring of deviations makes them positive and the difficulty about algebraic signs which was experienced in case of mean deviation is removed.

Demerits:

(1) Standard deviation is not easy to calculate, nor is it easily understood.

(2) It gives more weight to extreme values, because the squares of the deviations that are big in size, would be proportionately greater than the squares of those deviations that are comparatively small.

Uses:

Despite the drawbacks mentioned above, the standard deviation is the best measure of dispersion and should be used wherever possible. Just as the mean is the best measure of central tendency (leaving some exceptional cases), standard deviation is the best measure of dispersion. However, since standard deviation gives greater weight to extreme items, it does not find much favour with economists and businessmen who are more interested in the results of the modal class.

Difference between Mean Deviation and Standard Deviation

(*i*) Mean deviation does not take into account the algebraic signs. Standard deviation does not ignore them but nullifies their effect by squaring the deviations.

(*ii*) Mean deviation can be calculated from mean, median or mode. Standard deviation is calculated from mean only.

(*iii*) Standard deviation possesses many more mathematical properties than mean deviation.

Standard Deviation in Case of Discrete Series: In discrete series, standard deviation can be calculated from following method:

1. Actual Mean Method or Direct Method.
2. Assumed Mean Method.
3. Step Deviation Method.

1. Actual Mean Method or Direct Method: In this method, deviations are taken from actual mean. The following formula is used here:

$$\sigma = \sqrt{\frac{\Sigma fx^2}{N}}$$

where, $x = X - \overline{X}$ (deviation taken from actual $\overline{X}$).

2. Assumed Mean Method: In this method, deviations are taken from assumed mean as $d = X - A$. The following formula is used here:

3. Step Deviation Method: This method is used to simplify the calculations. This can be used through following formula:

$$\sigma = \sqrt{\frac{\Sigma fd^2}{N} - \left(\frac{\Sigma fd'}{N}\right)^2} \times i$$

where, $d' = d = \dfrac{m - A}{i}$

i = common factor.

Combined Standard Deviation

Combined standard deviation is defined as the combined value of standard deviation more than two groups. It can be computed by using following formula:

In case of two groups :

$$\sigma_{12} = \sqrt{\frac{N_1\sigma_1^2 + N_2\sigma_2^2 + N_1d_1^2 + N_2\sigma_2^2}{N_1 + N_2}}$$

where, σ_{12} = Combined standard deviation

σ_1 = Standard deviation of one group

σ_2 = Standard deviation of second group

$d_1 = | \bar{X}_1 - \bar{X}_{12} |, d_2 = | \bar{X}_2 - \bar{X}_{12} |$

X_{12} = Combined mean

X_1 = Mean of one group

X_2 = Mean of second group

N_1 = No. of items in one group

N_2 = No. of items in second group

In case of more than two groups :

$$\sigma_{123} = \sqrt{\frac{N_1\sigma_1^2 + N_2\sigma_2^2 + N_3\sigma_3^2 + N_1\sigma_1^2 + N_2\sigma_2^2 + N_3d_3^2 + \ldots}{N_1 + N_2 + N_3 + \ldots}}$$

where, $d_1 = \bar{X}_1 - \bar{X}_{123}, d_2 = \bar{X}_2 - \bar{X}_{123}, d_3 = \bar{X}_3 - \bar{X}_{123}$

Properties of Standard Deviation

There are following properties of standard deviation:

(*i*) The standard deviation of first natural numbers

1, 2, 3, ... n is taken as $\sqrt{\dfrac{1}{12}(n^2 - 1)}$

(*ii*) Standard deviation is always calculated from arithmetic mean because the sum of squares of the deviations from the arithmetic mean is always minimum than other measures.

Symbolically: $\Sigma(x-\bar{x})^2$ is always minimum.

(*iii*) Mean and standard deviation depends upon the change of scale because if every item in a series is multiplied by the constant then value of $\bar{x}$ and σ will also increase by constant value its, but if each value is divided by constant value it results decease in the value of $\bar{x}$ and σ.

(*iv*) If the number of groups two or more than two with their different N (numbers), X (mean) and σ (standard deviations) are given we can calculate the combined standard deviation by using the following formulae:

$$\sigma_{123} = \sqrt{\frac{N_1\sigma_1^2 + N_2\sigma_2^2 + N_3\sigma_3^2 + N_1\sigma_1^2 + N_2\sigma_2^2 + N_3 d_3^2 + \ldots}{N_1 + N_2 + N_3 + \ldots.}}$$

where, $d_1 = \bar{X}_1 - \bar{X}_{123}, d_2 = \bar{X}_2 - \bar{X}_{123}, d_3 = \bar{X}_3 - \bar{X}_{123}$

(*v*) The standard deviation has relation with mean deviation (MD) and quartile deviation (QD) which can be defined as follows:

$$\text{Q.D.} = \frac{2}{3}\sigma \qquad \text{M.D.} = \frac{4}{5}\sigma$$

(*vi*) The standard deviation has a relation with arithmetic mean in a symmetrical distribution which is shown in following way :

$\bar{X} \pm (0.6745)\ \sigma$ (It includes the 50% of the items)

$\bar{X} \pm 1\ \sigma$ (It includes the 68.27% of the items)

$\bar{X} \pm 2\sigma$ (It includes the 95.45% of the items)

$\bar{X} \pm 3\sigma$ (It includes the 99.73% of the items)

This relation can be shown graphically through the following way :

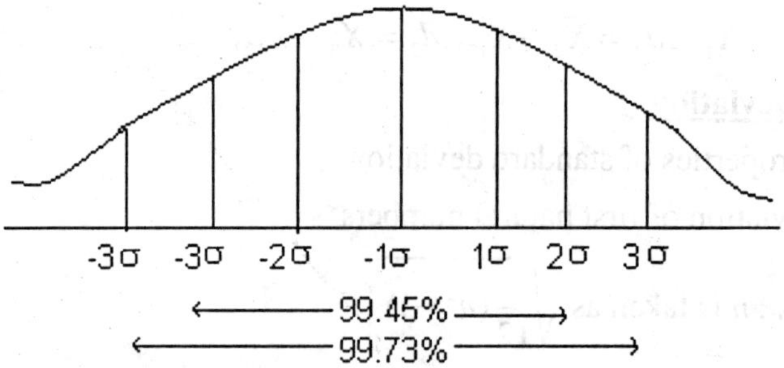

1.20 Co-efficient of Variation

Co-efficient of variation is an important relative measure of dispersion. It was invented by Karl Pearson. It is based on standard deviation. It is the best and an comparing their variability in them. It can also be used to compare the consistency, stability, an homogeneity of two or more series. If one series has less coefficient of variation than other series then this series will be more consistent than another one. It can be calculated by following formula:

$$\text{Coefficient of variation (CV)} = \frac{\sigma}{\bar{X}} \times 100$$

where σ = Standard deviation

$\bar{X}$ = Arithmetic mean.

Variance: Variance is defined as the square of standard deviation. In this way, it is also based on standard deviation. It was invented by R.A. Fisher in 1918. It can be calculate applying following formula :

$$\text{Variance} = \sigma^2$$

σ = Standard deviation

Example 1: *A security analysis studied hundred companies and obtained the following data in the year* 2003:

Dividend declared (%)	0-8	8-16	16-24	24-32	32-40
No. of companies	5	30	40	10	15

Calculate the SD and variance of the dividend declared.

Solution:

Dividend Declared	***No. of Co.' S***	*m*	*dx*	*fdx*	fdx^2
0-8	5	4	-16	-8	1280
8-16	30	12	-8	-240	1920
16-24	40	20	0	0	0
24-32	10	28	8	80	640
32-40	15	36	16	240	3840
	100			$\Sigma fdx = 0$	$\Sigma fdx^2 = 7680$

$$\sigma = \sqrt{\frac{\Sigma fdx^2}{N} - \left(\frac{\Sigma fdx}{N}\right)^2}$$

$$\sqrt{\frac{7680}{100} - \left(\frac{0}{100}\right)^2} = \sqrt{76.8} = 8.76$$

$$\text{Variance} = (\sigma)^2$$

$$\text{Variance} = \frac{\sum fdx^2}{N} - \left(\frac{\sum fdx}{N}\right)^2 = \frac{7680}{100} = 76.8$$

Example 2: ***A company paid bonus to its employees as under :***

Monthly salary (Rs.)	100-120	120-140	140-160	160-180	180-200	200-220	220 and over
Bonus paid (Rs.)	500	600	700	800	900	1000	1100

The actual salaries of the employees given below are in Rs.

205	162	125	148	190	168	168
184		145	125	195	250	170
150		154	150	218	168	175
130	110	165	175	187	190	178

Restate the data in the form of a frequency distribution and find out

(*i*) The total bonus paid.

(*ii*) The average salary paid,

(*iii*) The standard deviation of the distribution.

Solution:

(*i*) To calculate the total bonus paid we classify the data and then determine the desired amount

Monthly Salary (Rs.)	**Tally Bar**	***f***	**Bonus (*x*)**	***fx***
100-120	I	1	500	500
120-140	III	3	600	1800
140-160	卌	5	700	3500
160-180	卌IIII	9	800	7200
180-200	卌	5	900	4500
200-220	II	2	1000	2000
220 and over	I	1	1100	1100
		26		$\sum fx = 20600$

$\therefore$ Total bonus paid = Rs. 20,600

(ii) To calculate average salary and standard deviation, let A = 170

Monthly Salary (Rs.)	Frequency (*f*)	*m*	*dx'*	*fdx'*	fdx'^2
100-120	1	110	-3	-3	9
120-140	3	130	-2	-6	12
140-160	5	150	-1	-5	5
160-180	9	170	0	0	0
180-200	5	190	1	5	5
200-220	2	210	2	4	8
220-240	1	230	3	3	9
	$N = 26$			$\Sigma fdx' = -2$	$\Sigma fdx' = 48$

$$\bar{X} = A + \frac{\Sigma fdx'}{N} \times i = 170 + \frac{-2}{26} \times 20$$

$$= 170 - 1.538 = \text{Rs. } 168.46$$

$\therefore$ Average salary = Rs. 168.46

$$\sigma = \sqrt{\frac{\Sigma fdx'}{N} - \left(\frac{\Sigma fdx'}{N}\right)^2} \times i = \sqrt{\frac{48}{26} - \left(\frac{-2}{26}\right)^2} \times 20$$

$$= \sqrt{1.846 - 0.0059} \times 20$$

$$= \sqrt{1.840} \times 20 = \text{Rs. } 27.13$$

Example 3: *Two sections of 50 students scored marks given below in house exams. Discuss this variability through co-efficient of variation which section gave better performance.*

(U.P.T.U.) (L.U.)

Marks percentage (CI)	40-50	50-60	60-70	70-80	80-90	90-100
Section (A) No.	6	9	16	12	5	2
Section (B) No.	1	3	8	32	4	2

Solution:

Section: "A"

C.I.	f	m	dx'	fdx'	fdx'²
40-50	6	45	-2	-12	24
50-60	9	55	-1	-9	9
60-70	16	65	0	0	0
70-80	12	75	1	12	12
80-90	5	85	2	10	20
90-100	2	95	3	6	18
	$N = 50$			$\Sigma fdx' = 7$	$\Sigma fdx' = 48$

$$\overline{X} = A + \frac{\Sigma fdx'}{N} \times i$$

$$= 65 + \frac{7}{50} \times 10 = 65 + 1.4 = 66.4$$

$$\text{S.D.} = \sqrt{\frac{\Sigma fdx'^2}{N} - \left(\frac{\Sigma fdx'}{N}\right)^2}\, i = \sqrt{\frac{83}{50} - \left(\frac{7}{50}\right)} \times 10$$

$$= \sqrt{1.66 - 0.0196 \times 10}$$

$$= \sqrt{1.6404} \times 10 = 1.2808 \times 10 = 12.808$$

$$\text{C.V.(A)} \quad \frac{S.D.}{X} \times 100 = \frac{12.808}{66.4} \times 100 = 19.29\%$$

Section "B"

C.I.	f	m	dx'	fdx'	fdx'²
40-50	1	45	-3	-3	9
50-60	3	55	-2	-6	12
60-70	8	65	-1	-8	8
70-80	32	75	0	0	0
80-90	4	85	1	4	4
90-100	2	95	2	4	8
	$N = 50$			$\Sigma fdx' = -9$	$\Sigma fdx'^2 = 41$

$$\bar{X} = A + \frac{\sum fdx'}{N} \times i$$

$$= 75 + \frac{-9}{50} \times 10 = 75 - 1.8 = 73.2$$

$$\text{S.D.} = \sqrt{\frac{\sum fdx'^2}{N} - \left(\frac{\sum fdx'}{N}\right)^2} i = \sqrt{\frac{41}{50} - \left(\frac{-9}{50}\right)^2} \times 10$$

$$= \sqrt{0.82 - 0.0324} \times 10$$

$$= \sqrt{0.7876} \times 10 = 0.8875 \times 10 = 8.875$$

$$\text{C.V.(B)} = \frac{S.D.}{X} \times 100 = \frac{8.875}{73.2} \times 100 = 12.12\%$$

As far as performance is concerned Section 'B' is also better as its average is much higher that Section 'A'.

Example 4: *The number of employees, wages per employee and variance of the wage per employee for two factories are given below* **(U.P.T.U.)**

No. of Employees	50	100
Average wage per employee per week (Rs.)	120	85
Variance of wage per employee per week (Rs.)	9	16

(*a*) In which factory there is greater variation in the distribution of wages per employees?

(*b*) Suppose in factory 'B' the wages of an employee were wrongly as Rs. 120 instead of Rs. 100 what would be the correct variance for factory "B"?

Solution: (A)

Factory 'A'
Co-efficient of variance

$$CV = \frac{\sigma}{X} \times 100$$

$$\sigma = \sqrt{9} = 3$$

$$\bar{X} = 120$$

$$CV = \frac{3}{120} \times 100$$

$$= 2.5$$

Factory 'A'
Co-efficient of variance

$$CV = \frac{\sigma}{X} \times 100$$

$$\sigma = \sqrt{16} = 4$$

$$\bar{X} = 85$$

$$CV = \frac{4}{85} \times 100$$

$$= 4.71$$

The co-efficient of variation is greater for factory 'B', hence there is greater variation in the distribution of wages per employees in factory 'B'.

(B) Correct variance: For finding correct variance, first we have to find the correct $\bar{X}$

$$\bar{X} = \frac{\Sigma X}{N} = 85 \Rightarrow \frac{\Sigma X}{100}$$

$$\Sigma X = 8500$$

Correct $\Sigma X = 8500 - 120 + 100 = 8480$

$\therefore$ Correct $\Sigma X = \frac{8480}{100} = 84.8$

$$\text{Variance } \sigma^2 = \frac{\Sigma X^2}{N} - \left(\frac{\Sigma X}{N}\right)^2 = \frac{\Sigma X^2 N}{N} - (\bar{X})^2$$

Subsisting the values of σ^2, X

$$16 = \frac{\Sigma X^2}{100} - (85)^2$$

or, $1600 = \Sigma X^2 = 722500$

$$\Sigma X^2 = 724100$$

But in this total 100 has been taken as 120

$$\text{Correct } \Sigma X^2 = 724100 - (120)^2 + (100)^2$$

$$= 724100 - 14400 + 10000 = 71970$$

$$\text{Correct variance} = \frac{\text{Correct } \Sigma X^2}{N} - (\text{Correct } \bar{X})^2$$

$$= \frac{719700}{100} - (84.8)^2 = 7197 - 7191.04$$

$$= 5.96$$

Example 5: *The mean of* 5 *observation of* 4.4 *and variance is* 8.24. *If there of the five observation are* 1, 2, 6 *find the other two.*

Solution: Let the missing observations be x and y

x	x2
1 2 6 x y	1 4 36 x^2 y^2
$\Sigma x = 9 + x + y$	$\Sigma x^2 = 41 + x^2 + y^2$

Now, $\bar{X} = \frac{\sum X}{N}$

$\therefore \quad 4.4 = \frac{x+y+9}{5}$

$\Rightarrow \quad x + y = 13 \quad \ldots(i)$

$$\sigma^2 = \frac{\sum X^2}{N} - (\bar{X})^2$$

$\therefore \quad 8.24 = \frac{41 + x^2 + y^2}{5} - (4.4)^2$

$$8.24 = \frac{41 + x^2 + y^2}{5} - 19.36$$

$$8.24 = \frac{41 + x^2 + y^2 - 96.8}{5}$$

$$41.2 = 41 - 96.8 + x^2 + y^2$$

$$x^2 + y^2 = 97 \quad \ldots(ii)$$

From (i) and (ii)

$$x^2 + (13 - x)^2 = 97$$

$$2x^2 - 26x + 169 = 97$$

$$2x^2 - 26x + 72 = 0$$

$$x^2 - 13x + 36 = 0$$

$$(x - 9)(x - 4) = 0$$

$$x = 9, 4$$

if $x = 9, y = 4$

if $x = 4, y = 9$

$$\boxed{CV = \frac{\sigma}{\bar{X}} \times 100}$$

Variance

Variance $= \sigma^2$

Thus, $\sigma = \sqrt{Variance}$

1.21 Skewness

So far, we have discussed the methods of measuring the central tendency of a frequency distribution and the methods of studying the concentration of items round the central value. However, these measures do not reveal whether the dispersal of values on either side of an

average is symmetrical or not. If observations are arranged in a symmetrical order round a measure of central tendency, we get a "symmetrical distribution." When plotted, such a distribution gives a normal or ideal curve. In a perfectly symmetrical distribution, the values of mean, median and mode coincide and the quartiles are equidistant from the median. A normal curve is a bell-shaped frequency curve in which the values on either side of a measure of central tendency are symmetrical.

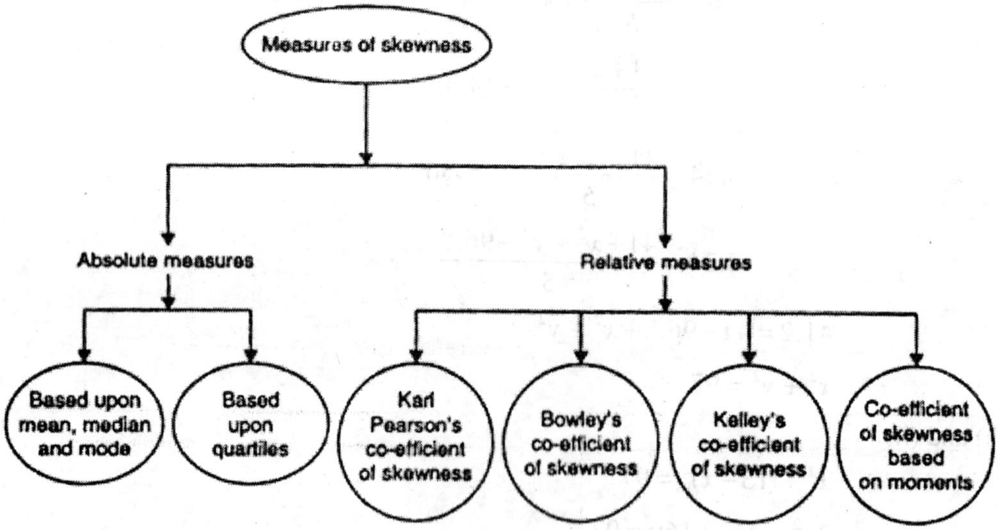

In order to study a frequency distribution, it would be of great use to know whether it would give a normal curve, and if not, to what extent it would deviate from a normal distribution. In fact measures of central tendency and measures of dispersion should always be supplemented by the measures of the third order, for instance the measure of skewness. Skewness is the opposite of symmetry and its presence tells us that a particular distribution is not symmetrical, or, in other words, it is skew.

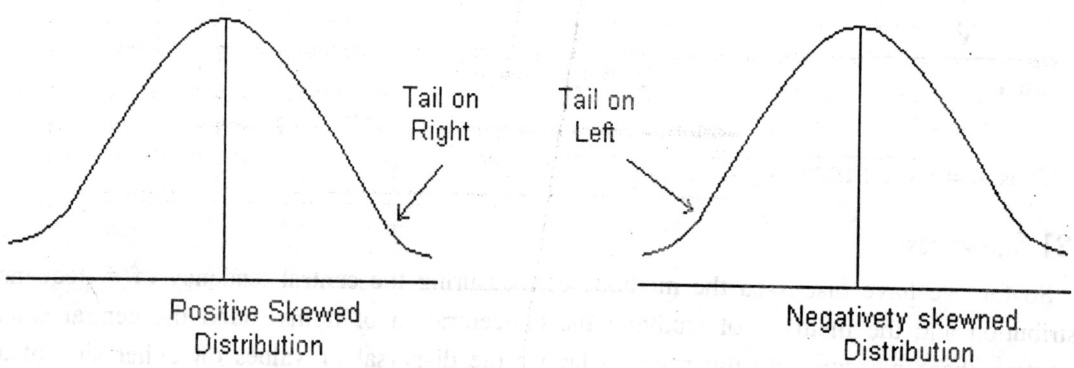

Definition

A distribution is said to be skewed when the mean and the median fall at different points in the distribution, and the balance of the curve (or its centre of gravity) is shifted to one side or to the other (left or right).

Symmetrical Distribution:

It is bell-shaped and in it, there is no skewness. The value of mean, median and mode is identical.

Positively Skewed Distribution:

It is skewed to the right. In it the value of mean is more than the value of median and median is greater than mode.

Negatively Skewed Distribution:

It is skewed to the left. In it the value of mode is more than the values of median and median is greater than mean.

Thus:

(*i*) In a symmetrical distribution, $\bar{x} = M = Z$

(*ii*) In a positively skewed distribution, $\bar{x} > M > Z$

(*iii*) In a negatively skew distribution, $\bar{x} < M < Z$

Difference between Measures of Dispersion and Skewness

(1) Dispersion deals with the spread of values around central value. Skewness on the other hand deals with the symmetry of distribution around a central value.

(2) Dispersion deals with the amount of variation and skewness deals with the direction of variation.

(3) Dispersion helps in finding out the extent to which a central value is a representative of the whole distribution. Skewness deals with the nature of variations on either side of a central value.

Test of Skewness

(*a*) In a skew distribution values of mean, median and mode would not coincide. The mean and mode would be pulled wide apart and median would usually lie between them.

(*b*) In a skew distribution the two quartiles would not be equidistant from the median.

(*c*) A skew distribution would not give a bell-shaped curve.

(*d*) The sum of positive deviations from median is not equal to the sum of negative deviations.

(*e*) Frequencies are not equally distributed at various points which are equidistant from mode on either side.

Method of measuring skewness

(*i*) Karl Pearson's method

(*ii*) Bowley's method

(*iii*) Kelly's method

(*iv*) Method of moments

Measures of Skewness

First Measures of Skewness:

(*i*) Mean – Mode ($\bar{x}$ - Z)

(*ii*) Mean – Median ($\bar{x}$ - M)

(*iii*) Median – Mode (M - Z)

These measures suffer from some drawbacks. These are:

(*i*) These measures are expressed in the units of a distribution and therefore cannot be compared with measures expressed in another distribution with a different unit.

(*ii*) There may be considerable variation in different distributions. In one distribution the difference between mean and median may be very large as compared to similar difference in another distribution and yet the two distribution may give similar curves. For example, the difference between mean and median in case of weights may be much larger than a similar difference in heights yet the two curves representing weight and height may look similar because relative variations are not studied by these absolute measures.

However, these measures of skewness are not as popular as those given by Karl Pearson, Bowley, Kelly. Thus the important measures of relative skewness are:

(1) Karl Pearson's Coefficient of Skewness:

$$S_k = \frac{\bar{X} - Z}{\sigma}$$

If mode is ill-defined:

$$S_k = \frac{3(\bar{X} - M)}{\sigma}$$

(2) Bowley's Coefficient of Skewness:

$$S_k = \frac{Q_2 + Q_1 - 2M}{Q_3 - Q_1}$$

(3) Kelly's Coefficient of Skewness:

$$S_k = \frac{D_1 + D_9 - 2D_5}{D_9 - D_1}$$

$$\text{or } S_k = \frac{P_{10} + P_{90} - 2P_{50}}{P_{90} - P_{10}}$$

(4) Method of Moments

$$\beta_1 - \frac{\mu_3^2}{\mu_2^3}$$

1.22 Moments

Moment is a familiar mechanical term for the measure of a force with reference to its tendency to produce rotation. The strength of this tendency depends on the amount of the force and the distance from the origin of the point at which the force is exerted.

$$Moment = \frac{\Sigma fx}{\Sigma f}$$

This is the same formula as used for calculation of mean. It is for this reason that the arithmetic average is also called the first moment about origin.

If the origin is not zero but the mean value then the first moment about mean would be $\frac{\Sigma d}{N}$, where d indicates the difference between the values of a variable (X) and the mean (X).

In case of grouped data, the first moment about mean would be

$$\frac{\Sigma fd}{N}$$

Moments about Mean

Series of Individual Observations

$$\mu_1 = \frac{1}{N}\Sigma(X - \overline{X}) = \frac{\Sigma d}{N}$$

$$\mu_2 = \frac{1}{N}\Sigma(X - \overline{X})^2 = \frac{\Sigma d^2}{N}$$

$$\mu_3 = \frac{1}{N}\Sigma(X - \overline{X})^3 = \frac{\Sigma d^3}{N}$$

$$\mu_4 = \frac{1}{N}\Sigma(X - \overline{X})^4 = \frac{\Sigma d^4}{N}$$

Grouped Data

$$\mu_1 = \frac{1}{N}\Sigma f(X - \overline{X}) = \frac{\Sigma fd}{N}$$

$$\mu_2 = \frac{1}{N}\Sigma f(X - \overline{X})^2 = \frac{\Sigma fd^2}{N}$$

$$\mu_3 = \frac{1}{N}\Sigma f(X - \overline{X})^3 = \frac{\Sigma fd^3}{N}$$

$$\mu_4 = \frac{1}{N}\Sigma f(X - \overline{X})^4 = \frac{\Sigma fd^4}{N}$$

Moments can be extended to μ_5 or μ_6 or more, but in actual practice the first four moments are enough to describe a series.

Objective

Moments are calculated to study the nature of a distribution. They tell us whether a distribution is symmetrical or not. They also tell us about the nature of symmetry – whether the symmetrical curve is

(*i*) Normal

(*ii*) More flat than a normal curve

(*iii*) More peaked than a normal curve

Thus we can study the skewness of a distribution with the help of moments. To study the nature of a distribution, two constants are calculated from the moments. They are

$$\beta_1 = \frac{\mu_3^2}{\mu_2^3}$$

$$\beta_2 = \frac{\mu_4}{\mu_2^2}$$

β_1 tells us whether a distribution is skewed or whether it is symmetrical.

B_2 tells us the difference between a symmetrical curve and a normal curve. This is known as Kurtosis.

1.23 Kurtosis

Kurtosis is another measure which tells us about the form of a distribution. It tells us whether the distribution, if plotted on a graph, would give us a normal curve, a curve more flat than the normal curve or a curve more peaked than the normal curve.

The word kurtosis in Greek language means 'bulginess'

Definition

The degree of kurtosis of a distribution is measured relative to the peakedness of a normal curve.

If a distribution is more peaked than the normal distribution, it is called 'leptokurtic.' If the distribution is more flat than the normal distribution, it is called 'platykurtic.' The normal distribution is known as 'mesokurtic.' (Platykurtic curves are like platypus, squat with short tails, leptokurtic curves are like kangaroos, high with long tails, noted for leaping.)

Measures of Kurtosis

Kurtosis is measured by coefficient β_2 or its derivation γ_2.

$$\beta_2 = \frac{\mu_4}{\mu_2^{\,2}}$$

$$\gamma_2 = \beta_2 - 3$$

The standard value of β_2 is taken as 3 and curves with β_2 less than 3 are called platykurtic while curves with β_2 more than 3 are called leptokurtic. In a normal or mesokurtic curve, β_2 is equal to 3. Therefore, for a normal curve γ_2 is 0, in a platykurtic curve, γ_2 is less than 0 and in a leptokurtic curve, γ_2 is greater than 0.

Coefficients of Skewness based on Moments

$$\beta_1 = \frac{\mu_3^{\,2}}{\mu_2^{\,3}}$$

$$\gamma_1 = \sqrt{\beta_1} = \frac{\mu_3}{\mu_2^{\frac{3}{2}}}$$

If there is no skewness in a distribution the value of $\beta_1 = 0$. If the value of β_1 is more than zero it is an indication of skewness and the greater the value of β_1, greater is the extent of skewness. However, a drawback of β_1 is that it cannot assume a negative value (μ_3^2 will be positive, as it is a square; μ_2 is also positive as it is square of deviations). This drawback is removed by γ_1.

If $\beta_2 = 3$, the curve is normal or mesokurtic

If $\beta_2 > 3$, the curve is peaked or Leptokurtic

If $\beta_2 < 3$, the curve is flat toped or platykurtic

Karl Pearson β and γ coefficients

Beta (β) Coefficients	Gamma (γ) Coefficients
$\beta_1 = \frac{\mu_3^2}{\mu_2^3}$	$\gamma_1 = \pm\sqrt{\beta_1}$
$\beta_2 = \frac{\mu_4}{\mu_2^2}$	$\gamma_2 = \beta_2 - 3$

Example 1: *The first four moments of a distribution about the value* 4 *of the variable are* = 1.5, 17,–30 *and* 108, Find the moments about mean, Karl Pearson coefficients β_1 and β_2. Find also the moments about (i) the origin (ii) about $x = 2$. **(U.P.T.U. 2006)**

Solution: We have $\mu'_1 = -1.5, \mu'_2 = 17, \mu'_3 = -30, \mu'_4 = 108$ where $a = 4$

Moments about Mean

$$\mu_1 = 0$$

$$\mu_2 = \mu'_2 - \mu'^2_1 = 17 - 2.25 = 14.75$$

$$\mu_3 = \mu'_3 - 3\mu'_2\mu'_1 + \mu'^3_1 = -30 - 3(17)(-1.5) + 2(-1.5)^3 = 39.75$$

$$\mu_4 = \mu'_4 - 4\mu'_3\mu'_1 + 6\mu'_2\mu'^2_1 - 3\mu'^4_1$$

$$= 108 - 4(-30)(-1.5) + 6(17)(-1.5)^2 - 3(1.5)^4 = 142.3125$$

$\therefore$ $$\beta_1 = \frac{\mu_3^2}{\mu_2^3} = \frac{(39.75)^2}{(14.75)^3} = 0.4926$$

$$\beta_2 = \frac{\mu_4}{\mu_2^2} = \frac{142.3125}{(14.75)^3} = 0.6543$$

(*i*) Moments about origin

$$v_1 = x = a + \mu'_1 = 4 - 1.5 = 2.5$$

$$v_2 = \mu_2 + v_1^2 = 14.75 + (2.5)^2 = 8.5$$

$$v_3 = \mu_3 + 3\mu_2 v_1 + v_1^2 + v_1^4$$

$$= 142.3125 + 4(39.75) + (2.5) + 6(14.75)(2.5)^2 + (2.5)^3 = 1108.5625$$

(*ii*) Moments about $x - 2$

Here $a = 2$

$\therefore$ $$\mu'_1 = \bar{x} - a = 2.5 - 2 = 0.5$$

$$\mu'_2 = \mu_2 + \mu'^2_1 = 14.75 + 0.25 = 15$$

$$\mu'_3 = \mu_3 + 3\mu'_1 + \mu'^3_1 = 39.75 + 3(14.75)(0.5) + (.5)^3 = 62$$

$$\mu'_4 = \mu_4 + 4\mu_3\mu'_1 + 6\mu_2\mu'^2_1 + \mu'^4_1.$$

$$= 142.3125 + 4(39.75)(0.5) + 6(14.75)(0.5)^2 + (0.5)^4 = 244$$

Example 2: *Compute the moment coefficient of skewness* (β_1) from the following data :

(L.U.)

Marks Obtained	0-10	10-20	20-30	30-40	40-50	50-60	60-70
Frequency	6	12	22	24	16	12	8

Solution: Here we construct the following table :

Let $a = 35$

Class intervals	*Frequency* (f_i)	*MId values* (x_i)	$u_i = \dfrac{x_i - 35}{10}$	$f_i u_i$	$f_i u_i^2$	$f_i u_i^3$
0-10	6	5	-3	-15	54	-162
10-20	12	15	-2	-24	48	-96
20-30	22	25	-1	-22	22	-22
30-40	24	35	0	0	0	0
40-50	16	45	1	16	16	16
50-60	12	55	2	24	48	96
60-70	8	65	3	24	72	216
Total	*N = 100*	-	-	$\Sigma f_i u_i = 0$	$\Sigma f_i u_i^2 = 260$	$\Sigma f_i u_i^3 = 48$

Now $$\mu'_2 = \frac{1}{N}\sum_{i=1}^{n} fu_1^2 \times h^2 = \frac{260}{100} \times 100 = 260$$

$$\mu'_3 = \frac{1}{N}\sum_{i=1}^{n} fu_1^3 \times h^3 = \frac{48}{100} \times 1000 = 480$$

Therefore,

$$\beta_1 - \frac{\mu'^2_3}{\mu'^2_2} = \frac{(480)^2}{(260)^3} = 0.01$$

$\Rightarrow$ $\beta_1 > 0.$

Hence, the distribution is slightly positively skewed.

Example 3: *Find the coefficient of skewness and kurtosis from the following data :*

x_i	4.5	14.5	24.5	34.5	44.5	54.5	64.5	74.5	84.5	94.5
f_i	1	5	12	22	17	9	4	3	1	1

Solution: Let a = 44.5

x_i	*Frequency* (f_i)	$u_i = \dfrac{x - 44.5}{10}$	$f_i u_i$	$f_i u_i^2$	$f_i u_i^3$	$f_i u_i^4$
4.5	1	–4	–4	16	–64	256
14.5	5	–3	–15	45	–135	405
24.5	12	–2	–24	48	–96	192
34.5	22	–1	–22	22	–22	22
44.5	17	0	0	0	–0	0

54.5	9	1	9	9	9	9
64.5	4	2	8	16	32	64
74.5	3	3	9	27	81	243
84.5	1	4	4	16	64	256
94.5	1	5	5	25	125	625
Total	$N=75$	–	$\Sigma f_i u_i = -30$	$\Sigma f_i u_i^2 = 224$	$\Sigma f_i u_i^3 = -6$	$\Sigma f_i u_i^4 = 2072$

Now

$$\mu'_1 = \frac{1}{N}\sum_{i=1}^{n} f_i u_i \times h = \frac{-30}{75}\times 10 = -4$$

$$\mu'_2 = \frac{1}{N}\sum_{i=1}^{n} f_i u_i^2 \times h^2 = \frac{224}{75}\times 100 = -299$$

$$\mu'_3 = \frac{1}{N}\sum_{i=1}^{n} f_i u_i^3 \times h^3 = \frac{-6}{75}\times 1000 = 80$$

$$\mu'_4 = \frac{1}{N}\sum_{i=1}^{n} f_i u_i^4 \times h^4 = \frac{2072}{75}\times 10000 = 276300$$

Thus moments about mean

$$\mu_2 = \mu'_2 - \mu'^2_1 = 299 - (-4)^2 = 283$$

$$\mu_3 = \mu'_3 - 3\mu'_2\mu'_1 + 2\mu'^3_1 = -80 - 3(299)(-4) + 2(-4)^3 = 3380$$

$$\mu_4 = \mu'_4 - 4\mu'_3\mu'_1 + 6\mu'_2\mu'^2_1 - 3\mu'^4_1$$

$$= 276300 - 4(-80)(-4) + 6(299)(-4)^2 - 3(-4)^4 = 302956$$

∴

$$\beta_1 - \frac{\mu'^2_3}{\mu'^2_2} = \frac{(3380)^2}{(283)^3} = 0.504$$

$$\beta_2 - \frac{\mu_4}{\mu'^2_2} = \frac{(302956)^2}{(283)^3} = 3.7827$$

Hence $\beta_1 > 0$, the distribution is slightly positively skewed.

And $\beta_2 > 3$, the distribution is leptokurtic.

Example 4: *The first four central moments of a distribution are* 0, 2.5, 0.7 *and* 18.75. *Examine the skewness and kurtosis of the distribution.*

Solution: We have $\mu_1 = 0, \mu_2 = 2.5, \mu_3 = 0.7$ and $\mu_4 = 18.75$

To examine skewness, we compute

$$\beta_1 - \frac{\mu_3^2}{\mu'^2_2} = \frac{(0.7)^2}{(2.5)^3} = 0.031$$

Since $\beta_1 > 0$ the distribution is positively skewed

Next, Kurtosis is given by the coefficient

$$\beta_2 - \frac{\mu_4}{\mu'^2_2} = \frac{18.75}{(2.5)^2} = 3.0$$

Since $\beta_1 > 3$. Hence the curve is mesokurtic.

Example 5: *Find the moment coefficient of kurtosis for the following data:*

Class	40-45	45-50	50-55	55-60	60-65	65-70	70-75	75-80	80-85
Frequency	8	25	38	49	51	32	24	22	18

Solution: Here we are taking $a = 62.5$ and $h = 5$, get the following table:

Class	*Mid value* (x_i)	f_i	$u_i = \frac{x-62.5}{5}$	f_iu_i	$f_iu_i^2$	$f_iu_i^3$	$f_iu_i^4$
40-45	42.5	8	–4	–32	128	–512	2048
45-50	47.5	25	–3	–75	225	–675	2025
50-55	52.5	38	–2	–76	152	–304	608
55-60	57.5	49	–1	–49	49	–49	49
60-65	62.5	51	0	0	0	0	0
65-70	67.5	32	1	32	32	32	32
70-75	72.5	24	2	48	96	192	384
75-80	77.5	22	3	66	198	594	1782
80-85	82.5	18	4	72	288	1152	4608
Total		$N = 267$	–	$\Sigma f_iu_i = -14$	$\Sigma f_iu_i^2 = 1168$	$\Sigma f_iu_i^3 = 430$	$\Sigma f_iu_i^4 = 11536$

Now

$$\mu'_1 = \frac{1}{N}\sum_{i=1}^{n} f_iu_i \times h = \frac{-14}{267} \times 5 = -0.26$$

$$\mu'_2 = \frac{1}{N}\sum_{i=1}^{n} f_iu_i^2 \times h^2 = \frac{1168}{267} \times 5^2 = 109.36$$

$$\mu'_3 = \frac{1}{N}\sum_{i=1}^{n} f_iu_i^3 \times h^3 = \frac{430}{267} \times 5^2 = 201.31$$

$$\mu'_4 = \frac{1}{N}\sum_{i=1}^{n} f_iu_i^4 \times h^4 = \frac{11536}{267} \times 5^4 = 27003.75$$

Thus moments about mean

$$\mu_2 = \mu'_2 - \mu'^2_1 = 109.36 - (-0.26)^2 = 109.29$$

$$\mu_4 = \mu'_4 - 4\mu'_3\mu'_1 + 6\mu'_2\mu'^2_1 - 3\mu'^4_1$$

$$= 27003.75 - 4\times 201.31\times(-0.26) + 6(109.36)(-0.26)^2$$

$$-3(-0.26)^4 = 27257.40$$

$\therefore$
$$\beta_2 - \frac{\mu'_4}{\mu'^2_2} = \frac{26242.86}{(109.29)^2} = 2.282$$

Hence $\beta_2 > 3$, the distribution is platykurtic.

Example 6: For a frequency distribution $\left(\frac{f_i}{x_i}\right)$ prove that $\beta_2 \geq 1$.

Solution: We know that

$$\beta_2 = \frac{\mu_4}{\mu_2^2}$$

To prove $\beta_2 \geq 1$, we must prove that $\mu_4 \geq \mu_2^2$.

Now
$$\mu_4 - \mu_2^2 = \frac{1}{N}\sum_{i=1}^{n} f_i(x_i - \bar{x})^4 - \left[\frac{1}{N}\sum_{i=1}^{n} f_i(x_i - \bar{x})^2\right]^2$$

Let
$$z_i = (x_i - \bar{x})^2$$

Then
$$\mu_4 - \mu_2^2 = \frac{1}{N}\sum_{i=1}^{n} f_i(z_i)^2 - \left[\frac{1}{N}\sum_{i=1}^{n} f_i z_i\right]^2$$

$\Rightarrow$
$$\mu_4 - \mu_2^2 = \sigma_2^2$$

Since $\sigma_2^2 \geq 0$ (always)

$\therefore$
$$\mu_4 - \mu_2^2 \geq 0 \Rightarrow \mu_4 \geq \mu_2^2$$

Hence $\beta_2 \geq 1$, prove

Example 7: *Find the first four moments of the following data. Also make Sheppard corrections.*

Interval	10-20	20-30	30-40	40-50	50-60	60-70	70-80
Frequency	1	20	69	108	78	22	2

Solution:

Interval	f_i	x_i	$u_i = x_i - 45$	$u_i = \frac{x-45}{10}$	$f_i u_i$	$f_i u_i^2$	$f_i u_i^3$	$f_i u_i^4$
10-20	1	15	–30	–3	–3	9	–27	81
20-30	20	25	–20	–2	–40	80	–160	320
30-40	69	35	–10	–1	–69	69	–69	69
40-50	108	45	0	0	0	0	0	0
50-60	78	55	10	1	78	78	78	78
60-70	22	65	20	2	44	88	176	352
70-80	2	75	30	3	6	18	54	162
Total	$N =$ 300	–	–	–	$\sum f_i u_i$ = 16	$\sum f_i u_i^2$ =342	$\sum f_i u_i^3$ = 52	$\sum f_i u_i^4$ =1062

Now
$$\mu'_1 = \frac{1}{N}\sum f_i u_i .10 = \left(\frac{16}{300}\right)10 = 0.53$$

$$\mu'_2 = \frac{1}{N}\sum f_i u_i^2 .(10)^2 = \left(\frac{342}{300}\right)(10)^2 = 114$$

$$\mu'_3 = \frac{1}{N}\sum f_i u_i^3 .(10)^3 = \left(\frac{52}{300}\right)(10)^3 = 173.33$$

$$\mu'_4 = \frac{1}{N}\sum f_i u_i^4 .(10)^4 = \left(\frac{1062}{300}\right)(10)^4 = 35400$$

Moments about mean

$$\mu_1 = 0 \quad \text{(always)}$$

$$\mu_2 = \mu'_2 - \mu'^2_1 = 114 - (0.53)^2 = 113.72$$

$$\mu_3 = \mu'_3 - 3\mu'_2\mu'_1 + 2\mu'^3_1 = 173.33 - 3(114)(0.53) + 2(0.53)^3 = -7.63$$

$$\mu_4 = \mu'_4 - 4\mu'_3\mu'_1 + 6\mu'_2\mu'^2_1 - \mu'^4_1$$
$$= 35400 - 4(173.33)(0.53) + 6(114)(0.53)^2 - 3(0.53)^4 = 35224.44$$

Sheppard's Correction. $h = 10$

$$\mu_1 \text{ (corrected)} = \mu_1 = 0$$

$$\mu_2 \text{ (corrected)} = \mu_2 - \frac{h^2}{12} = 113.72 - \frac{(10)^2}{12} = 105.39$$

$$\mu_3 \text{ (corrected)} = \mu_3 = -7.63$$

$$\mu_4 \text{ (corrected)} = \mu_4 - \frac{1}{2}\mu_2 + \frac{7}{240}h^2$$

$$= 35224.44 - \frac{1}{2}(113.72) + \frac{7}{240}(10)^2 = 35170.4966 \quad \textbf{Ans.}$$

Example 8. *Calculate the coefficient of the skewness from the following data:*

Wages in rupees	0-10	10-20	20-30	30-40	40-50	50-60	60-70
No. of labours	185	77	34	180	136	23	50

Solution. Let assumed mean = 35

Classes	f_i	*Mid value* x_i	$u_i = \frac{x_i - 35}{10}$	$f_i u_i$	$f_i u_i^2$	$f_i u_i^3$
0-10	185	5	-3	-555	1665	-4995
10-20	77	15	-2	-154	308	-616
20-30	34	25	-1	-34	34	-34
30-40	180	35	0	0	0	0
40-50	136	45	1	136	136	136
50-60	23	55	2	46	92	184
60-70	50	65	3	150	450	1350
	$N = 685$			$\Sigma f_i u_i = -411$	$\Sigma f_i u_i^2 = 2685$	$\Sigma f_i u_i^3 = -3975$

Here $h = 10$

$$\mu'_1 = \frac{1}{N}\sum f_i u_i \times h = \frac{-411}{685} \times 10 = -6$$

$$\mu'_2 = \frac{1}{N}\sum f_i u_i^2 \times h^2 = \frac{2685}{685} \times 100 = 391.97$$

$$\mu'_3 = \frac{1}{N}\sum f_i u_i^3 \times h^3 = \frac{3975}{685} \times 1000 = -5802.9$$

$$\mu_1 = a + \mu'_1 - 35 - 6 = 29$$

$$\mu_2 = \mu'_2 - \mu'^2_1 = 391.97 - 36 = 355.97$$

$$\mu_3 = \mu'_3 - 3\mu'_2\mu'_1 + 2\mu'^3_1$$

$$= -5802.9 - 3 \times 391.97 \times (-6) + 2(-2)(-6)^3$$

$$= -5802.9 + 7055.46 - 432$$

$$= -6234.9 + 7055.46$$

$$= -820.56$$

$$\beta_1 = \frac{\mu_3^2}{\mu_2^3} = \frac{(820.56)^2}{(355.97)^3} = 0.0149$$

Since $\beta_1 > 0$.

Therefore, the curve is positively skewed.

Example 9: *In two frequency distributions the second moments about mean are 36 and 49 respectively, while third moments about mean are 43.2 and 85.75. Compare the skewness in the two frequency distributions.*

Solution:

(i) In first frequency distribution, we have

$$\mu_2 = 36 \text{ and } \mu_3 = 43.2$$

$$\therefore \quad \beta_1 = \frac{\mu_3^2}{\mu_2^3} = \frac{(43.2)^2}{(36)} = 0.04$$

$$\Rightarrow \quad \beta_1 > 0 \text{ (positive)}$$

Hence the distribution is positively skewed.

(ii) In second frequency distribution, we have

$$\mu_2 = 49 \text{ and } \mu_3 = 75.75$$

$$\therefore \quad \beta_1 = \frac{\mu_3^2}{\mu_2^3} = \frac{(85.75)^2}{(49)^3} = 0.0625$$

$$\Rightarrow \quad \beta_1 > 0 \text{ (positive)}$$

Hence again the distribution is positively skewed.

Example 10: *For a distribution with the mean* $\bar{x} = 10$ variance $\sigma^2 = 16$, $\gamma_1 = 1$ and $\beta_2 = 4$, find the first four moments about origin.

Solution: We have $\bar{x} = 10$; $\sigma^2 = \mu_2 = 16, \gamma_1 = 1$ and $\beta_2 = 4$

We know that

$$\gamma_1 = \sqrt{\beta_2} = \frac{\mu_3}{\mu_2^{3/2}} = 1 \qquad \text{As } \beta_1 = \frac{\mu_3^2}{\mu_2^3}$$

$$\Rightarrow \quad \mu_2^{3/2} = (16)^{3/2} = (4)^{23/2} = 4^3 = 64$$

and $$\beta_2 = \frac{\mu_4}{\mu_2^2} = 4 \Rightarrow \mu_4 = 4(\mu_2^2) = 4\times 16^2 = 1024$$

Next moments about origin are

$$v_1 = \bar{x} = 10$$

$$v_2 = \mu_2 + v_1^2 = 16 + 10^2 = 116 \quad | v_1 = \bar{x}$$

$$v_3 = \mu_3 + 3\mu_2 v_1 + (v_1)^2 = 64 + 3\times 16\times 10 + 10^3$$

$$= 64 + 480 + 1000 = 1544$$

$$v_4 = \mu_4 + 4\mu_3 v_1 6\mu_2 (v_1)^2 + (v_1)^4$$

$$= 1024 + 4\times 64\times 10 + 6\times 16\times 10^2 + 10^4$$

$$= 1024 + 2560 + 9600 + 1000 = 23184$$

Example 11: *The first three moments about the origin are given by*

$$\mu'_1 = \frac{n+1}{2}, \mu'_2 = \frac{(n+1)(2n+1)}{6}, \mu'_3 := \frac{n(n+1)^2}{4}$$

examine the skewness of the data.

Solution: We know that

$$\mu_3 = \mu'_3 - 3\mu'_2\,\mu'_1 + 2(\mu'_1)^3$$

$$= \frac{n(n+1)^2}{4} - \frac{n(n+1)(2n+1)}{6}.\frac{n+1}{2} + 2\left(\frac{n+1}{2}\right)^3$$

$$= \frac{(n+1)^2}{4}[-(2n+1) + (n+1)]$$

$$= \frac{(n+1)^2}{4}[-2n + 1 + n + 1)$$

$$= \frac{(n+1)^2}{4}[0] = 0$$

$$\therefore \quad \beta_1 = \frac{\mu_3^2}{\mu_2^3} = \frac{0}{\mu_2^3} = 0$$

Since $\beta_1 = 0$.

Thus there is no skewness in the data.

Example 12: *The fourth moment mean of a frequency distribution is* 48. *What must be the value of its S.D. in order that the distribution be (i) Leptokurtic (ii) Mesokurtic (iii) Platykurtic?*

Solution: We now that

$$\beta_2 = \frac{\mu_3}{\mu_2^2} = \frac{\mu_4}{\sigma^4} = \frac{48}{\sigma^4} \qquad \text{As } \sigma^4 = \mu_2$$

(*i*) For Deptokurtic,

$$\beta_2 > 3$$

$$\Rightarrow \quad \frac{48}{\sigma^4} > 3$$

or $$\sigma^4 < \frac{48}{\sigma^4} \Rightarrow \sigma^4 < 16$$

or $$\sigma < 2$$

(*ii*) For Mesokurtic,

$$\beta_2 = 3$$

$$\Rightarrow \quad \frac{48}{\sigma^4} = 3 \Rightarrow \sigma = 2$$

(*iii*) For Platy kurtic,

$$\beta_2 < 3$$

$$\Rightarrow \quad \beta > 2.$$

Exercise 1.1

1. Define statistics, it's scope and significance in economics, commerce and various areas of management. **(UPTU-07, 08) (L.U.)**
2. "Statistics is the Science of Estimates and Probabilities." Explain and illustrate.
3. "Statistics are like clay of which you can make a God or Devil as you please." Comment on the statement. **(UPTU-09) (A.U.)**
4. "Statistics affects everybody and touches life at many points. It is both a science and an art." Comment.
5. Explain the properties of a good average. In the light of these properties which average do you think is the best and why? **(UPTU -07)**
6. Discuss the merits and demerits of median as a measure of central tendency.**(UPTU-07)**
7. What do you understand by coefficient of variation? Discuss its importance in business problems. Also distinguish between variance and coefficient of variation.

8. Compute mean and median from the following data :

Income More than (In Rs.)	1000	2000	3000	4000	5000	6000	7000	8000
No. of Persons	72	67	59	50	36	29	4	0

(UPTU-07)

9. For two firms A and B belonging to same industry, the following details are available :

	Firm A	**Firm B**
Number of Employees	100	200
Average wages per month	240	170
Standard deviation of the wage per month	6	8

Find :

(*i*) Which of the firm pays out larger amount as monthly wages?

(*ii*) Which firm show greater variability in the distribution of wages?

(*iii*) Find average monthly wage and the standard deviation of the wages of all employees in both the firms.

10. Calculate coefficient of variation form the following data :

Age- groups (less than)	10	20	30	40	50	60	70
Population (in '000)	10	26	51	81	107	120	125

11. Form the given distribution of 30 units, calculate mean, median and mode :

Sales (in '000)	0-10	10-20	20-30	30-40	40-50	50-60
Units	3	6	10	8	2	1

12. What are various measures of dispersion? Critically examine them. **(UPTU-CO-09)**

13. The following distribution shows the turnover to the branches of a group of multiple shops in March, 1989 :

Turnover (in Rs. '000)	**No. of Shops**
5 and under 10	8
10 and under 15	18
15 and under 20	42
20 and under 25	62
25 and under 30	30
30 and under 35	10
35 and under 40	4

Calculate coefficient of variation from the data given above.

14. What do you understand by skewness? Explain different methods for measuring it. **(UPTU-07)**
15. What do you understand by kurtosis? Explain different methods for measuring it.
16. What are the different measures of central tendency?
17. Distinguish between dispersion and skewness.
18. What is kurtosis? How does it differ from skewness?
19. From the Data given below; Calculate,
    (*a*) Karl Pearson's Coefficient of Skewness.
    (*b*) Bowley's Coefficient of Skewness.
    Mean = 150; Median = 142; $Q_1 = 6_2$; $Q_3 = 195$
20. Calculate the first four moments about the mean and also the value of β_1 and β_2 form the following data :

Marks	0-10	10-20	20-30	30-40	40-50	50-60	60-70
No. of Students	8	12	20	30	15	10	5

21. Calculate the first four moments about the mean from the following data. Also calculate the value of β_1 and β_2 first

Marks	0-10	10-20	20-30	30-40	40-50	50-60	60-70
No. of Students	5	12	18	40	15	7	3

22. Following distribution gives the pattern of overtime work done by 100 employees of a company. Calculate median, first quartile and third quartile:

Overtime Hours	10-15	15-20	20-25	25-30	30-35	35-40
No. of Employees	11	20	35	20	8	6

23. Calculate standard deviation from the following data :

Profit (Rs. Crores)	No. of Companies
Less than 10	8
Less than 20	20
Less than 30	40
Less than 40	70
Less than 50	90
Less than 60	100

24. What is measure of dispersion? List the methods known to you.

25. In the following table, distribution of students is shown according to their weights in kg. Find the coefficient of variation of each series. Which series show greater variation in weights?

Weight (kg)	30-40	40-50	50-60	60-70
Class A	10	20	18	4
Class B	9	21	15	6

26. Below are given the number of runs scored by two batsmen in 10 matches.

Batsman A :	27	0	100	39	45	103	80	40	52	2
Batsman B :	13	16	80	70	5	62	40	10	131	13

Who is better run scorer? Also find which of the two batsmen is more consistent in scoring.

27. In a statistical investigation in two villages A and B, the following data was obtained :-

Particulars	Village A	Village B
Number of Respondents	600	500
Average Income (Rs.)	175	186
Standard deviation (Rs.)	10	9

(*i*) What is the average income of the respondents in the villages A and B put together?

(*ii*) In which village is the variation in income greater?

28. Find arithmetic mean and standard deviation from the following data. Also find coefficient of variation.

Age (less than) :	10	20	30	40	50	60	70	80
No. of persons :	15	30	50	75	100	110	115	125

29. 'Measure of central tendency, dispersion and skewness are complementary to one another in understanding a frequency distribution. Elucidate.

Find the coefficient of variation, if the sum of squares of the deviations of 10 observations taken from mean 50 is 250.

30. Calculate standard deviation from the following data :

Age (in years)	4-6	6-8	8-10	10-12	12-14	14-16	16-18
No. of students	30	90	120	150	80	60	20

31. The following table shows the profits earned by 750 small-scale industrial units in U.P. in the year 2006-07 in Rs. lakhs :-

Profits (Rs. laksh)	20-25	25-30	30-35	35-40	40-45	45-50	50-55	55-60
No. of units	50	70	80	180	150	120	70	30

Calculate median and mode of the above frequency distribution and account for the difference, if any.

32. In a statistical investigation, the daily incomes of 50 retailers in a market located in Kanpur were found distributed as follows :-

Daily Income	0-150	150-160	160-170	170-180	180-190	190-200	200 and above
No. of Retailers	1	3	5	16	11	8	6

Find the Median, Q_1 and Q_3 and calculate the Coefficient of Skewness by Bowley's Method.

33. Calculate the mean, median and mode from the following data :

Marks	Students
Less than 36	10
Less than 40	47
Less than 44	112
44-48	80
48-52	51
52-56	35
56-60	18
60-64	4

34. Calculate Karl Pearson's coefficient of skewness form the data given below :

Marks	70-80	60-70	50-60	40-50	30-40	20-30	10-2	0-10
No. of candidates	11	22	30	35	21	11	6	5

35. Compute the mean deviation (M.D.) from the following data. Also find the coefficient of M.D.

Classes	0-20	20-40	40-60	60-80	80-100	100-120
Frequency	5	50	84	32	10	6

36. The mean and the standard deviation of a characteristic of 100 items were found be 60 and 10 respectively. At the time of calculations, two items were wrongly taken as 5 and 45 instead of 30 and 20. Calculate the corrected mean and corrected standard deviation.

37. The figures of weights of boys and girls studying in a school are as under :-

	Number	Mean weight	variance
Boys	100	60 kg	9
Girls	50	45 kg	4

(*a*) Compute the combined standard deviation.

(*b*) Which distribution is more variable?

38. Calculate the Karl Pearson's coefficient of skewness from the following data :

Size	14.5	15.5	16.5	17.5	18.5	19.5	20.5	21.5
Frequency	35	40	48	100	125	87	43	22

39. The mean and S.D. of size 10 values were found to be 9.5 and 2.5 respectively. Later on, an additional observation became available. This was 15.0 and was included in the original sample. Find the mean and S.D. of the 11 observations.

40. Share prices of two companies A Ltd. And B Ltd. Were recorded as follow:

A Ltd	12	13	15	14	14	14	13	17
B.Ltd	113	114	113	115	117	114	112	114

Which company's share prices are more variable? **(UPTU-08)**

41. Compute an appropriate measure of skewness for the following data:

Sales (Rs. Lakhs)	0-50	50-60	60-70	70-80	80-90	90-100	100-110	110-120	120-above
No. of companies	12	30	65	78	80	55	45	25	10

(UPTU-08)

42. (*a*) What is the distinction between median and mode? Under what condition would you make use of each one of them in the analysis of business problems?

(UPTU-CO-08)

(*b*) Calculate mean deviation of number of heads in 20 tosses of five coins as given below:

No. of Heads (x)	0	1	2	3	4	5
Frequency (y)	1	2	7	6	3	1

43. (*a*) The mean of 5 observation is 4 and the variance is 5.20. Three of these observation s are given by 1,2 and 6. What are the remaining two observations? **(UPTU-CO-08)**

(*b*) A person takes a trip which consists of traveling 900 miles by rain at an average speed of 30 m.p.h., 3000 miles by plane at an average of 400 m.p.h., 400 miles by bus at 25 m.p.h. and finally 15 miles by taxi at 25 m.p.h. What is the average speed for the entire distance? **(UPTU-CO-08)**

44. The mean annual salary of employees of a company is Rs. 30,000/- .The mean annual salaries of male and female employees are Rs. 35,000/- and Rs. 23,000/- respectively. Find out the percentage of male and female employees working in the company. **(UPTU-09)**

45. An incomplete frequency distribution is given as follows :

Variable	Frequency
10 – 20	12
20 – 30	30
30 – 40	?
40 – 50	65
50 – 60	?
60 – 70	25
70 – 80	18
Total	**229**

Given that the median value is 46, determine the missing frequencies using the median formula.

46. What is statistics ? Explain important function of statistics. **(UPTU-CO-09)**

47. Find mean and mode from the following table : **(UPTU-CO-09)**

Income (Rs.) :	100 – 200	100 – 300	100 – 400	100 – 500	100 – 600
No. of Persons :	15	33	63	83	100

48. In a batch of 13 students, 4 have failed. The marks of the successful candidates were 41, 57, 38, 61, 36, 35, 71, 50 and 40. Find the median marks. **(UPTU-CO-09)**

49. (*a*) Write the empirical relationship between Mean, Mode and Median. If Mean = 5, Median = 6 then computer Mode. **(TMU-CO-09)**

(*b*) Consider the following situation.

	Mean	S.D
Player A	30	5
Player B	25	3

Which player is more consistent ? **(TMU-CO-09)**

50. Consider the following distribution.

Variable	Frequency
10 – 20	10
20 – 30	15
30 – 40	50
40 – 50	52
50 – 60	40
60 – 70	12

Computer Mean, Mode & Median. **(TMU-CO-09)**

51. The score of students in internal exams are found to be distribution as

10, 12, 15, 11, 3, 12, 10, 9, 8, 7, 5

Computer standard derivation & skewness **(TMU-CO-09)**

52. (*a*) Discuss relative merits and demerits of median .

(*b*) Explain the superiority of standard deviation over other measures of dispersion. **(TMU-09)**

53. What is the role of measure of dispersion? Define various measures of dispersion in brief. Below are given the number of runs scored by two batsmen in eight matches.

Batsman A:	27	16	39	45	101	80	40	52
Batsman B:	0	100	80	5	60	40	10	121

Who is better run scorer? Also find which of the two batsman is more consistent in scoring.

54. Find the coefficient of variation, if the sum of squares of the deviation of 10 obsertions taken from mean 50 is 250. **(UPTU 2006)**

55. What do you mean by dispersion? Enlist the important of measure of dispersion. **(UPTU 2006)**

56. Statistic affects everybody and touches life at many points it is both a science and an art?" comment. **(UPTU 2006)**

57. Distinguish between primary data and secondary data, what are the various techniques the collecting primary data? Explain briefly. **(UPTU 2003)**

58. Statistics play an important role not only in the study of economics and commerce, but also in managerial decision making, Explain briefly. **(UPTU 2005)**

59. Discuss the merit and demerits of mode as a measure of central tendency? **(UPTU 2005)**

60. Define statistics in singular and plural sense. **(UPTU 2005)**

61. Write short note on Qualitative Statistics?

Objective type Questions

1. The algebraic sum of the deviation of 10 observations measured from 15 is 7. Thus the mean is **(UPTU-08)**
   (a) 10.5 (b) 70
   (c) 15.7 (d) 10.7
2. The algebraic sum of the deviation from mean is
   (a) maximum (b) least
   (c) zero (d) None of these
3. The sum of square of deviations from mean is
   (a) least (b) zero
   (c) maximum (d) None of these
4. An additional observation 15 is include in a series of all observation and its mean remains unaffected. The mean of the series was
   (a) 11 (b) 15
   (c) 165 (d) 4
5. The median of a series is 10. Two additional observation, 7 and 20, are added to the series. The median of the new series will be
   (a) 9 (b) 20
   (c) 7 (d) 10
6. A distribution has mean = 8.5, median = 8.3, and mode= 7.4. The distribution is
   (a) positively skewed (b) negatively skewed
   (c) symmetrical (d) None of these
7. In a moderately asymmetrical distribution, the mean and median are 22 are 26 respectively. Then, the value of mode will be
   (a) 25 (b) 24
   (c) 34 (d) None of these
8. In a batch of 13 students, 4 have failed. The marks of the successful candidates were 41,57, 38, 61, 36, 35, 71, 50 and 40. find the median marks
   (a) 40 (b) 50
   (c) 41 (d) None of these

9. The arithmetic mean of 9 observations is 100 and that of 6 is 80, the combined mean of all the 15 observation will be

   (a) 100 (b) 80

   (c) 90 (d) 92

10. The arithmetic mean of the first N natural numbers, 1, 2, 3, ...N is

    (a) $\frac{N}{2}$ (b) $\frac{N+1}{2}$

    (c) $\frac{2N+1}{2}$ (d) None

11. In a symmetrical distribution:

    (a) (Median – Q1) = (Q3 – Median)

    (b) (Median – Q1) >(Q3 – Median)

    (c) (Median – Q1)<(Q3 – Median)

    (d) None of these

12. The following information-mean = 144, median =142 and mode = 174 describes a

    (a) positively skewed distribution

    (b) negatively skewed distribution

    (c) symmetrical distribution

    (d) None of these

13. For a symmetrical distribution, Q1 and Q3 are 20 and 40 respectively. The value of 50th percentile will be

    (a) 40 (b) 20

    (c) 30 (d) None of these

14. For a symmetrical distribution P25 and P75 are 40 and 60 respectively. The value of median will be

    (a) 50 (b) 40

    (c) 60 (d) None of these

15. For a symmetrical distribution, Q1 and Q2 are 30 and 45 respectively. Then the value of Q3 is

    (a) 60 (b) 45

    (c) 30 (d) None of these

16. The sum of squares of deviation for 10 observations taken from mean 50 is 250. The coefficient of variation is

    (a) 50 % (b)10 %

    (c) 40 % (d) None of these

17. For a symmetrical distribution $Q_1 = 25$ and $Q_3 = 45$, the median is. **(UPTU-08, 10)**

(a) 20 (b) 25

(c) 35 (d) None of these

18. The median is

(a) 4th decile (b) 50th percentile

(c) 8th decile (d) None of these

19. Which measure of dispersion is least affected by extreme values

(a) S.D. (b) Range

(c)M.D. (d) Q.D.

20. The mean of squared deviation about the mean is called

(a) S.D. (b) Variance

(c) M.D. (d) Q.D.

21. The mean of absolute deviations from an average is called

(a) S.D. (b) M.D.

(c) Variance (d) Q.D.

22. Mean ± 3σ range of a normal distribution curve covers............percent area of the curve **(UPTU-08)**

(a) 90.67 (b) 99.73

(c) 95.45 (d) None of theses

23. Quartile deviation is

(a) (2/3) σ (b) (4/5) σ

(c) (3/2) σ (d) None of these

24. $\bar{x} = 10$, $\sigma = 3.2$. All the observations increased by 4 would give the result

(a) $\bar{x} = 10, \sigma = 7.2$ (b) $\bar{x} = 10, \sigma = 3.2$.

(c) $\bar{x} = 14, \sigma = 3.2$ (d) $\bar{x} = 14, \sigma = 7.2$

25. The father of statistics is **(U.P.T.U. 2010)**

(a) Marshal (b) Gottfried Achenwall

(c) Galton (d) None of these

26. $\bar{x} = 50, \sigma = 25$; the C.V. is

(a) 200 (b) 25

(c) 50 (d) None of these

27. If Q.D. is 16, the most likely value of S.D. will be

(a) 24 (b) 42

(c) 16 (d) None of these

28. If M.D. is 12, the value of S.D. will be
    (a) 15 (b) 12
    (c) 24 (d) None of these
29. Which of the following measures is most affected by extreme values
    (a) S.D. (b) Q.D.
    (c) M.D. (d) Range
30. If each and every value of a set of observations is multiplied by a constant, then the variance is
    (a) unaltered (b) increases
    (c) decreases (d) None of these
31. Which of the following is a unit free number
    (a) S.D. (b) Variance
    (c) M.D. (d) C.V.
32. If mean is 10 and coefficient of variation is 5, then the standard deviation will be
    (a) 10 (b) 50
    (c) 5 (d) none
33. The standard deviation of a set of 50 items is 6.5. If every item is increased by 5, then the standard deviation will be
    (a) 11.5 (b) 1.5
    (c) 6.5 (d) none
34. Find the coefficient of variation, if the sum of squares of the deviation of 10 observations taken from mean (=50) is 250.
    (a) 50 (b) 25
    (c) 10 (d) none
35. When coefficient of skewness is zero, the distribution is :
    (a) J shaped (b) U shaped
    (c) Bell shaped (d) V shaped
36. A negative coefficient of skewness implies that :
    (a) Mean is greater than mode (b) Mean is less than Mode
    (c) Mean is equal to Mode (d) None of these
37. Karl Pearson's coefficient of skewness is
    (a) always positive (b) always negative
    (c) always zero (d) Can be positive, negative and zero
38. If β_2 is greater than 3, then the curve is called :
    (a) Mesokurtic (b) Leptokurtic

(c) Platykurtic (d) All of these

39. In a frequency curve of scores the mode was found to be less than the mean. This shows that the distribution is :

(a) Negative skewed (b) Positively skewed

(c) Normal (d) None of these

40. For a symmetric distribution :

(a) $\mu_3 = 0$ (b) $\mu_3 > 0$

(c) $\mu_3 < 0$ (d) None of these

41. β_2 is always____________

(a) positive (b) negative

(c) zero (d) one

42. Skewness is positive when mean is .... mode.

(a) equal to (b) less than

(c) more than (d) None of these

43. For a symmetrical distribution $\beta 1$ is equal to-

(a) zero (b) one

(c) three (d) two

44. The first central moment is always

(a) zero (b) one

(c) two (d) three

45. The second central moment is always equal to

(a) One (b) zero

(c) two (d) three

46. The flat curve is also known as

(a) Leptokurtic (b) Platykurtic

(c) Mesokurtic (d) None of these

47. Statistics deals with only .... Data

(a) Quantitative (b) Qualitative

(c) both (d) None of these

48. Statistics can be considered as

(a) An art (b) Science

(c) Both art as well as science (d) None of these

49. Statistics does not study individuals

(a) True (b) false

(c) can't say (d) None of these

50. Which of the following is /are true

    (1) A single figure is not statistics

    (2) Statistics are affected by a number of factors.

    (3) Statistics cannot be misused.

    (a) All (b) 1,2

    (c) 1,3 (d) 2,3

51. The value of median and mode can be determined

    (a) Graphically (b) Mathematically

    (c) Both (d) None of these

52. The point of intersection of the 'less than' and 'more than' Ogives corresponds to-

    (a) Mean (b) Median

    (c) Mode (d) Geometric mean

53. Sum of the absolute deviation taken from .... is least.

    (a) Mean (b) Median

    (c) Mode (d) Geometric mean

54. Variance is the square of -------

    Coefficient of variation

    S.D., M.D., Q.D.

55. Which of the following is/are true

    1. Range is the best measure of dispersion.
    2. C.V. is expressed in same units as the original data.
    3. M.D. can never be negative.

    1, 2 2, 3

    Only 2. Only 3.

56. S.D. is always....... Range.

    (a) More than (b) Less than

    (c) Equal to (d) None

57. Mode can be graphically located with the help of ....

    (a) Bar diagram (b) Ogives

    (c) Histogram (d) Frequency curve

57. Mode can be graphically located with the help of ....

    (a) Bar diagram (b) Ogives

    (c) Histogram (d) Frequency curve

58. $\beta_2 =$

(a) $\dfrac{\mu_3}{\mu_2^2}$ (b) $\dfrac{\mu_4}{\mu_2^2}$

(c) $\dfrac{\mu_4}{\mu_3^2}$ (d) $\dfrac{\mu_3}{\mu_4^2}$

59. ______ reveals the shape of the distribution at the top.

(a) Skewness (b) Kurtosis

(c) Dispersion (d) Central value

60. The coefficient of skewness based on quartiles is also known as _____

(a) Karl Pearson's coefficient (b) Bowley's coefficient

(c) M oments (d) Kurtosis

61. In a series, 20 percent values are greater than 90, then …… is 90. **(UPTU-08)**

62. In computing the average ratio of increase in GNP………. is the most suitable measures. **(UPTU-08)**

Answer

1	C	11	A	21	B	31	D	41	A	51	C	61	GM
2	C	12	D	22	B	32	B	42	A	52	B	62	P80
3	A	13	C	23	A	33	C	43	A	53	B		
4	B	14	A	24	C	34	C	44	A	54	B		
5	D	15	A	25	D	35	C	45	A	55	D		
6	A	16	B	26	C	36	B	46	B	56	B		
7	C	17	C	27	A	37	D	47	A	57	C		
8	D	18	B	28	A	38	B	48	C	58	B		
9	D	19	D	29	D	39	B	49	A	59	B		
10	B	20	A	30	B	40	A	50	B	60	B		

List of Important Formula

1. Arithmetic Mean

Method	Individual Series	Discrete Series	Continuous Series
(a) Direct Method	$\bar{X}=\frac{\Sigma X}{N}$	$\bar{X}=\frac{\Sigma fX}{N}, N=\Sigma f$	$\bar{X}=\frac{\Sigma fX}{N}, N=\Sigma f$
(b) Short-cut Method	$\bar{X}=A+\frac{\Sigma d}{N}$, $d=(X-A)$	$\bar{X}=A+\frac{\Sigma fd}{N}$, $d=(X-A)$	$\bar{X}=A+\frac{\Sigma fd}{N}$, $d=(X-A)$
(d) Step-deviation Method		$\bar{X}=A+h\frac{\Sigma fd}{N}$, $d'=\frac{X-A}{h}$	$\bar{X}=A+h\frac{\Sigma fd}{N}$, $d'=\frac{X-A}{h}$

(d) Combined arithmetic mean (i) $\bar{X}_{12}=\frac{N_1\bar{X}_1+N_2\bar{X}_2}{N_1+N_2}$

(ii) $\bar{X}_{12}=\frac{N_1\bar{X}_1+N_2\bar{X}_2+\ldots+N_k\bar{X}_k}{N_1+N_2+\ldots..+N_k}$

(e) Weighted A.M. $\bar{X}_w=\frac{W_1\bar{X}_1+W_2\bar{X}_2+\ldots+W_k\bar{X}_k}{W_1+W_2+\ldots..+W_k}=\frac{\Sigma WX}{\Sigma W}$

2. Median and Partition values

Partition value	Individual Series	Discrete Series	Continuous Series
(a) Median	Size of $\left(\frac{M+1}{2}\right)^{th}$ item	Size of $\left(\frac{M+1}{2}\right)^{th}$ item	Size of $\left(\frac{N}{2}\right)^{th}$ item determines the median class. Then Median $=l_1+\frac{\frac{N}{2}-c}{f}(l_2-l_1)$
(b) Q_1	Size of $\left(\frac{M+1}{4}\right)^{th}$ item	Size of $\left(\frac{M+1}{4}\right)^{th}$ item	Size of $\left(\frac{N}{4}\right)^{th}$ item determines the I quartile class, then

			$Q_1 = l_1 + \dfrac{\frac{N}{4} - c}{f}(l_2 - l_1)$
(c) Q_1	Size of $3\left(\dfrac{M+1}{4}\right)^{th}$ item	Size of $3\left(\dfrac{M+1}{4}\right)^{th}$ item	Size of $\left(\dfrac{3N}{4}\right)^{th}$ item determines the III quartile class. Then $Q_3 = l_1 + \dfrac{\frac{3N}{4} - c}{f}(l_2 - l_1)$
(d) D_r, r^{th}	Size of $r\left(\dfrac{M+1}{10}\right)^{th}$ item	Size of $r\left(\dfrac{M+1}{10}\right)^{th}$ item	Size of $\left(\dfrac{rN}{10}\right)^{th}$ item determines the rth decile class. Then $D_r = l_1 + \dfrac{\frac{rN}{10} - c}{f}(l_2 - l_1)$
decile (e) $r = 1, 2 \ldots., 9$ P_r, r^{th} percentile $r = 1, 2 \ldots., 90$	Size of $r\left(\dfrac{M+1}{100}\right)^{th}$ item	Size of $r\left(\dfrac{M+1}{100}\right)^{th}$ item	Size of $\left(\dfrac{rN}{100}\right)^{th}$ item determines the rth percentile class. Then $P_r = l_1 + \dfrac{\frac{rN}{100} - c}{f}(l_2 - l_1)$

3. Mode

Individual Series	Discrete Series	Continuous Series
The value having the maximum frequency	The value having the maximum frequency to be determined by observation or grouping method	First determine the modal class by observation or grouping method. Then $\text{Mode} = l_1 + \dfrac{f_1 - f_0}{2f_1 - f_0 - f_2} \times (l_2 - l_1)$ $\text{Mode} = l_1 + \dfrac{\lvert f_1 - f_0 \rvert}{\lvert f_1 - f_0 \rvert + \lvert f_1 - f_2 \rvert} \times h$

4. Geometric Mean

Individual Series	Discrete Series	Continuous Series
G.M. = $\sqrt[N]{*X_1 \times X_2 \times .... \times X_N)}$ G.M. = Antilog $\left[\frac{\Sigma \log X}{N}\right]$	G.M. = Antilog $\left[\frac{\Sigma f \log X}{N}\right]$	G.M. = Antilog $\left[\frac{\Sigma f \log X}{N}\right]$

$$\text{Combined G.M.} = \text{Antilog}\left[\frac{N_1 \log G_1 + N_2 \log G_2}{N_1 + N_2}\right]$$

$$\text{Weight G.M.} = \text{Antilog}\left[\frac{\Sigma W \log X}{\Sigma W}\right]$$

Compound interest formula,

$$P_n = P_0(1+r)^n$$

5. Harmonic Mean

Individual Series	Discrete Series	Continuous Series
H.M. = Reciprocal $\left(\frac{\Sigma(1/X)}{N}\right)$ $= \frac{N}{\Sigma(1/X)}$	H.M. = Reciprocal $\left(\frac{\Sigma(f/X)}{N}\right)$ $= \frac{N}{\Sigma(f/X)}$	H.M. = Reciprocal $\left(\frac{\Sigma(f/X)}{N}\right)$ $= \frac{N}{\Sigma(f/X)}$

6. Empirical Relationship between Means

(a) Mode = 3 Median – 2 Mean.

(b) H.M. ≤ G.M. ≤ A.M.

7. Range

Individual Series	Discrete and continuous series
Range – $L - S$ Coeff. of Range = $\frac{L-S}{L+S}$	Range –$L - S$ Coeff. of Range = $\frac{L-S}{L+S}$ Here, L is the upper limit of the highest class and S the lower limit of the lowest class

8. Quartile Deviation (Q.D.)

Individual Series	Discrete and continuous series
$\text{Q.D.} = \dfrac{Q_3 - Q_1}{2}$ $\text{Coeff. of Q.D.} = \dfrac{Q_3 - Q_1}{Q_3 + Q_1}$	$\text{Q.D.} = \dfrac{Q_3 - Q_1}{2}$ $\text{Coeff. of Q.D.} = \dfrac{Q_3 - Q_1}{Q_3 + Q_1}$

9. Mean Deviation (M.D.)

Individual Series	Discrete and continuous series
$\text{M.D.} = \dfrac{1}{N} \Sigma \mid X = \bar{X} \mid$ $\text{Coeff. of M.D.} = \dfrac{\text{M.D.}}{\text{Mean}} = \dfrac{\text{M.D.}}{x}$	$\text{M.D.} = \dfrac{1}{N} \Sigma \mid X = \bar{X} \mid$ $\text{Coeff. of M.D.} = \dfrac{\text{M.D.}}{\text{Mean}} = \dfrac{\text{M.D.}}{x}$

10. Standard Deviation (S.D.)

Individual Series	Discrete and continuous series
(i) Actual Mean Method : $\sigma = \sqrt{\left[\dfrac{1}{N}\Sigma(X - \bar{X})^2\right]}$ $= \sqrt{\left[\dfrac{\Sigma X^2}{N} = \left(\dfrac{\Sigma X}{N}\right)^2\right]}$ $\sqrt{\left[\dfrac{1}{N}\left(\Sigma X^2 - N\bar{X}^2\right)\right]}$ (ii) Short-cut Method: $\sigma = \sqrt{\left[\dfrac{\Sigma d^2}{N} - \left(\dfrac{\Sigma d}{N}\right)^2\right]}$ where $d = (X - A)$ (iii) Step deviation Methods : $\sigma = h \times \sqrt{\left[\dfrac{\Sigma d'^2}{N} - \left(\dfrac{\Sigma d'}{N}\right)^2\right]}$ where, $d' = \left(\dfrac{X - A}{h}\right)$	(i) Actual Mean Method : $\sigma = \sqrt{\left[\dfrac{1}{N}\Sigma f(X - \bar{X})^2\right]}$ $= \sqrt{\left[\dfrac{\Sigma fX^2}{N} = \left(\dfrac{\Sigma fX}{N}\right)^2\right]}$ $\sqrt{\left[\dfrac{1}{N}\left(\Sigma fX^2 - N\bar{X}^2\right)\right]}$ (ii) Short-cut Method: $\sigma = \sqrt{\left[\dfrac{\Sigma d^2}{N} - \left(\dfrac{\Sigma d}{N}\right)^2\right]}$ where $d = (X - A)$ (iii) Step deviation Methods : $\sigma = h \times \sqrt{\left[\dfrac{\Sigma fd'^2}{N} - \left(\dfrac{\Sigma fd'}{N}\right)^2\right]}$ where, $d' = \left(\dfrac{X - A}{h}\right)$

11. Coefficient of variation or C.V. = $(\sigma / \bar{X}) \times 100$

$$\textbf{Combined S.D.} = \sigma_{12} = \sqrt{\left[\frac{N_1(\sigma_1^2 + D_1^2) + N_2(\sigma_2^2 + D_2^2)}{}\right]}$$

where, $D_1 = (\bar{X}_1 - \bar{X}_{12})$ and $D_2 = (\bar{X}_2 - \bar{X}_{12})$

Variance = $\sigma^2 = (S.D.)^2$.

12. Percentage of items lying between specific σ times

Limits	Percentage of items
(i) within $\bar{X} \pm 1\sigma$ or one σ limits $\bar{X} \pm 1\sigma$	

Individual Series	Discrete and continuous series
(i) Actual Mean Method : $\sigma = \sqrt{\left[\frac{1}{N}\Sigma(X - \bar{X})^2\right]}$ $= \sqrt{\left[\frac{\Sigma X^2}{N} - \left(\frac{\Sigma X}{N}\right)^2\right]}$ $\sqrt{\left[\frac{1}{N}\left(\Sigma X^2 - N\bar{X}^2\right)\right]}$	(i) Actual Mean Method : $\sigma = \sqrt{\left[\frac{1}{N}\Sigma f(X - \bar{X})^2\right]}$ $= \sqrt{\left[\frac{\Sigma fX^2}{N} - \left(\frac{\Sigma fX}{N}\right)^2\right]}$ $\sqrt{\left[\frac{1}{N}\left(\Sigma fX^2 - N\bar{X}^2\right)\right]}$
(ii) Short-cut Method: $\sigma = \sqrt{\left[\frac{\Sigma d^2}{N} - \left(\frac{\Sigma d}{N}\right)^2\right]}$ where $d = (X - A)$ (iii) Step deviation Methods : $\sigma = h \times \sqrt{\left[\frac{\Sigma d'^2}{N} - \left(\frac{\Sigma d'}{N}\right)^2\right]}$ where, $d' = \left(\frac{X - A}{h}\right)$	(ii) Short-cut Method: $\sigma = \sqrt{\left[\frac{\Sigma d^2}{N} - \left(\frac{\Sigma d}{N}\right)^2\right]}$ where $d = (X - A)$ (iii) Step deviation Methods : $\sigma = h \times \sqrt{\left[\frac{\Sigma fd'^2}{N} - \left(\frac{\Sigma fd'}{N}\right)^2\right]}$ where, $d' = \left(\frac{X - A}{h}\right)$

13. Coefficient of variation or C.V. = $(\sigma / \bar{X}) \times 100$

$$\text{Combined S.D.} = \sigma_{12} = \sqrt{\left[\frac{N_1(\sigma_1^2 + D_1^2) + N_2(\sigma_2^2 + D_2^2)}{N_1 + N_2}\right]}$$

where, $D_1 = (\bar{X}_1 - \bar{X}_{12})$ and $D_2 = (\bar{X}_2 - \bar{X}_{12})$

$$\text{variance} = \sigma^2 = (\text{S.D.})^2.$$

14. Percentage of items lying between specific σ times

Limit	Percentage of items
(*i*) within $\bar{X} \pm 1\sigma$ or one σ limits	68.27%
(ii) within $\bar{X} \pm 2\sigma$ or one σ limits	95.45%
(iii) within $\bar{X} \pm 3\sigma$ or three σ limits	99.73%

15. Skewness

Positively Skewed Distribution
(longer bail on the right)

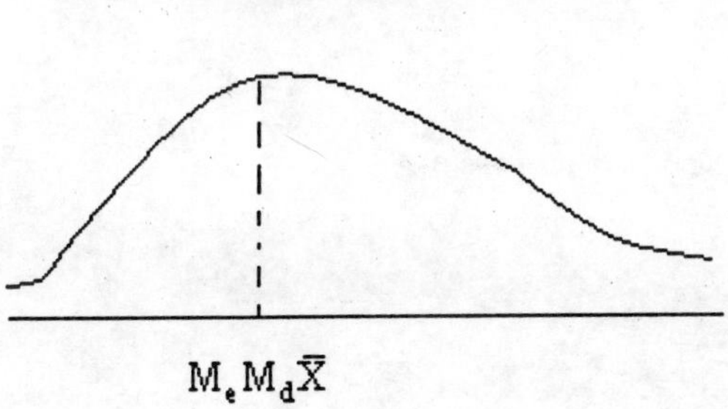

Negatively Skewed Distribution
(longer tail on the left)

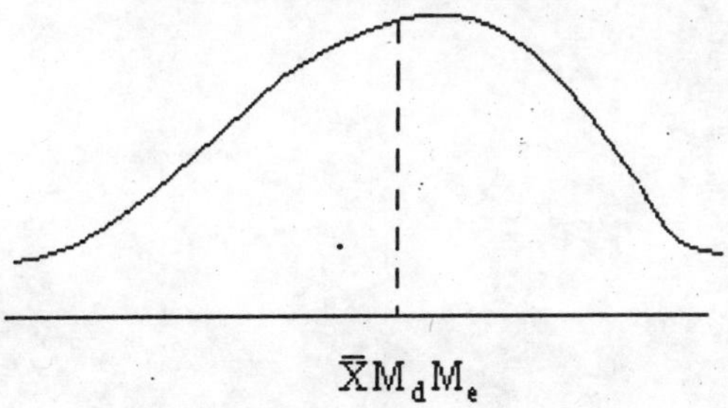

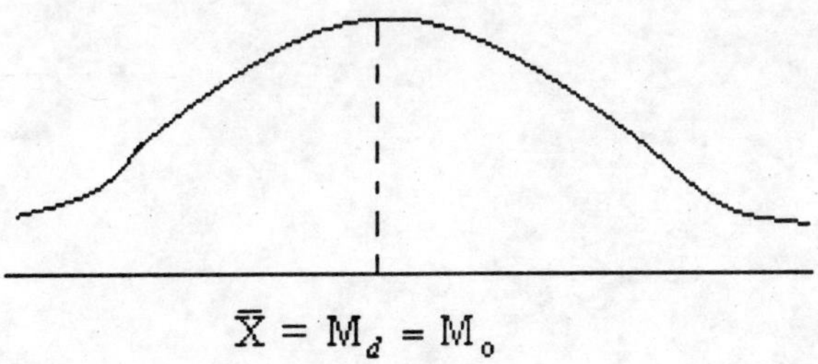

Symmetrical Distribution

Lack of Symmetry or departure from symmetry

$$S_{KP} = \frac{\bar{X}}{\sigma} - M_o \text{ or } \frac{3(\bar{X} - M_d)}{\sigma}$$

$$S_{KB} = \frac{(Q_3 - Q_1) - (Q_2 - Q_1)}{(Q_3 - Q_1)} \text{ or } \frac{Q_3 + Q_1 - 2M_d}{Q_3 - Q_1}$$

$$S_{KX} = \frac{P_{90} - 2P_{50} + P_{10}}{P_{90} - P_{10}} - M_o \text{ or } \frac{D_9 - 2D_5 + D_1}{D_9 - D_1} - M_o$$

2 TIME SERIES/INDEX NUMBER

2.1 Introduction and Application

Time series refers to such a series in which one variable is time. In other words, if we have a chronologically arranged values of a variable over successive time periods, it would be a time series. Examples of time series would be the figures of national income, or production or costs or prices spread over a period of time.

The analysis of such figures is called the Analysis of Time Series. Time series analysis is done primarily for the purpose of making forecasts for the future and also for the purpose of evaluating past performances. An economist or a businessman is very naturally interested in estimating the future figures of national income, population, prices and wages, etc. In fact, the success or failure of an economist or a businessman depends to a large extent on the accuracy of his future forecasts. Forecasting is done by analyzing the past behavior of the variable under study. Hence the analysis of time series assumes great importance in the study of all economic problems.

However, it should not be concluded from the above discussion that analysis of time series is useful only to economists and businessmen. Analysis of past data is done in a variety of other fields also. A sociologist may find the analysis of past data relating to crimes very useful for studying the crime situation in a country and suggesting appropriate measures for controlling it. Similarly, in a study of weather conditions, or in studying the incidence of cancer or in studying the body temperature of a patient, an analysis of past data is very useful. Thus we can conclude by saying that the analysis of time series is helpful in studying any phenomenon whose values are or can be chronologically arranged over successive time periods.

Definition **(U.P.T.U. 2006, 07, 08, 10)**

A time series may be defined as a collection of readings belonging to different time periods, of some economic variable or composite of variables such as production of steel, per capita income, gross national product, price of tobacco or index of industrial production.

Utility of Time Series Analysis

(*i*) It helps in the analysis of past behavior of a variable.

(*ii*) It helps in forecasting.

(*iii*) It helps in evaluation of current achievement.

(*iv*) It helps in making comparative studies.

2.2 Components of a Time Series

1.Secular Trend or Long Term Movements (T) **(L.U.) (U.P.T.U. 2006, 07, 08, 10)**

The general tendency of the time series data to increase or to decrease or to remain segregated during a long period of time is called secular trend.

(*i*) The secular trend is generally either upward or downward.

(*ii*) General trend is the result of such forces which are more or less constant for a long time or which change very gradually.

(*iii*) The term 'long period of time' is a relative term.

(*iv*) The secular trend may be linear or non-linear.

(*v*) It is not necessary that a time series should always have a rising or falling tendency.

2. Seasonal Variations (S)

Seasonal variations refer to such movements in a time series which are due to forces which are rhythmic in nature and which repeat themselves periodically every season. The seasonal variations may be attributed to the following causes:

(*i*) Causes resulting from natural forces.

(*ii*) Causes resulting from local customs and traditions.

3. Cyclical Variations (C)

The cyclical variations in a series are the recurrent variations whose duration is more than one year. The difficulty associated with business cycles is that their period is not uniform and further, cyclical variations are mixed up with erratic and irregular variations which are difficult to be isolated.

4. Irregular Variations (I)

Irregular variations are the effect of random factors. These are generally mixed up with seasonal and cyclical variations and are caused by irregular and accidental factors like floods, famines, wars, strikes, lockouts, etc.

Time Series Decomposition Models

The analysis of time series consists of two major steps:

1. Identifying the various factors or influences which produce the variations in the time series, and
2. Isolating, analyzing and measuring the effects of these factors independently, by holding other things constant.

The purpose of decomposition models is to break a time series into its components: Trend (T), Cyclical (C), Seasonality (S), and Irregularity (I). Decomposition of time series aims to isolate influence of each of the four components on the actual series so as to provide a basis for forecasting. There are many models by which a time series can be analysed; two models commonly used for decomposition of a time series are:

Multiplicative Model. The actual values of a time series, represented by Y can be found by multiplying four components at a particular time period. The effect of four components on the time series is interdependent. The multiplicative time series model is defined as:

$$Y = T \times C \times S \times I$$

The multiplicative model is appropriate in situations where the effect of C, S and I is measured in relative sense and not in absolute sense. The geometric mean of C, S and I is assumed to be less than one.

Additive Model. In this model, it is assumed that the effect of various components can be estimated by adding the various components of a time series. It is stated as:

$$Y = T + C + S + I$$

Here C, S and I are absolute quantities and can have positive or negative values. It is assumed that these four components are independent of each other. However, in real-life time series data this assumption does not hold good.

2.3 Measurement of Trend (various methods)

The various methods by which trend values can be determined are: **(U.P.T.U. 2006, 2010)**

1. **Freehand or Graphic Method :** This is the simplest of all the methods of finding out the trend values. First of all the values of a time series are plotted on a graph paper in the form of a histogram. After this a freehand smoothed curve is drawn through these points in such a way that the curve represents the general tendency of the data. The trend values can then be read for various time periods by locating them on the trend line against each time period.
2. **Method of Semi-Averages :** In this method, as the name suggests, semi-averages are calculated to find out the trend values. By semi-averages is meant the averages of the two halves of a series. Thus, if we have a time series running from 1994 to 2003, it would be divided into two halves – one half from 1994 to 1998 and the other half from 1999 to 2003. The averages of the values of these two halves would be found out. These averages would be plotted against the mid-value of each half. The two points are then joined by a straight line which can be extended on either side. This is the trend line.
3. **Method of Moving Averages:** Moving average method is a simple device of reducing fluctuations and obtaining trend values with a fair degree of accuracy. In this method the average value of a number of years is taken as the trend value for the middle point of the period of moving average. The process of averaging smoothes the curve and reduces the fluctuations.

   The first thing to be decided in this method is the period of the moving average – that is, to decide about the number of consecutive items whose average would be calculated each time. Suppose it has been decided that the period of the moving average would be 5 years, then the arithmetic average of the first 5 items would be placed against the item no. 3 and then the average of item numbers 2, 3, 4, 5 and 6 would be placed against item no. 4. This process would be repeated till the average of the last five items has been calculated.
4. **Method of Least Squares** (Fitting Straight Line Trend : One of the best ways of obtaining trend values is the method of least squares. With this method, a straight line trend is obtained, this line is called the Line of the Best Fit. It is a line from which the sum of the deviations of various points on either side is equal to zero. Also, the sum of the squares of these deviations would be the least as compared to the sums of squares of the deviations obtained by using other lines. That is why this method is known as the method of least squares.

Methods of measuring trend

(1) Free hand or graphic method

(2) Semi-average method

(3) Moving average method

(4) Least square method

2.4 Free hand or graphic method

This is the simplest and most flexible method of estimating the secular trend and consists of first obtaining a histogram by plotting the time series value on a graph paper and then drawing it free hand smooth curve through these points so that it accurately reflect the long term tendency of the data.

Important Points for drawing a curve

(1) It should be smooth.

(2) Number of points above and below should be nearly equal.

(3) The sum of the vertical deviations of the given points about the trend line should be approximately equal to sum of the vertical deviation of the points below the trend lone.

(4) Sum of the squares of the vertical deviation of the given points from the trend line should be minimum possible.

Merits:

This method is

(1) Simple and time saving method, does not require any mathematical calculation.

(2) Flexible method for all types of trends.

Demerits

(1) This method is subjective in nature.

(2) Not suitable for forecasting and for making decisions.

Example 1. *From the following data of the sales determine the trend line by free hold curve.*

Year	1980	1981	1982	1983	1984	1985	1986	1987	1988	1989	1990
Sale	50	70	60	90	70	110	100	130	120	150	140

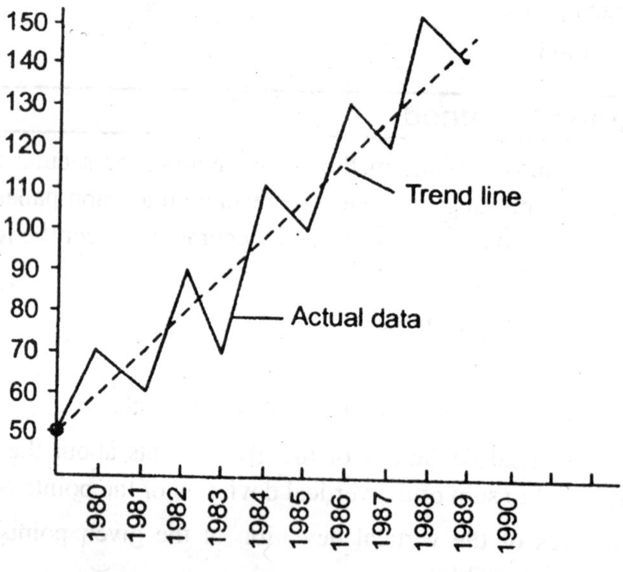

2.5 Method of Semi-Averages

Under this method the data for which trend values are to be computed are divided into two equal parts and averages are computed for both the part. If there is odd number of years, the value of the middle year is omitted.

The average value of these two halves should be calculated. These average values would be plotted against the mid value of each half. By joining these two points we get the trend line. This line can be extended on both ways.

Merits

(1) It is a simple method.

(2) The trend figures are objective.

(3) Future and past estimate can be obtained by extending the lines.

Demerits

(1) This method is based on linear relationship but fails is non-linear relationship.

(2) This method ignores the extreme values.

(3) The prediction is not reliable.

Example 2. *Calculate trend values from the following data by the method of semi-averages.*

Year:	1974	1975	1976	1977	1978	1979	1980	1981
Sales:	10	11	13	8	14	12	9	14
Year:	1982	1983	1984	1985	1986	1987	1988	
Sales:	13	10	12	16	14	16	17	

Solution: We have off number of years, therefore we neglect the value of middle year 1981.

Average for 1974 to 1980 $= \frac{1}{7}(10+11+13+8+14+12+9) = \frac{77}{7} = 11$

Average for 1982 to 1988 $= \frac{1}{7}(13+10+12+16+14+16+17) = \frac{98}{7} = 14$

11 is plotted the mid year 1977 of the first half and 14 should be plotted against the mid year 1985 of the other half. These two points are joined to get a trend line.

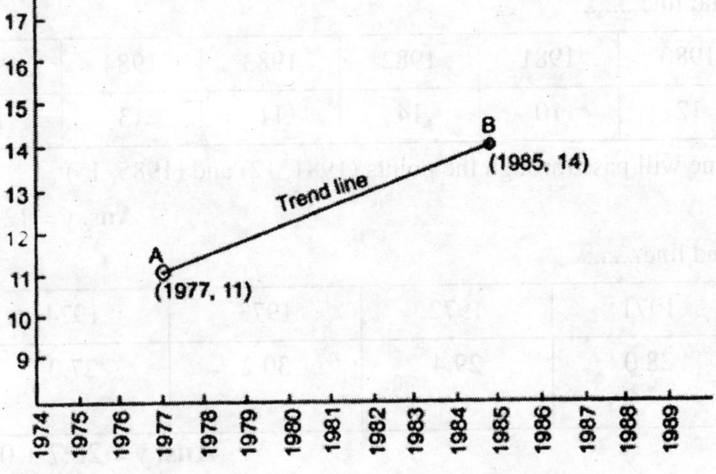

The equation of the trend line

The trend line passes through the point A (1977, 11) and the point B (1985, 14).

$$\left[y - y_1 = \frac{y_2 - y_1}{x_2 - x_1}(x - x_1) \right]$$

$$y - 11 = \frac{14-11}{1985-1977}(x-1977)$$

$$\Rightarrow \quad y - 11 = \frac{3}{8}(x-1977)$$

$$\Rightarrow \quad y = 11 + 0.375(x-1977)$$

Exercise 2.1

1. Fit a trend line by the method of semi average to the following data and estimate the sales for 1987:

Year:	1979	1980	1981	1982	1983	1984	1985	1986
Sales (in '000):	412	438	444	454	470	482	490	500

Hint: The trend line will pass through the points (1980.5, 437) and (1984.5, 480.5)

2. Fit a trend line........

Year:	1980	1981	1982	1983	1984	1985	1986
Production:	12	10	14	11	13	15	17

Hint: The trend line will pass through the points (1981, 12) and (1985, 15)

Ans. $y = 12 + 0.75\ (x - 1981)$

3. Fit a trend line........

Years	1971	1972	1973	1974	1975
Profit (in Rs. lakhs)	28.0	29.4	30.2	27.0	32.5

Ans. $y = 28.7 + 0.35\ (x - 1971.5)$

4. The sales of a commodity in tonnes varied from 1985 to 1997 as follows:

280 300 280 270 240 230 230 220 200 210 200 230

Fit a trend line by the method of semi-averages.

Ans. $y = 275 + 8.57\ (x - 1994.5)$

2.6 Method of Moving Averages

Moving averages consists of a series of arithmetic means calculated from overlapping groups of successive values of a time series.

Case I. When period is odd:

Let the period of moving averages be 3 years and the items $a, b, c, d, e,$

$$\text{Average of first three} = \frac{a+b+c}{3}$$

Dropping the first year value and adding the value of the next year the average becomes

$$= \frac{b+c+d}{3}$$

Next average $= \dfrac{c+d+e}{3}$

It this way moving averages are

$$= \frac{a+b+c}{3}, \frac{b+c+d}{3}, = \frac{c+d+e}{3}$$

$= \dfrac{a+b+c}{3}$ is to be written against the mid year b

$= \dfrac{b+c+d}{3}$ is to be written against the mid year c

$= \dfrac{c+d+e}{3}$ is to be written against the mid year d.

Case II. When period is even.

Let the period of moving averages be 4-years then the average of first four figures will be placed between second and third year like-wise the average of second group of four years will be replaced between third and fourth year. These two moving averages will then be averaged and this average would be written as against the third year. This process is called centering of the averages.

1	2	3	4	5	6	7	8
a	*b*	*c*	*d*	*e*	*f*	*g*	*h*

$\dfrac{a+b+c+d}{4}$ against to be placed between 2 and 3.

$\dfrac{b+c+d+e}{4}$ against to be placed between third and fourth and so on.

These two moving averages will then be average and this new average would be written against the third year. This process is called centering of the averages.

In case of even period of moving averages the trend values are obtained after centering the averages.

Note: Centering of the moving averages is required only in the even period and not in odd period.

Merits: This method is

(1) Simple

(2) Flexible to add more figures

(3) Objective

(4) To eliminate the fluctuation

(5) Used for determining seasonal cyclic and irregular variations.

Demerits

(1) There is no trend values for some years in the beginning and summing the end.
It means there will be no trend values for the first three years and the last three years.

(2) There is no fluctuation relationship between the values and time.

(3) This method is not helpful in forecasting and predicting the value.

(4) Selection of period of moving average is a difficult task.

(5) In case of non-linear trend the values obtained by this method are biased.

Example 3. *Computation of moving average taking a 3 years period and find a trend.*

Years	1985	1986	1987	1988	1989	1990	1991	1992
Profits (in Rs.)	15420	14470	15520	21020	26120	31950	35370	35670

Solution. Procedure:

(1) Put the original data of years and profits in column (i) & (ii) as shown in Table:

(2) Obtain the 3 years moving totals starting from first year and put against the middle of the years.

(3) Now, leaving first year value, add a successive year value in the group. Find the total of this group and place it against the middle of the years.

(4) Keep on continuing unless all values are utilized.

(5) Now, divide each 3 years moving total by 3 to get the moving average as per the years and shown in (iv) column.

(6) We can plot the moving averages on a graph paper by taking years along x-axis and moving averages along y-axis by choosing suitable scales. The resulting graph provides the trend.

Table

Year (i)	Profits (in Rs) (ii)	3- Year moving totals (iii)	3- year moving average (iv)
1985	15420	—	—
1986	14470	45410	15136.7
1987	15520	51010	17003.3
1988	21020	62660	20886.7
1989	26120	79090	26363.3
1990	31950	93440	31146.7
1991	35370	102990	34330.0
1992	35670		

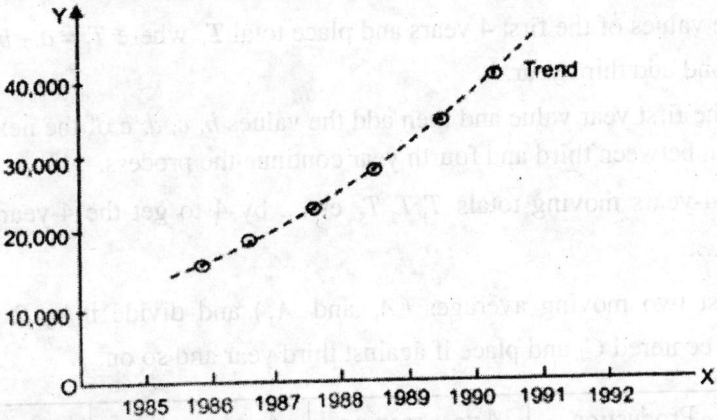

Example 4. *Calculate the five yearly moving average of acres under tea in India from the following data:*

Year	1925	1926	1927	1928	1929	1930	1931	1932	1933	1934
Area (in '000 acres)	672	679	690	702	712	802	807	809	816	821

Solution.

Year (i)	Area in '000 acres (ii)	5 yearly moving total III	Trend 5 yearly moving average
1925	672	—	—
1926	679	—	—
1927	690	3455	691.0
1928	702	3585	717.0
1929	7012	3713	742.6

1930	802	3832	766.4
1931	807	3946	789.2
1932	809	4055	811.0
1933	816	—	—
1934	821	—	—

Example 5. *Calculate trend by four years moving average of the data given below:*

Year:	1978	1979	1980	1981	1982	1983	1984	1985	1986	1987	1988
Production:	614	615	652	678	681	655	717	719	708	779	757

Solution. Calculation of moving averages when period is even (say 4 years)

Working Rule:

Step 1. Add the values of the first 4 years and place total T_1, where $T_1 = a+b+c+d$ in between the second add third year.

Step 2. Leave the first year value and then add the values *b, c, d, e* of the next 4-years and place this T_2 in between third and fourth year continue the process.

Step 3. Divide 4-years moving totals T_1, T_2, T_3 etc.... by 4 to get the 4-years moving averages A_1, A_2.......

Step 4. Add first two moving averages (A_1 and A_2) and divide it by 2 to get the moving average centered C_1 and place if ägainst third year and so on.

Year	Production	4 year moving Total T_1	4 year moving average A_1	4 year moving average centered C_1
1978	614			
1979	615		639.75	
1980	652	2559	656.50	648.125
1981	678	2626	666.50	661.500
1982	681	2666	682.75	674.625
1983	655	2731	693.00	687.875
1984	717	2772	699.75	696.375
1985	719	2799	730.75	715.250
1986	708	2923	740.75	735.750
1987	779	963		
1988	757			

5. Find trend values from the following data by the 3- yearly moving average method.

Year :	1982	1983	1984	1985	1986	1987	1988
Production :	412	438	446	454	470	483	490

6. Construct a four-year centered moving average from the following data

Year :	1920	1930	1940	1950	1960	1970	1980
Imported : Cotton consumption in India (in '000 bales)	129	131	106	91	95	84	93

7. Find the 5- yearly moving average from the following data :

Year :	1995	1996	1997	1998	1999	2000	2001	2002	2003	2004
Production : (in quintals)	50	40	30	52	60	50	70	85	80	87

8. Compute the 4- year centered moving average for the following data

Year	1	2	3	4	5	6	7	8	9	10	11	12	13	14
Values	53	79	76	66	69	94	105	87	79	104	98	97	100	105

9. Obtain the 5- yearly moving average of the following data:

Year :	1982	1983	1984	1985	1986	1987	1988	1989	1990
Sales : (in crores of Rs.)	36	43	43	34	44	54	52	24	15

10. Find trend by three- yearly moving average for the following data :

Year	1979	1980	1981	1982	1983	1984	1985	1986	1987	1988
Production (in million tonnes)	60	69	81	78	23	102		109	118	117

2.7 Method of Least Squares

The method of least squares has already been explained in the context of regression analysis in Chapter 9 of the present book. *As observed, the method is very useful for fitting mathematical functions to a given set of data.* The method is objective, and therefore, gives correct and accurate estimation of trend, once the form of equation representing trend is determined.

An examination of graphical plot of the time series often provides an adequate basis for deciding the functional form of the trend. Some of the common curves used for representing trend are

(1) $Y = a + bX$: Linear or Straight line trend.

(2) $Y = a + bX + cX^2$: Parabolic or Quadratic trend.

(3) $Y = ab^x$: Exponential trend.

Fitting of Linear (or Straight Line) Trend

The simplest type of trend equation is the linear equation of the form

$$\boxed{Y = a + bX} \quad \text{...(1)}$$

where X represents time and Y the value of the variable Here Y is the dependent and A[1] is an independent variable

Now for the set of given data $(X_1, Y_1)(X_2, Y_2)....,(X_n, Y_n)$, the constants a and b are determined by solving simultaneously the equations:—

$$\boxed{\begin{aligned} \Sigma Y &= Na + b\Sigma X \\ \Sigma XY &= a\Sigma X + b\Sigma X^2 \end{aligned}} \quad \text{...(2)}$$

The equations in (2). called normal equations for the least square line in (1), gives

$$a = \frac{(\Sigma Y)(\Sigma X^2) - (\Sigma X)(\Sigma XY)}{N\Sigma X^2 - (\Sigma X)^2} \quad \text{...(3)}$$

$$b = \frac{N(\Sigma XY) - (\Sigma X)(\Sigma Y)}{N\Sigma X^2 - (\Sigma X)^2} \quad \text{...(4)}$$

If the values of X are equidistant, the calculations involved in the estimation of a and b can be further simplified by shifting the origin to the appropriate mid-point in time, so that $\Sigma X = 0$. Obviously, the normal equations in (2) becomes

$$\left.\begin{aligned} \Sigma Y &= Na \\ \Sigma XY &= b\Sigma X^2 \end{aligned}\right\} \quad \text{...(5)}$$

Therefore, $a = \dfrac{\Sigma Y}{N}$ and $b = \dfrac{\Sigma XY}{\Sigma X^2}$ ...(6)

Substituting the estimated values of a and b in (1), the fitted linear trend will be

$$Y = a + bX. \quad \text{...(7)}$$

we can find the trend values, say Y, by putting different values of X in (7). When writing the trend equation, the origin and unit of time must be clearly specified, as an equation without such specification will be useless.

Shifting the Origin

In shifting the origin, two cases arise according as the number of years N covered by the series is odd or even.

Shifting the Origin when *N* is odd

If we take the origin as middle year, then the transformed variable

$$x = \frac{(X - \text{Middle year})}{\text{Interval in } X \text{ values}} \quad \ldots(8)$$

Shifting the Origin when *N* is even

In this case we have two middle values. So we take the origin at the average of these two middle values and lake half the interval as unit. Thus, the transformed variable will be

$$x = \frac{(X - \text{Average of two middle values})}{\frac{1}{2}(\text{Interval in } X \text{ values})} \quad \ldots(9)$$

obviously, the transformed variable *r* assume values

x = (-5,-3,-1,1,3,5.......), and consequently we also have $\sum x = 0$. More so, the sum of all odd powers of x will also be zero.

Example 1: *Fit a trend line to the following data by the method of least squares. Obtain trend values and estimate the production for 2000 and 2005.* **(U.P.T.U. 2008)**

Year X	Production ('000 units) Y	$x = \frac{(X-1999)}{2}$	XY	X^2	Trend values $Y = a + bx$
1995	18	-2	-36	4	$Y = 21 + 0.2(-2) = 20.6$
1997	21	-1	-21	1	$Y = 21 + 0.2(-1) = 20.8$
1999	23	0	0	0	$Y = 21 + 0.2(0) = 21.0$
2001	27	1	27	1	$Y = 21 + 0.2(1) = 21.2$
2003	16	2	32	4	$Y = 21 + 0.2(2) = 21.4$
$N = 5$	$\sum Y = 105$	$\sum Y = 0$	$\sum xY = 2$	$\sum x^2 = 10$	

Let the trend time to be fitted be

$$Y = a + bX \quad \ldots(i)$$

For suitably shifting the origin, we use the transformation

$$x = \frac{(X - 1999)}{2}$$

Thus, the transformed trend line becomes

$$Y = a + bx \quad \ldots(ii)$$

The normal equations giving the values of a and b are

$$\left.\begin{aligned} \sum Y &= Na + b\sum x \\ \sum xY &= a\sum x + b\sum x^2 \end{aligned}\right\} \quad \ldots(iii)$$

Putting the values from the table in (iii), one gets

$$105 = 5a \Rightarrow a = \frac{105}{5} = 21$$

and $$2 = 10b \Rightarrow b = \frac{2}{10} = 0.2$$

Thus, the fitted trend line is obtained by putting the values of a and b in (ii), *i.e.*,

$$Y = 21 + 0.2x; \quad \text{where} \quad x = \frac{X - 1999}{2} \qquad \text{...(iv)}$$

or we can also write

$$y = a + b\left(\frac{X - 1999}{2}\right) \qquad \text{...(v)}$$

Putting the transformed values of x corresponding to the given values of X in (iv) or directly using (v) we get the trend values as shown in the above table. For example,

The Estimate for X = 2000 is : $Y = 21 + 0.2\left(\frac{2000 - 1999}{2}\right) = 21.1$

The Estimate for X = 2005 is : $Y = 21 + 0.2\left(\frac{2005 - 1999}{2}\right) = 21.6$

Example 2: *Obtain trend values by fitting trend line by least squares method to the given data. Also estimate the trend for* 2003.

Year	1997	1998	1999	2000	2001	2002
Sales (in '000 Rs.)	10	12	15	16	18	19

(L.U.) (U.P.T.U. 2006)

Solution:

Computation of trend by least squares method

Year X	Sales ('000 Rs.) Y	x = 2(X- 1999.5)	x^2	xY	Trend $\hat{Y} = 15 + 0.914x$
1997	10	-5	25	50	10.430
1998	12	-3	9	36	12.258
1999	15	-1	1	15	14.086
2000	16	+1	1	16	15.914
2001	18	+3	9	54	17.742
2002	19	+ 5	25	95	19.570
N- 6	$\Sigma Y = 90$	$\Sigma x = 0$	$\Sigma x^2 = 70$	$\Sigma xY = 64$	

In this example, the number of years given is six. *i e..* even. So for shifting the origin we make use of the transformation in (9), *i.e.*

$$x = \frac{[X - \text{Average of two middle values}]}{\frac{1}{2}[\text{Internal in } x \text{ values}]} = \frac{X - 1999.5}{\frac{1}{2}}$$

$$= 2(X - 1999.5) \quad \text{...(i)}$$

Now, the trend line becomes :

$$Y = a + bx. \quad \text{...(ii)}$$

The values of a and b are obtained by using the normal equations ;

$$\Sigma Y = Na + b\Sigma x \quad \text{or} \quad 90 = 6a \Rightarrow a = 15$$

$$\Sigma xY = a\Sigma x + b\Sigma x^2 \quad \text{or} \quad 64 = 70b \Rightarrow b = 0.914$$

Thus the fitted trend line becomes

$$Y = 15 + 0.914x, \quad \text{where } x = 2(X\text{- }1999.5) \quad \text{...(iii)}$$

Putting x = - 5, - 3, - 1, 1,3, and 5 in (iii), we get trend values as shown in the above table. For estimating sales in 2003, we first use the transformation in (i) to obtain die value of x forgiven X- 2003, *i.e.,*

$$x = 2[X \;\; 1999.5] = 2[2003 - 1999.5] - 7.0$$

Thus, the estimate of sales in 2003 is

$$\hat{Y} = 15 + 0.914(7.0) = 21.4 \text{ thousand Rs.}$$

Example 3: *The following table shows the number of salesman working for a certain concern:*

Year	1998	1999	2000	2001	2002	2003
Number	28	38	46	40	56	60

[U.P.T.U. 2005]

Solution: Use the method of least squares to fit a straight line trend.

Year (X)	Number (Y)	x = 2(X-2000.5)	x^2	xY
1998	28	-5	25	140
1999	38	-3	9	114
2000	46	-1	1	46
2001	40	1	1	40
2002	56	3	9	168
2003	60	5	25	300
$N = 6$	$\Sigma Y = 268$	$\Sigma x = 0$	$\Sigma x^2 = 70$	208

In this case, we consider the transformation

$$x = \frac{X - 2000.5}{1/2} = 2(X - 2000.5)$$

Thus, the trend becomes

$$Y = a + bx$$

Solving, $\sum Y = Na + b\sum x$

$$\Rightarrow \quad a = \frac{\sum Y}{N} = 44.66$$

$$\sum xy = a\sum x + b\sum x^2$$

$$\Rightarrow \quad b = \frac{\sum xY}{\sum x^2} = \frac{208}{70} = 2.97$$

Putting a and b in (i), the trend line is

$$Y = 44.66 + 2.97x$$

where $x = 2(X\text{-}200.5)$

Example 4: Fit a straight line trend by least square method data given below and estimate trend for 2008.

Year	2002	2003	2004	2005	2006	2007
Sales (in '000 Rs.)	10	12	15	16	18	19

(A.U.) [U.P.T.U. 2009]

Solution: Use the method of least squares to fit a straight line trend.

Year (X)	Sales (Y)	$x = 2(X\text{-}2004.5)$	x^2	xY
2002	10	-5	25	–50
2003	12	-3	9	–36
2004	15	-1	1	–15
2005	16	1	1	16
2006	18	3	9	54
2007	19	5	25	95
$N = 6$	$\sum Y = 90$	$\sum x = 0$	$\sum x^2 = 70$	64

$$a = \frac{\sum y}{N} = \frac{90}{6} = 15$$

$$b = \frac{\sum xy}{\sum x^2} = \frac{64}{70} = 0.914$$

Then straight line $y = a + b\,x$

$= 15 + 0.914\,x$

Estimate sales for the year 2008 put x = 7 in above the equation.

$$Y_{2008} = 15 + 0.914(7)$$

$$= 21.398 \quad \text{thousand Rs.}$$

Fitting of Parabolic or Quadratic Trend

When we plot original time series data on a graph, we may sometimes observe that a curved 'tine is more appropriate to the data. *This is especially true for a long series, and then we may consider, instead of linear trend represented by a first degree equation, the fitting of a curved line given by higher degree equation. If there is one band in the original data, the trend can be best filled bv a* parabola *or a* second degree *polynomial* which is of the form

$$\boxed{Y = a + bX + cX^2} \qquad \ldots(10)$$

For the set of data $(X_1, y_1,), (X_2, Y_2), \ldots\ldots (X_{N,}Y_N)$, the constant *a, b* and *c* are determined by solving the following normal equations.

$$\Sigma Y = Na + b\Sigma X + c\Sigma X^2$$

$$\Sigma XY = a\Sigma X + b\Sigma X^2 + c\Sigma X^3$$

$$\Sigma X^2Y = a\Sigma X^2 + b\Sigma X^2 + c\Sigma X^4 \qquad \ldots(11)$$

The normal equations in (11) *are remembered as they can be obtained by multiplying equation* (10) *by* 1, *X and* X^2 *respectively and summing on both sides of the resulting equations.*

For simplifying the calculations, the origin and unit may be appropriately chosen according to the shifting schemes discussed in fitting the linear trend. Accordingly, $\Sigma x = \Sigma x^3 = 0$. and the set of normal equations in (11) providing estimates for *a, b* and *c* in (11) reduces to

$$\Sigma Y = Na + c\Sigma x^2$$

$$\Sigma xY = b\Sigma x^2$$

$$\Sigma x^2Y = a\Sigma x^2 + c\Sigma x^4 \qquad \ldots(12)$$

On substituting the values of *a, b* and *c* in (10), the fitted parabolic curve becomes

$$Y = a + bx + cx^2 \qquad \ldots(13)$$

Always mention the origin and unit of time while mentioning the trend equation. Estimated trend values, *Y* are obtained by putting different values of *x* in (13).

Example 5: *Fit a non-linear trend of the form* $Y = a + bx + cX^2$ *for the given data* :

x:	0	1	2	3	4
y:	1.0	1.5	1.5	2.5	3.5

Solution:

Fitting a non-linear trend by least squares method

X	Y	$x = (X-2)$	x^2	x^3	x^4	xY	x^2Y
0	1.0	-2	4	-8	16	-2.0	4.0
1	1.5	- 1	1	-1	1	1.5	1.5
2	1.5	0	0	0	0	0	0
3	2.5	1	1	1	1	2.5	2.5
4	3.5	2	4	8	16	7.0	14.0
	$\sum Y = 10$	$\sum x = 0$	$\sum x^2 = 10$	$\sum x^3 = 0$	$\sum x^4 = 34$	$\sum xY = 6.0$	$\sum x^2Y = 22.0$

For making $\sum x = \sum x^2 = 0$, we use the Information $x = (X\ 2)$.

Now, let the trend fitted be :

$$Y = a + bx + cx^2 \text{ where } x = (X-2) \qquad \text{...(i)}$$

The normal equations giving the values of a, b and c are

$$\sum Y = Na + b\sum x + c\sum x^2 \quad \text{or} \quad 10 = 5a + 0 + 10c \qquad \text{...(ii)}$$

$$\sum xY = a\sum x + b\sum x^2 + c\sum x^3 \quad \text{or} \quad 6.0 = 0 + 10b + 0 \qquad \text{...(iii)}$$

$$\sum x^2Y = a\sum x^2 + b\sum x^3 + c\sum x^4 \quad \text{or} \quad 22 = 10a + 0 + 34c \qquad \text{...(iv)}$$

Equation (iii) gives $b = \dfrac{6}{10} = 0.6$

Solving (ii) and (iv), one gets easily ; $a = 1.7243$ and $c = 0.1429$.

Putting the values of a, b and c in (i), one get the non-linear trend as

$$Y = 1.7243 + 0.6x + 0\ 1429x^2,$$

where $x = (X-2)$.

Example 6: *The prices of a commodity during* 1995-2000 *are given below. Fit a parabola* $Y = a + bX + cX^2$ *to these data. Estimate the price of the commodity for the year* 2001.

Year	1995	1996	1997	1998	1999	2000
Price	100	107	128	140	181	192

Solution:

Fitting a Parabolic Trend

Year X	Price Y	$x = 2(X - 1997.5)$	x^2	x^3	x^4	xY	x^2Y
1995	100	-5	25	125	625	-500	2500
1996	107	-3	9	- 27	81	-321	963
1997	128	- 1	1	- 1	1	- 128	128
1998	140	+ 1	1	1	1	140	140
1999	181	3	9	27	81	543	1629
2000	192	5	25	125	625	960	4800
$N = 6$	$\sum Y = 848$	$\sum x = 0$	$\sum x^2 = 70$	$\sum x^3 = 0$	$\sum x^4 = 1414$	$\sum xY = 694$	$\sum x^2Y = 10160$

Let the parabolic curve be

$$Y = a + bx + cx^2 \quad \ldots\text{(i)}$$

where $x = 2(X - 1987.5)$. The normal equations giving the values of *a, b* and *c* are

$$\sum Y = Na + b\sum x + c\sum x^2 \quad \text{or} \quad 848 = 6a + 0 + 70c \quad \ldots\text{(ii)}$$

$$\sum xY = a\sum x + b\sum x^2 + c\sum x^3 \quad \text{or} \quad 694. = 70b \quad \ldots\text{(iii)}$$

$$\sum x^2Y = a\sum x^2 + b\sum x^3 + c\sum x^4 \quad \text{or} \quad 10160 = 70a + 1414c \quad \ldots\text{(iv)}$$

Equation (iii) gives $b = \dfrac{694}{70} = 9.91$

Multiplying (ii) by 70 and (iv) by 6 and subtracting, one gets

$$420a + 4900c = 59360$$

$$420a + 8484c = 60960$$

Solving, we get

$$-3584c = -1600$$

$$c = 0.4464$$

Thus from (ii), $6a = 848 - 31.248 = 816.752$

$\therefore$ $a = 136.125$

Thus, the fitted trend parabola is :

$$Y = 136.125 + 9.91x + 0.4464x^2,$$

where, $x = 2(X - 1997.5)$. For estimating the price in 2001. we put $x = 2(2001 - 1997.5) - 7.0$ in fitted curve: Thus, the estimated price is

$$\hat{Y} = 136.125 + 9.91 \times 7 + 0.4464\,(7)^2 = 227.37.$$

Fitting Exponential Trend

The trends discussed so far can be plotted an arithmetic scales. However, there are other types of mathematical equations, which arc appropriate in some cases for fitting nonlinear trends One such equation is represented by exponential function. Many time series data concerning with business and economic activities showing constant initial growth and not approaching certain upper limit can best be described by exponential function. *To decide about the exponential trend, it is helpful to obtain a scatter diagram of log ' Y values with X. In case the scatter diagram so obtained indicates a linear trend, then the functional relationship between Y and X is of the exponential type*

$$\boxed{Y = ab^X} \quad \text{...(14)}$$

where a and b are constants to be determined by the set of data $(X_1, Y_1), (X_2, Y_2), ...(X_N, Y_N)$ For this we first take logarithms of both sides of equation (14) and get

$$\log Y = \log a + X \log b$$

which is of the linear form.

$$y = A+BX \quad \text{...(15)}$$

where $y = \log Y$, $A = \log a$ and $B = \log b$.

Now we can apply the usual procedure of fitting the linear trend as discussed above. By suitable choice of origin and unit of time, the values of A and B in (15) can be obtained as

$$A = \frac{\Sigma y}{N} = \frac{\Sigma \log Y}{N}$$

and

$$B = \frac{\Sigma Xy}{\Sigma X^2} = \frac{\Sigma X \log y}{\Sigma X^2}$$

Finally, the values of a and b can be determined by taking antilogarithms of A and B respectively, *i.e.*,

$$a = \text{antilog } A \text{ and } b = \text{antilog } B$$

Putting these estimated values of a and b in (14), we get the required exponential trend.

Example 7 : *The following table gives the profits of a concern for five years ending* 2004 :

Year (X)	2000	2001	2002	2003	2004
Profit (Y) Rs. ('000)	1.6	4.5	13.8	40.2	125

Find the trend values for the years 2000-2004 *using an equation of the form* $Y = ab^X$

Solution: The equation to be fitted is : $Y = ab^X$. ...*(i)*

or $$\log Y = \log a + X \log b \quad \text{...(ii)}$$

$$y = A + BX.$$

where $y = \log Y$, $A = \log a, B = \log b$. The values of A and B can be obtained from the following normal equations :

$$\sum y = NA + B\sum X$$

$$\sum Xy = A\sum X + B\sum X^2 \qquad ...(iii)$$

Fitting of Exponential Trend

Year X	Profit ('000 Rs.) Y	$y = \log Y$	$x = (X - 2002)$	x^2	yx
2000	1.6	0.2041	-2	4	0.4082
2001	4.5	0.6532	- 1	1	0.6532
2002	13.8	1.1399	0	0	0
2003	40.2	1.6042	1	1	1 6042
2004	125.0	2.0969	2	4	4.1938
$N = 5$		$\sum y = 5.6983$	$\sum x = 0$	$\sum x^2 = 10$	$\sum yx = 4.7366$

Putting the values from the table in (iii)

$5.6983 = 5A \quad \Rightarrow A = 1.1397 \quad \Rightarrow a = \text{antilog}\ (1.1397)$
$= 13.79$

$4.7366 = 10A \quad \Rightarrow B = 0.4737 \quad \Rightarrow b = \text{antilog}\ (0.4737)$
$= 2.977$

Putting the values of a and b in (i), the fitted trends is

$$Y = (13.79)\ (2.997)^X, \text{ where } X = (x - 2002)$$

For computation of trend values, we make use of equation (ii) *i.e* $\quad y = 1.1397 + 0.4737X$

For computation procedure is clarified in the following table :

Computation of Trend values

Year x	$X = (x - 2002)$	$y = \log Y = 1.1397 + 0.4737X$	Trend values $\hat{Y}$ = antilog y
2000	-2	$1.1397 + 0.4737(-2) = 0.1923$	1.56
2001	-1	$1.1397 + 0.4737(-1) = 0.6660$	4.63
2002	0	$1.1397 + 0 = 1.1397$	13.79
2003	1	$1.1397 + 0.4737(1) = 1.6134$	41.06
2004	2	$1.1397 + 0.4737(2) = 2.0871$	122.22

Merits and Demerits of the Method of Least Square

Merits

1. It is a mathematical method which does not leave any scope of subjectivity, *i.e* . it is free from any bias.
2. Unlike the method of moving averages, this method provides trend values for all given time points in the series

3. The fitted trend equation can be used for purposes of estimation, prediction and forecasting.

Demerits

1. The method involves lot of calculations as compared to other methods of trend determination.
2. It is not flexible in the sense that an addition of even a single value to initial data needs fresh calculations for determining the trend equation
3. Predictions or forecasts are based only on long-term variations, it., trend, while the impact of remaining (cyclical, seasonal and irregular) is ignored.
4. The choice of a particular trend equation or curve is largely a subjective matter In '.hi absence of no hard and fast rule, the choice of the equation depends on the person concerned.

There are several methods for the construction of index numbers. The following diagram illustrates the various methods.

2.8 Index Numbers

Introduction **(L.U.) (A.U) (U.P.T.U. 2005, 08)**

Index numbers are devices that measure the change in the level of a phenomenon with respect to time, geographical location or some other characteristic. Initially, index numbers were designed to study the change in the price level or the purchasing power of money. Today there is hardly any phenomena which does not make use of the device of index numbers. Wherever a comparative study has to be made, index numbers are very handy. In present day situation changes in production, consumption, exports, imports, national income, cost of living, incidence of crime, number of road accidents, business failures and a very wide variety of other phenomena are studied with the help of index numbers. Index numbers are supposed to be barometers which measure the change in the level of a phenomenon. Their importance in the realm of quantitative techniques cannot be over emphasized.

Definition

An index number is a statistical measure designed to show changes in variable or a group of related variables with respect to time, geographical location or other characteristic.

We now explain the various methods in details. There are mainly two classes of index numbers, namely

(*i*) Unweighted index numbers

(*ii*) Weighted index numbers.

Characteristics of Index Numbers

1. Index numbers are a specialized type of average.
2. Index numbers study the effects of such factors which cannot be measured directly.
3. Index numbers bring out the common characteristics of a group of items.
4. The changes measured by index numbers can be either in relation to time or in relation to place.

Uses of Index Numbers

1. Help in studying trends.
2. Help in policy formulation.
3. Help in measuring the purchasing power of money.
4. Help in deflating various values.
5. Act as economic barometers.

Types of Index Numbers

(*a*) Price Index Numbers (Wholesale and Retail).

(*b*) Quantity Index Numbers.

(*c*) Value Index Numbers.

(*d*) Special Purpose Index Numbers.

Selection of the Base

Index numbers measure the relative changes in the level of a phenomenon as compared to the level of the same phenomenon on a previous date. This previous date or the period on which the current variations are based is known as the Base Period of Index Number. In the construction of index numbers the selection of the base period is a very important step. There are two methods by which the base period can be selected:

(*i*) **Fixed Base Method :** As the name suggests, in this method the base period is fixed. A particular year is generally chosen arbitrarily and the prices of the subsequent years are expressed as relatives of the prices of the base year. Sometimes instead of choosing a single year as the base, a period of a few years is chosen and the average price of this period is taken as the base year price. Fixed base can be used for an indefinite period. The year which is selected as a base should be a normal year. Or, in other words, the price level in this year should neither be abnormally low nor abnormally high. If an abnormal year is chosen as the base, the price relatives of the current year calculated on its basis would give misleading conclusions. In order to remove this difficulty associated with the selection of a normal year, the average price of a few years is sometimes taken as the base price, as stated earlier. The idea is that if a few years' average is taken, abnormalities in one direction would be set off against abnormalities in another direction. Sometimes when an index number is being constructed for a past period, the average of the whole period may be taken as the base. But this is possible only if the index number relates to the past.

(ii) **Chain Base Method :** In this method, there is no fixed base period. The year immediately preceding the one for which price relatives have to be calculated is assumed as the base year. In this way there is no fixed base. It goes on changing. The chief advantage of this method is that the price relatives of a year can be compared with the price levels of the immediately preceding year. Businessmen and others are more interested in comparison of this type rather than in comparisons relating to distant past. Yet another advantage of the chain base method is that under it, it is possible to include new items in an index number or to delete old items which are no more important. In fixed base method, this is not possible. But chain base method has a drawback and it is that with it, comparisons cannot be made over a long period.

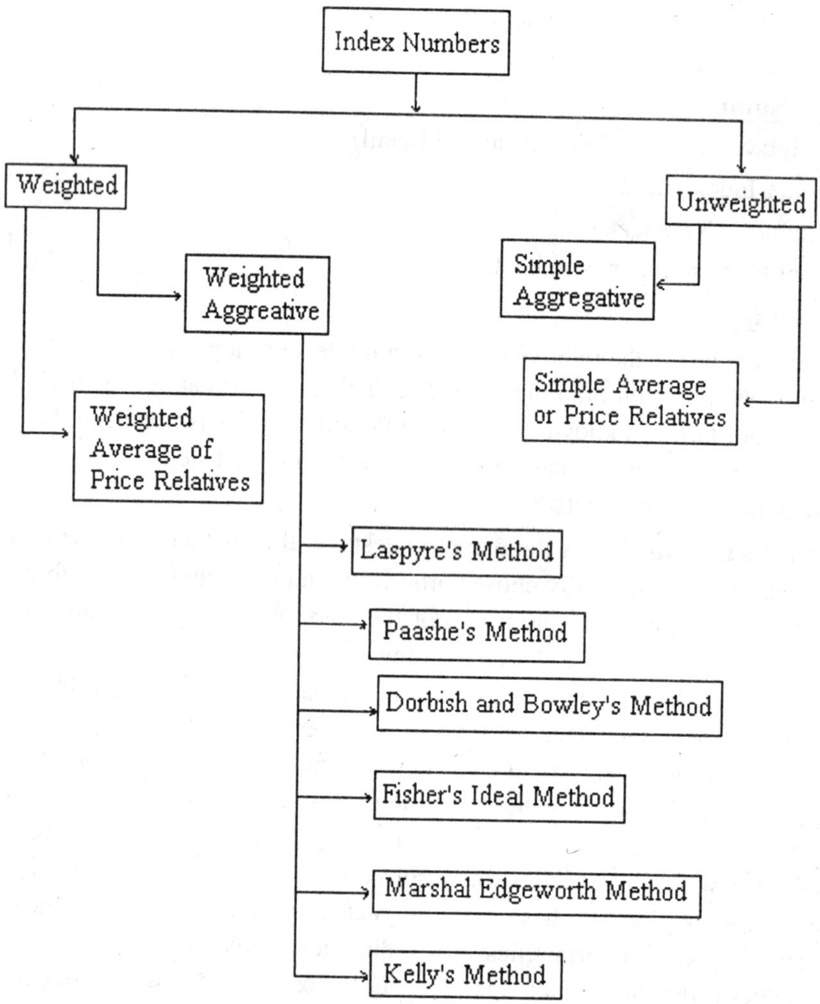

Methods of Constructing Index Numbers

A. Un-weighted Index Numbers. (each item is supposed to have the same weight.)

B. Weighted Index Numbers. (weights are assigned to various items in accordance with their importance.)

Un-weighted index numbers can be further divided in two categories:

(*i*) Simple Aggregative Method.

$$P_{01} = \frac{\Sigma p_1}{\Sigma p_0} \times 100$$

(*ii*) Simple Average of Relatives Method.

$$P_{01} = \frac{\Sigma\left(\frac{p_1}{p_0} \times 100\right)}{N}$$

Similarly, weighted index numbers can also be divided in two categories:

(*i*) Weighted Aggregative Method.

1. Laspeyres Method.

$$P_{01} = \frac{\Sigma p_1 q_0}{\Sigma p_0 q_0} \times 100$$

2. Paasche's Method.

$$P_{01} = \frac{\Sigma p_1 q_1}{\Sigma p_0 q_1} \times 100$$

3. Drobish and Bowley's Method.

$$P_{01} = \frac{\frac{\Sigma p_1 q_0}{\Sigma p_0 q_0} + \frac{\Sigma p_1 q_1}{\Sigma p_0 q_1}}{2} \times 100$$

4. Fisher's Ideal Method.

$$P_{01} = \sqrt{\frac{\Sigma p_1 q_0}{\Sigma p_0 q_0} \times \frac{\Sigma p_1 q_1}{\Sigma p_0 q_1}} \times 100$$

5. Marshall-Edgeworth Method.

$$P_{01} = \frac{\Sigma(q_0 + q_1)p_1}{\Sigma(q_0 + q_1)p_0} \times 100$$

$$or\ P_{01} = \frac{\Sigma p_1 q_0 + \Sigma p_1 q_1}{\Sigma p_0 q_0 + \Sigma p_0 q_1} \times 100$$

6. Walsh Method.

$$P_{01} = \frac{\Sigma p_1 \sqrt{q_0 q_1}}{\Sigma p_0 \sqrt{q_0 q_1}} \times 100$$

7. Kelly's Method.

$$P_{01} = \frac{\Sigma p_1 q}{\Sigma p_0 q} \times 100$$

(*ii*) Weighted Average of Relatives Method. (beyond the scope of our discussion.)

Quantity or Volume Index Numbers

The quantity index numbers measure average change in quantities and enable us to compare changes in physical quantity of goods produced or sold.

Laspeyres Method

$$Q_{01} = \frac{\Sigma q_1 p_0}{\Sigma q_0 p_0} \times 100$$

Paasche's Formula

$$Q_{01} = \frac{\Sigma q_1 p_1}{\Sigma q_0 p_1} \times 100$$

Fisher's Formula

$$Q_{01} = \sqrt{\frac{\Sigma q_1 p_0}{\Sigma q_0 p_0} \times \frac{\Sigma q_1 p_1}{\Sigma q_0 p_1}} \times 100$$

Value Index Numbers

Value is the product of price and quantity. A simple value ration is equal to the value of the current year divided by the value of the base year. If this ration is multiplied by 100, we get the value index number.

$$V = \frac{\Sigma p_1 q_1}{\Sigma p_0 q_0} \times 100$$

$$or\ V = \frac{\Sigma v_1}{\Sigma v_0} \times 100$$

Tests of Adequacy of Index Number Formulae

1. **Unit Test :** This test requires that the formula for the construction of index number should be such which is not affected by the unit in which the prices or quantities have been quoted. This test is satisfied by all the formulae discussed above except the simple (un-weighted) aggregative index formula.

2. **Time Reversal Test :** If the formula for calculating an index number is such that it will give the same ratio between one point of comparison and the other, no matter which of the two is taken as base, it satisfies the time reversal test. That is

$$P_{01} \times P_{10} = 1$$

This test is not satisfied by Laspeyres and Paasche's formulae. It is satisfied by:

(1) Fisher's Ideal Formula

(2) Kelly's Formula

(3) Marshall-Edgeworth Method

(4) Walsch Formula

1. **Factor Reversal Test :** A formula that permits inter-changing the price and quantities without giving inconsistent result, that is, the two results multiplied together should give the true value ratio. That is

$$P_{01} \times Q_{01} = \frac{\Sigma p_1 q_1}{\Sigma p_0 q_0}$$

This test is satisfied only by the Fisher's Ideal Index Number.

2. **Circular Test :** It is a sort of extension of the time reversal test. Suppose an index number is constructed for the year 2003 with the base of 2002 and another index number for 2002 on the base of 2001, then it should be possible for us to directly get an index number for 2003 on the base of 2001. If this is possible, then the circular test is satisfied. If P_{01} represents the price change of the current year on the base year and P_{12} the price change of the base year on some other base, and P_{20} the price change of the current year on this second base, then the following equation should be satisfied:

$$P_{01} \times P_{12} \times P_{20} = 1$$

This test is fulfilled only by un-weighted index numbers.

2.9 Cost of Living Index Numbers

(L.U.) (U.P.T.U. 2006)

These index numbers are also called consumer price index numbers, retail price index numbers, cost of living price index numbers and price of living index numbers. Cost of living index numbers do not actually measure the actual cost of living nor the fluctuations in the cost of living due to causes other than the changes in the price level. Cost of living index numbers only tell us how much the consumers of a particular class have to pay to get a basket of goods and services at a particular point of time in comparison to what they paid for this basket in the base year.

The necessity of the construction of cost of living index numbers arises on account of the fact that wholesale price index numbers measure the variations only in the general level of prices.

These variations do not throw light on the effects of rise and fall of prices on the cost of living of different classes of people in a society. Different groups of people consume different types of commodities and even the same type of commodities are not consumed in the same proportion by different classes of people. The relative importance of different commodities is therefore different in case of different types of people. In order to measure the effects of the rise and fall in the prices of various commodities on the cost of living of different classes of people, separate index numbers are constructed for different groups.

It should be remembered that a cost of living index number tells us about the variations in the cost of living of only one group of persons living in a particular region. By region, we mean an area within which retail process are almost equal and by groups we mean classes distinguished from each other on the basis of incomes. Thus, there cannot be one cost of living index number for textile workers of the whole country, because retail process in different places differ and the pattern of consumption is also not alike in different localities. Similarly, we cannot have a cost of living index number for the whole population of a particular town because groups of persons with different incomes spend their income on various commodities in different ways and the relative importance of various commodities to all persons is not identical.

Limitations of Index Numbers

(1) They are only approximate indicators of the relative level of a phenomenon.

(2) Index numbers use only limited number of items in their calculation.

(3) The quality of the product is very difficult to be accounted for in the construction of index numbers.

(4) Index numbers are liable to be misused.

(5) Indices constructed for one purpose cannot be used for another purpose.

Example 1: From the following compute price Index Numbers all four methods:

Commodities	1970		1980	
	Price	Quantity	Price	Quantity
A	20	8	40	6
B	50	10	60	5
C	40	15	50	15
D	20	20	20	25

Solution:

Commodities	1970		1980		$p_0 q_0$	$p_0 q_1$	$p_1 q_0$	$p_1 q_1$
	p_0	q_0	p_1	q_1				
A	20	8	40	6	160	120	320	240
B	50	10	60	5	500	250	600	300
C	40	15	50	15	600	600	750	750
D	20	20	20	25	400	500	400	500
					1660	**1470**	**2070**	**1790**

Laspeyre's Index Number

$$=\frac{\Sigma P_1 q_0}{\Sigma P_0 q_0}\times 100=\frac{2070}{1660}\times 100=124.699$$

Paasche's Index number

$$\frac{\Sigma p_1 q_1}{\Sigma p_0 q_1}\times 100=\frac{1790}{1470}\times 100=121.77$$

Fisher's Ideal Index Number

$$\left[P_{01}\times = P_{01^{Pa}} * P_{01^{La}}\right]^{1/2}=[124.699*121.77]^{1/2}=123.32$$

Marshall Edgeworth Index Number

$$\frac{\Sigma p_1 q_1+\Sigma p_1 q_0}{\Sigma p_0 q_1+\Sigma p_0 q_0}\times\frac{1790+2070}{1470+1660}\times 100=123.23$$

Example 2: *From the following, construct index number of the group of four commodities by using Fishers Ideal method.*

Commodities	Base Year		Current Year	
	Price	Expenditure	Price	Expenditure
A	2	40	5	75
B	4	16	8	40
C	1	10	2	24
D	5	25	10	60

Solution:

Commodities	Base Year		Current Year		q_0	q_1	$p_1 q_0$	$p_0 q_1$
	p_0	p_0q_0	p_1	p_1q_1				
A	2	40	5	75	20	15	100	30
B	4	16	4	8	4	5	32	20
C	1	10	2	24	10	12	20	12
D	5	25	10	60	5	6	50	30
		91		199			**202**	**92**

Fisher's Ideal Price Index

$$\left[P_{01}^{F} = P_{01}^{La}\right]^{1/2} = \sqrt{\frac{202\times199}{91\times92}}\times100 = 219.12$$

Test of Consistency

- *Unit Test:* This test requires that the index number formula should be independent of the units in which the prices or the quantities of various commodities are quoted. All those formulas which were discussed earlier other than Simple Aggregate of Prices (Quantities) satisfy this test.
- Time Reversal Test : $P_{01}\times P_{10} = 1$
- Other than Laspeyre's & aasche's Index Numbers all others satisfy this test.
- Factor Reversal Test: $P_{01}\times P_{10} = [\Sigma P_1q_1 / \Sigma P_0q_0]$

Example 3: *From the following check whether (i) Laspeyre's (ii) Paasche's (iii) Fishers Index Numbers Satisfy the Time and factor Reversal Tests.*

Commodities	Base Year		Current Year	
	Price	Quantity	Price	Quantity
A	6.5	500	10.8	560
B	2.8	124	2.9	148
C	4.7	69	8.2	78
D	10.9	38	13.4	24
E	8.6	49	10.8	27

Solution:

Commodities	$p_0 q_0$	$p_1 q_0$	$p_0 q_1$	$p_1 q_1$
A	3250	5400	3640	6048
B	347.2	359.6	414.4	429.2
C	324.3	565.8	366.6	63.6
D	414.2	509.2	261.6	321.6
E	421.4	529.2	232.2	291.6
	4757.1	**7363.8**	**4914.8**	**7730**

Laspeyre's Price Index Number: 154.80, Laspeyre's Quantity Index Number: 101.21

Paasche's Price Index Number: 157.28 Paache's Quantity Index Number: 104.97

Fisher's Ideal Price Index Number: 156.03, Fisher's Ideal Quantity Index Number: 103.01

By trail we can find that Fisher's Index Number satisfies both the tests.

Example 4: *From the following, calculate Cost of Living Index Number:*

Commodities	Base Year Price	Current Year Price	Weights
A	30	47	4
B	8	12	1
C	14	18	3
D	22	15	2
E	1	25	30

Solution:

Commodities	P	WP
A	156.67	626.67
B	150.00	150.00
C	128.57	385.71
D	68.18	136.36
E	120.00	12.00
		1418.74

1418.74/11 = 128.98

Example 5: Calculate price index number for the year 2001 with 1999 as the base year from the following data using.

(i) Laspyre's method

(ii) Paasche's Index

(iii) Fisher's Index

(U.P.T.U. 2009)

Commodity	Unit	1991		2001	
		Pric (Rs.)	Value	Qty. consumed	Value
A	Kg.	10	1500	160	1760
B	Kg.	12	1080	100	1300
C	Metre	15	900	60	960
D	Packets	9	450	40	480

Solution:

1991 (base year)		2001 (Current year)		p_1q_0	p_0q_0	p_1q_1	p_0q_1
p_0	q_0	p_1	q_1				
10	150	11	160	1650	1500	1760	1600
12	90	13	100	1170	1080	1300	1200
15	60	16	60	960	900	960	900
9	50	12	40	600	450	480	360
Total				**4380**	**3930**	**4500**	**4060**

(i) Laspyre's method:

$$=\frac{\Sigma p_1q_0}{\Sigma p_0q_0}\times 100=\frac{4380}{3930}\times 100=111.45$$

(ii) Paasche's Index

$$=\frac{\Sigma p_1q_1}{\Sigma p_0q_1}\times 100=\frac{4500}{4060}\times 100=110.84$$

(iii) Fisher's Index

$$=\sqrt{\frac{\Sigma p_1q_0}{\Sigma p_0q_0}\times\frac{\Sigma p_1q_1}{\Sigma p_0q_1}}\times 100$$

$$=\sqrt{1.2321}\times 100=111$$

Objective type Questions

1. An overall tendency of rise or fall in a time series is called:
   (a) Seasonal (b) Trend
   (c) Cyclical (d) Irregular
2. The component useful for short term forecasting is :
   (a) Cyclical (b) Trend
   (c) Seasonal (d) Irregular
3. The component useful for long term forecasting is : **(UPTU-08)**
   (a) Trend (b) Seasonal
   (c) Cyclical (d) Irregular
4. In an additive model, the component measurements are:
   (a) Positive (b) Negative
   (c) Absolute (d) None of these
5. In a multiple model, C,S and I have:
   (a) Positive value (b) Positive or negative value
   (c) Absolute value (d) Indexing value
6. The method of moving average is useful for determining:
   (a) Trend (b) seasonal indices
   (c) Irregular variation (d) None of these
7. Seasonal variations repeat with in:
   (a) Five years (b) Seven years
   (c) Two years (d) A years
8. Loss of working days due to fire in a factory is associated to the:
   (a) Trend (b) Seasonal component
   (c) Cyclical component (d) Random component
9. A boom is business activity is associated to the:
   (a) Cyclical component (b) Seasonal component
   (c) Random component (d) Trend
10. Decline in steel production due to work's strike is associated to the:
    (a) Random component (b) Cyclical component
    (c) Trend (d) Seasonal variation

11. The seasonal indices are obtained by using:
    (a) Link relative method (b) Moving average method
    (c) Free hand curve method (d) None of these
12. The trend is determined by:
    (a) The link relative method (b) Ratio-to-trend method
    (c) Ratio-to-moving average method (d) None of these
13. The weight used in Laspeyres' quantity index are donated as:
    (a) q_0 (b) q_1
    (c) p_0 (d) p_1
14. The weight used in Paasche's price index are denoted as:
    (a) q_0 (b) q_1
    (c) p_0 (d) p_1
15. The weight used in Paasche's quantity index are denoted as:
    (a) q_0 (b) q_1
    (c) p_0 (d) p_1
16. Dorbish-Bowely's price index uses as weights
    (a) base year quantity
    (b) current year and base year quantities
    (c) average of base year and current year quantity
    (d) None of these
17. The arithmetic mean of Laspeyres and Paasche's indices is: **(UPTU-08)**
    (a) Fisher index (b) Bowley's index
    (c) Marshall and Edgeworth index (d) Walsh index
18. The geometric mean of Laspeyres' and Paasche's indices is:
    (a) Fisher's ideal index (b) Bowley's index
    (c) Marshall and Edgeworth index (d) None of these
19. Symbolically $P_{01} \times P_{10}=1$ stand for
    (a) Unit test (b) Circular test
    (c) Factor reversal test (d) Time reversal test
20. Symbolically $P01 \times Q10 = \frac{\Sigma p_1q_1}{\Sigma p_0q_0}$ stand for
    (a) Unit test (b) Circular test
    (c) Factor reversal test (d) Time reversal test

21. Fisher's ideal index formula satisfies

(a) Circular test (b) Time reversal test

(c) Factor reversal test (d) Both, the factor and time reversal

22. In usual symbols, $P_{01} \times P_{12} = 1 / P_{02}$ gives:

(a) Circular test (b) Unit test

(c) Time reversal test (d) Factor reversal test

23. Fixed base index numbers and chain indices are

(a) The same (b) Different

(c) Always 100 (d) None of these

24. The time reversal test is satisfied if:

(a) $P_{01} \times P_{10} = \frac{1}{\sum P_0 q_0}$ (b) $P_{01} \times Q_{01} = \sum P_1 q_1$

(c) $P_{01} \times Q_{01} = 1$ (d) $P_{01} \times P_{01} = 1$

25. Which of the following Index satisfied the circular test **(U.P.T.U. 2010)**

(a) Laspeyer's Index (b) Paasche's Index

(c) Bowley's Index (d) Fisher's Index

Answers

1. b	6. a	11. a	16. d	21. d
2. c	7. d	12. d	17. b	22. a
3. a	8. d	13. a	18. a	23. a
4. c	9. a	14. b	19. d	24. a
5. d	10. a	15. d	20. c	25. c

Exercise 2.2

1. What is a time series? Explain the objectives of the analysis of a time series?
2. Describe the components of a time series. Illustrate them with suitable examples. **(UPTU-07)**
3. Define trend in a time series. What are the objectives behind the study of trend in a time series?
4. Explain the method of moving averages. Describe the merits and demerits of this method.

(*a*) Distinguish between the seasonal and cyclical variations.

(*b*) Describe models of a time series. How do they differ?

(*c*) Agricultural outputs in million tones for 5 years are given below :

Year	1998	1999	2000	2001	2002
Output	80	85	87	93	100

Obtain a least square linear estimate of the output for the year 2004.

5. The following table shows the number of salesman working for a certain concern :

Year :	1998	1999	2000	2001	2002	2003
Number :	28	38	46	40	56	60

Use the method of least squares to fit a straight line trend.

6. The number of units of a product exported during 1997-2004 is given below. Fit straight line trend by the method of least square. Estimate the export for 2005.

Year	No. of units (in 000)
1997	15
1998	20
1999	24
2000	29
2001	35
2002	45
2003	60
2004	85

7. Fit a straight line trend by the method of Least squares to the following data. Assuming that the same rate of change continues, what would be the predicted sales for the year 1997:

Year	Sales (1000 rupees)
1998	38
1989	40
1990	65
1991	72
1992	69
1993	60
1994	87
1995	95

What is an index number? What are the uses of index numbers? **(UPTU-07)**

8. State and explain Fisher's Ideal Formula for Price Index Numbers. Show how it satisfies the time reversal and the factor reversal tests?
9. What is meant by family budget enquiry? Discuss briefly the method of construction cost of living index numbers.
10. Explain the significance of index numbers. Also mention their limitations. **(U.P.T.U. 2007)**
11. "Index number are economic barometers". Explain this statement and mention the limitations of index numbers.
12. Explain clearly (i) Time Reversal Test, and (ii) Factor Reversal Test. **(L.U.)**
    What do you understand by the terms base shifting, splicing and deflating?
13. On the basis of the following information, calculate
    (*i*) Laspeyres' index
    (*ii*) Paasche's index
    (*iii*) Fisher's index.

Commodity	Base year		Current year	
	Price	Quantity	Price	Quantity
A	2	40	6	50
B	4	50	8	40
C	6	20	9	30
D	8	10	6	20
E	10	10	5	20

14. Using the following data, construct Fisher's ideal index, and show that it satisfies factor reversal test and time reversal test.

Commodity	Price		Quantity	
	Base year	Current year	Base year	Current year
A	6	10	50	56
B	2	2	100	120
C	4	6	60	60
D	10	12	30	24
E	8	12	40	36

15. Convert the following fixed base index numbers into chain base index numbers:

Year	1995	1996	1997	1998	1999	2000
F.B.I.	188	196	204	190	196	200

16. Convert the following fixed base index numbers into fixed base index numbers:

Year	1995	1996	1997	1998	1999	2000
F.B.I.	92	102	104	98	103	101

17. Shift the base year from 1991 to 1993 in the following series of index number :

Year	1991	1992	1993	1994	1995	1996
Index	100	115	125	130	140	185

18. Below are given the figures of production (in thousand tones) of a fertilizer factory :

Year :	1997	1998	1999	2000	2001	2002	2003
Production :	70	75	90	98	84	91	99

Fit a straight line trend by the method of least squares and estimate trend value for 2005.

(UPTU-07)

19. Construct Fisher's Ideal Index from the following data and show that it satisfies time reversal and factor reversal tests : **(UPTU-08)**

Commodity	2006		2007	
	Price	**Value**	**Price**	**Value**
A	10	100	12	144
B	15	75	20	120
C	8	80	10	110
D	20	60	25	50
E	50	5000	60	540

20. Fit a straight line trend by least squares method data given below and estimate trend for 2008 : **(UPTU-08)**

Year	2002	2003	2004	2005	2006	2007
Sales (in '000 Rs.)	10	12	15	16	18	19

21. Fit a straight line trend by method of least squares of the following data tabulate the trend value and estimate the value for 2011 from the same: **(UPTU-2010)**

Year	2001	2002	2003	2004	2005	2006	2007	2008
Value	380	400	650	720	690	695	600	850

List of Formulae

1. Price Relative $= P_{0n} = \frac{P_n}{P_0} \times 100$

Quantity Relative $= Q_{0n} = \frac{q_n}{q_0} \times 100$

Value Relative $= V_{0n} = \frac{\sum p_n q_n}{\sum p_0 q_0} \times 100 = \frac{\sum v_n}{\sum v_0} \times 100$

2. Unweighted Index Numbers

Simple Aggregate Price Index $P_{0n} = \frac{\sum p_n}{\sum p_0} \times 100$

Simple Average of Price Relative $= P_{0n} = \frac{\sum \frac{P_n}{P_0} \times 100}{N}$

Simple Geometric mean of Price Relative $= P_{0n} = Anti\log\left[\frac{\sum \log\left(\frac{P_n}{P_0} \times 100\right)}{N}\right]$

$$= Anti\log\left[\frac{\sum \log R}{N}\right]$$

where, $R = \frac{P_m}{P_0} \times 100$

3. Weighted Index Numbers

(a) Weighted Aggregative Method :

Simple Aggregative with fixed weight $= P_{0n} = \frac{\sum p_n W}{\sum p_0 W} \times 100$

Laspeyres' Price Index $= P_{0n} = \frac{\sum p_n q_0}{\sum p_0 q_0} \times 100$

Paaxhe's Price Index $= P_{0n} = \frac{\sum p_n q_n}{\sum p_0 q_n} \times 100$

Marshall-Edgeworth's Index $= P_{0n} = \frac{\sum p_n (q_0 + q_n)}{\sum p_0 (q_0 + q_n)} \times 100$

Dorbish and Bowley Index $= P_{0n} = \frac{1}{2}\left[\frac{\sum p_n q_0}{\sum p_0 q_0} + \frac{\sum p_n q_n}{\sum p_0 q_0}\right] \times 100$

Fisher's Ideal Index $= P_{0n} = \sqrt{\left[\frac{\sum p_n q_0}{\sum p_0 q_0} + \frac{\sum p_n q_n}{\sum p_0 q_0}\right]} \times 100$

(b) Weighted Average of Relatives :

Weighted Average of Relative Method $= P_{0n} = \frac{\left(\frac{P_m}{P_0} \times 100\right) W}{\Sigma W} = \frac{\Sigma RW}{\Sigma W}$

4. Quantity Index Numbers

(a) Unweighted Quantity Index:

Simple Aggregative Quantity Index $= Q_{0n} = \frac{\Sigma q_n}{\Sigma q_0} \times 100$

Quantity Index (Average of quantity Relative) $= Q_{0n} = \frac{\Sigma\left(\frac{q_n}{q_0} \times 100\right)}{N}$

(b) Weighted quantity Index:

Quantity Index (Simple Aggregative with fixed weights) $= Q_{0n} = \frac{\Sigma q_n W}{\Sigma q_n W} \times 100$

Laspeyre's Quantity Index $= Q_{0n} = \frac{\Sigma q_n p_0}{\Sigma q_n p_0} \times 100$

Paasche's Quantity Index $= Q_{0n} = \frac{\Sigma q_n p_n}{\Sigma q_0 p_n} \times 100$

Fisher's Quantity Index $= Q_{0n} = \sqrt{\left[\frac{\Sigma q_n p_0}{\Sigma q_0 p_0} \times \frac{\Sigma q_n p_n}{\Sigma q_0 p_n}\right]} \times 100$

5. Tests for Consistency or Adequacy

Time Reversal Test : $P_{0n} \times P_{n0} = 1$

Factor Reversal Test : $P_{0n} \times Q_{0n} = \frac{\sum p_n q_n}{\sum p_0 q_0}$

Circular Test : $P_{01} \times P_{10} \times P_{20} = 1$ (Fre three circular periods)

$P_{01} \times P_{12} \times P_{23} \times P_{30} = 1$ (Fre three circular periods)

6. Link Relative (L.R.) $= \frac{\text{Current year price}}{\text{Price of the preceding year}} \times 100$

Chain Index (C.I.) $= \frac{\text{Current year's Link Relative} \times \text{Preceding year's Chain Index}}{100}$

7. Conversion of Chin Base Index Numbers (C.B.I.) to Fixed Base Index Numbers (F.B.I.)

$$\text{F.B.I.} = \frac{\text{Curent year's C.B.I} \times \text{Prevous year's F.B.I.}}{100}$$

8. Base Shifting

Recasted Index Number of any year $= \frac{\text{Index no. of old base}}{\text{Index no. of new base}} \times 100$

9. Splicing

(a) Forward Splicing :

Required Index $= \frac{\text{Old Index on the exisiting base} \times \text{Index to be spliced}}{100}$

(b) For Backward Splicing :

Required Index $= \frac{100}{\text{Old Index on the exisiting base} \times \text{Index to be spliced}}$

10. Deflating

Deflated value $= \frac{\text{Current value}}{\text{Def lator}} \times 100$

Real wages (Income) $= \frac{\text{Normal wages (Income)}}{\text{Price Index}} \times 100$

3 CORRELATION AND REGRESSION

3.1 Correlation

Introduction

In various types of analysis discussed so far, we have confined ourselves to such series where various items assumed different values of one variable. There can be, however, such series also where each item assumes the values of two or more variables. For example, if the heights and weights of a group of persons are measured we shall get such series where each member of the group would assume two values – one relating to height and another relating to weight. If, besides heights and weights, the chest measurements were also taken, each member of the group would assume three values relating to three different variables.

In such situations, sometimes it appears that the values of the various variables so obtained are inter-related. It is likely that such relationship may be obtained in two series relating to the heights and weights of a group of persons. It may be observed that weights increase with increase in heights so that tall people are heavier than short sized people. Similarly, if data are collected about the prices of a commodity and the quantities sold at different prices, two series would be obtained. In these two series we are again likely to find some relationship. With an increase in the price of the commodity, the quantity sold is bound to decrease. Such relationships can be find in many other types of series also.

The term correlation (or co-variation) indicates the relationship between two such variables in which with changes in the value of one variable, the value of the other variable also changes.

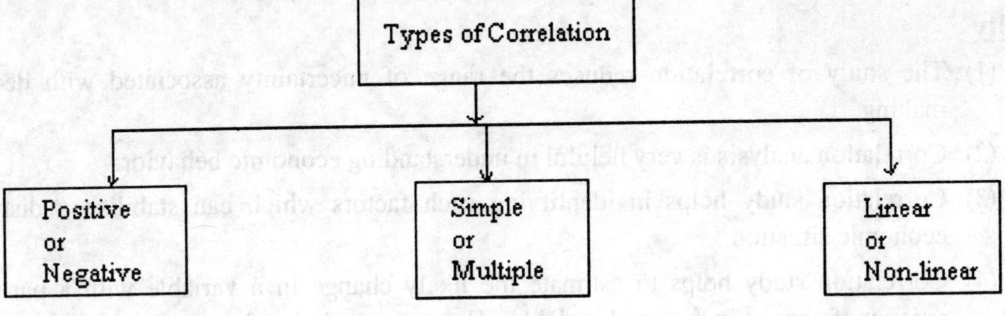

$$-1 \leq r \leq +1$$

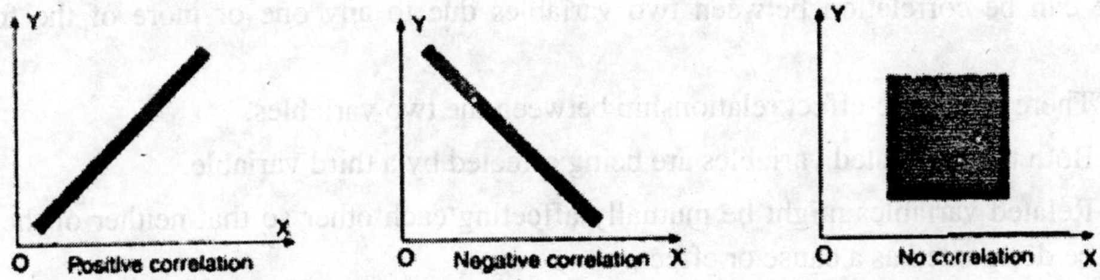

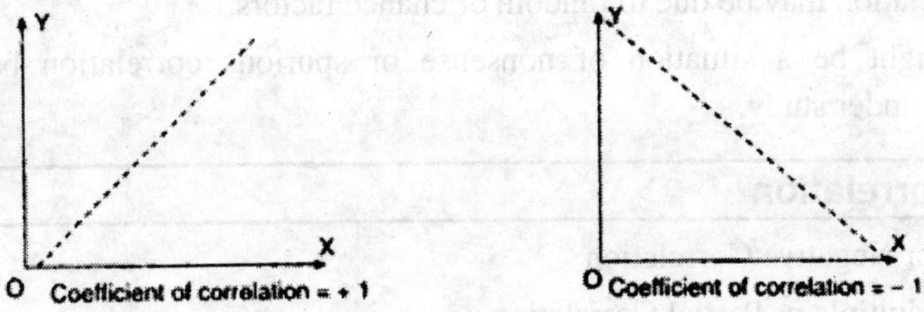

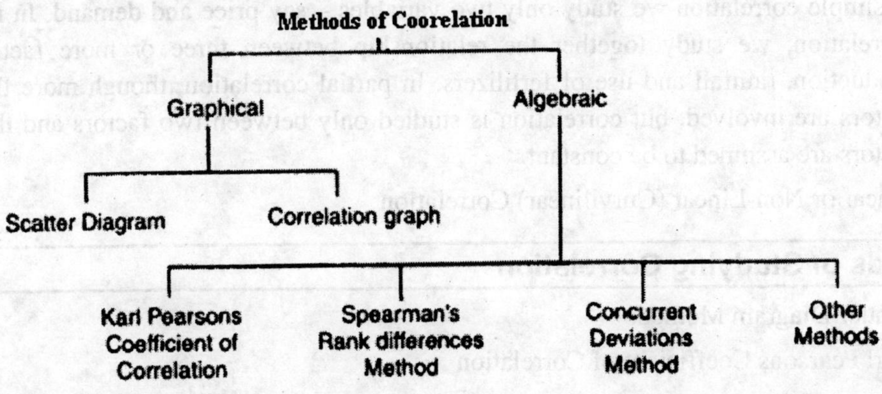

Definition

If two or more quantities vary in sympathy so that movements in the one tend to be accompanied by corresponding movements in the other(s) then they are said to be correlated.

Utility

(1) The study of correlation reduces the range of uncertainty associated with decision making.

(2) Correlation analysis is very helpful in understanding economic behavior.

(3) Correlation study helps in identifying such factors which can stabilize a disturbed economic situation.

(4) Correlation study helps to estimate the likely change in a variable with a particular amount of change in a related variable. (Here we take help of regression analysis.)

(5) Inter-relationship studies between different variables are very helpful tools in promoting research and opening new frontiers of knowledge.

There can be correlation between two variables due to any one or more of the following reasons:

(1) There is a cause-effect relationship between the two variables.

(2) Both the correlated variables are being affected by a third variable.

(3) Related variables might be mutually affecting each other so that neither of them could be designated as a cause or effect.

(4) The correlation may be due to random or chance factors.

(5) There might be a situation of nonsense or spurious correlation between the two variables under study.

3.2 Types of Correlation

(*i*) Positive or Negative Correlation

(*ii*) Simple, Multiple or Partial Correlation

In simple correlation we study only two variables – say price and demand. In multiple correlation, we study together the relationship between three or more factors like production, rainfall and use of fertilizers. In partial correlation, though more than two factors are involved, but correlation is studied only between two factors and the other factors are assumed to be constant.

(*iii*) Linear or Non-Linear (Curvilinear) Correlation

3.3 Methods of Studying Correlation

(*i*) Scatter Diagram Methods

(*ii*) Karl Pearsons Coefficient of Correlation

(*iii*) Spearman's Coefficient of Rank Correlation

(*iv*) Coefficient of Concurrent Deviation

Karl Pearson's Coefficient of Correlation

$$r = \frac{\sum_{i=1}^{n}(x_i y_i)}{n\sigma_x \sigma_y}$$

$$\text{or } r = \frac{\text{Covariance }(x,y)}{\sigma_x \sigma_y}$$

$$\text{or } r = \frac{N.(\sum xy) - \sum x.\sum y}{\sqrt{N.\sum x^2 - (\sum x)^2}\sqrt{N.\sum y^2 - (\sum y)^2}}$$

In case of group data

$$r = \frac{(\sum f.d_x.d_y) - \sum f.d_x.\sum f.d_y}{\sqrt{N.\sum f.d_x{}^2 - \frac{(\sum f.d_x)^2}{N}}\sqrt{N.\sum f.d_y{}^2 - \frac{(\sum f.d_y)^2}{N}}}$$

$$\text{Covariance} \quad (X,Y) = \frac{\sum d_x d_y}{N}$$

Mathematical Properties of Coefficient of Correlation

(1) It lies between -1 and +1. It cannot exceed unity. $(-1 < r < +1)$

(2) It is not affected by change of scale or origin.

Coefficient of Correlation by the Method of Least Squares

Will be discussed while studying Regression Analysis.

Spearman's Rank Correlation Coefficient

$$\boxed{r = 1 - \frac{6.\sum d^2}{N(N^2-1)}} \quad \text{where, d = deviation} = R_1 - R_2$$

$$\text{or} \quad \boxed{r = 1 - \frac{6.\sum d^2}{(N^3 - N)}}$$

In case of equal ranks

$$\boxed{r = 1 - \frac{6.\left[\sum d^2 + \sum \frac{1}{12}(m_1^3 - m_1) + \sum \frac{1}{12}(m_2^3 - m_2) + ...\right]}{(N^3 - N)}}$$

Coefficient of Concurrent Deviation

$$r_c = \pm\sqrt{\left(\frac{2c-N}{N}\right)}$$

3.4 Karl Pearson's Co-Efficient of Correlation (or Product Moment Correlation Co-Efficient)

(U.P.T.U. 2006, 2007)

Correlation co-efficient between two variables x and y, usually denoted by $r(x, y)$ or r_{xy} is a numerical measure of linear relationship between them and is defined as

$$r_{xy} = \frac{\Sigma(x_i - \bar{x})(y_i - \bar{y})}{\sqrt{\Sigma(x_i - \bar{x})^2 \Sigma(y_i - \bar{y})^2}} = \frac{\frac{1}{n}\Sigma(x_i - \bar{x})(y_i - \bar{y})}{\sqrt{\frac{1}{n}\Sigma(x_i - \bar{x})^2 \frac{1}{n}\Sigma(y_i - \bar{y})^2}} = \frac{\frac{1}{n}\Sigma(x_i - \bar{x})(y_i - \bar{y})}{\sigma_x \sigma_y}$$

$$\therefore \quad \boxed{r_{xy} = \frac{\Sigma(x-\bar{x})(y-\bar{y})}{n\sigma_x\sigma_y}}$$

Alternate from of r(x, y) :

$$\boxed{r(x, y) = \frac{n\Sigma xy - \Sigma x\Sigma y}{\sqrt{n\Sigma x^2 - (\Sigma x)^2}\sqrt{n\Sigma y^2 - (\Sigma y)^2}}}$$

Here n is the no. of pairs of values of x and y.

Note. Correlation co-efficient is independent of change of origin and scale.

Let us define two new variables u and v as

$$u = \frac{x-a}{h}, \; v = \frac{y-b}{k} \text{ where } a, b, h, k \text{ are constants, then } r_{xy} = r_{uv}.$$

Then, $$\boxed{r(u,v) = \frac{n\Sigma uv - \Sigma u\Sigma v}{\sqrt{n\Sigma u^2 - (\Sigma u)^2}\sqrt{n\Sigma v^2 - (\Sigma v)^2}}}$$

Example 1. *Find the coefficient of correlation between the values of x and y:*

[U.P.T.U. (C.O.) 2008]

x	1	3	5	7	8	10
y	8	12	15	17	18	20

Solution: Here, $n = 6$

The table is as follows :

x	y	x^2	y^2	xy
1	8	1	64	8
3	12	9	144	36
5	15	25	225	75
7	17	49	289	119
8	18	64	324	144
10	20	100	400	200
$\Sigma x = 34$	$\Sigma y = 90$	$\Sigma x^2 = 248$	$\Sigma y^2 = 1446$	$\Sigma xy = 582$

Karl Pearson's coefficient of correlation is given by

$$r(x, y) = \frac{n\Sigma xy - \Sigma x \Sigma y}{\sqrt{n\Sigma x^2 - (\Sigma x)^2}\sqrt{n\Sigma y^2 - (\Sigma y)^2}}$$

$$= \frac{(6 \times 582) - (34 \times 90)}{\sqrt{(6 \times 248) - (34)^2}\sqrt{(6 \times 1446) - (90)^2}}$$

$$= \frac{432}{\sqrt{333}\sqrt{576}} = 0.9879 \qquad \text{(highly positive)}$$

Example 2. *The following data regarding the heights (y) and weight s(x) of 100 college students are given:*

$$\Sigma x = 15000, \quad \Sigma x^2 = 2272500, \quad \Sigma x = 6800,$$

$$\Sigma y^2 = 463025 \text{ and } \Sigma xy = 1022250.$$

Find the correlation coefficient between height and weight. **(U.P.T.U. 2001)**

Solution: Here $n = 100$

Correlation co-efficient $r(x, y)$ is given by

$$r = \frac{n\Sigma xy - \Sigma x \Sigma y}{\sqrt{n\Sigma x^2 - (\Sigma x)^2}\sqrt{n\Sigma y^2 - (\Sigma y)^2}}$$

$$= \frac{(100 \times 1022250) - (15000 \times 6800)}{\sqrt{(100 \times 2272500) - (15000)^2}\sqrt{(100 \times 463025) - (6800)^2}}$$

$$= \frac{102225000 - 12000000}{\sqrt{227250000 - 225000000}\sqrt{46302500 - 46240000}}$$

$$= \frac{225000}{\sqrt{2250000}\sqrt{62500}} = \frac{225000}{1500 \times 250} = 0.6.$$

Example 3: *Find the co-efficient of correlation for the following table :*

x:	10	14	18	22	26	30
y:	18	12	24	6	30	36

Solution: Let $u = \frac{x-22}{4}, v = \frac{y-24}{6}$

x	y	u	v	u^2	v^2	uv
10	18	-3	-1	9	1	3
14	12	-2	-2	4	4	4
18	24	-1	0	1	0	0
22	6	0	-3	0	9	0
26	30	1	1	1	1	1
30	36	2	2	4	4	4
Total		$\Sigma u = -3$	$\Sigma v = -3$	$\Sigma u^2 = 19$	$\Sigma v^2 = 19$	$\Sigma uv = 12$

Here, $n = 6, u = \frac{1}{n}, \Sigma u = \frac{1}{6}(-3) = -\frac{1}{2}; v = \frac{1}{n}\Sigma v = \frac{1}{6}(-3) = -\frac{1}{2}$

$$r_{uv} = \frac{n\Sigma uv - \Sigma u \Sigma v}{\sqrt{n\Sigma u^2 - (\Sigma u)^2}\sqrt{n\Sigma v^2 - (\Sigma v)^2}}$$

$$= \frac{(6\times12)-(-3)(-3)}{\sqrt{(6\times19)-(-3)^2}\sqrt{(6\times19)-(-3)^2}} \frac{63}{\sqrt{105}\sqrt{105}} = 0.6$$

Hence, $r_{xy} = r_{uv} = 0.6$

Example 4: *Ten students got the following percentage of marks in Principles of Economics and Statistics:*

Roll Nos.	1	2	3	4	5	6	7	8	9	10
Marks in Economics	78	36	98	25	75	82	90	62	65	39
Marks in Statistics	84	51	91	60	68	62	86	58	53	47

Calculate the co-efficient of correlation.

Solution: Let the marks in the two subjects be denoted by *x* and y respectively.

x	y	*u = x- 65*	*v* = y - *66*	u^2	V^2	*uv*
78	84	13	18	169	324	234
36	51	-29	15	841	225	435
98	91	33	25	1089	625	825
25	60	- 40	-6	1600	36	240
75	68	10	2	100	4	20
82	62	17	-4	289	16	-68
90	86	25	20	625	400	500
62	58	-3	-8	9	64	24
65	53	0	- 13	0	169	0
39	47	- 26	- 19	676	361	494
Total		$\sum u = 0$	$\sum v = 0$	$\sum u^2 = 5398$	$\sum v^2 = 2224$	$\sum uv = 2734$

Here, $\quad n = 10, \bar{u} = \frac{1}{n}\sum u_i = 0, \bar{v} = \frac{1}{n}\sum v_i = 0$

$$r_{uv} = \frac{n\sum uv - \sum u \sum v}{\sqrt{n\sum u^2 - (\sum u)^2}\sqrt{n\sum v^2 - (\sum v)^2}}$$

$$= \frac{(10\times 2734) - (0\times 0)}{\sqrt{(10\times 5398) - (0)^2}\sqrt{(10\times 2224) - (0)^2}}$$

$$= \frac{27340}{\sqrt{53980}\sqrt{22240}} = 0.789$$

Hence, $r_{xy} = r_{nv} = 0.789$.

Example 5. *A computer while calculating correlation co-efficient between two variables X and Y from 25 pairs of observations obtained the following results :*

n=25, $\quad \sum X = 125, \quad \sum X^2 = 650,$

$\sum Y = 100, \quad \sum Y^2 = 460, \quad \sum XY = 508.$

It was, however, later discovered at the tune of checking that he had copied down two pairs as

X	Y
6	14
8	6

while the correct values were

X	Y
8	12
6	8

Obtain the correct value of correlation co-efficient.

Solution: Corrected $\sum X = 125 - 6 - 8 + 8 + 6 = 125$

Corrected $\sum Y = 100 - 14 - 6 + 12 + 8 = 100$

Corrected $\sum X^2 = 650 - 6^2 - 8^2 + 8^2 + 6^2 = 650$

Corrected $\sum Y^2 = 460 - 14^2 - 6^2 + 12^2 + 8^2 = 436$

Corrected $\sum XY = 508 - 6 \times 14 - 8 \times 6 + 8 \times 12 + 6 \times 8 = 520$

(Subtract the incorrect values and add the corresponding correct values)

$$\bar{X} = \frac{1}{n}\sum X = \frac{1}{25}\times 125 = 5;\ \bar{Y} = \frac{1}{n}\sum Y = \frac{1}{25}\times 100 = 4$$

Corrected $r_{xy} = \dfrac{n\sum XY - \sum X \sum Y}{\sqrt{n\sum X^2 - (\sum X)^2}\sqrt{n\sum Y^2 - (\sum Y)^2}}$

$$= \frac{(25\times 520) - (125\times 100)}{\sqrt{(25\times 650) - (125)^2}\sqrt{(25\times 436) - (100)^2}} = 0.67.$$

Example 6: *If* $z = ax + by$ *and r is the correlation coefficient between x and y, show that*

$$\sigma_2^2 = a^2\sigma_x^2 + b^2\sigma_y^2 + 2abr\sigma_x\sigma_y$$

Solution: $z = ax + by$

$\Rightarrow \quad \bar{z} = a\bar{x} + b\bar{y}, \quad z_i = ax_i + by_i$

$$z_i - \bar{z} = (x_i - \bar{x}) + b(y_i - \bar{y})$$

Now $\sigma_z^2 = \frac{1}{n}\sum(z_i - \bar{z})^2 = \frac{1}{n}\sum[a(x_i - \bar{x}) + b(b_i - \bar{y})]^2$

$$= \frac{1}{n}\sum[a^2(x_i - \bar{x})^2 + b^2(y_i - \bar{y})^2 + 2ab(x_i - \bar{x})(y_i - \bar{y})]$$

$$= a^2.\frac{1}{n}\sum(x_i - \bar{x})^2 + b^2.\frac{1}{n}\sum(y_i - \bar{y})^2 + 2ab.\frac{1}{n}\sum(x_i - \bar{x}) + (y_i - \bar{y})$$

$$= a^2\sigma_x^2 + b^2\sigma_y^2 + 2ab\sigma_x\sigma_y$$

$$\therefore r = \frac{\frac{1}{n}\sum(x_i - \bar{x})(y_i - \bar{y})}{\sigma_x\sigma_y}$$

Example 7. *(i) Establish the formula:*

where r_{xy} is the correlation coefficient between x and y. Using the above formula, calculate the correlation coefficient from the following data relating to the marks of 10 *candidates in aptitude test (x) and Achievement rating (y).*

						Marks					
Aptitude (x)	:	22	53	46	67	43	35	88	11	95	13
Achievement (y)	:	18	39	31	42	55	64	82	10	96	14

(ii) Establish the formula

$$r = \frac{\sigma_x^2 + \sigma_y^2 - \sigma_{x-y}^2}{2\sigma_x \sigma_y}$$

where r is the coefficient of correlation between x and y and $\sigma_x, \sigma_y, \sigma_{x-y}$ are concerned standard deviations. Hence evaluate r from the following data :

x:	21	23	30	54	57	58	72	78	87	90
y:	60	71	72	83	110	84	100	92	113	135

Sol.: (i) Let $z = x - y$

$\therefore \quad \bar{z} = \bar{x} - \bar{y}$

$\therefore \quad z - \bar{z} = (x - \bar{x}) - (y - \bar{y})$

or, $\quad (z - \bar{z})^2 = (x - \bar{x})^2 + (y - \bar{y})^2 - 2(x - \bar{x})(y - \bar{y})$

Summing up for n terms,

$$\Sigma(z - \bar{z})^2 = \Sigma(x - \bar{x})^2 + \Sigma(y - \bar{y})^2 - 2\Sigma(x - \bar{x})(y - \bar{y})$$

or, $$\frac{\Sigma(z - \bar{z})^2}{n} = \frac{\Sigma(x - \bar{x})^2}{n} + \frac{\Sigma(y - \bar{y})^2}{n} - \frac{2\Sigma(x - \bar{x})(y - \bar{y})}{n}$$

$\Rightarrow \quad \sigma_z^2 = \sigma_x^2 + \sigma_y^2 - 2r\sigma_x\sigma_v$ where $r = \dfrac{\Sigma(x - \bar{x})(y - \bar{y})}{n\sigma_x\sigma_y}$

$$\Rightarrow \quad \boxed{\sigma_{x-y}^2 = \sigma_x^2 + \sigma_y^2 - 2r\sigma_x\sigma_y}$$

or, $$\boxed{r = \frac{\sigma_x^2 + \sigma_y^2 - \sigma_{x-y}^2}{2\sigma_x\sigma_y^h}}$$

Now, $\quad n = 10$

$$\bar{x} = \frac{22+53+46+67+43+35+88+11+95+13}{10} = \frac{473}{10} = 47.3$$

$$\bar{y} = \frac{18+39+37+42+55+64+82+10+96+14}{10} = \frac{451}{10} = 45.1$$

Now we form the table as

x	y	$z = x - y$	$x-\bar{x}$	$y-\bar{y}$	$z-\bar{z}$	$(x-\bar{x})^2$	$(y-\bar{y})^2$	$(z-\bar{z})^2$
22	18	4	-25.3	-27.1	1.8	640.09	734.41	3.24
53	39	14	5.7	-6.1	11.8	32.49	37.21	139.24
46	31	15	- 1.3	-14.1	12.8	1.69	198.81	163.84
67	42	25	19.7	-3.1	22.8	38.09	9.61	519.84
43	55	- 12	-4.3	9.9	-14.2	18.49	98.01	201.64
35	64	-29	- 12.3	18.9	-31.2	151.29	357.21	973.44
88	82	6	40.7	36.9	3.8	1656.49	1361.61	14.44
11	10	1	- 36.3	-35.1	- 1.2	1317.69	1232.01	1.44
95	96	- 1	47.7	50.9	- 3.2	2275.29	2590.81	10.24
13	14	- 1	-34.3	-31.1	-3.2	1176.49	967.21	10.24
						$\Sigma(x-\bar{x})^2 =$ 7658.1	$\Sigma(y-\bar{y})^2$ = 7586.9	$\Sigma(z-\bar{z})^2 =$ 2037.6

where, $$\bar{z} = \frac{\Sigma z}{n} = \frac{22}{10} = 22$$

Now, $$\sigma_x^2 = \frac{\Sigma(x-\bar{x})^2}{n} = \frac{7658.1}{10} = 765.81$$

$$\sigma_y^2 = \frac{\Sigma(y-\bar{y})^2}{n} = \frac{7586.9}{10} = 758.69$$

$$\sigma_{x-y}^2 = \sigma_z^2 = \frac{\Sigma(z-\bar{z})^2}{n} = \frac{2037.6}{10} = 203.76$$

Substituting the values in the formula (1),

$$\sigma_{x-y}^2 = \sigma_z^2 = \sigma_{x-y}^2 = \sigma_x^2 + \sigma_y^2 - 2r_{xy}\sigma_x\sigma_y$$

$\Rightarrow$ $$203.76 = 765.81 + 758.69 - 2r_{xy}\ (27.67)\ (27.54)$$

$$r_{xy} = \frac{1524.5 - 203.76}{1524.06} = 0.866$$

(ii) The formula is established in part (*i*). Now we shall procee[d ...] the given data. Here, $n = 10$,

$$\bar{x} = \frac{\Sigma x}{n} = \frac{21 + 23 + 30 + 54 + 57 + 58 + 72 + 78 + 87 + 90}{10} \quad \frac{0}{10} = 5$$

$$\bar{y} = \frac{\Sigma y}{n} = \frac{60+71+72+83+110+84+100+92+113+135}{10} = \frac{920}{10} = 92$$

Now we form the table in

x	y	$z=x-y$	$x-\bar{x}$	$y-\bar{y}$	$z-\bar{z}$	$(x-\bar{x})^2$	$(y-\bar{y})^2$	$(z-\bar{z})^2$
21	60	-39	- 36	-32	- 4	1296	1024	16
23	71	-48	-34	-21	- 13	1156	441	169
30	72	-42	-27	-20	-7	729	400	49
54	83	-29	-3	-9	6	9	81	36
57	110	- 53	0	18	- 18	0	324	324
58	84	-26	1	-8	9	1	64	81
72	100	-28	15	8	7	225	64	49
78	92	- 14	21	0	21	441	0	441
87	113	- 26	30	21	9	900	441	81
90	135	-45	33	43	- 10	1089	1849	100
		$\Sigma z=-350$				$\Sigma(x-\bar{x})^2 = 5846$	$\Sigma(y-\bar{y})^2 = 4688$	$\Sigma(z-\bar{z})^2 = 1346$

where, $\bar{z}=\dfrac{\Sigma z}{n}=\dfrac{-350}{10}=-35$

Now, $\sigma_x^2=\dfrac{1}{n}\Sigma(x-\bar{x})^2=\dfrac{1}{10}(5846)=584.6$

$$\sigma_y^2=\frac{1}{n}\Sigma(y-\bar{y})^2=\frac{1}{10}(4688)=468.8$$

$$\sigma_{x-y}^2=\sigma_z^2=\frac{1}{n}\Sigma(z-\bar{z})^2=\frac{1}{10}(1346)=134.6$$

Substituting the values in the formula (2), we get

$$r=\frac{584.6+4688-134.6}{2\sqrt{584.6\sqrt{468.8}}}=\frac{918.8}{2(523.50786)}=0.8775$$

Example 8. *(i) Calculate Karl Pearson's coefficient of correlation between X and Y for the following information :* **(U.P.T.U.)**

$$n=12,\ \Sigma X=120,\ \Sigma Y=130,\ \Sigma(X-8)^2=150$$

$$\Sigma(Y-10)^2=200 \text{ and } \Sigma(X-8)(Y-10)=50=200$$

(ii) Calculate coefficient of correlation from the following results :

$$n=10,\ \Sigma X=100,\ \Sigma Y=150,\ \Sigma(X-10)^2=180$$

$$\Sigma(Y-15)^2=215 \text{ and } \Sigma(X-10)(Y-15)=60.$$

Solution: *(i)* $\Sigma x=\Sigma(X-8)=\Sigma X-\Sigma 8=120-(8\times 12)=24$

$$\Sigma y=\Sigma(Y-10)=\Sigma Y-\Sigma 10=130-(10\times 12)=10$$

$\sum xy = \sum(X - 8)(Y-10) = 50$ (given)

$\sum x^2 = \sum(X - 8)^2 = 150$

$\sum y^2 = \sum(Y - 10)^2 = 200$

Now, $$r = \frac{n\sum xy - \sum x \sum y}{\sqrt{n\sum x^2 - (\sum x)^2}\sqrt{n\sum y^2 - (\sum y)^2}} = \frac{(12\times50)-(24\times10)}{\sqrt{(12\times150)-(24)^2}\sqrt{(12\times200)-(10)^2}}$$

$$= \frac{360}{\sqrt{1224}\sqrt{2300}} = 0.2146$$

(i) Mean of first series, $\bar{X} = \frac{\sum X}{n} = \frac{100}{10} = 10$

Mean of second series, $\bar{Y} = \frac{\sum Y}{n} = \frac{150}{10} = 15$

Now, $$r = \frac{\sum(X-\bar{X})(Y-\bar{Y})}{\sqrt{\sum(X-\bar{X})^2(Y-\bar{Y})^2}}$$

$$= \frac{\sum(X-10)(Y-5)}{\sqrt{\sum(X-10)^2(Y-15)^2}}$$

$$= \frac{60}{\sqrt{180\times215}} = 0.305$$

Example 9. *The Personnel Manager of a large chain of retail stores is interested in studying the relationship between the experience of his sales personnel and their sales performance. For this purpose, he took a sample of 5 sales personnel at random and recorded data regarding their experience in years and sales in Rs. lakhs as follows :*

Sales Personnel	*Experience (in yrs.)*	*Sales performance (Rs. lakhs)*
1	2	20
2	4	12
3	6	18
4	8	10
5	10	40

Calculate Karl Pearson's coefficient of correlation between the experience and sales performance of the sales personnel. **[U.P.T.U. (MBA) 2004]**

Solution: Let the experience be denoted by x and sales performance be denoted by y. Let us form the table as :

x	y	xy	x^2	y^2
2	20	40	4	400
4	12	48	16	144
6	18	108	36	324
8	10	80	64	100
10	40	400	100	1600
$\sum x = 30$	$\sum y = 100$	$\sum xy = 676$	$\sum x^2 = 220$	$\sum y^2 = 2568$

Here, $n = 5$

Karl Pearson's Coeff. of correlation is given by

$$r = \frac{n\sum xy - \sum x \sum y}{\sqrt{n\sum x^2 - (\sum x)^2}\sqrt{n\sum y^2 - (\sum y)^2}}$$

$$= \frac{(5\times 676) - (30\times 100)}{\sqrt{(5\times 220) - (30)^2}\sqrt{(5\times 2568) - (100)^2}}$$

$$= \frac{380}{\sqrt{200}\sqrt{2840}} = 0.5042$$

Correlation of Bivariate Group data

When we have to find coefficient of correlation from bivariate group data table, the following formulae is applicable.

$$r = \frac{N.\sum fd_x d_y - \sum fd_x . \sum fd_y}{\sqrt{N\sum fd_x^2 - (\sum fd_x)^2}\sqrt{N\sum fd_y^2 - (\sum fd_y)^2}}$$

Example 10: *Find the coefficient of correlation between the age and marks from the following table*

Age in years

Test Marks	18	19	20	21	Total
200-250	4	4	2	1	11
250-300	3	5	4	2	14
300-350	4	6	8	5	21
350-400	1	4	9	10	21
Total	10	19	20	18	67

Solution: Let the age of student and marks obtained by them is represented by X and Y

(MBA, Delhi Univ.)

y \ x	d_y \ d_x	*Age in years* 18 (−1)	19 (0)	20 (1)	21 (2)	Total, f	fd_y	fd_y^2	fd_xd_y
200–250	−1	(4) 4	(0) 4	(−2) 2	(−2) 1	11	−11	11	0
250–300	0	(0) 3	(0) 5	(0) 4	(0) 2	14	0	0	0
300–350	1	(−2) 2	(0) 6	(8) 8	(10) 5	21	21	21	16
350–400	2	(−2) 1	(0) 4	(12) 6	(40) 10	21	42	84	50
Total, f		10	19	20	18	n = 67	Σfd_y = 52	Σfd_y^2 = 116	Σfd_xd_y = 66
fd_x		−10	0	20	36	Σfd_x = 46			
fd_x^2		10	0	20	72	Σfd_x^2 = 102			
fd_xd_y		0	0	18	48	Σfd_xd_y = 66			

where $d_x = x - 19$, $d_y = (m - 275)/50$

Substituting values in the formula of Karl Pearson's correlation coefficient, we have

$$r = \frac{n\Sigma fd_xd_y - (\Sigma fd_x)(\Sigma fd_y)}{\sqrt{n\Sigma fd_x^2 - (\Sigma fd_x)^2}\sqrt{n\Sigma fd_y^2 - (\Sigma fd_y)^2}} = \frac{67\times 66 - 46\times 52}{\sqrt{67\times 102 - (46)^2}\sqrt{67\times 116 - (52)^2}}$$

$$= \frac{4422 - 2392}{\sqrt{6834 - 2116}\sqrt{7772 - 2704}} = \frac{2030}{\sqrt{4718}\sqrt{5068}}$$

$$= \frac{2030}{68.688\times 71.19} = 0.415$$

Interpretation: Since the value of r is positive, therefore age of students and marks obtained in an intelligence test are positively correlated to the extent of 0.415. Hence, we conclude that as the age of students increases, score of marks in intelligence test also increases.

Example 11: *Calculate the co-efficient of correlation between the age of mother and age of daughter from the under noted data and comment upon the result obtain and its probable error between the age of* 100 *mother and daughter age.* **(U.P.T.U. 2010)**

Age of Mother in Years	Age of daughters in Years					Total
	5-10	10-15	15-20	20-25	25-30	
15-25	6	3	–	–	–	9
25-35	3	16	10	–	–	29
35-45	–	10	15	7	–	32
45-55	–	–	7	10	4	21
55-65	–	–	–	4	5	9
Total	9	29	32	21	9	100

Solution: Calculation of coefficient of correlation

Calcualtion of the coefficient of correlation

Ages of Mothers in Years	*Age of Daughters* *5–10* *7.5*	*10–15* *12.5*	*15–20* *17.5*	*20–25* *22.5*	*25–30* *27.5*	*Total*	*dy*	*d'y*	*fd'y*	*fd'y²*	*fdx dy*
15–25 20	24 6 +4	6 3 +2				9	–20	–2	–18	36	30
25–35 30	6 3 +2	16 16 +1	0 10 0			29	–10	–1	–29	29	22
35–45 40		0 10 0	0 15 0	0 7 0		32	0	0	0	0	0
45–55 50			0 7 0	10 10 +1	8 4 +2	21	10	1	21	21	18
55–65 60				8 4 +2	20 5 4	9	20	2	18	36	28
Total	9	29	32	21	9	100			–8	122	98
dx	–10	– 5	0	5	10						
d'x	–2	– 1	0	+1	+ 2						
fd'x	–18	–29	0	21	18	–8					
fd'x²	36	29	0	21	36	122					
fdxy	30	22	0	18	28	98					

$$r = \frac{N.\Sigma fd_x d_y - \Sigma fd_x . \Sigma fd_y}{\sqrt{N \Sigma fd_x^2 - (\Sigma fd_x)^2} \sqrt{N \Sigma fd_y^2 - (\Sigma fd_y)^2}}$$

$$r = \frac{10(98) - (-8)(-8)}{\sqrt{10(122) - (8)^2} \sqrt{10(122) - (8)^2}}$$

$$= \frac{980 - 64}{34 \times 34} = +0.79$$

P.E. = 0.6745 × S.E.

$$= 0.6745 \times \frac{1 - r^2}{\sqrt{n}}$$

$$= 0.6745 \times \frac{1 - (.80)^2}{10}$$

$$= 0.067$$

Merits and Demerits of Karl Pearson's Coefficients of Correlation

Merits

(1) It is most important and popular method of meaning the relationship between two variables.

(2) The value of r is easily interpretable.

(3) It measures the direction as well as the relationship between the two variables

(4) In regression analysis it is used for estimating the value of dependent variables from the known value of the independent variables.

Demerits

(1) The value of the coefficient is affected by extreme items.

(2) Its computational procedure is difficult as compared to other methods.

(3) Coefficients value lies between (-1) and (+1) therefore 1 its value needs a careful interpretation.

(4) It assume the linear relationship between the two variables, whether such relationship exists or not.

3.5 Rank Correlation (Spearman's Rank Correlation)

Sometimes we have to deal with problems in which data cannot be quantitatively measured but qualitative assessment is possible.

Let a group of *n* individuals be arranged in order of merit or proficiency in possession of two characteristics A and B. The ranks in the two characteristics are, in general, different. For example, if A stands for intelligence and B for beauty, it is not necessary that the most intelligent individual may be the most beautiful and *vica versa.* Thus an individual who is ranked at the top for the characteristic A *may be* ranked at the bottom for the characteristic B. Let (x_i, y_i), $i = 1, 2, \ldots\ldots\ldots n$ be the ranks of then individuals in the group for the characteristics A and B respectively. Pearsonian co-efficient of correlation between the ranks x_i-'s and y_is is called the *rank correlation co-efficient* between the characteristics A and B for that group of individuals.

Thus rank correlation co-efficient

$$r = \frac{\Sigma(x_i - \bar{x})(y_i - \bar{y})}{\sqrt{\Sigma(x_i - \bar{x})^2 (y_i - \bar{y})^2}} = \frac{\frac{1}{n}\Sigma(x_i - \bar{x})(y_i - \bar{y})}{\sigma_x \sigma_y}$$

Now x_i's and y_i' s are merely the permutations of n numbers from 1 to n. Assuming that no two individuals are bracketed or tied in either classification *i.e.*, $(x_i, y_i) \neq (x_j, y_j)$ for $i \neq j$ both x and y take all integral values from 1 to n.

$$\therefore \quad \bar{x} = \bar{y} = \frac{1}{n}(1+2+3+\ldots.+n) = \frac{1}{n}.\frac{n(n+1)}{2} = \frac{n+1}{2}$$

$$\Sigma x_i = 1+2+3+\ldots.+n = \frac{n(n+1)}{2} = \Sigma y_i$$

$$\Sigma x_i^2 = 1^2 + 2^2 + \ldots.+n^2 = \frac{n(n+1)(2n+1)}{6} = \Sigma y_i^2$$

If d_i denotes the difference in ranks of the ith individual, then

$$d_i = x_i - y_i = (x_i - \bar{x}) - (y_i - \bar{y})$$

$$\frac{1}{n}\Sigma d_i^2 = \frac{1}{n}\Sigma[(x_i - \bar{x}) - (y_i - \bar{y})]^2$$

$$= \frac{1}{n}\Sigma x_i - \bar{x})^2 + \frac{1}{n}\Sigma[(y_i - \bar{y})^2 - 2.\frac{1}{n}\Sigma(x_i - \bar{x})(y_i - \bar{y})^2$$

$$= \sigma_x^2 + \sigma_y^2 - 2r\sigma_x\sigma_y \qquad \ldots(2) \qquad | \text{ using } (1)$$

But $\quad \sigma_x^2 = \frac{1}{n}\Sigma x_{i^2} - \bar{x}^2 = \frac{1}{n}\Sigma(y_i^2 - \bar{y}^2) = \sigma_y^2$

$$\therefore \text{ From (1), } \frac{1}{n}\Sigma d_i^2 = 2\sigma_x^2 - 2r\sigma_x^2 = 2(1-r)\sigma_x^2 = 2(1-r)\left[\frac{1}{n}\Sigma x_i^2 - \bar{x}^2\right]$$

$$= 2(1-r)\left[\frac{1}{n}.\frac{n(n+1)(2n+1)}{6} - \frac{(n+1)^2}{4}\right]$$

$$= (1-r)(n+1)\left[\frac{4n+2-3n-3}{6}\right] = \frac{(1-r)(n^2-1)}{6} \text{ or } 1 - r = \frac{6\Sigma d_i^2}{n(n^2-)}$$

Hence $$r = 1 - \frac{6\sum d_i^2}{n(n^2-1)}$$

Note: This is called Spearman's Formula for Ran Correlation.

$$\sum d_i = \sum(x_i - y_i) = \sum x_i - \sum y_i = 0 \text{ always}$$

This serves as a check on calculations

The following three case are exist

(1) When Rank are given

(2) When Rank are not given

(3) When Rank are equal

1. When Rank are given

Example 1: *Compute the rank correlation coefficient for the following data :*

Person	:	*A*	*B*	*C*	*D*	*E*	*F*	*G*	*H*	*I*	*J*
Rank in Maths	:	9	10	6	5	7	2	4	S	1	3
Rank in Physics		1	2	3	4	5	6	7	8	9	10

Solution: Here the rank are given and $n = 10$.

Person	R_1	R_2	$d = R_1 - R_2$	d^2
A	9	1	8	64
B	10	2	8	64
C	6	3	3	9
D	5	4	1	1
E	7	5	2	4
F	2	6	-4	16
G	4	7	-3	9
H	8	8	0	0
I	1	9	-8	64
J	3	10	- 7	49
				$\sum d^2 = 280$

$$\therefore \quad r = 1 - \left\{\frac{6\sum d^2}{n(n^2-1)}\right\} = 1 - \left\{\frac{6\times 280}{10(100-1)}\right\} = 1 - \frac{168}{99} = 1 - 1.697 = -0.697.$$

(2) When Rank are not given

Example 2. *The marks secured by recruits in the selection test (X) and in the proficiency test CY) are given below:*

Serial No.	1	2	3	4	5	6	7	8	9
X :	10	15	12	17	13	16	24	14	22
Y :	30	42	45	46	33	34	40	35	39

Calculate the rank correlation co-efficient.

Solution: Here the marks are given. Therefore, first of all, write down ranks. In each series, the item with the largest, size is ranked 1, next largest 2 and so on.

X	10	15	12	17	13	16	24	14	22	Total
Y	30	42	45	46	33	34	40	35	39	
Ranks in X (x)	9	5	8	3	7	4	1	6	2	
Ranks in Y (y)	9	3	2	1	8	7	4	6	5	
$d = x - y$	0	2	6	2	- 1	-3	-3	0	-3	0
d^2	0	4	36	4	1	9	9	0	9	72

$$\therefore \quad r = 1 - \left\{\frac{6\sum d^2}{n(n^2-1)}\right\} = 1 - \left\{\frac{6\times 72}{10\times 80}\right\} = 1 - .6 = 0.4, \text{ where } n = 9,$$

Example 3: *Rank correlation co-efficient of marks obtained by 10 students in Mathematics and English was found to be 0.5. It was later discovered that the difference in ranks in two subjects obtained by one of the students was wrongly taken as 3 instead of 7. Find the correct rank correlation co-efficient.*

Solution: Incorrect $r_k = 0.5, n = 10$

$$\therefore \quad \text{Incorrect } \sum d^2 = \frac{n(n^2-)(1-r_k)}{6} = \frac{10\times 99\times 0.5}{6} = 82.5$$

Now, correct $\sum d^2$ = Incorrect $\sum d^2 - (3)^2 + (7)^2 = 82.5 - 9 + 49 = 122.5$

$$\therefore \quad \text{Correct } r_b = 1\left\{\frac{6\sum d^2}{nn^2-1}\right\} = 1 - \left\{\frac{6\times 122.5}{10(100-1)}\right\} = 0.2676.$$

Example 4. *Ten competitors in a beauty contest were ranked by three judges in the following orders :*

First Judge	1	6	5	10	3	2	4	9	7	8
Second Judge	3	5	8	4	7	10	2	1	6	9
Third Judge	6	4	9	8	1	2	3	10	5	7

Use the method of rank correlation to determine which pair of judges has the nearest approach to common taste in beauty ?

Solution: Let R_1, R_2, R_3 be the ranks given by three judges.

Calculation of Rank Correlation Coefficient

Competitor	R_1	R_2	R_3	$d_{12} = R_1 - R_2$	$d_{13} = R_1 - R_3$	$d_{23} = R_2 - R_3$	$d_{12}^2 =$	$d_{13}^2 =$	$d_{23}^2 =$
A	1	3	6	-2	-5	-3	4	25	9
B	6	5	4	1	2	1	1	4	1
C	5	8	9	-3	-4	- 1	9	16	1
D	10	4	8	6	2	4	36	4	16
E	3	7	1	-4	2	6	16	4	36
F	2	10	2	-8	0	8	64	0	64
G	4	2	3	2	1	- 1	4	1	1
H	9	1	10	8	-1	-9	64	1	81
I	7	6	5	1	2	1	1	4	1
J	8	9	7	-1	1	2	1	1	4
$n = 10$							$\Sigma d_{12}^2 = 200$	$\Sigma d_{13}^2 = 60$	$\Sigma d_{23}^2 = 214$

Rank correlation coefficient between first and second judges,

$$r_{k_{12}} = 1 - \left\{\frac{6\Sigma d_{12}^2}{n(n^2-1)}\right\} = 1 - \left\{\frac{6\times 200}{10(99)}\right\} = -0.212$$

Rank correlation coefficient between first and third judges,

$$r_{k_{13}} = 1 - \left\{\frac{6\Sigma d_{13}^2}{n(n^2-1)}\right\} = 1 - \left\{\frac{6\times 60}{10\times 99}\right\} = 0.636$$

Rank correlation coefficient between second and third judges,

$$r_{k_{23}} = 1 - \left\{\frac{6\Sigma d_{23}^2}{n(n^2-1)}\right\} = 1 - \left\{\frac{6\times 214}{10\times 99}\right\} = -0.297$$

Correlation between first and second judges is negative *i.e.,* their opinions regarding beauty test are opposite to each other. Similarly, opinions of second and third judges are opposite to each other, but the opinions of first and third judges are of similar type as their correlation is positive. It means that their likings and dislikings are very much common.

Example 5. *The coefficient of rank correlation between the debenture prices and share prices of a company was* 0.8. *If the sum of the squares of the difference in ranks was 33, find the value of n.*

Sol. $$r_h = 1 - \left\{\frac{6\Sigma d^2}{n(n^2-1)}\right\} \qquad \ldots(1)$$

Here, $r_k = 0.8, \Sigma d^2 = 33$

$\therefore$ From (1), $$0.8 = 1 - \left\{\frac{6\times 33}{n(n^2-1)}\right\}$$

$$n(n^2-1) = \left\{\frac{198}{0.2}\right\} = 990$$

$$\Rightarrow \quad n^3 - 1000 - n + 10 + 0$$

$$\Rightarrow \quad (n-10)(n^2+10n+100-1) = 0$$

$$\Rightarrow \quad n = 10 \qquad |\therefore n \text{ cannot be imaginary}$$

Hence no. of items in the group is 10.

(3) When Rank are equal REPEATED RANKS

If any two or more individuals have same rank or the same value in the series c/f marks, then the above formula *fails* and requires an adjustment. In such cases, each individual is given an average rank. *This common* average *rank* is the average of the ranks which these individuals would have assumed if they were slightly different *from* each other. Thus, if two individual are ranked equal at the sixth place, they would have assumed the 6th and 7th ranks if they were ranked slightly different. Their common rank $= \frac{6+7}{2} = 6.5$. If three individuals are ranked equal at fourth place, they would have assumed the 4th, 5th and 6th ranks if they were ranked slightly different. Their common rank $= \frac{4+5+6}{3} = 5$.

Adjustment. Add $\frac{1}{2}m(m^2-1)$ to Σd^2 where m stands for the number of times an item is repeated.

This adjustment factor is to be added for each repeated item.

Thus $$r = 1 - \frac{6.\left[\Sigma d^2 + \Sigma\frac{1}{12}(m_1^3 - m_1) + \Sigma\frac{1}{12}(m_2^3 - m_2) + \ldots\right]}{(N^3 - N)}$$

Example 6. Obtain the rank correlation co-efficient for the following data :

X :	68	64	75	50	64	80	75	40	55	64
Y :	62	58	68	45	81	60	68	48	50	70.

Solution: Here, marks are given, so write down the ranks.

X	68	64	75	50	64	80	75	40	55	64	Total
Y	62	58	68	45	81	60	68	48	50	70	
Ranks in X (x)	4	6	2.5	9	6	1	2.5	10	8	6	
Ranks in Y (y)	5	7	3.5	10	1	6	3.5	9	8	2	
$d = x - y$	- 1	- 1	- 1	- 1	5	-5	- 1	1	0	4	0
d^2	1	1	1	1	25	25	1	1	0	16	72

In the X-series, the value 75 occurs twice. Had these values been slightly different, they would have been given the ranks 2 and 3. Therefore, the common rank given to them is $\frac{2+3}{2} = 2.5.$ The value 64 occurs thrice. Had these values been slightly different, they would have been given the ranks 5, 6, and 7. Therefore the common rank given to them is $\frac{5+6+7}{3} = 6.$ Similarly, in the Y-series, the value 68 occurs twice. Had these values been slightly different, they would have been given the ranks 3 and 4, Therefore, the common rank given to them is $\frac{3+4}{2} = 3.5.$

Thus, m has the values 2, 3, 2.

$$\therefore \quad r = 1 - \frac{6\left\{\Sigma d^2 + \frac{1}{12}m(m^2-1) + \frac{1}{12}m_2(m_2^2-1) + \frac{1}{12}m_3(m_3^2-1)\right\}}{n(n^2-1)}$$

$$= 1 - \frac{6\left\{72 + \frac{1}{12}2(2^2-1) + \frac{1}{12}3(3^2-1) + \frac{1}{12}.2(2^2-1)\right\}}{10(10^2-1)}$$

$$= 1 - \left\{\frac{6 \times 75}{990}\right\} = \frac{6}{11} = 0.545$$

Example 7: *The value of Spearman's rank correlation coefficient of a certain number of observations was found to be 2/3. The sum of the squares of difference between the corresponding ranks was 55. Find the number of pairs.*

Solution : It is given that $p = 2/3$ and $D^2 = 55$, Putting these values in formula (13), *i e.,*

$$\rho = 1 - \frac{6\Sigma D^2}{N(N^2-1)}$$

one gets $\frac{2}{3}=1-\frac{6\times55}{N(N^2-1)}$ or $\frac{330}{N(N^2-1)}=\frac{1}{3}$

or $N(N^2-1)=990$

or $N(N^2-1)=10\times99$

or $N(N^2-1)=10(10^2-1)$

$\therefore$ $N=10.$

Thus, the number of pairs of observations is 10.

Example 8: *The coefficient of rank correlation of the marks obtained by 10 students in Statistics and Accountancy was found to be 0.2. It was later discovered that the difference in ranks in the two subjects obtained by one of the students was wrongly taken as 9 instead of 7. Find the corrected value of coefficient of rank correlation.*

Solution: Here, the rank correlation coefficient is given as

$\rho=+0.2$ and $N=10.$

Using these values we can obtain the incorrect value of $\sum D^2$ as under :

$$\rho=1-\frac{6\sum D^2}{N(N^2-1)}$$

or $0.2=1-\frac{6\times\sum D^2}{10(100-1)}$ or $0.2=1-\frac{6\times\sum D^2}{990}$

Now, the corrected $\sum D^2$ incorrect $\sum D^2$ - (square of the wrong difference)

+ (square of the correct difference)

$$=132-9^2+7^2=132-81+49-100$$

$\therefore$ Corrected $\rho=1-\frac{6\times\text{ Corrected }\sum D^2}{N(N^2-1)}=i-\frac{6\times100}{10\times99}=1-0.606=0.394$

Merits and Demerits of Rank Correlation Method

Merits

1. The method is simple and easily understandable as compared to the Karl Pearson's method. However, where ranks are treated as scores, ρ will be equal lo r. This is due to the fact that ρ is Karl Pearson's coefficient between two sets of ranks
2. The method is specially useful when precise measurements on the variables under study are not given or cannot be obtained. In other words, when the factors under study are qualitative in nature.

3. This method is applicable even when precise quantitative information on the two variables is available.
4. The method can be applied to irregular data also as it does not assume that the data should be normal.

Demerits

1. The method can be applied to ungrouped data only.
2. The ranking procedure involved in this procedure ignores the actual magnitude of data and, as such, the results obtained are only approximate.
3. The computation procedure becomes difficult as the number of paired observations increases.

3.6 Concurrent Deviation Method

This is the simplest method of studying correlation between two variables. In this method, only the direction of change (+ or -) and not the magnitude of variations, is taken in to consideration. The method ρ. gives a general idea of the direction of covariation between the two variables. *The co-efficient of correlation by the concurrent deviation method is obtained by the formula :*

$$r_e = \pm\sqrt{\left[\pm\left(\frac{2C-n}{n}\right)\right]} \qquad \ldots(15)$$

Here, r_c The coefficient of correlation by the concurrent deviation method.

C = The number of concurrent deviations, *i.e.*, the number of positive products of D_x and D_y

D_x, D_y = Stand tor deviations of X and Y-series. Here each value in the series is compared with the proceeding one. If the value is greater than the proceeding, deviation is taken positive (+) otherwise negative (-). If the value is equal to the proceeding, deviation will be zero (0).

n = The number of pairs of deviations compared. This number is one less than N (The number of paired observations in the series), *i.e.*, $n = (N-1)$.

The method involves the following steps :

Steps

1. Determine deviations D_x and D_y for X and Y-series as defined above.
2. Multiply the corresponding deviations signs and count the number of positive products which is denoted as C.
3. Find $n-(N-1)$.
4. Use formula (13) to find the coefficient of correlation by concurrent deviation method. Important point in its use is to note that:

(*i*) If (2*C*- *n*) is positive, then only positive sign is to be retained at both the places in formula (15) which now reads as,

$$r_e = +\sqrt{\left[+\left(\frac{2C-n}{n}\right)\right]}$$

(*ii*) If $(2C-n)$ is negative then only negative sign is to be retained at both the places in formula (15) which now reads as.

$$r_e = -\sqrt{\left[-\left(\frac{2C-n}{n}\right)\right]}$$

The procedure will be more clear from the following examples.

Example 9: *Calculate co-efficient of concurrent deviations from the following data:*

Price	368	384	385	361	347	384	395	403	400	385
Imports	22	21	24	20	22	26	24	29	28	27

Solution:

Computation of Concurrent Deviations

Price *X*	Deviation D_x	Imports *Y*	Deviation D_y	$D_x \times D_y$
368		22		
384	+	21	-	-
385	+	24	+	+
361	–	20	-	+
347	–	22	+	-
384	+	26	+	+
395	+	24	-	-
403	+	29	+	+
400	–	28	-	+
3.85	–	27	-	+
$N = 10$				$C = 6$

Here, $n = N - 1 = 10 - 1 = 9$. Also the value of $(2C - n) = 12 - 9 = 3$ which is positive. Therefore,

$$r_e = +\sqrt{\left[+\left(\frac{2C-n}{n}\right)\right]} = \sqrt{\left[+\left(\frac{12-9}{9}\right)\right]} = +\sqrt{0.3333} = +0.577$$

Thus, there is a moderate degree of positive correlation between prices and imports.

Example 10. *Calculate the co-efficient of correlation, using the method of concurrent deviations, between supply and demand from the following data. Also comment on your result.*

Year	1980	1981	1982	1983	1984	1985	1986	1987	1988	1989
Supply ('000 tons)	120	110	120	119	140	125	127	119	140	160
Demand ('000 tons)	240	250	260	266	232	245	255	267	268	239

[C.A. (Inter); May 1992]

Solution: **Computation of Concurrent Deviation**

Year	Supply (X)	Demand (Y)	Deviations D_x	Deviations D_y	$D_x D_y$
1980	120	240			
1981	110	250	–	+	–
1982	120	260	+	+	+
1983	119	266	–	+	–
1984	140	232	+	–	–
1985	125	245	–	+	–
1986	127	255	+	+	+
1987	119	267	–	+	–
1988	140	268	+	+	+
1989	160	239	+	–	–
$N = 10$					$C = 3$

Here, $n = N - 1 = 10 - 1 = 9$. Since the value of $(2C - n) = 6 - 9 = -3$ is negative, therefore co-efficient of correlation by concurrent deviation will be

$$r_c = -\sqrt{\left[-\left(\frac{2C-n}{n}\right)\right]} = -\sqrt{\left[-\left(\frac{3}{9}\right)\right]} = -\sqrt{0.333} = -0.577$$

$r_c = -0.577$ indicates a moderate degree of negative correlation between supply and demand.

Example 11. *From the data given below, find the correlation coefficient by the method of concurrent deviations :*

Year	1975	1976	1977	1978	1979	1980	1981
Supply	150	155	160	173	160	165	180
Price	200	181	170	160	185	180	70

Solution:

Computation of Concurrent Deviations

Year	*Supply (X)*	*Price (Y)*	*Deviation D_x*	*Deviation D_y*	$D_x D_y$
1975	150	200			
1976	155	181	+	–	–
1977	160	170	+	–	–
1978	173	160	+	–	–
1979	160	185	–	+	–
1980	165	180	+	–	–
1981	180	170	+	–	–
$N = 7$					$C = 0$

Hence $n = N - 1 = 7 - 1 = 6$. The value of $(2C - n) = 0 - 6 = -6$ is negative, Thus

$$r_e = -\sqrt{\left[-\left(\frac{2C-n}{n}\right)\right]} = -\sqrt{\left[-\left(\frac{6}{6}\right)\right]} = -1.0.$$

which shows a perfect negative correlation between supply and demand.

Merits and Demerits of Concurrent Deviation Method

Merits

1. It is a simple method of determining coefficient of correlation.
2. The method is specially useful when the number of items is very large and one wishes to get a quick idea of covariation or relationship between the two variables.
3. The coefficient is easily calculated and is useful for the study of short time fluctuations in a time series.

Demerits

1. The method has the weakness of assigning the same weight to small and big changes in the values of the series. For example the deviation form increase from ISO to 151 or from 150 to 175 will be positive (+). Thus, small and big changes get the same weight as their magnitude of change are not taken into consideration.
2. The results obtained by this method are only a rough indicator of correlation.

3.7 Coefficient of Determination

The coefficient of determination is denoted by r^2. It measures the extent of relationship between two variables x and y. The coefficient of determination is used to interpret the values of r. It is the proportionate variation independent variable due to independent variables

$$\text{if } r = 0.4 \qquad r^2 = 0.16$$

It shows that 0.16% variations in dependent variable is due to independent variable.

$$r^2 = \frac{\text{explained variance}}{\text{Total variance}}$$

Coefficient of determination is always between 0 and 1 and r is always greater than r^2 except when $r = 0$ and 1.

Coefficient of determination = r^2

Coefficient of non-determination = $1 - r^2$

Also, coefficient of alienation $= \sqrt{1-r^2}$.

Illustrative Example

Example 12: *Compute standard error and probable error through coefficient of correlation following data:*

Age in year	18	20	24	28	35	40
Height (cm)	155	168	160	178	162	168

Also calculate:

(*a*) Coefficient of determination.

(*b*) Coefficient of non-determination.

(*c*) Coefficient of alienation.

(*d*) Significance of correlation.

Solution:

X	Y	$x = (X-29)$	$y = (Y-168)$	x^2	y^2	xy
18	155	-11	-13	121	169	143
20	168	-9	0	81	0	0
24	160	-5	-8	25	64	40
28	178	-1	10	1	100	-10
35	162	6	-6	36	36	-36
40	168	11	0	121	0	0
		$\sum x = -9$	$\sum y = -17$	$\sum x^2 = 385$	$\sum y^2 = 369$	$\sum xy = 137$

$$r = \frac{\sum xy - \frac{(\sum x)(\sum y)}{N}}{\sqrt{\sum x^2 - \frac{(\sum x)^2}{N}}\sqrt{\sum y^2 - \frac{(\sum y)^2}{N}}}$$

$$r=\frac{137-\frac{(-9)(-17)}{6}}{\sqrt{385-\frac{(-9)^2}{6}}\sqrt{369-\frac{(-17)^2}{6}}}$$

$$r=\frac{137-\frac{153}{6}}{\sqrt{385-\frac{81}{6}}\sqrt{369-\frac{289}{6}}}=\frac{137-25.5}{\sqrt{371.5}\sqrt{320.83}}=\frac{111.5}{19.5\times17.91}$$

$$=\frac{111.5}{345.126}=0.323$$

(*a*) Coefficient of determination = $r^2 = (0.323)^2 = 0.104$

(*b*) Coefficient of non-determination = $1 - r^2 = 1 - 0.104 = 0.896$

(*c*) Coefficient of determination of alienation = $\sqrt{1-r^2}$

$\sqrt{0.896}=0.947$

(*d*) To check the significance

$$PE = .6745\frac{1-r^2}{\sqrt{N}}=0.6745\frac{1-.(323)^2}{\sqrt{N}}=\frac{0.6745\times0.896}{2.4495}$$

$$=\frac{0.604352}{2.4495}=0.246$$

Exercise 3.1

1. Calculate the coefficient of correlation for the following data :

Height of father (in inches)	65	66	67	67	68	69	70	72
Height of son (in inches)	67	68	65	68	72	72	69	71

2. Find the correlation coefficient between x and y from the given data : **(L.U.)**

x	78	89	97	69	59	79	68	57
y	125	137	156	112	107	138	123	108

3. Find the correlation coefficient from the following data :

x	92	89	87	86	83	77	71	63	53	50
y	86	88	91	77	68	85	52	82	37	57

4. Calculate the coefficient of correlation for the following data **(U.P.T.U. 2006)**

Husband's age (in yrs.) x	23	27	28	28	29	30	31	33	35	36
Wife's age (in yrs.) y	18	20	22	27	21	29	27	29	28	29

5. Find Karl Pearson's coefficient of correlation between the values of x and y given below:

x	78	89	96	69	59	79	68	61
y	125	137	156	112	107	136	123	108

6. Define Karl Pearson's coefficient of correlation. How would you interpret the sign and magnitude of a correlation coefficient ? **[U.P.T.U. (MBA) 2005]**

7. The marks of the same 15 students in two subjects A and B are analysed. The two numbers within the brackets denote the ranks of the same student in A' and B respectively :

   (1, 10) (2, 7) (3, 2) (4, 6) (5, 4) (6, 8) (7, 3) (8, 1) (9, 11) (10, 15) (11, 9) (12, 5) (13, 14) (14, 12) (15, 13)

   Use Spearman's formula to find the rank correlation coefficient.

8. Calculate the coefficient of correlation from the following data by the Spearman's Rank difference method :

Price of Tea (Rs.) :	75	88	95	70	60	80	81	50
Price of Coffee (Rs.) :	120	134	150	115	110	140	142	100

9. Ten students got the following percentage of marks in Chemistry and Physics :

Students	1	2	3	4	5	6	7	8	9	10
Marks in Chemistry :	78	36	98	25	75	82	90	62	65	39
Marks in Physics	84	51	91	60	68	62	86	58	63	47

Calculate the rank correlation co-efficient.

10. A sample of 12 fathers and their eldest sons gave the following data about their heights in inches :

Father :	65	63	67	64	68	62	70	66	68	67	69	71
Son :	68	66	68	65	69	66	68	65	71	67	68	70

Calculate the co-efficient of rank correlation.

11. A firm not sure of the response to its product in ten different colour shades decides to produce them in those colour shades, if the ranking of these colour shades by two typical consumer judges is highly correlated.

The two judges rank the ten colours in the following order :

Colour	*Red*	*Green*	*Blue*	*Yellow*	*White*	*Black*	*Pink*	*Purple*	*Orange*	*Ivory*
Ranking by I Judge	6	4	3	1	2	7	9	8	10	5
Ranking by II Judge	4	1	6	7	5	8	10	9	3	2

Is there any agreement between the two judges, to allow the introduction of the product by the firm in the market ?

Assume 69 and 112 as the mean values for *x* and *y* respectively.

12. Two judges in a music competition rank the 12 entries as follows :

x	1	2	3	4	5	6	7	8	9	10	11	12
y	12	9	6	10	3	5	4	7	8	2	11	1

What degree of agreement is there between the judgement of the two judges?

Answer

(1) 0.603, (2) 0.96, (3) 0.7291, (4) 0.82, (5) 0.995

(7) 0.51, (8) 0.929, (9) 0.089, (10) 0.722, (11) 0.454

(12) –0.454

3.8 Regression Analysis

The dictionary meaning of the word regression is 'stepping back' or 'going back.' Regression implies going back or returning towards the mean. Regression lines study the average relationship between two series, and throw light on their covariance. For example, if the coefficient of correlation between the heights of fathers and sons is +0.7, it means that if a group of fathers have heights which are more than the average by *x* inches, their sons could have heights which would be more than average by 0.7*x* inches. Thus, the heights of the sons regress towards the mean. The study of this tendency is the subject matter of regression.

Definition

Regression analysis attempts to establish the nature of the relationship between variables – that is, to study the functional relationship between the variables and thereby provide a mechanism for predicting, or forecasting.

Utility

The definition makes it clear that regression analysis is done for estimating or predicting the unknown value of one variable from the known value of the other variable. This is a very useful statistical tool which is used both in natural as well as social sciences.

In the field of business this tool of statistical analysis is very widely used. Businessmen are interested in predicting future production, consumption, investment, prices, profits, sales, etc. In fact the success of a businessman depends on the correctness of the various estimates that he is required to make. In sociological studies and in the field of economic planning, projections of population, birth rates, death rates and other similar variables are of great use.

With the help of regression analysis we can estimate or predict the effect of one variable on the other. However, in social sciences there often is multiple causation which means that a large number of factors affect various variables. The regression study which confines itself to a study of two variables is called simple regression. The regression analysis which studies more than two variables at a time is called multiple regression.

In simple regression analysis there are two variables – one of which is known as an independent variable or regresser or predictor or explanator. On the basis of the values of this variable the values of the other variable are predicted. This other variable is called the dependent or regressed or explained variable.

With the help of regression studies we can also calculate the value of the coefficient of correlation. The coefficient of determination (square of coefficient of correlation), which measures the effect of the independent variable on the dependent variable gives us an indication about the predictive value of the regression studies.

Comparison of Correlation and Regression Studies

(1) Correlation studies are meant for studying the co-variation of two variables. Regression analysis tells us about the relative movement in the variables under study and with its help we can also predict the value of one variable by taking into account the value of the other variable.

(2) Correlation between two series is not necessarily a cause-effect relationship. Regression, on the other hand, presumes one variable as a cause and the other as its effect.

(3) The coefficient of correlation varies between ±1. The regression coefficients have the same sign as the correlation coefficient. Further, regression coefficients can have a value higher than unity but the product of the two regression coefficients can never exceed unity because the correlation coefficient is the square root of the product of the two regression coefficients.

For regression analysis, a graph is needed to be drawn. For this, first we have to draw a scatter diagram. When all related pairs or values of X and Y have been plotted, we draw two regression lines to predict the values of X and Y variables. The regression line which is used to predict the values of Y for corresponding values of X is called the Regression Line of Y on X. similarly the regression line used to predict a value of X for a value of Y is called the Regression Line of X on Y. If the coefficient of correlation between X and Y is perfect, that is, its value is either +1 or -1, the two regression lines will coincide; there will be only one regression line, as the variations in the two series in such cases always increases or decreases by a constant figure.

Regression can be linear or non-linear. We shall limit our discussion to linear regression only.

Regression lines can be drawn by:

(*a*) **Free Hand Curve Method :** In the free hand curve method, we first plot the pairs of the values of X and Y in the form of a scatter diagram – one point for one pair of values. After this we draw two free hand straight lines. One of these lines is drawn in such a way that the positive deviations of Y-series from its mean are cancelled by the negative deviations. That is, the sum of the deviations on one side of the line shall be equal to the sum of the deviations on the other side. This will be the regression line of Y on X. The other regression line would be drawn in such a way that the positive deviations of X-series from its mean would cancel the negative deviations. This is the regression line of X on Y. The two regression line cut each other at the point, the coordinates of which give the mean values of the two series.

However, it is very difficult to draw regression lines by freehand curve method. Usually a piece of thread is repeatedly adjusted in such a manner in the scatter diagram that the positive and negative deviations cancel each other. Once these lines are drawn, we can predict or estimate the values of Y from the regression line of Y on X, and similarly the values of X can be predicted from the regression line of X on Y.

(*b*) **Method of Least Squares :** In order to avoid the difficulties associated with the drawing of regression lines by the free hand curve method, a mathematical relationship is established between the movements of X and Y series and algebraic equations are obtained to represent the relative movements of X and Y series.

One such method is the method of least squares. In this method we minimize the sum of squares of the deviations between the given values of a variable and its estimated values given by the line of best fit. Line of regression of Y on X is the line which gives the best estimate for the value of Y for a specified value of X. similarly the line of regression of X on Y is the line which gives the best estimate for the value of X for a specified value of Y.

If the values of Y are plotted on the Y-axis (that is, the vertical axis) then the regression line of Y on X will be such that it minimizes the total of the squares of the vertical deviations. Similarly, if the values of X are plotted on the X-axis (the horizontal axis) the regression line of X on Y will be such which minimizes the total of the squares of the horizontal deviations.

The line of best fit is obtained by the equation of straight line

$$Y = a + bX$$

And that in the method of least squares this line is obtained with the help of the following two normal equations:

$$\Sigma Y = na + b(\Sigma X)$$

$$\Sigma XY = a\Sigma(X) + b\Sigma(X^2)$$

If the values of X and Y variables are substituted in the above equations we get the values of a and b and thus get the regression line of Y on X. Here Y is the dependent variable and X the independent variable. To get the regression line of X on Y, we will have to assume X as the dependent variable and Y as the independent variable. We will then get the two equations for the two regression lines.

Regression line of X on Y

$$X = a + bY$$

Will be given by the normal equations:

$$\Sigma X = na + b(\Sigma Y)$$

$$\text{and } \Sigma XY = a\Sigma(Y) + b\Sigma(Y^2)$$

After obtaining the two regression equations, from the first equation (Y on X) we obtain any two values of Y for some values of X, plot them, and join them with a straight line to get the regression line of Y on X.

Similarly, from the regression equation of X on Y, we get two values of X for any two values of Y, plot and join them with a straight line to obtain the regression line of X on Y. The two lines cut each other at the point which gives the average values of X and Y.

After drawing the regression lines, in order to find any value of Y for a given value of X we will draw a perpendicular from the X-series (for the given value of X) and the point at which it cuts the regression line of Y on X will indicate the coupled value of Y which can be read on the Y-scale (by drawing a line parallel to X-axis form the point where the perpendicular joins the regression line of Y on X). Similarly values of X-series can be found by using the regression line of X on Y.

3.8.1 Why Two Regression Lines?

The answer to the above question is that one regression line cannot minimize the sum of squares of deviations for both the X and Y series unless the relationship between them indicates perfect positive or negative correlation. In case of perfect correlation, one line is enough because X and Y series have the same type of deviations. Ordinarily in social sciences perfect correlation is very rarely found. For this reason one regression line minimizes the sum of the squares of deviations of the Y-series and the other regression line takes care of the deviations of the X-series.

Regression Equations

Regression equation of Y on X:

$$Y = a + bX$$

Regression equation of X on Y:

$$X = a + bY$$

In these equations *a* and *b* are constants which determine the positions of the lines of regression. The parameter *a* indicates the level of the line of regression (the distance of the line above or below the origin). The parameter *b* determines the slope of the line, that is, the corresponding change in Y in relation to per unit change in X or vice versa.

The values of *a* and *b* in these equations will be given by the normal equations discussed above.

Method of Deviations from the Means

This method is much simpler than the method of least squares. Here, instead of taking the actual values of X and Y, we take their deviations from the mean values. According to this method, the regression equation of Y on X is given by

$$(Y-\bar{Y}) = r\frac{\sigma_y}{\sigma_x}(X-\bar{X})$$

$r\frac{\sigma_y}{\sigma_x}$ is called the Regression Coefficient of Y on X and is denoted by b_{yx}

Regression equation of X on Y is given by

$$(X-\bar{X}) = r\frac{\sigma_x}{\sigma_y}(Y-\bar{Y})$$

$r\frac{\sigma_x}{\sigma_y}$ is called the Regression Coefficient of X on Y and is denoted by b_{xy}

Thus, the two regression equations can be rewritten as

Regression equation of Y on X

$$(Y-\bar{Y}) = \frac{\Sigma xy}{\Sigma x^2}(X-\bar{X})$$

Regression equation of Y on X

$$(X-\bar{X}) = \frac{\Sigma xy}{\Sigma y^2}(Y-\bar{Y})$$

3.8.2 Properties of Regression Coefficients

(1) The geometric mean of b_{yx} and b_{xy} gives the value of the coefficient of correlation. That is

$$r = \pm\sqrt{b_{yx}.b_{xy}}$$

(2) The sign of *r* will be the same as the sign of the two regression coefficients.

(3) Both the regression coefficients will have the same algebraic sign. Either both will be positive, or both will be negative.

(4) The values of both the regression coefficients cannot be greater than one. At most, only one of them can be greater than one, not both.

When deviations are taken from assumed mean

$$b_{yx} = \frac{n.\Sigma xy - \Sigma x.\Sigma y}{n.\Sigma x^2 - (\Sigma x)^2} \text{ and}$$

$$b_{xy} = \frac{n.\Sigma xy - \Sigma x.\Sigma y}{n.\Sigma y^2 - (\Sigma y)^2}$$

Example 13: *If the regression coefficients are* 0.8 *and* 0.2, *what would be the value of coefficient of correlation?* **(U.P.T.U. 2004)**

Solution: We know that,

$$r^2 = b_{yx}b_{xy} = 0.8 \times 0.2 = 0.16$$

Since r has the same sign as both the regression coefficients b_{yx} and b_{xy}

Hence $r = \sqrt{0.16} = 0.4.$

Example 14: *Calculate linear regression coefficients from the following :*

[U.P.T.U. (MCA) 2001]

x :	1	2	3	4	5	6	7	8
y :	3	7	10	12	14	17	20	24

Solution: Linear regression coefficients are given by

$$b_{yx} = \frac{n\Sigma xy - \Sigma x \Sigma y}{v\Sigma x^2 - (\Sigma x)^2}$$

$$b_{xy} = \frac{n\Sigma xy - \Sigma x \Sigma y}{v\Sigma y^2 - (\Sigma y)^2}$$

Let us prepare the following table :

x	y	x^2	y^2	xy
1	3	1	9	3
2	7	4	49	14
3	10	9	100	30
4	12	16	144	48
5	14	25	196	70
6	17	36	289	102
7	20	49	400	140
8	24	64	576	192
$\Sigma x = 36$	$\Sigma y = 107$	$\Sigma x^2 = 204$	$\Sigma y'^2 = 1763$	$\Sigma xy = 599$

Here $n = 8$

$$b_{yx} = \frac{(8\times599)-(36\times107)}{(8\times204)-(36)^2} = \frac{940}{336} = 2.7976 \quad \text{and}$$

$$b_{xy} = \frac{(8\times599)-(36\times107)}{(8\times1763)-(107)^2} = \frac{940}{2655} = 0.3540$$

Example 15: *The following table gives age (x) in years of cars and annual maintenance cost (y) in hundred rupees :*

X :	1	3	5	7	9
Y :	15	18	21	23	22

Estimate the maintenance cost for a 4 year old car after finding the regression equation.

Sol.

X	y	xy	x^2
1	15	15	1
3	18	54	9
5	21	105	25
7	23	161	49
9	22	198	81
$\sum x = 25$	$\sum y = 99$	$\sum xy = 533$	$\sum x^2 = 165$

Here, $n = 5$

$$\bar{x} = \frac{25}{5} = 5, \bar{y} = \frac{\sum y}{n} = \frac{99}{5} = 19.8$$

$$\therefore \quad b_{yx} = \frac{\sum xy - \sum x \sum y}{n\sum x^2 - (\sum x)^2} = \frac{(5\times533)-(25\times99)}{(5\times165)-(25)^2} = 0.95$$

Regression line of y on x is given by

$$y - \bar{y} = b_{yx}(x - \bar{x})$$

$$\Rightarrow \quad y - 19.8 = 0.95(x-5)$$

$$\Rightarrow \quad y = 0.95x + 15.05$$

When $x = 4$ years $\quad y = (0.95\times4)+15.05 = 18.85$ hundred rupees = Rs. 1885.

Example 16. *In a partially destroyed laboratory record of an analysis of a correlation data, the following results any are eligible :*

Variance of x = 9

Regression equations ; $8x-10y+66=0, 40x-18y=214.$

What were (a) the mean values of x and y (b) the standard deviation of y and the co-efficient of correlation between x and y. **(U.P.T.U. 2003, 2008)**

Solution: (a) Since both the lines of regression pass through the point $(\bar{x}, \bar{y})$ therefore, we have

$$8\bar{x}-10\bar{y}+66=0 \quad ...(1)$$

$$40\bar{x}-18\bar{y}-214=0 \quad ...(2)$$

Multiplying (1) and 5, $40\bar{x}-50\bar{y}+330=0$ ...(3)

Subtracting (3) from (2), $32\bar{y}-544=0 \quad \therefore \quad \bar{y}=17$

$\therefore$ From (1), $8\bar{x}-170+66=0$ or $8\bar{x}=104$: $\bar{x}=13$

Hence $\bar{x}=13 \quad \bar{y}=17$

(b) Variance of $x=\sigma_x^2=9$ (given)

$\sigma_x=3$

The equations of lines of regression can be written as

$$y=.8x+6.6 \text{ and } x=.45yx+5.35$$

$\therefore$ The regression co-efficient of y on x is $\dfrac{r\sigma_y}{\sigma_x}=.8$ ...(4)

The regression co-efficient of x on y is $\dfrac{r\sigma_x}{\sigma_y}=.45$ ...(5)

Multiplying (4) and (5), $r^2 = .8 \times .45 = .36 \qquad \therefore \; r = 0.6$

(+ve sign with square root is taken because regression co-efficients are +ve)

From (4), $\sigma_y=\dfrac{.8\sigma_x}{r}=\dfrac{.8\times}{0.6}=4.$

Example 17. *The following results were obtained from marks in Applied Mechanics and Engineering Mathematics in an examination :*

	Applied Mechanics (x)	*Engineering Mathematics (y)*
Mean	47.5	39.5
Standard Deviation	16.8	10.8

$r=0\,95.$

Find both the regression equations. Also estimate the value of y for x = 30.

Sol. $\bar{x} = 47.5$ $\bar{y} = 39.5$

$\sigma_x = 16.8$ $\sigma_x = 10.8$ and $r = 0.95.$

Regression coefficients are

$$b_{yx} = r\frac{\sigma_y}{\sigma_x} = 0.95 \times \frac{10.8}{16.8} = 0.6107$$

and

$$b_{xy} = r\frac{\sigma_x}{\sigma_y} = 0.95 \times \frac{16.8}{10.8} = 1.477$$

Regression line of y on x is

$$y - \bar{y} = b_{yx}(x - \bar{x})$$

$$\Rightarrow \quad y - 39.5 = 0.6107(x - 47.5) = 0.6107x - 29.008$$

$$y = 0.6107x + 10.49 \quad \ldots(1)$$

Regression line of x on y is

$$x - \bar{x} = b_{xy}(y - \bar{y})$$

$$x - 47.5 = 1.477(y - 39.5)$$

$$x = 1.477y - 10.8415 \quad \ldots(2)$$

Putting $x = 30$ in equation (1), we get

$$y = (0.6107)(30) + 10.49 = 18.321 + 10.49 = 28.81.$$

Example 18. *From the following data. Find the most likely value of y when x = 24 :*

	y	*x*
Mean	985.8	18.1
S.D.	36.4	2.0

r = 0.58.

Solution: Given: $\bar{y} = 985.8$, $\bar{x} = 18.1$, $\sigma_y = 36.4, \sigma_x = 2, r = 0.58$

Regression coefficient,

$$b_{yx} = r\frac{\sigma_y}{\sigma_x} = (0.58)\frac{36.4}{2} = 10.556.$$

Regression line of y on x is

$$y - \bar{y} = b_{yx}(x - \bar{x})$$

$$\Rightarrow \quad y - 985.8 = 10.556(x - 18.1)$$

$$\Rightarrow \quad y = 10.556 + 794.73$$

Where $x = 24$,

$$y = (10.556 \times 24) + 794.73 = 1048 \text{ (approximately)}.$$

Example 19: *The equations of two regression lines, obtained in a correlation analysis of 60 observations are :*

$$5x = 6y + 24 \text{ and } 1000y = 768x - 3608.$$

What is the correlation coefficient ? Show that the ratio of coefficient of variability of x to that of y is $\frac{5}{24}$ *What is the ratio of variances of x and y?*

Solution: Regression line of x on y is

$$5x = 6y + 24$$

$$x = \frac{6}{5}y + \frac{24}{5}$$

$$\therefore \qquad b_{xy} = \frac{6}{5} \qquad \ldots(1)$$

Regression line of y on x is

$$1000y = 768x - 3608$$

$$y = 0.768x - 3.608$$

$$\therefore \qquad b_{yx} = 0.768 \qquad \ldots(2)$$

From (1), $$r\frac{\sigma_x}{\sigma_y} = \frac{6}{5} \qquad \ldots(3)$$

From (2), $$r\frac{\sigma_y}{\sigma_x} = 0.768 \qquad \ldots(4)$$

Multiplying equations (3) and (4), we get

$$r^2 = 0.9216 \Rightarrow r = 0.96 \qquad \ldots(5)$$

Dividing (4) by (3), we get

$$\frac{\sigma_x^2}{\sigma_y^2} = \frac{6}{5 \times 0.768} = 1.5625.$$

Taking square root, we get

$$\frac{\sigma_x}{\sigma_y} = 1.25 = \frac{5}{4} \qquad \ldots(6)$$

Since the regression lines pass through the point $(\bar{x}, \bar{y})$, we have

$$5\overline{x} = 6\overline{y} + 24$$

$$1000\overline{y} = 768\overline{x} - 3608$$

Solving the above equations for $\overline{x}$ and $\overline{y}$, we get $\overline{x} = 6, \overline{y} = 1$.

Coefficient of variability of $x = \frac{\sigma_x}{\overline{x}}$,

Coefficient of variability of $y = \frac{\sigma_y}{\overline{y}}$.

$\therefore$ Required ratio $= \frac{\sigma_x}{\overline{x}} \times \frac{\overline{y}}{\sigma_y} = \frac{\overline{y}}{\overline{x}}\left(\frac{\sigma_x}{\sigma_y}\right) = \frac{1}{6} \times \frac{5}{4} = \frac{5}{24}$. | Using (6)

Example 20: *A study of prices of a certain commodity at Hapur and Kanpur yields the following data:*

	Hapur (Rs.)	*Kanpur (Rs.)*
Average price/kilo	2.463	2.797
S.D.	0.326	0.207

'r' between prices at Hapur and Kanpur is 0.774 **[U.P.T.U. (C.O.) 2004]**

Estimate, from the above data, the most likely price at Hapur corresponding to the price of Rs. 3.052 per kilo at Kanpur.

Solution: Here, $\overline{x} = 2.463$, $\overline{y} = 2.797$, $\sigma_x = 0.326$, $\sigma_y = 0.207$ and $r = 0.774$

Regression coefficient $b_{xy} = r\frac{\sigma_x}{\sigma_y} = (0.774)\left(\frac{0.326}{0.207}\right) = 1.218956522$

Regression line of x on y is given by

$$x - \overline{x} = b_{xy}(y - \overline{y})$$

$$\Rightarrow \qquad x - 2.463 = 1.218956522(y - 2.797)$$

$$x = 1.218956522y - 0.9464213$$

when $y = 3.052$, $\quad x = 1.218956522\,(3.052) - 0.9464213 = 2.7738$

Hence the most likely price at Hapur is Rs. 2.7738 per kilo, corresponding to the given price at Kanpur

Example 21: *A panel of two judges, A and B, graded seven T.V. serial performances by awarding marks independently as shown in the following table :*

Performance	1	2	3	4	5	6	7
Marks by A	46	42	44	40	43	41	45
Marks by B	40	38	36	35	39	37	41

The eighth T.V. performance which judge B could not attend, was awarded 37 marks by judge A. If the judge B had also been present, how many marks would be expected to have been awarded by him to the eighth T.V. performance ?

Use regression analysis to answer this question. **[U.P.T.U. (MBA) 2003]**

Solution: Let the marks awarded by judge A be denoted by x and the marks awarded by judge B be denoted by y.

Here, $n=7$; $\bar{x}=\frac{\Sigma x}{n}=\frac{46+42+44+40+43+41+45}{7}=43$

$$\bar{y}=\frac{\Sigma y}{n}=\frac{40+38+36+35+39+37+41}{7}=38$$

Let us form the table as

x	y	xy	x^2
46	40	1840	2116
42	38	1596	1764
44	36	1584	1936
40	35	1400	1600
43	39	1677	1849
41	37	1517	1681
45	41	1845	2025
$\Sigma x = 301$	$\Sigma y = 266$	$\Sigma xy = 11459$	$\Sigma x^2 = 12971$

Regression coefficient,

$$b_{yx}=\frac{n\Sigma xy-\Sigma x\Sigma y}{n\Sigma x^2-(\Sigma x)^2}=\frac{(7\times11459)-(301\times266)}{(7\times12971)-(301)^2}$$

Regression line of y on x is given by

$$y-\bar{y}=b_{yx}(x-\bar{x})$$

$$y-38=0.75(x-43)$$

$$\Rightarrow \quad y=0.75x+5.75$$

when $x = 37$

$$y = 0.75(37) + 5.75 = 33.5 \text{ Marks}$$

Hence, if judge B had also been present, 33.5 marks would be expected to have been awarded to the eighth T.V. performance.

Example 22: *The following results were obtained from records of age (x) and systolic blood pressure (y) of a group of 10 men.*

	x	y
Mean	53	142
Variance	130	165

and $\Sigma(x-\overline{x})(y-\overline{y})=1220$

Find the approximate regression equation and use it to estimate the blood pressure of a man whose age is 45.

Solution: Coefficient of correlation

$$r=\frac{\Sigma(x-\overline{x})(y-\overline{y})}{n\sigma_x\sigma_y}=\frac{1220}{10\sqrt{130\times165}}=0.83$$

Since we are to estimate blood pressure y of a 45 years old man we will find relation line of y on x.

Regression Coefficient $b_{yx}=r\frac{\sigma_y}{\sigma_x}=0.83\sqrt{\frac{165}{130}}=0.935$

Relation line of y on x is given by:

$$y-\overline{y}=b_{yx}(x-\overline{x})$$

$$y-142=0.935(x-53)$$

$$y=0.935x+92.445$$

when $x = 45$ then $y=0.935(45)+92.445$

$= 134.52$

Hence, the required blood pressure = 134.52

3.9 Difference Between Correlation and Regression

(U.P.T.U. 2007, 09)

Aspects	Correlation Analysis	Regression Analysis
Definition	Correlation analysis deals with the association between two or more variables.	It is measure of average relationship between two or more variables in terms of original units of data.
Type of Relationship	It measures the degree of covariability between two	It study the nature of relationship between the

	variables.	variables so that we can predict the value of one on the basis of another.
Cause and effect Relationship	In correlation, we cannot study cause an effect relationship.	In regression, we have one dependent and one independent variable which makes it possible to determine cause and effect relationship.
Symmetry of coefficient	Correlation coefficient of X and Y and Y on X are symmetric i.e., $r_{xy} = r_{ux}$	Regression coefficient of X on Y and Y on X are not symmetric $b_{xy} \neq b_{yx}$
Change of origin and scale	Correlation coefficient is independent of change of scale and origin.	Regression coefficient are independent of change of origin but not of scale.
Measurement	(a) Scatter diagram is one of the graphical method of measuring correlation. (b) We can also measure correlation coefficient by using formula $r = \frac{Cov(X,Y)}{\sigma_x \sigma_y}$	We have two regression equation Regression equation of *X* on Y is X = a + b *Y* Regression equation of Y on X is Y = a + bX. To determine a, b we use normal equation.
Application	Correlation analysis is on fined only to the study of linear relationship between variables and has limited use.	Regression analysis has wider application as it studies linear as well as non linear relationship between the variables.
Absolute/ Relative Measure of Relationship	Co-relation coefficient is the relative "measure of linear relationship between X and Y and is independent of the units of measurement. It is a pure number lying between ±1.	Regression co-efficient are absolute measures representing the change in the value of the variable y(x) for a unit change in the value of the variable x(y).
Non-sense correlation/	There may be a non-sense correlation between two	There is no such thing like non-sense regression.

regression	variable which is due to pure chance and has no practical relevance, e.g., The correlation between the size of shoe and intelligency of a group of variable.	

Regression lines: Consider the case of two variables *X* and *Y*, then we have two Regression lines which are as follows:

1. Regression line of Y on X: This line gives the most probable values of Y forgiven values of X.
2. Regression line of X on Y: This line gives the most probable values of X forgiven values Y.

3.10 Partial and Multiple Correlation and Regression

Social and natural phenomena are generally affected simultaneously by a large number of factors. The effect of these factors on one another is studied by correlation and regression studies. In simple correlation between two variables, as we have studied earlier, our assumption was that the effect of other factors on the phenomenon under study is ignored. For example, when we study correlation between price and demand and treat price as a dependent factor and demand as an independent factor, we ignore the other independent factors like money in circulation, exports, and imports, which also affect price. Another assumption that we make in a study of simple correlation or regression is that the various independent variables affecting a dependent variable are not interrelated. It was assumed that they are mutually independent. However, in actual practice there is an association between different independent variables affecting a dependent variable.

Thus, our study of simple correlation and regression makes such assumptions which are not true and to this extent the relationship studied is not absolutely dependable. It is necessary to study the effect of all the factors. Partial and multiple correlation and regression analysis is done to achieve this objective.

In partial correlation we study the effect of one independent variable on a dependent variable by excluding the effect of other independent factors. Thus if price (a dependent variable) is being affected by

(*i*) demand,

(*ii*) money in circulation, and

(*iii*) exports,

We can study the relationship between price and demand by excluding the effects of money supply and exports. This will be called a study of partial correlation between price and demand. In simple correlation the effect of these factors was not excluded. It was just ignored.

In multiple correlation we study the effects of all the independent variables simultaneously on a dependent variable. Thus, if we study the effects of demand, money supple and exports (all independent variables) on price (dependent variable) at the same time or if we study their combined effect on price it would be called multiple correlation study.

Multiple and partial correlation and regression studies are very complex in nature if many independent variables are involved. The calculations in such cases are possible only through the use of computers.

4.0.1 Partial Correlation

Partial correlation is also called net correlation. It is a study of the relationship between one dependent variable and one independent variable by keeping the other independent variables constant.

Simple correlation between two variables is called zero order coefficient as no factor is held constant. If a partial correlation is studied between two variables by keeping a third variable constant, it would be called a first order coefficient, as one variable is kept constant. Similarly, if two variables are kept constant, we get the second order coefficient, and so on.

A first order coefficient may be indicated by $r_{12.3}$ (or $r_{21.3}$), which means that a partial correlation is being studied between variables (1) and (2), while variable (3) is kept constant.

$$r_{12.3} = \frac{r_{12} - r_{13}r_{23}}{\sqrt{1-r_{13}^2}\sqrt{1-r_{23}^2}}$$

Partial Correlation Analysis: Utility and Limitations

The analysis of partial correlation is of great significance particularly in the field of social sciences, where most of the phenomena have multiple causation. A number of variables are in operation at the same time and their effects cannot be studied in isolation as is done in physical and experimental sciences where the variables can be controlled and the effect of each variable can be studied separately. The partial correlation analysis is one such technique where it is possible to keep some variables constant and study the effects of only one independent variable on a dependent variable. In partial correlation analysis the effects of independent variables other than the one which is being studied are not ignored as is done in the case of simple correlation.

The utility of partial correlation is great in interrelated series and in various experimental designs where interrelated phenomena are to be studied.

However, partial correlation analysis has some limitations:

(1) It is presumed in the calculation of partial correlation coefficient that the simple correlations or zero order correlations from which partial correlation is computed have linear relationships between the variables. In actual practice, particularly in social sciences, this assumption may lead to misleading results as a linear relationship generally does not exist in such phenomena.

(2) The effects of the independent variables are studied additively not jointly. It means that it is presumed that the various independent variables are independent of each other. In actual practice this may not be true and there may be an interaction among the factors.

(3) The reliability of the partial correlation coefficient decreases as their order gores up. Therefore it is necessary that the size of the items in the gross correlation should be large.

(4) It involves a lot of calculation and its analysis is not easy.

4.0.2 Multiple Correlation

In multiple correlation we study three or more variables at a time. The effect of all the independent factors on a dependent factor is studied simultaneously.

If it is desired to study the relationship between output, soil fertility, chemical manures and rainfall we will have to pick up the variable whose value has to be estimated. It will be called the dependent variable. If, for example, we wish to know how output is related to soil fertility, chemical manures and rainfall, then output would be the dependent factor and soil fertility, chemical manures and rainfall would be the independent factors. We shall then study the effect of all these three independent factors on output which is the dependent factor. Which factor should be chosen as the dependent factor would depend on the purpose of the enquiry.

A dependent variable is indicated by X_1 and the independent variables by X_2, X_3, X_4, …. The Coefficient of Multiple Linear Correlation is represented by R and the necessary subscripts are added to it. Thus

$R_{1.23}$ = Multiple Correlation Coefficient with X_1 as dependent variable and X_2 and X_3 as independent variables.

$$R_{12.3} = \sqrt{\frac{r_{12}^2 + r_{13}^2 - 2r_{12}r_{13}r_{23}}{1 - r_{23}^2}}$$

The following points should be noted about the multiple correlation coefficient:

(*i*) It is a non-negative coefficient. Its value ranges between 0 and 1.

$$R_{1.23} \geq r_{12}, R_{1.23} \geq r_{13}$$

(*ii*) If $R_{1.23} = 0$ then $r_{12} = 0$ and $r_{13} = 0$.

(iii) $R_{1.23}$ is the same thing as $R_{1.32}$. the position of the subscript to the right of the dot does not make a difference.

(iv) By squaring $R_{1.23}$ we get the coefficient of multiple determination.

Utility and Limitations

The utility and the limitations of the multiple correlation coefficient are the same as those of partial correlation coefficient. Multiple correlation coefficient gives the effects of all independent variables on a dependent variable. This is very useful in understanding the movements in the dependent variable. If multiple and partial correlation coefficients are studied together, a very useful analysis of the relationship between the various variables is possible.

The chief limitation of the multiple correlation coefficient is that like partial correlation coefficient it also presumes that a linear relationship exists between the zero order coefficients. It also assumes that the independent variables affect the dependent variable in an independent manner and have an additive property. If, however, there is inter-relation between independent variables their effects cannot be distinct nor can they be additive. The multiple correlation coefficient is cumbersome in calculation and difficult in interpretation. As such, it should be calculated with care and interpreted with caution.

4.0.3 Multiple Regression Analysis

In case of a simple regression study between two variables X and Y we find out the relative movement of Y-series for a unit movement of X-series and vice-versa. We therefore have two regression equations – one of Y on X and the other of X on Y.

In multiple regression analysis there are three or more variables – say X_1, X_2 and X_3. We now take X_1 as the dependent variable and try to find out its relative movement for movements in both X_2 and X_3 which are independent variables. Thus in multiple regression analysis the effect of two or more independent variables on one dependent variable is studied.

The procedure for studying multiple regression is similar to the one we have for simple regression, with the difference that the other variables are added in the regression equation. If there are three variables X_1, X_2 and X_3, the multiple regression would take the following form:

$$X_1 = a_{1.23} + b_{12.3}X_2 + b_{13.2}X_3$$

In the above equation $b_{12.3}$ indicates the slope of the regression line of X_1 on X_2 when X_3 is held constant. Similarly $b_{13.2}$ indicates the slope of the regression line of X_1 on X_3 when X_2 is held constant.

In most problems the changes in X_1 are due partially to changes in X_2 and partially to changes in X_3. It is for this reason that $b_{12.3}$ is called the partial regression coefficient of X_1 on X_2, keeping X_3 constant and $b_{13.2}$ is called the partial regression coefficient of X_1 on X_3, keeping X_2 constant.

Assumptions of Linear Multiple Regression Analysis

(*i*) The dependent variable is a random variable. The independent variable need not necessarily be random.

(*ii*) The relationship between independent and dependent variables is linear.

Exercise 3.2

1. Explain the concept of regression and point out its usefulness in dealing with business. For bivariate distribution coefficient of regression of Y On X and X on Y worked out 1.5 and 0.5 respectively. What is the correlation between the two variables?
2. Define correlation and discuss its significance in statistical analysis. Does it signify 'cause and effect' relationship between the two variables? **(L.U.)**
3. A computer while calculating the correlation coefficient between two variable, X and Y, obtained the following results:

   $n = 25, \Sigma X = 125, \Sigma X^2 = 650, \Sigma Y = 100$

   $\Sigma Y^2 = 460, \Sigma XY = 508.$

   It was, however, discovered later at the time of checking that it had copied down two pairs of observations as :

X	Y
6	14
8	6

   in place of the correct pairs :

X	Y
8	12
6	8

   Obtain the correct value of r.
4. The following data relate to advertising expenditure (in lakhs of rupees) and their corresponding sales (in crores of rupees)

Ad. Expenditures	Sales
10	14
12	17
15	23
23	25
20	21

Estimate : (i) the sales corresponding to advertising expenditure of Rs. 30 lakhs and

(ii) the Advertising expenditure for a sales target of Rs. 35 crores.

5. Define correlation & Calculate karl Pearson's coefficient of correlation between price and demand of a commodity from the following data :

Price (in Rs.)	Demand (in '000 tonnes)
17	38
18	37
19	38
20	33
21	32
22	33
23	34
24	29
25	26
26	23

6. You are given the following informations about the advertisement costs and sales :

	Ad. Costs (X) (Rs. in Lacs)	Sales (Y) (Rs. in Lacs)
Mean	10	90
Standard Deviation	3	12

Calculate :

(*a*) Likely sales when advertising cost is Rs. 15 lacs.

(*b*) Likely Ad. costs if the company wants to attain a sale target of Rs. 120 lacs.

7. Find Karl Pearson's coefficient of correlation between age and playing habit of the following students :

Age	15	16	17	18	19	20
No. of Students	250	200	150	120	100	80
Regular Players	200	150	90	48	30	16

8. What is regression analysis? Explain its use in business problems with suitable examples. **(L.U.) (A.U.) (U.P.T.U.)**

9. Write two regression equations form the following data :

X	65	66	67	07	68	69	71	73
Y	67	68	64	68	72	70	69	70

10. Explain the meaning and significance of the term correlation. the following data relates the advertising expenses and the respective sales :

Ad' expenses (in '00)	50	40	20	10	5
Sales (in '000)	700	600	500	400	400

Calculate Karl Pearson's coefficient of correlation and interpret its value.

11. From the following data obtain the two regression equations :

Sales	91	97	108	121	67	124	51	73	111	57
Purchases	71	75	69	97	70	91	39	61	80	47

12. Explain scatter diagram method correlation. Calculate coefficient of correlation and check whether it is significant?

X	22	24	38	35	69	78	46
Y	66	59	53	68	75	86	68

13. Explain the concept of regression and point out its usefulness in dealing with business problems. Obtain the regression equations for the following :

X	15	27	27	30	34	38	46
Y	120	140	150	170	180	200	250

14. Obtain regression line of x and y for the given data **(U.P.T.U. 2007)**

X	1	2	3	4	5	6
Y	50	8.1	10.6	13.1	16.2	20.0

15. Distinguish between correlation and regression analysis. Write the mathematical properties of Coefficient of Correlation **(UPTU – 08)**

16. How are regression equations useful in business-forecasting? Calculate the coefficient of correlation between x and y from the following data :

X	2	4	6	8	10
Y	12	14	16	18	20

17. What is regression? Why are there two regression lines? From the following data, obtain the two regression equations the figures are in Rs. thousands :

Sales	91	97	106	121	67	124	51
Purchase	91	75	69	97	70	91	39

18. Given below are data relating to prices of a share in Kolkata and Mumbai Stock Exchanges :-

Particulars	Kolkata (X)	Mumbai (Y)
Average Price	Rs. 130	Rs. 134
Standard Deviation	Rs. 5	Rs. 7

Coefficient of Correlation between the prices of the share in Kolkata and Mumbai is + 0.8. Fit the two lines of regression and find the most likely price of the share in the Mumbai Stock Exchange corresponding to a price of Rs. 140 in Kolkata.

19. Find the Coefficient of Correlation when the two regression equations are—

$X = -0.2y + 4.2$ $\qquad$ $Y = -0.8x + 8.4$

20. In the following table X is advertising cost (in thousand rupees) and Y is sales (in lakh rupees)

X	12	18	24	30	36	42	48
Y	5.7	6.9	7.1	8.3	10.1	12.2	13.6

Find Karl Pearson Correlation Coefficient between X and Y.

21. Discuss the meaning of correlation and distinguish between positive and negative correlation. Regression equation of two valuables X and Y are as follows :

$3X + 2Y = 26$ and $6X + Y = 31$ **(U.P.T.U. 2010)**

Find (i) The mean of X and Y series.

(ii) The coefficient of correlation and

(iii) The most probable value of Y when X = 5.

22. Derive regression lines for the following data :

$n = 5, \Sigma X = 30, \Sigma X^2 = 190, \Sigma Y = 30, \Sigma Y^2 = 190, \Sigma XY = 192.$

23. Define ' Coefficient of Regression'. What will be the value of the Coefficient of Correlation of a bivariate series if $b_{yx} = 0.84$ and $b_{xy} = 0.45$?

24. In the following table X is advertising cost (in thousand rupees) and Y is sales (in lakh rupees)

X :	12	18	24	30	16	42	48
Y :	5.7	6.9	7.1	8.3	10.1	12.2	13.6

Find Karl Pearson Correlation Coefficient between X and Y.

25. The following are two regression equations :

$3X + 4Y = 15,$ $\qquad$ $5X + 6Y = 20$

Predict the value of Y for X = 20.

26. Given :-

X :	1	2	3	4	5
Y :	15	18	20	25	30

Obtain two regression lines.

27. Distinguish between Correlation and Regression. Why there are two regression lines?

28. From the following data, find out :

(*i*) two regression equations, and

(*ii*) the value of X when Y=75

	X	Y
Arithmetic Mean	36	85
Standard Deviation	11	8

Correlation coefficient between X and Y = 0.66

29. What is regression? How it is different from correlation? **(UPTU- 07)**

30. You are given the following data :

Variable	X	Y
Mean	47	96
Variance	64	81

Coefficient of correlation between X and Y = 0.36. Determine the equations of regression lines. Calculate Y when X = 50 and X when Y = 88. **(UPTU- 07)**

31. State some of the decision problems in which one is required to do correlation analysis. What methods would you use in order to do correlation analysis under various conditions? Does the choice of method depend on the nature of data? **(UPTU CO-08)**

32. Find the means of X and Y variables and the coefficient of correlation between them from the following two regression equations:

2Y – X = 50

3Y–2X = 10 **(UPTU-08)**

33. Two lines of regression are given by

$x+2y-5=0$ and $2x+3y-8=0$ and $\sigma_x^2=12$,

Calculate:

(*i*) the mean values of *x* and *y* (*ii*) variance of *y*

(*iii*) the coefficient of correlation between *x* and *y* **[U.P.T.U. (MBA) 2008]**

34. (i) Find both the lines of regression of following data :

x :	5.60	5.65	5.75	5.81	5.85
y :	5.80	5.70	5.80	5.79	6.01

[U.P.T.U. MBA (C.O.) 2005]

(*ii*) Obtain regression line of x and y for the given data :

x :	1	2	3	4	5	6
y :	5.0	8.1	10.6	13.1	16.2	20.0

[U.P.T.U. (MBA) 2007]

(*iii*) Given that

x :	1	3	5	7	8	10
y :	8	12	15	17	18	20

Find the equations of both lines of regression **[U.P.T.U. (C.O.) 2008]**

Objective type Questions

1. r will be positive when:
   (a) X increases, Y decreases (b) X decreases, Y increases
   (c) both X and Y increases (d) none of these
2. If two variables have the linear relationship X+Y=100,
   The correlation will be:
   (a) –1 (b) +1
   (c) +0.80 (d) 0.20
3. If $X'=2X$ and $Y'=Y+3$ and $r_{xy}=+0.80$ then $r_{x'y'}$ will be
   (a)–0.80 (b) 0.40
   (c) +0.80 (d) none of these
4. If X-Y=50, the correlation between X and Y will be:
   (a) –1 (b) +1
   (c) 0.50 (d) none of these
5. If r=0, the P.E. (r) will be
   (a) 0 (b) 1
   (c) $(0.6745/\sqrt{N})$ (d) none of these
6. If r=1, the P.E.(r) will be
   (a) 0 (b) 1
   (c) –1 (d) None of these
7. The coefficient of correlation
   (a) has no limit (b) is less than 1
   (c) is more than –1 (d) none of these

8. Most probable limits for population correlation coefficient are:

(a) r±0.6745 P .E .(r) (b) r± P .E. (r)

(c) r±3S.E.(r) (d) none of these

9. If the sum of the product of deviations of X and Y series from their means is zero, the correlation coefficient will be

(a) 0 (b) 1

(c) –1 (d) none of these

10. If cov (X,Y)=0, the value of r will be

(a) 1 (b) $\sigma_x . \sigma_y$

(c) 0 (d) σ_x

11. If ΣD^2 is zero, the coefficient of rank correlation will be:

(a) 0 (b) 1

(c) –1 (d) none of these

12. For the bivariate data

X:	20	21	22	23
Y:	5	4	3	2

The value of r is

(a) 0 (b) –1

(c) +1 (d) 0.4

13. If r=0, the cov(X,Y) is **(UPTU-08)**

(a) 1 (b) –1

(c) 0 (d) none of these

14. If r=1, then

(a) cov (X,Y) < $\sigma_x . \sigma_y$ (b) cov (X,Y) > $\sigma_x . \sigma_y$

(c) cov (X,Y) = $\sigma_x . \sigma_y$ (d) none of these

15. In regression of Y on X, X is

(a) a dependent variable (b) an independent variable

(c) a constant (d) none of these

16. In regression of X on Y, Y is

(a) The explained variable (b) Explanatory variable

(c) A constant (d) None of these

17. For predicting the best value of X for given Y, we make use of

(a) regression of Y on X (b) regression of X on Y

(c) means of X and Y series (d) none of these

18. In case of perfect correlation between X and Y, there will be
    (a) only one regression line (b) two regression line
    (c) more than two regression lines (d) no regression line
19. When r = -1, the two regression lines **(U.P.T.U. 2010)**
    (a) will coincide (b) will be perpendicular
    (c) will be parallel (d) none of these
20. When r = 0, the two regression lines
    (a) will be perpendicular (b) will be parallel
    (c) will coincide (d) none of these
21. If b_{yx} is greater than one, then b_{xy} is
    (a) less than one (b) equal to one
    (c) more than one (d) none of these
22. If b_{yx} is positive, then b_{xy} is
    (a) negative (b) positive
    (c) zero (d) none of these
23. If b_{yx} and b_{xy} are both positive, then the algebraic sign of r will be
    (a) negative (b) positive
    (c) undeterminable (d) none of these
24. If b_{yx}=3/2, b_{xy}=1/6, the value of r will be
    (a) –0.5 (b) +0.5
    (c) 1/6 (d) 3/2
25. If b_{yx}=-4/3, b_{xy}=-1/12, the value of r will be
    (a) –0.5 (b) –1/12
    (c) –4/3 (d) none of these
26. The product of two regression coefficient is
    (a) 1 (b) greater than 1
    (c) less than 1 (d) none of these
27. According to least square method, the residual sum of square is
    (a) minimized (b) maximized
    (c) increased (d) decreased
28. The standard form of the line of regression of Y on X is
    (a) X=a +b.Y (b) Y=a +b.X
    (c) a.X+ b.Y+c=0 (d) none of these

29. The standard form of the line of regression of X on Y is

(a) a.X+b.Y+c=0 (b) Y=a+b.X

(c) X=a+b.Y (d) none of these

30. If 2x+3y=10 is the regression of y on x, then b_{yx} is

(a) 2 (b) 10 (c) –3/2 (d) –2/3

31. If x+2y=6 is the regression of x on y, then the algebraic sign of b_{xy} is

(a) positive (b) negative

(c) undeterminable (d) none of these

32. If we have only one regression line between the two variables, then the value of r will be

(a) +1 (b) –1 (c) –1 or +1 (d) 0

33. Regression equation is also known as

(a) prediction equation (b) line of average relationship

(c) estimating equation (d) all the above

34. If b_{yx} >1, then b_{xy} is

(a) <1 (b) >1 (c) equal to 0 (d) equal to 1

35. If $\rho = \pm 1$, the two lines of regression are

(a) parallel (b) perpendicular

(c) coincident (d) none

36. If $\rho = 1$, the angle between the two lines of regression is

(a) 0^0 (b) 90^0

(c) 60^0 (d) 30^0

37. If ρ=0, the lines of regression are

(a) parallel (b) coincident (c) perpendicular (d) none

38. If r is more than six times ---- Than r is called significant.

(a) Probable error (b) Standard error

(c) Sampling error (d) Non- Sampling error

39. The coefficient of Correlation is geometric mean of. **(UPTU-08)**

(a) b_{xy} and b_{yx} (b) r and b_{yx}

(c) b_{xy} and r (d) sk and r

40. Which of the following are true-

1. The coefficient of correlation is never negative.
2. The rank correlation coefficient was developed by spearman
3. The coefficient of correlation is independent of change of scale and origin.

(a) 1 and 2 (b) 1 and 3 (c) 2 and 3 (d) Only 2

41. The regression lines cut each other at the point of
    (a) $\overline{x}$ and $\overline{y}$ (b) $\overline{x}$ only
    (c) $\overline{y}$ only (d) None of these
42. Which of the following are true-
    1. Regression coefficient are independent of change of scale and origin
    2. The regression lines cut each other at average of x and average of y
    3. Both the regression coefficient cannot more than 1.

    (a) 1 and 3 (b) 1 and 2 (c) 2 and 3 (d) Only 3
43. When the regression line of y on x and the regression line of x on y form a 90^0 Angle then **(U.P.T.U. 2010)**
    (a) r = 1 (b) r = 0 (c) r = 0.5 (d) None of these
44. Which of the following correlation coefficient show the highest degree of association **(U.P.T.U. 2010)**
    (a) 0.95 (b) 1 (c) – 1 (d) both b & c
45. If r = 0.90, then the coefficient of determination is **(U.P.T.U. 2009)**
    (a) 0.30 (b) 0.45 (c) 0.81 (d) 0.18

Answers

1. c	11. b	21.a	31. b	41. a
2. a	12. b	22. b	32. c	42. c
3. c	13. c	23. b	33. d	43. b
4. b	14. c	24. b	34. a	44. d
5. c	15. b	25. d	35. c	45. c
6. a	16. b	26. c	36.a	
7. d	17. b	27. a	37. c	
8. c	18. a	28. b	38. a	
9. a	19. a	29. c	39. a	
10. c	20. a	30. d	40. c	

List of Formulae

1. Karl Pearson's coefficient of correlation (Ungrouped data)

(a) When deviations are taken from mean :

$$r = \frac{\Sigma(X-\bar{X})(Y-\bar{Y})}{\sqrt{\Sigma(X-\bar{X})^2 \times \Sigma(Y-\bar{Y})^2}}$$

$$= \frac{\Sigma X'Y'}{\sqrt{[\Sigma(X'^2.(\Sigma Y'^2)}} \quad ; \quad X' = (X-\bar{X}),\ Y' = (Y-\bar{Y})$$

or $$r = \frac{\Sigma X'Y'}{N\sigma_x\sigma_y} \quad \text{or} \quad r = \frac{Cov(X,Y)}{\sqrt{[V(X)V(Y)]}}$$

(b) When deviations are taken from assumed means:

$$r = \frac{N\Sigma fd_x d_y --(\Sigma fd_x)(\Sigma fd_y)}{\sqrt{[(N\Sigma fd_x^2 - (\Sigma fd_x)^2\}\{N\Sigma fd_y^2 - (\Sigma fd_y)^2\}]}}$$

3. Probable error and standard error of correlation coefficient

$$\text{P.E. } (r) = 0.6745\left(\frac{1-r^2}{N}\right)$$

$$\text{S.E.} \quad (r) = \left(\frac{1-r^2}{N}\right)$$

4. Coefficient of determination and non-determination :

$$\text{The coefficient of determination} = r^2 = \frac{\text{Explained variation}}{\text{Total variation}}$$

$$\text{Coefficient of non-determination } K^2 = 1 - r^2 = \frac{\text{Unexplained variation}}{\text{Total variation}}$$

5. Spearman's coefficient of rank correlation

(a) United ranks

$$p = 1 - \frac{6\Sigma D^2}{N(N^2-1)}$$

(b) Fled ranks

$$p = 1 - \frac{6\left[\Sigma D^2 + \Sigma \frac{m(m^2-1)}{12}\right]}{N(N^2-1)}$$

6. Coefficient of correlation by the method of concurrent deviation

$$r_e = \pm\sqrt{\left[\pm\left(\frac{2C-n}{n}\right)\right]}$$

7. Fitting Regression Lines : (Ungrouped data)

(a) Using Least Square Method:

(i) The standard form of the line of regression of Y on X is :

$$Y = a + bX$$

The values of a and b are obtained by solving the normal equations:

$$\Sigma Y = Na + b\Sigma X$$

$$\Sigma XY = a\Sigma X + b\Sigma X^2$$

(ii) The standard form of the line of regression of X on Y is :

$$X = c + bY$$

The values of c and b are obtained by solving the normal equations:

$$\Sigma X = Nc + d\,\Sigma Y$$

$$\Sigma XY = c\,\Sigma Y + d\,\Sigma Y^2.$$

(b) Using the regression coefficients:

Regression of Y on $X : (Y - \bar{Y}) = b_{YX}(X - \bar{X})$

Regression of X on $Y : (X - \bar{X}) = b_{XY}(Y - \bar{Y})$

b_{YX} and b_{XY} can be computed as:

(i) Direct Method:

The regression coefficient of Y on X.

$$b_{YX} = \frac{N\Sigma XY - (\Sigma X)(\Sigma Y)}{N\Sigma X^2 - (\Sigma X)^2}$$

The regression coefficient of X on Y.

$$b_{XY} = \frac{N\Sigma XY_Y - (\Sigma X)(\Sigma Y)}{N\Sigma X^2 - (\Sigma Y)^2}$$

(ii) Using deviation method:

The regression coefficient of *Y* on *X*:

$$b_{YX} = \frac{N\Sigma d_x d_y - (\Sigma d_x)(\Sigma d_y)}{N\Sigma d_y^2 - (\Sigma d_x)^2}$$

The regression coefficient of *X* on *Y*:

$$b_{XY} = \frac{N\Sigma d_x d_y - (\Sigma d_x)(\Sigma d_y)}{N\Sigma d_y^2 - (\Sigma d_y)^2}$$

Here $d_x = (X - a), d_y = (Y - b)$

(c) Using the values of *r*, σ_X and σ_Y :

Regression of *Y* on $X : (Y - \bar{Y}) = r\frac{\sigma_Y}{\sigma_X}(X - \bar{X})$

Regression of *X* on $Y : (X - \bar{X}) = r\frac{\sigma_X}{\sigma_Y}(Y - \bar{Y})$

8. Fitting Regression Lines (Grouped data)

Regression of *Y* on $X : (Y - \bar{Y}) = b_{YX}(X - \bar{X})$

Regression of *X* on $Y : (X - \bar{X}) = b_{XY}(Y - \bar{Y})$

Here the regression coefficients b_{YX} and b_{XY} are obtained by using:

$$b_{YX} = \frac{N\Sigma f\, d_x d_y - (\Sigma f\, d_x)(\Sigma f\, d_y)}{N\Sigma f\, d_x^2 - (\Sigma f\, d_x)^2} \times \frac{k}{h}$$

and $$b_{XY} = \frac{N\Sigma f\, d_x d_y - (\Sigma f\, d_x)(\Sigma f\, d_y)}{N\Sigma f\, d_y^2 - (\Sigma f\, d_y)^2} \times \frac{k}{h}$$

where, $$d_x = \frac{X - a}{h},\ d_y = \frac{Y - b}{k}$$

9. Relation between correlation coefficient and regression coefficient

$$r = \pm[b_{YX} . b_{XY}]$$

10. Standard error of estimate

If $Y = a + bX$ is the regression line, then

$$S_{YX} = \sqrt{\left[\frac{\Sigma(Y - Y_{est})^2}{N}\right]} = \sqrt{\left[\frac{\Sigma Y^2 - a\Sigma Y - b\Sigma XY}{N}\right]}$$

Also $S_{YX} = \sigma_Y \sqrt{\left[1 - r^2\right]}$

Similarly, if $X = c + dY$ is the regression line, then:

$$S_{XY} = \sqrt{\left[\frac{\Sigma(X - X_{est})^2}{N}\right]} = \sqrt{\left[\frac{\Sigma X^2 - c\Sigma Y - bd\Sigma XY}{N}\right]}$$

Also $S_{XY} = \sigma_X \sqrt{\left[1 - r^2\right]}$

4 PROBABILITY

4.1 Introduction

In common parlance, the term probability refers to the chance of happening or not happening of an event. The theory of probability provides a numerical measure to the element of chance or uncertainty. It enables us to take decision under conditions of uncertainty with a calculated risk.

Today the theory of probability has been very extensively developed and there is hardly any discipline – physical or social – where it is not being used. In the field of business and economics it is very widely used for quantitative analysis of various problems and it forms the very basis of the modern theory of decision making.

Terminology

Random Experiment. it is an experiment which, if conducted repeatedly under homogeneous conditions, does not give the same result. The result may be any one of the various possible 'outcomes.' For example, if an unbiased die is thrown, it will not always fall with any particular number up. Any of the six numbers on the die may come up.

Trial and Event. The performance of a random experiment is called a trial and the outcome an event. Thus, throwing of a die would be called a trial and the result (falling of any one of the six numbers on a face of the die) an event.

Events can be either *simple* (*elementary*) or *compound* (*composite*). An event is called simple if it corresponds to a single possible outcome. Thus in throwing a die, the chance of getting 3 is a simple event. However, the chance of getting an odd number is a compound event.

A compound event can further be decomposed into simple events. For example, in the above-mentioned compound event, there are three simple events.

Exhaustive Cases. All possible outcomes of an event are known as exhaustive cases. In the throw of a single die, there are six exhaustive cases.

Favourable Cases. The number of outcomes which result in the happening of a desired event are called favourable cases. Thus, in a single throw of a die the number of favourable cases of getting an odd number are three, that is, 1, 3 and 5.

Mutually Exclusive Events. Two or more events are said to be mutually exclusive if the happening of any one of them excludes the happening of all others in single (same) experiment. Thus, in the throw of a single die, the events 5 and 6 are mutually exclusive because both cannot occur simultaneously.

Equally Likely Cases. Two or more events are said to be equally likely if the chance of their happening is equal, that is, there is no preference of any one event over the other. Thus in a throw of an unbiased die, the coming up of 1, 2, 3, 4, 5 or 6 is equally likely.

Independent and Dependent Events. An event is said to be independent if its happening is not affected by the happening of other events and if it itself also does not affect the happening of other events. Thus, in the throw of a die repeatedly, coming up of 5 on the first throw is independent of the coming up of 5 again in the second or subsequent throws.

However, if we are successively drawing cards from a pack, without replacement, the events would be dependent. For example, the chance of getting a King on the first draw is 4/52. However, if this card is not replaced, the chance of getting a King in the second draw would depend on whether we got a King in the first draw or not.

Permutations and Combinations

The word permutation refers to the arrangements and the word combination refers to groups. These terms find their usage in the calculation of probability.

The number of permutations of n dissimilar things taken r at a time

$$^nP_r = \frac{n!}{(n-r)!}$$

The number of combinations of n dissimilar things taken r at a time

$$^nC_r = \frac{n!}{r!\,(n-r)!}$$

Therefore,

$$^nP_r = {^nC_r}.r!$$

Some Basic Concepts of Set Theory

Set. A set is a collection of distinct and well defined objects. The objects forming the set are called the elements or members of the set. Distinct means that no two elements in a set are the same and well defined means that on the basis of a rule, it should be absolutely clear whether a particular object belongs to a particular set or not.

Subset. A set A is called a subset of a set B if each element of set A also belongs to set B. Set A can be smaller or equal to set B.

Equal Sets. Two sets A and B are said to be equal if all the elements of set A belong to set B and all the elements of set B belong to set A.

Null/Empty/Void Set. It is a set having no element. It is denoted by { } or φ.

Disjoint Sets. Two sets A and B are said to be disjoint if there is no element common in them, that is, if there is no element which belongs to both set A and set B.

Union of Two Sets. If A and B are two given sets then their union is the set of those elements which belong either to set A or set B or to both. The union of sets A and B is denoted as $A \cup B$.

Intersection of Sets. If A and B are two sets then their intersection is the set of those elements which are common to both the sets A and B. it is denoted as $A \cap B$.

Complement of a Set. Let U be any set (the universal set) and set A be its subset. Then the complement of set A in relation to U is that set B whose elements belong to U but not to A. Complement of A is denoted by $\bar{A}$, A' or A^c.

Sample Space. The set of all possible outcomes of an experiment is called the sample space of the experiment and is denoted by S. Each outcome is called an element or a sample point of the sample space. Sample space is also called the *universal set* or *event space* or *possibility set*. An event is a subset of the sample space. An event may consist of one or more sample points.

De Morgan's Laws

(i) $(A \cup B)^c = (A^c \cap B^c)$

(ii) $(A \cap B)^c = (A^c \cup B^c)$

4.2 Probability

Ordinarily speaking, the probability of an event denotes the likelihood of its happening. The value of probability ranges between 0 and 1. If an event is certain to happen, its probability would be 1, and if it is certain that the event would not take place, then the probability of its happening is 0. Ordinarily, in social sciences, the probability of the happening of an event is neither 0 nor 1. The reason is that in social sciences we deal with situations where there is always an element of uncertainty about the happening or not happening of an event. For this reason the probability of the events is generally between 0 and 1.

The general rule of the happening of an event is that if an event can happen in m ways and fail to happen in n ways, then the probability p of the happening of the event is given by

$$p = \frac{m}{m+n}$$

or $$p = \frac{\text{Number of cases favourable to the occurrence of the event}}{\text{Total number of mutually exclusive and exhaustive cases}}$$

Odds in Favour of the Occurrence of the Event

$$= \frac{m}{n} = \frac{\text{Number of cases favourable to the occurrence of the event}}{\text{Number of cases against the occurrence of the event}}$$

Odds Against the Occurrence of the Event

$$= \frac{m}{n} = \frac{\text{Number of cases against the occurrence of the event}}{\text{Number of cases favourable to the occurrence of the event}}$$

$P(A) + P(\bar{A}) = 1$

Note: if n events are mutually exclusive and exhaustive, the sum of their individual probabilities = 1

Classical or a priori Probability

This is the earliest approach to the theory of probability. It is based on the definition of probability given by Laplace – the ratio of the number of favourable cases to the total number of equally likely cases.

This theory assumes that the various outcomes of an event are equally likely and so the probability of their happening is also equal. Since this theory was one of the first attempts to determine the probability of an event even before the event has taken place, and often it tries to determine the probability of events which have never taken place before (that is, there is no past data available) it is called a priori probability.

This theory is suitable for calculating the probabilities of various events in games of chance, where various events are equally likely to happen. Thus, while throwing a die there are six possible events that can happen. They are supposed to be equally likely and the probability of getting any particular number (say 5) would be 1/6. And the probability that this event will not take place = $1 - \frac{1}{6} = \frac{5}{6}$

It means that P + q = 1 or 1 – q = p or 1 – p = q.

Relative Frequency Theory of Probability

The relative frequency approach to the theory of probability is not based on a priori probabilities. In many situations it is not possible to have equally likely events, on which assumption the classical theory of probability is based. For example, whether the prices of the shares of a company would go up or down are not two events which may be called equally likely. No doubt there are three alternatives here:

(*i*) The prices may remain constant.

(*ii*) The prices may go up.

(*iii*) The prices may go down.

But these events are not equally likely to happen. Similarly, whether a machine would turn out an acceptable article or an unacceptable article are two alternatives but they also are not equally likely. Therefore the a priori probability theory cannot be applied.

In such situations the probability of the happening of an event is determined on the basis of past experience or on the basis of relative frequency of success in the past. Thus, if a machine has been turning out 10% unacceptable articles in past the relative frequency for unacceptable articles would be 10% of the total items. However, relative frequency should always be estimated on the basis of a large number of readings in the past. The larger the number of past readings, the greater will be the accuracy of the result. Since in relative frequency approach probabilities are calculated on the basis of past experience these probabilities are called *posterior probabilities* as contrasted with a priori probabilities calculated through the classical approach.

It should be understood that a priori probabilities are generally calculated in games of chance and posterior probabilities in problems relating to various types of economic and social phenomena where prior probabilities are not constant. A priori probabilities are deductive in nature, and are based on theory instead of evidence or experience or experimentation. Posterior probabilities, also called *empirical probabilities*, are based on experience of the past and on experiments conducted. It is thus empirical in nature. For example, mortality tables, tables relating to expectation of life at various ages, birth rates, death rates, rates of depreciation of machinery, etc. are all based on past experience.

The posterior probability of an event

$$p = \frac{\text{Relative frequencey}}{\text{Number of items}}$$

Subjective Theory of Probability

This theory is also known as Personalistic Theory of Probability because it presumes that any decision reflects the personality of the decision maker, and subjective elements are important in assigning a probability to an event. This is very true in actual life. Suppose we have data relating to the price of a share for the last 2 years and further supposing that out of 1000 quotations relating to this share price, there was a price rise on 400 occasions, then the empirical probability of a price rise in this share is $\frac{400}{1000}$ or 0.4

However, with these data, some people would buy the shares and others would sell them for the reason that their subjective estimate coupled with relative frequency approach may give them is reflected in the ultimate decision. The decision under this theory is taken on the basis of the available data plus the effects of other factors, many of which may be subjective in nature.

This theory is very commonly used in business decision making. The approach in this theory is very broad based and flexible.

Axiomatic Approach to Probability

This approach is entirely mathematical in character and is based on set theory. To start with, some concepts are laid down and certain properties or postulates commonly known as *axioms* are defined. From these axioms alone the entire theory of probability is derived by deductive logic. The axiomatic probability includes the concepts of both the classical as well as the empirical definitions of probability.

In this concept, for mutually exclusive (disjoint) events, the probability of the happening of either A or B is given by

$P(A \cup B) = P(A) + P(B)$

For events of simultaneous occurrence, or the probability of both A and B happening together is given by

$P(A \cap B) = P(A) \times P(B)$

4.3 Conditional Probability

Two events A and B are said to be dependent when B can occur only when A is known to have already occurred or vice versa. The probabilities associated with such events are called conditional probabilities.

The probability of the occurrence of event A when event B has already occurred is called the conditional probability of the occurrence of A given that event B has already occurred and is denoted by P(A/B) (read as: Probability of A, given B).

4.4 Theorems of Probability

(*i*) **Addition Theorem** **(U.P.T.U. 2006)**

If A and B are any two events then the probability that at least one of them occurs

$P(A \cup B) = P(A) + P(B) - P(A \cap B)$

If A and B are mutually exclusive events, then $A \cap B = \varphi$, $P(A \cap B) = 0$, therefore

$P(A \cup B) = P(A) + P(B)$

If there are three events A, B and C, the probability of the occurrence of at least one of them

$P(A \cup B \cup C) = P(A) + P(B) + P(C) - P(A \cap B) - P(B \cap C) - P(C \cap A) + P(A \cap B \cap C)$

If the events are mutually exclusive

$P(A \cup B \cup C) = P(A) + P(B) + P(C)$

(*ii*) **Multiplication Theorem**

The probability of the simultaneous occurrence of the events A and B

P(A∩B) = P(AB) = P(A) x P(B/A) = P(B) x P(A/B)

If the events A and B are independent

P(B/A) = P(B), P(A/B) = P(A)

Therefore, for independent events

P(A∩B) = P(A) x P(B)

4.5 Bayes' Theorem and Inverse Probability

Bayes' theorem is based on the proposition that probabilities should be revised when new information is available. The idea of revising probabilities is used by us in our daily life. Probabilities are often revised as soon as some new information is available about the problem concerned.

The need for revising probabilities arises from a need to make better use of available information, and thereby reduce the element of risk involved in decision making.

Bayes' theorem is very widely used in decision theory. On the basis of this theorem, probabilities of various outcomes are revised upwards or downwards depending on the evidence obtained.

The probabilities before revision are called prior probabilities and those after revision, posterior probabilities.

Theorem

Imagine a situation where two uncertain events (A and Not A) are possible. Suppose we know their probability, that is, we know the probability of A's happening and also the probability of A's not happening. These probabilities are prior probabilities because they are probabilities before any further information is available. Suppose an investigation is now conducted. The investigation may have several outcomes which would be dependent on event A. For any particular outcome (which may be called B) the conditional probabilities P(B/A) and P(B Not A) are available.

The result itself serves to revise the probabilities for event A and event Not A. The resulting values would be posterior probabilities since they have been obtained after the results of the investigation.

The posterior probabilities are actually conditional probabilities of the form P(A/B) or P(Not A/B).

Thus, according to Bayes' Theorem, the posterior probability of event A for a particular result of an investigation B may be found as

$$P(A/B) = \frac{P(A)P(B/A)}{P(A)P(B/A) + P(Not\,A)P(B/Not\,A)}$$

Inverse Probability

It is the probability of the happening of an event as a result of factor (a) if the event could have happened as a result of factors (a) or (b) or (c) or ... or (n).

With this concept of inverse probability, the Baye's theorem can be stated as:

An event A can occur only if any one of the set of exhaustive and mutually exclusive events $B_1, B_2, B_3, \ldots, B_n$ occurs. The probabilities $P(B_1), P(B_2), P(B_3), \ldots, P(B_n)$ and the conditional probabilities $P(A/B_i)$ where $i = 1, 2, 3, \ldots, n$ are known. Then the conditional probability $P(B_i/A)$ when A has actually occurred is given by

$$P(B_i/A) = \frac{P(B_i)P(A/B_i)}{\sum_{i=1}^{n} P(B_i)P(A/B_i)}$$

Where $i = 1, 2, 3, \ldots, n$

Joint and Marginal Probabilities

Joint probabilities are arrived at by multiplying two or more probabilities depending on the number of events involved. Marginal probabilities are the sum of probabilities (prior or posterior) of two or more events. Both joint and marginal probabilities are used in the Bayes' theorem.

Mathematical Expectation

Mathematical expectation is the weighted mean of expected values of a variable. The mean is weighted in the sense that the various values of a variable are multiplied by their probabilities.

If X is a random variable which can assume any one of the values $x_1, x_2, x_3, \ldots, x_n$, with respective probabilities $p_1, p_2, p_3, \ldots, p_n$, then the mathematical expectation of X (or the expected value of X) which is denoted by $E(x)$ would be

$$E(x) = p_1x_1 + p_2x_2 + p_3x_3 + \ldots + p_nx_n$$

In a game of chance if a player would gain a sum 'a' if he wins and would lose a sum 'b' if he loses then the mathematical expectation would be

$$(a \times p) + (-b \times q) = ap - bq$$

Here loss is regarded as a negative gain.

If the mathematical expectation of a game is zero, it is a fair game. If it is more than zero, it is biased to the player, that is, the game is in favour of the player. If the mathematical expectation is negative, the game is biased against the player. At most gambling places, the mathematical expectation for the players is negative.

Addition and Multiplication Laws of Expectation

If X and Y are two random variables then the expected value of X and Y together, that is

$$E(X+Y) = E(X) + E(Y)$$

If X and Y are two *independent* random variables then the expected value of XY, that is

$$E(XY) = E(X) \times E(Y)$$

Variance of X in terms of expectation

$$\sigma^2{}_x = \frac{\Sigma(X - \bar{X})}{N}$$

$$or\ \sigma^2{}_x = \frac{1}{N}\Sigma X^2 - \bar{X}^2$$

$$or\ \sigma^2{}_x = [arithmetic\ average\ of\ X^2] - \bar{X}$$

Since the expected value of X is the arithmetic mean of X series over a period of time

$$\therefore Variance\ of\ X = E[X - E(X)]^2$$

$$or\ \sigma^2{}_x = E(X^2) - [E(X)]^2$$

Some more results

$E(ax + b) = aE(x) + b$

$Var(ax) = a^2Var(x)$

$Var(a + bx) = b^2Var(x)$

$Var(ax + by) = a^2Var(x) + b^2Var(y)$

$Var(a) = 0$

Where a and b are constants.

4.6 Chemistry of Cards

A pack of cards consist of four suits viz. Spade, Heart, Club, Diamond/Brick. Each suits consist of 13 cards, 9 cards number 2, 3, 4, 5, 6, 7, 8, 9, 10 and an Ace, a King, a Queen & Jack or Knave.

Face Card

Ace, King, Queen & Jack or Knave or known as face card.

Four Suits

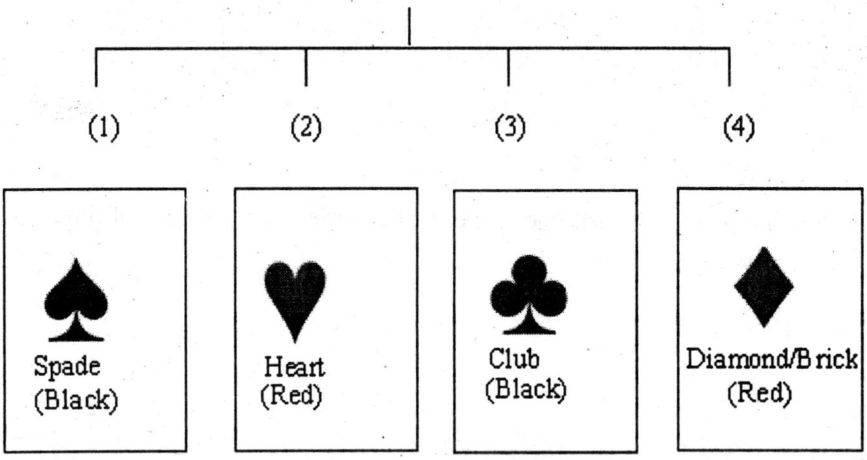

Example 1: *(Two events) Two cards are drawn from a pack of 52 cards what is the probability that either both or red or both are king.* **(U.P.T.U. 2004)**

Solution: Out of 52 cards, 2 cards can be drawn in ${}^{52}C_2$ ways.

So, Exhaustive number of cases = ${}^{52}C_2$

Consider the following events.

A = Two cards drawn are red card

B = Two cards drawn are king

By Addition Law of Theorem

Required probability $= P(A \cup B)$

$$= P(A) + P(B) - P(A \cap B) \quad \text{...(1)}$$

We have find $P(A)$, $P(B)$ and $P(A \cap B)$

There are 26 (13 + 13) red cards out of which 2 red cards can be drawn in ${}^{26}C_2$ ways

$$P(A) = \frac{{}^{26}C_2}{{}^{52}C_2}$$

Since there are 4 kings out of which 2 king can be drawn ${}^{4}C_2$ ways

So, $$P(B) = \frac{{}^{4}C_2}{{}^{52}C_2}$$

There are 2 cards which are both red and king therefore

$P(A \cap B)$ = Prob. of getting 2 cards which are both red and king.

$$= \text{Prob. of getting 2 red king cards } = \frac{^{2}C_2}{^{52}C_2}$$

Then equ. 1

$$\text{Required Prob.} = P(A) + P(B) - P(A \cap B) \quad ...(1)$$

$$= \frac{^{26}C_2}{^{52}C_2} + \frac{^{4}C_2}{^{52}C_2} - \frac{^{2}C_2}{^{52}C_2}$$

$$= \frac{55}{281}$$

Example 2: ***(Three events)*** *A card is drawn from a pack of 52 cards. Find of probability of getting a king or a heart or a red card.*

Solution: Let the following events A = getting a king

B = getting a heart

C = getting a red

$$P(A) = \frac{^{4}C_1}{^{52}C_1} = \frac{4}{52}, \quad P(B) = \frac{^{13}C_1}{^{52}C_1} = \frac{13}{52}, \quad P(C) = \frac{^{26}C_1}{^{52}C_1} = \frac{26}{52}$$

$$P(A \cap B) = P \text{ (getting a king of heart)} = \frac{1}{52}$$

$$P(B \cap C) = P \text{ (getting a heart card)} = \frac{13}{52}$$

$$P(C \cap A) = P \text{ (getting a red king)} = \frac{2}{52}$$

$$P(A \cap B \cap C) = P \text{ (getting a king of heart)} = \frac{1}{52}$$

So, Required probability

$$P(A \cup B \cup C)$$

$$= P(A) + P(B) + P(C) - P(A \cap B) - P(B \cap C) - P(C \cap A) + P(A \cup B \cup C)$$

$$= \frac{4}{52} + \frac{13}{52} + \frac{26}{52} - \frac{1}{52} - \frac{13}{52} - \frac{2}{52} + \frac{1}{52} = \frac{28}{52} = \frac{7}{13}$$

Example 3: *A problem in Business Statistics is given to four students A, B, C & D their respective chance of solving it are 1/2, 1/3, 1/5 and 1/6. What is the probability that the problem will be solved by any two of them.* **(U.P.T.U. 2006)**

Solution: The probability that the problem will be solved by any two of them

= P (A and B) + P (A and C) + P (A and D) + P (B and C) + P (B and D) + P (C and D)

= P (A).P(B) + P (A).P(C) + P (A).P(D) + P (B).P(C) + P (B).P(D) + P (C).P(D)

$$=\left(\frac{1}{2}\times\frac{1}{3}\right)+\left(\frac{1}{2}\times\frac{1}{5}\right)+\left(\frac{1}{2}\times\frac{1}{6}\right)+\left(\frac{1}{3}\times\frac{1}{5}\right)+\left(\frac{1}{3}\times\frac{1}{6}\right)+\left(\frac{1}{5}\times\frac{1}{6}\right)=\frac{91}{180}=0.505$$

4.7 Probability Theoretical Distributions

Introduction

Frequency distribution can be obtained in two ways, namely,

(*i*) By compiling actual frequencies through collection of data or by conducting experiments,

(*i*) By deriving the frequencies on the basis of some mathematical relationships.

The actual or observed frequency distributions (also called empirical or experimental distribution) are used to estimate certain values in the universe on the basis of sample studies. Thus, when we are finding the average height of adult males through a sample study our purpose is to estimate the average height of the adult males in the universe from which the sample has been taken.

However, there are certain situations where we can derive expected values on the basis of some mathematical relationship. For example, if we toss a coin we know that the probability of heads is ½ and of tails is also ½. If we toss a coin 100 times the expected number of heads is 50. This is the theoretical or derived frequency of heads. In actual practice, if we toss a coin 100 times and heads come up 60 times, then this is the observed frequency of heads. Thus, in such cases, we have an observed frequency of 60 and an expected frequency of 50. If we toss 10 coins 256 times we can have a set of observed frequencies by conducting the experiment and getting observed frequencies. We can also have theoretical frequencies by finding out the value of $256\left(\frac{1}{2}+\frac{1}{2}\right)^{10}$. This distribution would be called a theoretical frequency distribution or a probability distribution.

Thus, we can define theoretical or probability distributions as such distributions which are not obtained by actual observations or experiments but are mathematically deduced on certain assumptions.

The importance of theoretical distributions cannot be overemphasized. They provide us data on the basis of which the results of actual observations or experiments can be assessed. In fact, where theoretical distributions are available, there is no need for having observed distributions. Theoretical distributions provide the decision maker with a sound basis for taking rational and dependable decisions.

Theoretical distributions are of many types. We will, however, discuss only three such distributions which are more popular than others and are widely used. These are

(*i*) **Binomial distribution, (or Bernoulli's Distribution)**

(*ii*) **Poisson distribution, and**

(*iii*) **Normal distribution.**

Out of the above, the first two, namely, the binomial and the Poisson distributions are discrete distributions and the normal distribution is a continuous distribution.

4.8 Binomial Distribution

(U.P.T.U. 2005, 2006, 2008)

It is a particular case of multinomial distribution and is of very great importance in research and problems connected with probability and sampling. Binomial distribution studies such experiments which can have only two possible outcomes. Let us consider the tossing of a coin. Suppose we toss two coins (a and b) simultaneously. The possible outcomes shall be

Coins	
a	**b**
H	H
H	T
T	H
T	T

H = Heads
T = Tails

Thus the coins can fall in any one of four different ways, as shown above. If p stands for the probability of a coin falling heads and q for falling tails, then

The probability of two heads = $p \times p = p^2$

The probability of one heads and one tails = $(p \times q) + (q \times p) = pq + pq = 2pq$

The probability of two tails = $q \times q = q^2$

The above results are the expansion of $(p + q)^2$

$(p + q)^2 = p^2 + 2pq + q^2$

Let us now analyse the sample of three coins.

Type of Event	Ways of Arising			Probability of Way	Probability of the Type of Result
	a	**b**	**c**		
Three heads	H	H	H	p^3	p^3
Two heads, one tails	H	H	T	p^2q	$3p^2q$
	H	T	H	pqp	
	T	H	H	qp^2	
One heads, two	H	T	T	pq^2	$3pq^2$

Type of Event	Ways of Arising			Probability of Way	Probability of the Type of Result
	a	b	c		
tails	T	H	T	qpq	
	T	T	H	q^2p	
Three tails	T	T	T	q^3	q^3

These are the terms in the expansion of $(p + q)^3$

In case of an unbiased coin, p = q = ½. Therefore

$p^3 = (½)^3 = 1/8$

$3p^2q = 3 \times (½)^2 \times ½ = 3/8$

$3pq^2 = 3 \times ½ \times (½)^2 = 3/8$

$q^3 = (½)^3 = 1/8$

Similarly, the terms of the binomial expansion of

$$(p+q)^n = p^n + np^{n-1}q + \frac{n(n-1)}{1 \times 2}p^{n-2}q^2 + \frac{n(n-1)(n-2)}{1 \times 2 \times 3}p^{n-3}q^3 + \ldots + q^n$$

$$or\ (p+q)^n = {}^nC_0p^nq^0 + {}^nC_1p^{n-1}q^1 + {}^nC_2p^{n-2}q^2 + \ldots + {}^nC_rp^{n-r}q^r + \ldots + {}^nC_np^0q^n$$

Now, probability of n successes

$$P(n) = {}^nC_0p^nq^0 = p^n$$

Probability of zero successes

$$P(0) = {}^nC_np^0q^n = q^n$$

Probability of at least one success

= P(1) + P(2) + P(3) + … + P(n)

= 1 – P(0)

$= 1 - q^n$

Probability of exactly r successes

$$\boxed{P(r) = {}^nC_rp^rq^{n-r}} \qquad \text{where} \qquad p + q = 1$$

Probability of at least r successes

= P(r) + P(r + 1) + P(r + 2) + … + P(n)

$$= {}^nC_0p^nq^0 + {}^nC_1p^{n-1}q^1 + {}^nC_2p^{n-2}q^2 + \ldots + {}^nC_rp^{n-r}q^r$$

Probability of at most r successes

= P(0) + P(1) + P(2) + … + P(r)

$$= {}^nC_rp^{n-r}q^r + {}^nC_{r+1}p^{n-(r+1)}q^{r+1} + \ldots + {}^nC_{n-1}p^1q^{n-1} + {}^nC_np^0q^n$$

If these n trials are repeated N times, the number of exactly r, (r-1), (r-2), ... successes can be obtained by the expansion of $N(p + q)^n$

In this manner we can obtain the theoretical or expected frequencies when, say, N = 256. The actual frequencies when n coins are tossed simultaneously 256 times shall most probably be different from these. However, if the value of N is very large (say, 2560 or 25600) then the difference between the expected and observed frequencies would not be significant.

Assumptions of Binomial Distribution

(*i*) The number of trials or 'n' is finite and fixed. The performance must be repeated a fixed number of times.

(*i*) The experiment must result in either of the two events happening or, in other words, there must be only two possible outcomes of the event which are mutually exclusive and exhaustive.

(*i*) The probability of the happening of the event (or success) in any trial of the event is constant for all trials. Similarly, the probability of not happening of the event (or failure) is also constant. In other words p and q shall remain constant in all trials.

(*i*) All trials must be independent of each other.

General Form of Binomial Distribution

The general form of binomial distribution depends on the following two things:

(1) The values of p and q, and

(2) The value of the exponent n.

If p = q = ½, the distribution would be symmetrical and the expected frequencies on either side of the central value would be identical. Thus, in the case where four coins are tossed 256 times, the frequencies for 0, 1, 2, 3 and 4 heads would be 16, 64, 96, 64 and 16, respectively. The distribution is therefore symmetrical. If, however, p is not equal to q, the distribution would not be symmetrical but skewed. If $p < q$, the distribution will be positively skewed (skewed towards right) and if $p > q$, the distribution will be negatively skewed (towards left). If p = q, the effect of increasing the value of the exponent n would be that the value of mean would increase and so would the value of measure of dispersion. If $p \neq q$, an increase in the value of n would raise the value of the mean and dispersion, but would reduce the asymmetry of the distribution. It means that even if p and q are not equal, even then we can obtain a more or less symmetrical distribution if the value of n is large.

Thus we can conclude that the type of distribution that we shall obtain would depend on the values of p and q and also on the value of n.

Constants in a Binomial Distribution

The following relationships hold good in a binomial distribution:

(*i*) The mean of a binomial distribution is np., **mean = np**

(*ii*) The standard deviation of a binomial distribution is $\sqrt{(npq)}$ and variance is npq.

$$S.D. = \sqrt{npq}$$

$$\text{Variance} = npq$$

(*iii*) The moments in a binomial distribution are as follows:

$\mu_1 = 0$

$\mu_2 = npq$

$\mu_3 = npq(q - p)$

$\mu_4 = 3n^2p^2q^2 + npq(1 - 6pq)$

(*iv*) The β_1 and β_2 (on the basis of the above moments) are

$$\beta_1 = \frac{\mu_3{}^2}{\mu_2{}^3} = \frac{n^2p^2q^2(q-p)^2}{n^3p^3q^3} = \frac{(q-p)^2}{npq}$$

$$\beta_2 = \frac{\mu_4}{\mu_2{}^2} = \frac{3n^2p^2q^2 + npq(1-6pq)}{n^2p^2q^2} = 3 + \frac{1-6pq}{npq}$$

(*v*) If $\beta_1 = 0$, the distribution is symmetrical.

The values of γ_1 and γ_2 are

$$\gamma_1 = \sqrt{\beta_1} = \sqrt{\frac{(q-p)^2}{npq}} = \frac{q-p}{\sqrt{npq}} = skewness$$

$$\gamma_1 = \beta_2 - 3 = 3 + \frac{1-6pq}{npq} - 3 = \frac{1-6pq}{npq} = kurtosis$$

If the distribution is normal, both γ_1 and γ_2 would be zero.

Note: In a binomial distribution, variance would always be less than mean as mean is np and variance is npq (neither p nor q = 0 and both p and q are less than 1 as p + q = 1).

Applications of Binomial Distribution

1. In problems concerning no. of defectives in a sample from production line.
2. In estimation of reliability of systems.
3. No. of rounds fired from a gun hitting a target.
4. In Radar detection.

Example 1: *(i) Comment on the following statement :*

For a Binomial distribution, mean is 6 and variance is 9.

(ii) A die is tossed thrice. A success is getting 1 or 6 on a toss. Find the mean and variance of the number of success. **(Q. Bank U.P.T.U. 2001)**

Solution: (i) $\mu = np = 6$ ...(1)

$\sigma^2 = npq = 9$ ...(2)

Dividing (2) by (1), we get

$$q = \frac{9}{6} = 1.5$$

which is impossible as $0 \le q \le 1$

The above statement is false.

(ii) Prob. of getting success (1 or (6) on a toss $= \frac{2}{6} = \frac{1}{3}$

$$p = \frac{1}{3}$$

$\Rightarrow$ $q = 1 - \frac{1}{3} = \frac{2}{3}$

No. of tosses of a dice, $n = 3$

(i) Mean $= np = 3\left(\frac{1}{3}\right) = 1$

(ii) Variance $= npq = (3)\left(\frac{1}{3}\right)\left(\frac{2}{3}\right) = \frac{2}{3}$

Example 2: *If* 10% *of the bolts produced by a machine are defective, determine the probability that out of* 10 *bolts chosen at random*

(i) 1 (ii) None (iii) at most 2 bolts will be defective. **(Q. Bank U.P.T.U. 2001)**

Solution: Here, $p(\text{defective}) = \frac{10}{100} = \frac{1}{10}$ (given)

$\therefore$ $q(\text{non-defective}) = 1 - \frac{1}{10} = \frac{9}{10}$

Also, $n = 10$, (n is no. of bolts chosen). (given)

The expression for determining the probability of r defective bolts out of n bolts chosen at random is given by

$$P(r) = nC_r p^r q^{n-r}$$

(*i*) Here $r = 1$

$$P(1) = {}^{10}C_1 \left(\frac{1}{10}\right)^1 \left(\frac{9}{10}\right)^{10-1}$$ | using (1)

$$=10\left(\frac{1}{10}\right)\left(\frac{9}{10}\right)^9=(.9)^9=0.3874 \qquad ...(2)$$

(*ii*) Here $r=0$,

$$\therefore \qquad P(0)={}^{10}c_0\left(\frac{1}{10}\right)^0\left(\frac{9}{10}\right)^{10-0} \qquad | \text{ using (1)}$$

$$=\left(\frac{9}{10}\right)^{10}=0.3486 \qquad ...(3)$$

(*iii*) Prob. that at most 2 bolts will be defective = $P(r \le 2)$

$$= P(0) + P(1) + P(2)$$

Now,
$$P(2)={}^{10}c_0\left(\frac{1}{10}\right)^2\left(\frac{9}{10}\right)^{10-2} \qquad ...(4)$$

$$=\frac{10!}{2!8!}\left(\frac{1}{100}\right)\left(\frac{9}{10}\right)^8=45\left(\frac{1}{100}\right)(0.43046)=0.1937$$

$\therefore$ From (4),

Required Probability $= P(0) + P(1) + P(2)$

$= 0.3486 + 0.3874 + 0.1937 = 0.9297.$

Example 3: *A binomial variable X satisfies the relation 9P(X = 4) = P(X = 2) when n = 6. Find the value of the parameter p and P (X = 1).* **(U.P.T.U. 2005)**

Solution: We know that

$$P(X=r)={}^nC_rp^rq^{n-r} \qquad ...(1)$$

$$P(X=4)={}^6C_4p^4q^2=15p^4q^2$$

and
$$P(X=2)={}^6C_2p^2q^4=15p^2q^4 \qquad | \text{ since } n=6$$

The given relation is

$$9P(X=4)=P(X=2)$$

$$\Rightarrow \qquad 9(15p^4q^2)=15P^2q^4$$

$$\Rightarrow \qquad 9p^2=q^2=(1-P)^2 \qquad | \therefore p+q=1$$

$$\Rightarrow \qquad 9p^2=1+p^2-2p$$

$$\Rightarrow \qquad 8p^2=2p-1=0$$

$$\Rightarrow \qquad (4p-1)(2p+1)=0$$

$\therefore$ $\boxed{p = \frac{1}{4}}$ | $\therefore$ p cannot be negative

Now, $P(X=1) = {}^6C_1 \left(\frac{1}{4}\right)^1 \left(\frac{3}{4}\right)^5 = .3559.$ | $\because q = 1 - p = \frac{3}{4}$

Example 4. *Fit a binomial distribution to the following frequency data :*

x:	0	1	2	3	4
f:	30	62	46	10	2

Solution: The table is as follows :

x	f	fx
0	30	0
1	62	62
2	46	92
3	10	30
4	2	8
	$N = \sum f = 150$	$\sum fx = 192$

Mean of observations $= \frac{\sum fx}{\sum f} = \frac{192}{150} = 1.28 = m$

$\Rightarrow$ $np = 1.28$

$\Rightarrow$ $4p = 1.28$

$\Rightarrow$ $p = 0.32$

$\therefore$ $q = 1 - p = 1 - 0.32 = 0.68$

Also, $N = 150$

Hence the binomial distribution is | $\therefore N = \sum f$

$$= N(q+p)^n = 150(0.68 + 0.32)^4.$$

Example 5. *If the moment generating function of a random variable X is* $\left(\frac{1}{2} + \frac{2}{3}e^t\right)^5$ *find*

$P(X = 2)$

Solution: Let $P(X = r) = {}^nC_r p^r q^{n-r}, r = 0, 1, 2, \ldots\ldots, n$

then $M_0(t) = (q + pe^t)^n$ ...(1)

Given $$M_0(t) = \left(\frac{1}{3} + \frac{2}{3}e^t\right)^5 \qquad \ldots(2)$$

Comparing (1) and (2), we get

$$p = \frac{2}{3}, q = \frac{1}{3} n = 5$$

$$\therefore \qquad P(X = r) = {}^5C_r \left(\frac{2}{3}\right)^2 \left(\frac{1}{3}\right)^{5-r}$$

$$P(X = 2) = {}^5C_r \left(\frac{2}{3}\right)^2 \left(\frac{1}{3}\right)^2 = \frac{40}{243} = .1646$$

Example 6: Four person in a group of 20 are graduates. If 4 persons are selected at random from 20. Find the probability that 10.

(*a*) All are graduate (*b*) At least one is a graduate **(U.P.T.U. 2008)**

Solution: Probability of finding one graduate is $= \frac{4}{20} = \frac{1}{5}$

Probability of 1 graduate out of four selected $= {}^4C_1 \left(\frac{1}{3}\right)^1 \left(\frac{2}{3}\right)^2 = \frac{8}{27}$

Probability of 2 graduate out of four selected $= {}^4C_2 \left(\frac{1}{3}\right)^2 \left(\frac{2}{3}\right)^1 = \frac{4}{27}$

Probability of 3 graduate out of four selected $= {}^4C_3 \left(\frac{1}{3}\right)^3 \left(\frac{2}{3}\right)^0 = \frac{1}{27}$

Therefore the probability of at least 1 graduate out of 4 selected

$$= \frac{8}{27} + \frac{4}{27} + \frac{1}{27} = \frac{13}{27}$$

Example 7: *Six dice are thrown 729 times. How many times do you expect at least 3 dice to show a five or six.*

Solution: p = the chance of getting five or six with one dice $= \frac{2}{6} = \frac{1}{3}$

$$q = 1 - p = 1 - \frac{1}{3} = \frac{2}{3}, \ n = 6, \ N = 729$$

Since dice are in sets of 6 and there are 729 sets.

The expected number of times at least three dice showing five or six.

$$= N.P(r \geq 3)$$

$$= 729\ [P(3) + P(4) + P(5) + P(6)]$$

$$= 729\left[{}^6C_3\left(\frac{2}{3}\right)^3\left(\frac{1}{3}\right)^3 + {}^6C_4\left(\frac{2}{3}\right)^2\left(\frac{1}{3}\right)^4 + {}^6C_5\left(\frac{2}{3}\right)^1\left(\frac{1}{3}\right)^5 + {}^6C_6\left(\frac{2}{3}\right)^0\left(\frac{1}{3}\right)^6\right]$$

$$= 233$$

Examples 8: *Assume that on the average one telephone number out of fifteen called between 2 P.M. and 3 P.M. on week-days is busy. What is the probability that if 6 randomly selected telephone numbers are called (i) not more than three, (ii) at least three of them will be busy?*

(U.P.T.U.)

Solution: Let p, the probability of a telephone number being busy between 2 P.M. & 3 P.M. on week-days $p = \dfrac{1}{15}$

Then $$q = 1 - P = 1 - \frac{1}{15} = \frac{14}{15},\ n = 6$$

The probability that not more than three will be busy

$$= P(r \leq 3)$$

$$= P(0) + P(1) + P(2) + P(3)$$

$$= {}^6C_0\left(\frac{14}{15}\right)^6\left(\frac{1}{15}\right)^0 + {}^6C_1\left(\frac{14}{15}\right)^5\left(\frac{1}{15}\right)^1 + {}^6C_2\left(\frac{14}{15}\right)^4\left(\frac{1}{15}\right)^2 + {}^6C_3\left(\frac{14}{15}\right)^3\left(\frac{1}{15}\right)^3$$

$$= \frac{(14)^3}{(15)^6}[2744 + 1176 + 210 + 20] = 0.9997$$

The probability that at least three of them will be busy $= P(r \geq 3)$

$$= P(3) + P(4) + P(5) + P(6)$$

$$= {}^6C_3\left(\frac{14}{15}\right)^3\left(\frac{1}{15}\right)^3 + {}^6C_4\left(\frac{14}{15}\right)^2\left(\frac{1}{15}\right)^4 + {}^6C_5\left(\frac{14}{15}\right)^1\left(\frac{1}{15}\right)^5 + {}^6C_6\left(\frac{14}{15}\right)^0\left(\frac{1}{15}\right)^6$$

$$= 0.005$$

Exercise 4.1

1. Ten coins are tossed simultaneously. Find the probability of getting at least seven heads.
2. The probability of any ship of a company being destroyed on a certain voyage is 0.02. The company owns 6 ships for the voyage. What is the probability of:

   (*i*) losing one ship (*ii*) losing at most two ships (*iii*) losing none.

3. The incidence of occupational disease in an industry is such that the workers have a 20% chance of suffering from it. What is the probability that out of six workers chosen at random, four or more will suffer from the disease ?

4. The probability that a pen manufactured by a company will be defective is $\frac{1}{10}$. If 12 such pens are manufactured, find the probability that

   (*i*) exactly two will be defective (*ii*) at least two will be defective

   (*iii*) none will be defective.

5. If the chance that one of the ten telephone lines is busy at an instant is 0.2.

   (*i*) What is the chance that 5 of the lines are busy ?

   (*ii*) What is the probability that all the lines are busy ?

6. A bag contains 5 white, 7 red and 8 black balls. If four balls are drawn, one by one, with replacement, what is the probability that.

   (*i*) none is white (*ii*) all are white

   (*iii*) at least one is white (*iv*) only 2 are white ?

7. In a hurdle race, a player has to cross 10 hurdles. The probability that he will clear each hurdle is $\frac{5}{6}$ What is the probability that he will knock down fewer than 2 hurdles ?

8. Fit a binomial distribution for the following data and compare the theoretical frequencies with the actual ones

x:	0	1	2	3	4	5
f:	2	14	20	34	22 .	8

9. If the sum of mean and variance of a binomial distribution is 4.8 for five trials, find the distribution.

10. If the mean of a binomial distribution is 3 and the variance is $\frac{3}{2}$, find the probability of obtaining at least 4 successes **(L.U. 2006)**

11. In 800 families with 5 children each, how many families would be expected to have

    (*i*) 3 boys and 2 girls, (*ii*) 2 boys and 3 girls,

    (*iii*) no girl (*iv*) at the most two girls.

(Assume probabilities for boys and girls to be equal.)

12. In 100 sets of ten tosses of an unbiased coin, in how many cases do you expect to get

    (*i*) 7 heads and 3 tails (*ii*) at least 7 heads ?

13. The following data are the number of seeds germinating out of 10 on damp filter for 80 sets of seeds. Fit a binomial distribution to this data :

x:	0	1	2	3	4	5	6	7	8	9	10	Total
f:	6	20	28	12	8	6	0	0	0	0	0	80

[**Hint.** Here $n = 10, N = 80$, Mean $\dfrac{\sum fx}{\sum f} = 2.175 \quad \therefore \quad np = 2.175$ etc.]

14. In a binomial distribution, for $n = 5$ if

$$P(x = 1) = 0.4096 \quad \text{and} \quad P(x = 2) = 0.2048$$

then find the value *of p*.

15. The prob. that a bulb produced by a factory will fuse after a use of 150 days is 0.05. Find the prob. that out of 5 such bulbs

(i)None *(ii)* Atmost one

(iii) More than one *(iv)* At least one will fuse after 150 days of use.

16. The probability that a bomb dropped from a plane will strike the target is $\frac{1}{5}$. If six bombs are dropped, find the probability that (i) exactly two will strike the target, *(ii)* at least two will strike the target.

17. Five cards are drawn successively with replacement from a well-shuffled deck of 52 cards. What is the prob. that

(*i*) all the five cards are spades (*ii*) only three are spades

(*iii*) none is spade

18. If the probability of a defective bolt is 0.1, find (a) The mean (b) The standard deviation for the distribution bolts in a total of 400.

19. The sum and product of the mean and variance of a binomial distribution are 24 and 128 respectively. Find the distribution. (A.U.)

20. Manish takes a step forward with probability 0.4 and backward with probability 0.6. Find the probability that at the end of 11 steps, he is one step away from the starting point. [Hint. Manish will take either 6 steps forward and 5 backward or 5 steps forward and 6 backward]

Answers

1. $\dfrac{11}{64}$ 2. (i) 0.1085, (ii) 0.9997, (iii) 0.8858 3. $\dfrac{53}{3125}$

4. (i) 0.2301 (ii) 0.3412 (iii) 0.2833 5. (i) 0.02579 (ii) 1.024×10^{-7}

6. (i) $\frac{81}{256}$ (ii) $\frac{1}{256}$ (iii) $\frac{175}{256}$ (iv) $\frac{27}{128}$

7. $\frac{2}{5}\left(\frac{5}{6}\right)^9$

8. $100\,(.432 + 0.568)^5$

9. $\left(\frac{1}{5}+\frac{4}{5}\right)^5$

10. $\frac{11}{32}$

11. (i) 250, (ii) 250, (iii) 25, (iv) 400

12. (i) 12 nearly (ii) 17 nearly

13. $80\,(0.7825+0.2175)^{10}$

14. $\frac{1}{5}$

15. (i) $\left(\frac{19}{20}\right)^5$ (ii) $\frac{6}{5}\left(\frac{19}{20}\right)^4$ (iii) $1-\frac{6}{5}\left(\frac{19}{20}\right)^4$ (iv) $1-\left(\frac{19}{20}\right)^5$

16. (i) 0.246 (ii) 0.345

17. (i) $\left(\frac{1}{4}\right)^5$ (ii) $90\left(\frac{1}{4}\right)^5$ (iii) $\left(\frac{3}{4}\right)^5$

18. (a) 40 (b) 6

19. ${}^{32}C_r\left(\frac{1}{2}\right)^r\left(\frac{1}{2}\right)^{32-r}$; $r = 0, 1, \ldots, 32$

20. 0.36787

4.9 Poisson Distribution

This is also a discrete probability distribution and is useful in such cases where the value of p is very small and the value of n is very large. In such cases the binomial distribution does not give appropriate theoretical frequencies. The Poisson distribution in such situations has been found to be quite suitable. Poisson distribution is a limiting form of binomial distribution as n moves towards infinity and p moves towards zero but np or mean remains constant and finite.

This distribution is used very widely both in physical sciences as well as social sciences. This distribution studies the probabilities of rare events. Rare events are common in all sciences. In physics the emission of radioactive substance is a rare event. In biology, the number of bacteria in a unit may be very small. The number of defective articles produced by a high quality machine may be very small. The number of accidental deaths by falling from a roof would again be a small number. These phenomena are rare in the sense that the probabilities of their happening is very small. In fact we do not know the probabilities of their not happening. For example, we do not know the number of people who did not die by accidentally falling from a roof. All we know is the number of a few people who died in this manner. In all such cases the Poisson distribution is used to give theoretical or expected values.

Conditions of Poisson Distribution

(*i*) The variable is discrete.

(*ii*) The number of trials, that is, n is very large.

(*iii*) The probability of success, that is, p is very small.

(*iv*) The probability of success in each trial is constant.

(*v*) np is constant and finite.

Form of Poisson Distribution

(*i*) It is a discrete distribution.

(*ii*) It has a single parameter – the mean of the distribution – denoted by m.

(*iii*) The probability of exactly 0, 1, 2, 3, ..., n successes is found by the successive term of the expansion

$$e^{-\lambda}\left(1+\lambda+\frac{\lambda^2}{2!}+\frac{\lambda^3}{3!}\right)+....+\frac{\lambda^r}{r!}+....$$

Where e = 2.71828

When x = 0, probability of exactly zero success

$$P(0)=\frac{e^{-\lambda}\lambda^0}{0!}=e^{-\lambda}$$

Similarly, probability of 1 success

$$P(1)=\frac{e^{-\lambda}\lambda^1}{1!}=e^{-\lambda}\lambda$$

Probability of 2 successes

$$P(2)=\frac{e^{-\lambda}\lambda^2}{2!}$$

Probability of r successes

$$\boxed{\mathbf{P(r)}=\frac{\mathbf{e^{-\lambda}\lambda^r}}{\mathbf{Lr}}}\ (\mathbf{r=0,1,2,3....})$$

Constants of Poisson Distribution

1. Mean of Poisson distribution is m

Mean = $\sum rp(r)$

$$=0xe^{-\lambda}+(\lambda xe^{-\lambda})+\left(2\frac{\lambda^2}{2!}.xe^{-\lambda}\right)+\left(3\frac{\lambda^3}{3!}xe^{-\lambda}\right)+...$$

$$=\lambda xe^{-\lambda}\left[1+\lambda+\frac{\lambda^2}{2!}+\frac{\lambda^3}{3!}+....\right]$$

$$= (\lambda x e^{-\lambda}) r^{\lambda} = \lambda e^{-\lambda+\lambda} = \lambda e^{0} = 0 = \lambda$$

2. Variance of Poisson distribution is also m

   Thus Mean = Variance = np λ, $\sigma = \sqrt{\lambda} = np$

3. The moments (about mean) of the Poisson distribution are

   $\mu_1 = 0$

   $\mu_2 =$ variance $= \lambda$

   $\mu_3 = \lambda$

   $\mu_4 = \lambda + 3\lambda^2$

$$\beta_1 = \frac{\mu_3^2}{\mu_2^3} = \frac{\lambda^2}{\lambda^3} = \frac{1}{\lambda}$$

$$\beta_2 = \frac{\mu_4}{\mu_2^2} = \frac{\lambda + 3\lambda^2}{\lambda^2} = +\frac{1}{\lambda}$$

$$\gamma_1 = \sqrt{\beta_1} = \frac{1}{\sqrt{\lambda}}$$

$$\gamma_1 = \beta_2 - 3 = 3 + \frac{1}{\lambda} - 3 = \frac{1}{\lambda}$$

Fitting of a Poisson Distribution

Finding out the theoretical values in a Poisson distribution is very easy. We have to first find out the value of mean and calculate the frequency of 0 success. Once this is done the other frequencies can be obtained very easily as shown below

When r = 0

$P(0) = e^{-m}$

If this probability is multiplied by N (total number of observations) we get the frequency for 0 success

Frequency of 0 success $= N(P_0) = Ne^{-\lambda}$

Frequency of 1 success $= N(P_1) = N(P_0) \times \frac{\lambda}{1}$

Frequency of 2 success $= N(P_2) = N(P_1) \times \frac{\lambda}{2}$

Frequency of 3 success $= N(P_3) = N(P_2) \times \frac{\lambda}{3}$

Frequency of *r* success $= N(P_r) = N(P_{r-1}) \times \frac{\lambda}{r}$

For Poison distribution, $P(r) = \dfrac{e^{-\lambda'}}{r!}$ and $P(r+1) = \dfrac{e^{-\lambda'}\lambda^{r+1}}{(r+1)!}$

$$\frac{P(r+1)}{P(r)} = \frac{\lambda r!}{(r+1)!} = \frac{\lambda}{r+1}$$

Recurrence Relationship

$$\boxed{P(r+1) = \frac{\lambda}{r+1} P(r)}, r = 0,1,2,3,......$$

This is called the recurrence or recursion formula for the Poisson for distribution.

For the Poisson distribution, $P(r) = \dfrac{e^{-x}\lambda^r}{r!}$

$$\text{Mean } \mu = \sum_{r=0}^{\infty} \text{Pr}\, P(r) = \sum_{r=0}^{\infty} \text{r}\frac{e^{-x}\lambda^r}{r!}$$

$$= e^{-\lambda}\sum_{r=0}^{\infty}\frac{\lambda^r}{(r-1)!} = e^{-\lambda}\left(\lambda + \frac{\lambda^2}{1!} + \frac{\lambda^3}{2!} + ...\right)$$

$$= \lambda e^{-\lambda}\left(1 + \frac{\lambda}{1!} + \frac{\lambda^2}{2!} + ...\right) = \lambda e^{-\lambda}.e^{\lambda} = \lambda$$

Thus, the mean of the Poisson distribution is equal to the parameter λ.

$$\text{Variance } \sigma^2 = \sum_{r=0}^{\infty} r^2 P(r) - \mu^2 = \sum_{r=0}^{\infty} r^2.\frac{\lambda^r e^{-\lambda}}{r!} - \lambda^2 = e^{-\lambda}\sum_{r=0}^{\infty}\frac{r^2\lambda^r}{r!} - \lambda^2$$

$$= e^{-\lambda}\left[\frac{1^2.\lambda}{1!} + \frac{2^2.\lambda^2}{2!} + \frac{3^2.\lambda^3}{3!} + \frac{4^2.\lambda^4}{4!} + ...\right] - \lambda^2$$

$$= \lambda e^{-\lambda}\left[1 + \frac{2\lambda^2}{1!} + \frac{3\lambda^2}{2!} + \frac{4\lambda^2}{3!} + ...\right] - \lambda^2$$

$$= \lambda e^{-\lambda}\left[1 + \frac{(1+1)\lambda}{1!} + \frac{(1+2)\lambda^2}{2!} + \frac{(1+3)\lambda^3}{3!} + ...\right] - \lambda^2$$

$$= \lambda e^{-\lambda}\left[\left(1 + \frac{\lambda}{1!} + \frac{\lambda^2}{2!} + \frac{\lambda^3}{3!} + ...\right) + \left(\frac{\lambda}{1!} + \frac{2\lambda^2}{2!} + \frac{3\lambda^3}{3!} + ...\right)\right] - \lambda^2$$

$$= \lambda e^{-\lambda}\left[e^{\lambda} + \lambda\left(1 + \frac{\lambda}{1!} + \frac{\lambda^2}{2!} + ...\right)\right] - \lambda^2$$

$$= \lambda e^{-\lambda}[e^{\lambda} + \lambda e^{\lambda}] - \lambda^2 = \lambda e^{-\lambda}.e^{\lambda}(1+\lambda) - \lambda^2 = \lambda(1+\lambda) - \lambda^2 = \lambda$$

Hence, the variance of the Poisson distribution is also λ.

Thus, the mean and the variance of the Poisson distribution are each equal to the parameter λ.

Note: The mean and the variance of the Poisson distribution can also be derived from those of the binomial distribution in the limiting case when $n \to \infty, p \to 0$ and $np = \lambda$

Mean of binomial distribution is *np*.

$\therefore$ Mean of Poisson distribution $\underset{n\to\infty}{Lt}\, np = \underset{n\to\infty}{Lt}\, ,\lambda = \lambda$

Variance of binomial distribution is $npq = np\ (1 - p)$

$\therefore$ Variance of Poisson distribution $\underset{n\to\infty}{Lt}\, np(1-p) = \underset{n\to\infty}{Lt}\, \lambda\left(1 - \frac{\lambda}{n}\right) = \lambda$

Applications of Poisson distribution **(LU 2006)**

This distribution is applied to problems concerning :

(*i*) Arrival pattern of defective vehicles in a workshop,

(*ii*) Patients in a hospital

(*iii*) Telephone calls

(*iv*) Demand pattern for certain spare parts.

(*v*) No. of fragments from a shell hitting a target.

(*vi*) Emission of radioactive (a) particles.

(*vii*) No. of printing mistakes at each page of the book.

(*viii*) No. of air accidents in some time.

(*ix*) No, of deaths in a district by rare disease.

(*x*) No, of cars passing through a street in some time.

Example 1: *If the variance of the Poisson distribution is* 2, *find the probabilities for* 1, 2, 3, 4 *from the recurrence relation of the Poisson distribution. Also find* $P(x \geq 4)$.

(U.P.T.U. 2001)

Solution: λ, the parameter of Poisson distribution = Variance = 2

Recurrence relation for the Poisson distribution is

$$P(r+1) = \frac{\lambda}{r+1}P(r) = \frac{2}{r+1}P(r) \qquad ...(1)$$

Now $$P(r) = \frac{e^{-\lambda}\lambda^r}{r!} \Rightarrow P(0) = \frac{e^{-2}}{0!} = e^{-2} = 0.1353$$

Putting $r = 0,1,2,3$ in (1), we get

$$P(1) = 2P(0) = 2 \times .1353 = .2706; \qquad P(2) = \frac{2}{2}P(1) = .2706$$

$$P(3) = \frac{2}{3}P(2) = \frac{2}{3} \times .2706 = .1804; \qquad P(4) = \frac{2}{4}P(3) = \frac{1}{2} \times .1804 = .0902.$$

Now, $P(x \geq 4) = 1 - [P(0) + P(1) + P(2) + P(3)]$

$$= 1 - [.1353 + .2706 + .2706 + .1804] = .1431.$$

Example-2: *Assume that the probability of an individual coalminer being killed in a mine accident during a year is* $\frac{1}{2400}$. *Use Poisson's distribution to calculate the probability that in a mine employing* 200 *miners theere will be at least one fatal accident in a year.*

Solution: Here, $p = \frac{1}{2400}, n = 200;$ $\quad \therefore \lambda = np = \frac{200}{2400} = \frac{1}{12} = .083$

$$P(r) = \frac{\lambda^r e^{-\lambda}}{r!} = \frac{(.083)^r e^{0.083}}{r!}$$

P(at least one fatal accident) = 1 – P (no fatal accident)

$$= 1 - P(0) = 1 - \frac{(.083)^0 e^{-0.083}}{0!} = 1 - 092 = .08.$$

Example 3: *(i) Data was collected over a period of 10 years, showing number of deaths from horse kicks in each of the 200 army corps. The distribution of deaths was as follows :*

No. of deaths :	0	1	2	3	4	Total
Frequency :	109	65	22	3	1	200

Fit a Poisson distribution to the data and calculate the theoretical frequencies :

(ii) Fit a Poisson distribution to the following data and calculate theoretical frequencies

Deaths :	0	1	2	3	4
Frequencies :	122	60	15	2	1

Given that $e^{-0.5} = 0.61$. **(U.P.T.U. Special Exam. 2001, U.P.T.U. 2003)**

Solution: (*i*) Mean of given distribution $= \frac{\Sigma fx}{\Sigma f} = \frac{65 + 44 + 9 + 4}{200} = \frac{122}{200} = 0.61$

This is the parameter (X) of the Poisson distribution.

$\therefore$ Required Poisson distribution is $N.\frac{e^{-\lambda}.\lambda^r}{r!}$. $\qquad$ where $N = \Sigma f = 200$

$$= 200.e^{-0.61}\frac{(0.61)^r}{r!} = 108.7 \times \frac{(0.61)^r}{r!}.$$

r	$N.P(r)$	*Theoretical Frequency*
0	108.7	109
1	$108.7 \times 0.61 = 66.3$	66
2	$108.7 \times \frac{(0.61)^2}{2!} = 20.2$	20
3	$108.7 \times \frac{(0.61)^3}{3!} = 4.1$	4
4	$108.7 \times \frac{(0.61)^4}{4!} = 0.7$	1
		Total = 200

(ii) Mean of given distribution $= \frac{\Sigma fx}{\Sigma f}$

$$\Rightarrow \qquad \lambda = \frac{60+30+6+4}{200} = 0.5$$

Required Poisson Distribution $= N\frac{e^{-\lambda}.\lambda^r}{r!}$ [N = 200]

$$= 200e^{-0.5}\frac{(.5)^r}{r!} = 122\frac{(.5)^r}{r!}$$

r	$N.P(r)$	*Theoretical Frequency*
0	122	122
1	$122 \times 0.5 = 61$	61
2	$122 \times \frac{(.5)^2}{2!} = 15.25$	15
3	$122 \times \frac{(.5)^3}{3!} = 2.54$	3
4	$122 \times \frac{(.5)^4}{4!} = 0.3177$	0

Example 4: *Using Poisson distribution, find the probability that the ace of spades will be drawn from a pack of well-shuffled cards at least once in* 104 *consecutive trials. (Given* : $e^{-2} = 0.136$ **(Q. Bank UP T.U. 2001)**

Solution: $$p = \frac{1}{52}, n = 104$$

$$\therefore \quad \lambda = np = 104 \times \frac{1}{52} = 2$$

Prob. (at least once) $= P(r \geq 1) = 1 - P(0)$

$$= 1 - \frac{e^{-\lambda}.\lambda^0}{0!} = 1 - e^{-2} = 1 - 0.135335 = 0.8647$$

Example 5: *A car-hire firm has two cars, which it hires out day by day. The number of demands for a car on each day is distributed as a Poisson distribution with mean 1.5. Calculate the proportion of days on which neither car is used and the proportion of days on which some demand is refused.* ($e^{-1.5}$ *= 0.2231)* **(Q. Bank U.P.T.U. 2001)**

Solution: Since the number of demands for a car is distributed as a Poisson distribution with mean $\lambda = 1.5$.

$\therefore$ Proportion of days on which neither car is used

= Probability of there being no demand for the car

$$= \frac{\lambda^0 e^{-\lambda}}{0!} = e^{-1.5} = 0.2231$$

Proportion of days on which some demand is refused

= probability for the number of demands to be more than two

$$= 1 - P(x \leq 2) = 1 - \left(e^{-\lambda} + \frac{\lambda e^{-\lambda}}{1!} + \frac{\lambda^2 e^{-\lambda}}{2!} \right)$$

$$= 1 - e^{-1.5}\left(1 + 1.5 + \frac{(1.5)^2}{2}\right) = 1 - 0.2231(1 + 1.5 + 1.125)$$

$$= 1 - 0.2231 \times 3.625 = 1 - 0.8087375 = 0.1912625.$$

Example 6: *Six coins are tossed* 6400 *times. Using the Poisson distribution, determine the approximate probability of getting six heads x times.* **[U.P.T.U. (CO.) 2008]**

Solution: Probability of getting one head with one coin $= \frac{1}{2}$.

$\therefore$ The probability of getting six heads with six coins $= \left(\frac{1}{2}\right)^6 = \frac{1}{64}$

∴ Average number of six heads with six coins in 6400 throws $= np = 6400 \times \frac{1}{64} = 100$

∴ The mean of the Poisson distribution = 100.

Approximate probability of getting six heads x times when the distribution is Poisson

$$\frac{\lambda^x e^{-\lambda}}{x!} = \frac{(100)^x . e^{-100}}{x!}$$

Example 7: *The no. of arrivals of customers during any day follows Poisson distribution with a mean of 5. What is the probability that the total no. of customers on two days selected at random is less than 2. (Given : e^{-10}.- 4.54×10^{-5})*

Solution: $\lambda = 5$

Arrival of Customers

I day	II day	Total
0	0	0
0	1	1
1	0	1

Reqd. probability $= P(0)P(0) + P(0)P(1) + P(1)P(0)$

$$= \frac{e^{-5}.5^0}{0!}.\frac{e^{-5}.5^0}{0!} + \frac{e^{-5}.5^0}{0!}.\frac{e^{-5}.5^1}{1!} + \frac{e^{-5}.5^1}{1!}.\frac{e^{-5}.5^0}{0!}$$

$$= e^{-10} + 2.5.e^{-10} = 11e^{-10} = 11 \times 4.54 \times 10^{-5}$$

$$= 4.994 \times 10^{-4}.$$

Example 8: *Suppose the number of telephone calls on an operator received from* 9: 00 *to* 9. 05 *follow a Poisson distribution with a mean* 3 *Find the probability that*

(i) The operator will receive no calls in that time interval tomorrow.

(ii) In the next three days, the operator will receive a total of 1 call in that time interval.

(Given : e^{-3}= 0.04978) **(Q. Bank U.P.T.U. 2001)**

Solution: Here $\lambda = 3$

(i) $P(0) = \frac{e^{-\lambda}.\lambda^0}{0!} = e^{-3} = 0.04978$

(ii) Reqd. probability = P(0) P(0) P(1) + P(0) P(1) P(0) + P(1) P(0) P(0)

$$= 3\left\{\frac{e^{-\lambda}.\lambda^0}{0!}\right\}^2 \frac{e^{-\lambda}.\lambda^1}{1!} = 9(e^{-3})^3 = 0.00111.$$

Example 9: *If the probabilities of a bad reaction from a certain injection is* 0.0002, *determine the chance that out of* 1000 *individuals more than two will get a bad reaction.*

(Q. Bank U.P.T.U. 2001)

Solution: Here, $p = 0.0002, \quad n = 1000$

$$\therefore \quad \lambda = np = 1000 \times .0002 = 0.2.$$

Since the prob. of bad reaction is very small and no. of trials is very high, we use Poisson distribution here.

The prob. that out of 100 individuals, more than 2 will get a bad reaction is

$$= p(r > 2) = 1 - P(r < 2)$$

$$= 1 - [P(0) + P(1) + P(2)] \quad ...(1)$$

Now, $$P(0) = \frac{e^{-2}(.2)^0}{0} = .8187 \quad \text{(Here } r = 0)$$

$$P(1) = \frac{e^{-2}(.2)^1}{1} = .1637 \quad \text{(Here } r = 1)$$

and $$P(2) = \frac{e^{-2}(.2)^2}{2} = .0164 \quad \text{(Here } r = 2)$$

$\therefore$ From (1),

Reqd. probability = 1 - [.8187 + .1637 + .0164] = .0012.

Example 10: *In a certain factory turning out razor blades, there is a small chance of* 0.002 *for any blade to be defective. The blades are supplied in packets of* 10. *Calculate the approximate number of packets containing no defective, one defective and two defective blades in a consignment of* 10,000 *packets. (Given :* $e^{0.02} = 0.9802$) **(U.P.T.U. 2002, 2009)**

Solution: $p(\text{defective}) = 0.002$

$n = 10$ (no. of blades in a packet)

$$\therefore \quad \lambda = np = 10 \times 0.002 = 0.02$$

No of packets in the consignment, N = 10,000.

(i) Probability of having no defective $= P(0) = \dfrac{e^{-02}(.02)^0}{0!} = 0.9802$ [Here $r = 0$]

Approximate no. of packets having zero defective in the consignment = 0.9802 ×10000

= 9802

(ii) Probability of having one defective $= P(1) = \dfrac{e^{-02}(.02)^1}{1!} = 0.9802 \times .02 = 0.019604$

Approximate no. of packet having two defectives in the consignment

$= 0.000196 \times 10000 = 196.$

(iii) Probability of having one defective blades

$$= P(2) = \frac{e^{-02}(.02)^2}{2!} = \frac{(0.980198)\times(.0004)}{2} = 0.000196.$$

$\therefore$ Approximate no. of packet having two defectives in the consignment

$= 0.000196 \times 10000 = 196 = 2.$

Example 11: *(a) The number of accidents in a year involving taxi drivers in a city follows a Poisson distribution with mean equal to 3. Out of 1000 taxi drivers, find approximately the number of drivers with (i) no accidents (ii) more than 3 accidents in a year.*

(Q. Bank U.P.T.U. 2001)

(b) The distribution of the number of road accidents per day in a city is Poisson with mean 4 Find the number of days out of 100 days when there will be

(i) no accident *(ii) at least 2 accidents*

(iii) at most 3 accidents *(iv) between 2 and 5 accidents.*

(U.P.T.U. 2005)

Solution: (a) Mean $\lambda = 3$

No. of taxi drivers, N = 1000.

(i) Probability that there will be no accident in a year $= P(0) = \frac{e^{-3}(3)^0}{0!} = e^{-3} = 0.4978.$

Hence Reqd. no. of taxi drivers = 1000 × .04978 = 49.78 = 50 (approximately).

(ii) Probability that there will be more than 3 accidents in a year

$$= P(r > 3) = 1 - P(r \leq 3) = 1 - [P(0) + P(1) + P(2) + P(3)]$$

$$= 1 - \left[\frac{e^{-3}(3)^0}{0!} + \frac{e^{-3}(3)^1}{1!} + \frac{e^{-3}(3)^2}{2!} + \frac{e^{-3}(3)^3}{3!}\right]$$

$$= 1 - e^{-3}[1 + 3 + 4.5 + 4.5] = 1 - (13 \times .04978) = 0.35276.$$

Hence Reqd. no. of taxi drivers = 1000 × .35276.76 = 353 (app.).

Answer (b) Mean $\lambda = 4$, No. of days N = 100

I give

(i) $$P(r = 0) = \frac{e^{-\lambda}\lambda^0}{0!} = e^{-4} = 0.01831$$

$\therefore$ Reqd. no. of days = $NP(r = 0)$

= 100 × .01831 = 1.831 = 2

(ii) $$P(r \geq 2) = 1 - P(r < 2) = 1 - [P(r = 0) + P(r = 1)]$$

$$= 1 - \left[e^{-4} + \frac{e^{-4}(4)}{1!} \right] = 1 - 5e^{-4} = .90842$$

$\therefore$ Reqd. no. of days $= NP(r \geq 2) = 100 \times .90842 = 90.842 = 91$

(iii) $P(r \leq 3) = P(r = 0) + P(r = 1) + P(r = 2) + P(r = 3)$

$$= \frac{e^{-4}(4)^0}{0!} + \frac{e^{-4}(4)^1}{1!} + \frac{e^{-4}(4)^2}{2!} + \frac{e^{-4}(4)^3}{3!}$$

$$= e^{-4} + 4e^{-4} + 8e^{-4} + \frac{64}{6}e^{-4} = .43347$$

reqd. no. of days $= N.\text{P}(r \leq 3) = 100 \times .43347 = 43.347 = 43$

(iv) $P(2 > r < 5) = P(r = 3) + P(r = 4)$

$$= \frac{e^{-4}(4)^3}{3!} + \frac{e^{-4}(4)^4}{4!} = \left(\frac{64}{6} + \frac{256}{24} \right) e^{-4} = 0.3907$$

$$= 100 \times 0.3907 = 39.07 = 39.$$

$\therefore$ Reqd. no. of days $N.P(2 < r < 5)$

Example 12: *The frequency of accidents per shift in a factory is shown in the following table :*

Accident per shift	*Frequency*
0	192
1	100
2	24
3	3
4	1
Total	320

Calculate the mean number of accidents per shift. Fit a Poisson distribution and calculate theoretical frequencies. **(U.P.T.U. 2004)**

Solution: Mean no. of accidents per shift

$$\bar{x} = \lambda = \frac{\Sigma fx}{\Sigma f} = \frac{100 + 48 + 9 + 4}{320} = .5031$$

$\therefore$ Required Poisson distribution

$$= N.\frac{e^{-\lambda}.\lambda^r}{r!} = 320.\frac{e^{-5031}(.5031)^r}{r!} = \frac{(193.48)(.5031)^r}{r!}$$

r	$N.P(r)$	*Theoretical frequencies*
0	193.48	193
1	97.34	97
2	24.48	24
3	4.10	4
4	0.51	1

Example 13. *Wireless sets are manufactured with 25 solders joints each, on the average 1 joint in 500 is defective. How many sets can be expected to be free from defective joints in a consignment of 10000 sets ?* **(Q. Bank U.P.T.U. 2001)**

Solution: $$p=\frac{1}{500}, n=25$$

$$\therefore \quad \lambda = np = 25\times\frac{1}{500}=\frac{1}{20}=.05$$

No. of sets in a consignment, N = 10000

Probability of having no defective joint = $P(r = 0) = \dfrac{e^{-.05}(.05)^0}{0!}=0.9512.$

$\therefore$ The expected no. of sets free from defective joints = 0.9512 x 10000 = 9512.

Example 14. *A manufacturer knows that the condensors he makes contain on an average 1% of defectives. He packs them in boxes of 100. What, is the probability that a box picked at random will contain 4 or more faulty condensors ?*

Solution: $p = 0.01$, $n= 100$

$$\lambda = np = 1$$

$$P(r)=\frac{e^{-\lambda}\lambda^r}{r!}=\frac{e^{-1}1^r}{r!}=\frac{e^{-1}}{r!}$$

P(4 or more faulty condensers) = (4) + P(5) + ...+ P(1000)

$$=1-\left[\frac{e^{-1}}{0!}+\frac{e^{-1}}{1!}+\frac{e^{-1}}{2!}+\frac{e^{-1}}{3!}+\right]$$

$$=1-e^{-1}\left[1+1+\frac{1}{2}+\frac{1}{6}\right]=1-\frac{8}{3e}=1-0.938=0.019.$$

Example 15. *Suppose that a book of* 600 *pages contains* 40 *printing mistakes. Assume that these errors are randomly distributed throughout the book and r, the number of errors per page has a Poisson distribution. What is the probability that* 10 *pages selected at. random will be free from errors ?*

Solution: $p=\frac{40}{600}=\frac{1}{15}, n=10$

$$\lambda=np=10\left(\frac{1}{15}\right)=\frac{2}{3}$$

$$P(r)=\frac{e^{-\lambda}\lambda^r}{r!}=\frac{e^{-2/3}(2/3)^r}{r!}$$

$$P(0)=\frac{e^{-2/3}(2/3)^0}{0!}=e^{2/3}=0.51$$

Example 16. An *insurance company finds that* 0.005% *of the population dies from a certain kind of accident each year What is the probability that the company must pay off no more than* 3 *of* 10,000 *insured risks against such incident in a given year ?* **(Q. Bank U.P.T.U. 2001)**

Solution: $p=\frac{.005}{100}=.00005,\quad n=10000$

$\therefore$ $\lambda=np=10000\times .00005=0.5$

Reqd. Probability $=1-P(r\le 3)=1-[P(0)+P(1)+P(2)+P(3)]$

$$=1-\left[\frac{e^{-.5}(.5)^0}{0!}+\frac{e^{-.5}(.5)^1}{1!}+\frac{e^{-.5}(.5)^2}{2!}+\frac{e^{-.5}(.5)^3}{3!}\right]$$

$$=1-e^{-5}[1+.5+.125+.021]=1-(0.6065\times 1.646)$$

$$=1-.9984=.0016.$$

Example 17: *For a Poisson distribution with mean m, show that*

$$\mu_{r+1}=mr\mu_{r-1}+m\frac{d\mu_r}{dm}$$

where, $\mu_r=\sum_{x=0}^{\infty}(x-m)^r\frac{e^{-m}.m^x}{x!}.$

Solution: $\mu_r=\sum_{x=0}^{\infty}(x-m)^r.\frac{e^{-m}.m^x}{x!}$

$$\frac{d\mu_r}{dm}=\sum_{x=0}^{\infty}\left[\frac{-e^{-m}}{x!}.m^x(x-m)^r+\frac{e^{-m}}{x!}\{xm^{x-1}(x-m)^r-r(x-m)^{r-1}.m^x\}\right]$$

$$\Rightarrow\quad m\frac{d\mu_r}{dm}=\sum_{x=0}^{\infty}\frac{-e^{-m}}{x!}m^x(x-m)^{r+1}-rm\sum_{x=0}^{\infty}\frac{-e^{-m}}{x!}m^x(x-m)^{r-1}=\mu_{r+1}-rm\mu_{r-1}$$

$$\Rightarrow\quad \mu_{r+1}=m\frac{d\mu_r}{dm}+mr\mu_{r-1}$$

Example 18: *A Poisson distribution has a double mode at x = 3 and x = 4. What is the probability that x will have one or the other of these two values.* **[U.P.T.U. (C.O.) 2008]**

Solution: Since 2 modes are given when λ is an integer, modes are $\lambda - 1$ and λ.

$$\therefore \quad \lambda - 1 = 3 \Rightarrow \lambda = 4$$

$$\text{Probability (when } r = 3) = \frac{e^{-4}(4)^3}{3!}$$

$$\text{Probability (when } r = 4) = \frac{e^{-4}(4)^4}{4!}$$

$$\therefore \quad \text{Required Probability} = P(r = 3 \text{ or } 4) = P(r = 3) + P(r = 4)$$

$$= \frac{e^{-4}(4)^3}{3!} + \frac{e^{-4}(4)^4}{4!} + \frac{64}{3}e^{-4} = .39073$$

Exercise 4.2

1. If X is a Poisson variate such that P(X = 2) = 9P(x = 4) + 90P (X = 6), and the standard deviation. (A.U.)
2. If a random variable has a Poisson distribution such that P(1) = P(2), find
   (i) mean of the distribution (ii) P(4).
3. Suppose that X has a Poisson distribution. If $P(x = 2) = \frac{2}{3}P(X = 1)$ find, $(i) P(X = 0) (ii) P(X = 3)$. (L.U.)
4. A certain screw making machine produces on average 2 defective screws out of 100, and packs them in boxes of 500. Find the probability that a box contains 15 defective screws.
5. The incidence of occupational disease in an industry is such that the workmen have a 10% chance of suffering from it. What is the probability that in a group of 7, five or more will suffer from it ?
6. Suppose a book of 585 pages contains 43 typographical errors. If these errors are randomly distributed throughout the book, what is the probability that 10 pages, selected at random, will be free from errors ?
7. A manufacturer of cotter pins knows that 5% of his product is defective. If he sells cotter pins in boxes of 100 and guarantee that not more than 10 pins will be defective, what is the approximate prob. that a box will fail to meet the guaranteed quality ?
8. Records show that the probability is 0.00002 that a car will have a flat tyre while driving over a certain bridge. Use Poisson distribution to find the probability that among 20,000 cars driven over the bridge, not more than one will have a flat tyre.
9. Between the hours of 2 and 4 P M., the average no. of phone calls per minute coming into the switch board of a company is 2.5. Find the probability that during a particular minute, there will be no phone call at all [Given : $e^{-2} = 0.13534$ and $e^{-0.5} = 0.60650$.)

10. Fit a Poisson distribution to the following data given the number of yeast cells per square for 400 squares :

No. of cells per sq.	0	1	2	3	4	5	6	7	8	9	10
No. of squares	103	143	98	42	8	4	2	0	0	0	0

If is given that $e^{-1.3225} = 0.2665$.

11. The experience shows that 4 industrial accidents occur in a plant on an average per month. Calculate the probabilities of less than 3 accidents in a certain month. Use Poisson distribution. (Given $e^{-4} = 0.01832$) **(U.P.T.U. 2010)**

Answer

1. 1 2. $(i) 2) ii) \frac{2}{3e^2}$ 3. $(i) e^{-(4/3)} (ii) \frac{32}{81} e^{-(4/3)}$ 4. 0.0355. 5. 0.0008

6. 0.4795 7. 0.0136875 8. 0.938 9. 0.08208

10. Theoretical frequencies are 107, 141, 93, 41, 14, 4, 1, 0, 0, 0, 0.

4.10 Normal Distribution

Normal distribution is a continuous probability distribution and is most important of all the theoretical distributions. Many physical measurements and natural phenomena have observed frequency distributions which very closely resemble the normal distribution. These include measurements of heights and weights of both persons and things, characteristics like IQ, etc. A more important reason for the importance of this distribution lies in the fact that a theoretical property of the sample mean allows us to use the normal distribution to find out the probabilities of various sample results.

This distribution is extremely useful in the analysis of data concerning economic and business problems. This distribution plays a basic role in situations where inferences are made regarding the value of the population mean when only the sample mean can be calculated directly. Such situations are very common in the field of social sciences.

The normal distribution is a limiting case of binomial distribution if

(*i*) The number of trials or the value of n is very large (nearly infinity)

(*ii*) If neither p nor q is very small.

If p and q are nearly equal, the normal distribution is very close to binomial distribution. The normal distribution can be regarded as a limiting case of Poisson distribution if the value of mean, that is, m is very large (nearly infinity).

Importance of Normal Curve

1. If a random sample is taken from any universe then as the sample size increases the mean of the sample approaches the normal distribution (with mean μ and standard

deviation σ/n). this is the central limit theorem. This property of normal distribution is very important and it enables us to draw inferences about the universe by making sample studies. According to this theorem we can estimate the upper and lower limits within which a value in the universe would lie, by conducting sample studies.

2. Even when the assumptions of a normal distribution are not satisfied, the results given by a normal distribution study, in many cases, are found to be highly satisfactory. However, theoretically the results hold good under the assumption that the properties of the normal distribution are applicable to the problem under study.
3. There are many mathematical properties possessed by this distribution which make its application possible in a wide variety of situations and for making varied types of studies.
4. It is very useful in statistical quality control where the control limits are set by using this distribution.

Properties of Normal Distribution

1. The normal curve is symmetrical about the mean, that is, there is no skewness in it.
2. The mean, median and mode have the same value.
3. The height of the normal curve is maximum at the mean value. ***This ordinate divides the curve into two equal and identical parts***.
4. Since the curve is symmetrical, the first and third quartiles are equidistant from the median.
5. Since there is only one point of maximum frequency, the normal distribution is uni-modal.
6. The mean deviation is 0.7979 of the standard deviation.
7. Semi-inter-quartile range is equal to the probable error which is 0.6745 of standard deviation.
8. The points of inflection (the points at which the curve changes direction) are each at a distance of one standard deviation from the mean.
9. The curve is asymptotic to the base line. It continues to approach but never touches the base line.
10. The various ordinates at different distances from mean ordinate (in terms of standard deviation) stand in a fixed proportion to the height of the mean ordinate. Thus the height of an ordinate at σ (one standard deviation) distance on either side of the mean ordinate is 60.653% of the height of the mean ordinate.
11. The most important relationship in the normal curve is the area relationship. Since the ordinate at a given σ distance from the mean has always the same relationship with the

mean ordinate, it follows that the area of the curve enclosed between the mean ordinate and an ordinate at σ distance from mean would always be the same proportion of the total area of the curve. Thus, the area enclosed between the mean ordinate and an ordinate at a distance of one standard deviation (σ) from the mean is always 34.134% of the total area of the curve. It means that the area enclosed between the two ordinates at σ distance from mean on either side would always be 68.268% of the total area. Similarly the area between the two ordinates at 2σ distance from mean on either side would be 95.45% of the total area. Ordinates at 3σ distance from mean on either side would enclose 99.73% of the total area.

Area of the Normal Curve between Mean Ordinate and the Ordinates at various Sigma Distances from the Mean as percentage of the Total Area

Distance from the Mean Ordinate	Percentage of Total Area	
	at one side of mean	at both sides of mean
0.5σ	19.146	38.292
$1.0\,\sigma$	34.134	68.268
$1.5\,\sigma$	43.319	86.638
$1.96\,\sigma$	47.500	95.000
$2.0\,\sigma$	47.725	95.450
$2.5\,\sigma$	49.379	98.758
$2.5758\,\sigma$	49.500	99.000
$3.0\,\sigma$	49.865	99.730

We have specifically mentioned the area enclosed between the ordinates at 1.96σ distance, 2.578σ distance and 3σ distance because in various tests of significance these figures are most commonly used.

Constants of Normal Distribution

(*i*) The mean of the normal distribution is X and the standard deviation is σ.

(*ii*) $\mu_2 = \sigma^2$

$\mu_3 = 0$

$\mu_3 = 3\sigma^4$

(*iii*) $\beta_1 = \frac{\mu_3^2}{\mu_2^3} = 0$ (normal distribution has no skewness)

(*iv*) $\beta_1 = \frac{\mu_4}{\mu_2^2} = \frac{3\sigma^4}{\sigma^4} = 3$ (normal distribution has no kurtosis)

The Standard Normal Curve

A normal curve in which mean is zero and standard deviation is unity is known as the standard normal curve. Its utility is very great because curves with mean X and standard deviation σ can be converted into a standard normal curve by change of origin and scale. This becomes necessary as otherwise in different distributions with different values of mean and standard deviation, it would be very difficult to find out the area between various ordinates. Once they are converted into standard normal curve, this problem is solved.

In the original scale the mean and standard deviation are X and σ but in the new scale which is called the z-scale, the mean is zero and standard deviation is unity. This process of changing the X-scale into z-scale is called z-transformation. z is called the standard normal variate and is given by

$$z = \frac{X - \bar{X}}{\sigma}$$

Where X is the mean and σ is the standard deviation of the given normal distribution, X is the observed value at which we want to find the value of z.

Mean and Variance of Normal distribution

1. The A.M. of a continuous distribution $f(x)$ is given by

$$A.M.(\bar{x}) = \frac{\int_{-\infty}^{\infty} xf(x)dx}{\int_{-\infty}^{\infty} f(x)dx} \qquad \text{(by definition)}$$

Consider the normal distribution with μ, σ as the parameters then

$$\bar{x} = \int_{-\infty}^{\infty} x.\frac{1}{\sigma\sqrt{2\pi}} e^{-\frac{1}{2}\left(\frac{x-\mu}{\sigma}\right)^2} dx$$

Since $\int_{-\infty}^{\infty} f(x)dx$ = area under normal curve = 1

Put $\frac{x-\mu}{\sigma} = z$ so that $x = \mu + \sigma z \quad \therefore \; dx = x = \sigma dz$

$$\bar{x} = \int_{-\infty}^{\infty} (\mu + \sigma z)\frac{1}{\sigma\sqrt{2\pi}} e^{-\frac{1}{2}z^2} (\sigma dz)$$

$$= \mu \int_{-\infty}^{\infty} \frac{1}{\sqrt{2\pi}} e^{-z^2/2} dz + \frac{\sigma}{\sqrt{2\pi}} \int_{-\infty}^{\infty} z e^{-\frac{1}{2}z^2} dz$$

$$= \mu + \frac{\sigma}{\sqrt{2\pi}} \int_{-\infty}^{\infty} e^{-z^2/2} d\left(\frac{z^2}{2}\right) \qquad \because \int_{-\infty}^{\infty} \frac{1}{\sqrt{2\pi}} e^{-z^2/2} dz = 1$$

$$=\mu+\frac{\sigma}{\sqrt{2\pi}}\left(\frac{e^{-z^2/2}}{-1}\right)_{-\infty}^{\infty}$$

$$\boxed{\bar{x}=\mu}$$

2. By definition,

$$\text{Variance} = \int_{-\infty}^{\infty}(x-\bar{x})^2 f(x)ds$$

$$= \int_{-\infty}^{\infty}x^2 f(x)dx + x^2\int_{-\infty}^{\infty}f(x)dx - 2x\int_{-\infty}^{\infty}xf(x)dx$$

$$= \int_{-\infty}^{\infty}x^2 f(x)dx + \bar{x}^2 - 2\bar{x}\bar{x} \qquad \left|\because \int_{-\infty}^{\infty}f(x)dx = 1 \text{ and } = \int_{-\infty}^{\infty}xf(x)dx = \bar{x}\right.$$

$$= \int_{-\infty}^{\infty}x^2 f(x)dx - \bar{x}^2 \qquad \ldots(1)$$

Now, Let $I = \int_{-\infty}^{\infty}x^2 f(x)dx = \int_{-\infty}^{\infty}x^2\frac{1}{\sigma\sqrt{2\pi}}e^{-\frac{1}{2}\left(\frac{x-\bar{x}}{\sigma}\right)^2}dx$

Put $\frac{x-\bar{x}}{\sigma} = z$ so that $x = \bar{x}+\sigma z$ $\qquad \therefore dx = \sigma dz$

Hence $$I = \int_{-\infty}^{\infty}(\bar{x}+\sigma z)^2\frac{1}{\sigma\sqrt{2\pi}}e^{-z^2/2}\sigma dz$$

$$= \frac{1}{\sqrt{2\pi}}\left[\sigma^2\int_{-\infty}^{\infty}z^2e^{-z^2/2}dz + \bar{x}^2\int_{-\infty}^{\infty}e^{-z^2/2}dz + 2\sigma\bar{x}\int_{-\infty}^{\infty}ze^{-z^2/2}dz\right]$$

$$= \frac{-\sigma^2}{\sqrt{2\pi}}\int_{-\infty}^{\infty}zd(e^{-z^2/2}) + \bar{x}^2.1 + 2\sigma\bar{x}.0$$

$$= -\frac{\sigma^2}{\sqrt{2\pi}}(ze^{-z^2/2})_{-\infty}^{\infty} + \frac{\sigma^2}{\sqrt{2\pi}}\int_{-\infty}^{\infty}e^{-z^2/2}dz + \bar{x}^2$$

$$= 0 + \sigma^2.1 + \bar{x}^2 = \sigma^2 + \bar{x}^2$$

$\therefore$ From (1), $\boxed{\text{Variance} = = \sigma^2 + \bar{x}^2 - \bar{x}^2 = \sigma^2}$

$\therefore$ The standard deviation of the normal distribution is σ.

Area under the Normal Curve

Bu taking $z = \frac{x-\mu}{\sigma}$, standard normal curve is formed. The total area under this curve is 1.

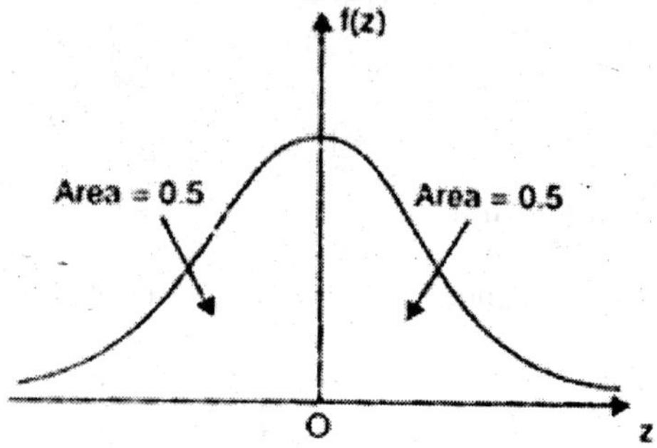

The area under the curve is divided into two equal parts by $z = 0$. The area between the ordinate $z = 0$ and any other ordinate can be noted from the supplied table. It should be noted that mean for the normal distribution is 0.

Applications of Normal Distribution

De Moivre made the discovery of this distribution in 1733.

This distribution has an important application in the theory of errors made by chance in experimental measurements.

Its more applications are in computation of hit probability of a shot and in statistical inference in a almost every branch of science.

Example 1. *A sample of 100 dry battery cells tested to find the length of life produced the following results:*

$$\bar{x} = 12 \text{ hours}, \ \sigma = 3 \text{hours}.$$

Assuming the data to be normally distributed, what precentage of battery cells are expected to have life

(i) more than 15 hours *(ii) less than 6 hours*

(iii) between 10 and 14 hours? (U.P.T.U. 2004)

Solution: Here x denotes the length of life of dry battery cells.

Also $$z = \frac{x-\bar{x}}{\sigma} = \frac{x-12}{3} \quad ...(1)$$

(i) Put $x = 15$, in eq. (1) $z = \frac{15-12}{3} = \frac{3}{3} = 1$

$\therefore$ P(more than 15) =

$P(x > 15) = P(z > 1)$

$= P(0 < z < \infty) - P(0 < z < 1)$

$= .5 - 0.3413 = 0.1587 = 15.87\%.$

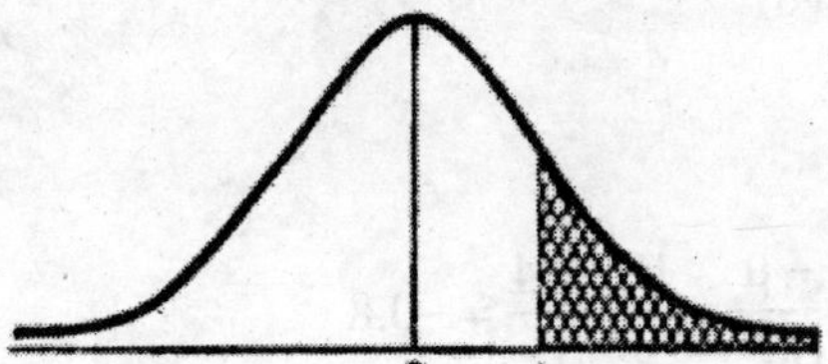

(ii) When $x = 6,\ z = -2$

$$\therefore \quad P(x > 6) = P(z > -2)$$

$$= P(z > 2) = P(0 < z < \infty) - P(0 < z < 2)$$

$$= .5 - 0.4772 = 0.0228 = 2.28\%.$$

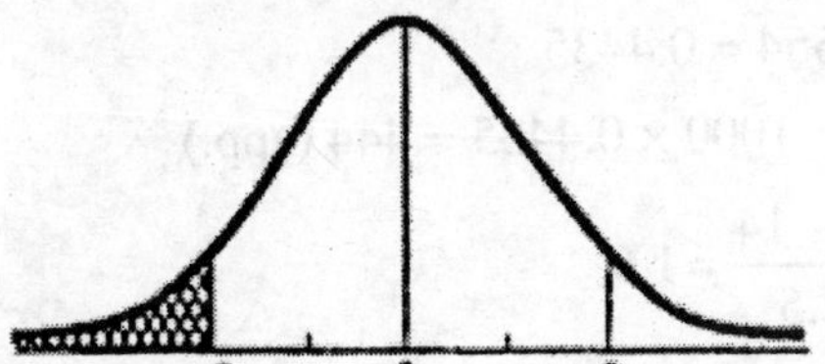

(iii) When $x = 10,\ z = -\dfrac{2}{3} = -0.67$

When $x = 14,\ z = \dfrac{2}{3} = 0.67$

$$P(10 < x < 14)$$

$$= P(-0.67 < z < 0.67)$$

$$= 2P(0 < z < 0.67) = 2 \times 0.2485$$

$$= 0.4970 = 49.70\%$$

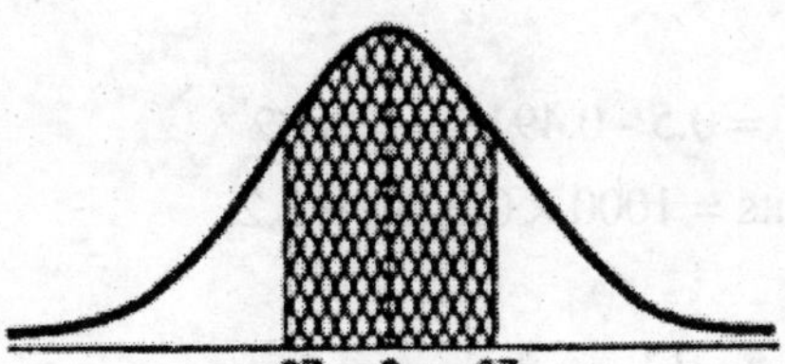

Example 2. *In a sample of* 1000 *cases, the mean of a certain test is* 14 *and S.D. is* 2.5. *Assuming the distribution to be normal, find*

(i) *how many students score between* 12 *and* 15?

(ii) *How many score above* 18?

(iii) *how many score below* 8?

(iv) *how many score* 16? **(U.P.T.U. 2001)**

Solution:

(i)
$$z_1 = \frac{x_1 - \mu}{\sigma} = \frac{12 - 14}{2.5} = -0.8$$

$$z_2 = \frac{x_2 - \mu}{\sigma} = \frac{15 - 14}{2.5} = 0.4$$

Area lying between - 0.8 and 0.4

= Area between 0 to 0.8 + Area between 0 to 0.4

= 0.2881 + 0.1554 = 0.4435

Reqd no. of students = 1000 × 0.4435 = 444 (app.)

(ii)
$$z = \frac{18 - 14}{2.5} = 1.6$$

Area right to 1.6 = 0.5 - (Area between 0 and 1.6)

= 0.5 - 0.4452 = 0.0548

Reqd. no of students = 1000 × 0.0548 = 54.8 = 55 (app.)

(iii)
$$z = \frac{8 - 14}{2.5} = -2.4$$

Area left to - 2.4 = 0.5 - (Area between 0 and 2.4)

= 0.5 - 0.4918 = 0.0082

∴ Reqd. no. of students = 1000 × 0.0082 = 8.2 = 8 (app.).

(iv)
$$z_1 = \frac{15.5 - 14}{2.5} = 0.6$$

$$z_2 = \frac{16.5 - 14}{2.5} = 1$$

Area between 0.6 and 1 = 0.3413 - 0.2257 = 0.1156

∴ Reqd. no. of students = 1000 × 0.1156 = 115.6 = 116 (app.).

Example 3. *Assume mean height of soldiers to be 68.22 inches with a variance of 10.8 inches square. How many soldiers in a regiment of 1,000 would you expect to be over 6 feet tall, given that the area under the standard normal curve between x = 0 and x = 0.35 is 0.1368 and between x = 0 and x = 1.15 is 0.3746.* (U.P.T.U. 2002)

Solution: $x = 6$ feets = 72 inches

$$\therefore \quad z = \frac{x-\mu}{\sigma} = \frac{72-68.22}{\sqrt{10.8}} = 1.15$$

$$P(x > 72) = P(z > 1.15)$$

$$= 0.5 - P(0 \le z \le 1.15)$$

$$= 0.5 - 0.3746 = 0.1254$$

$\therefore$ Expected no. of soldiers = 1000 × 0.1254 = 125.4 = 125 (app.)

Example 4. *The mean height of 500 students of 151 cm and the standard deviation is 15 cm. Assuming that the heights are normally distributed, find how many students have heights between 120 and 155 cm?* **(U.P.T.U. 2010)**

Solution: No. of students = 500 $\quad \therefore \quad N = 500$

Mean, $\mu = 151$ cm.

When $x_1 = 129$ cm.,

Standard normal variable $\quad z_1 = \dfrac{x_1-\mu}{\sigma} = \dfrac{120-151}{15} = \dfrac{-31}{15} = -2.07.$

When $x_2 = 155$ *cm.*,

Standard normal variable $\quad z_2 = \dfrac{x_2-\mu}{\sigma} = \dfrac{155-151}{15}$

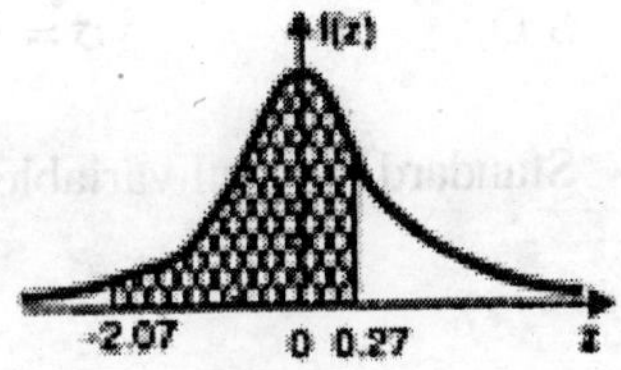

$= 0.27.$

$$\therefore \quad P(120 < x < 155) = P(-2.07 < z < 0.27)$$

$$= P(-2.07 \le z \le 0) + P(0 \le z \le 0.27)$$

$$= P(0 \le z \le 2.07) + P(0 \le z \le 0.27)$$

$$= 0.4808 + 0.1084 \qquad \text{(By table)}$$

$$= 0.5892.$$

$\therefore$ The required no. of students = 0.5892 × 500 = 294 (approximately).

Example 5. *A manufacturer knows from experience that the resistance of resistors he produces is normal with mean μ = 100 ohms and standard deviation σ = 2 ohms. What precentage of resistors will have resistance between 98 ohms and 102 ohms?*

(Q. Bank U.P.T.U. 2001)

Solution: $\mu = 100\Omega, \ \sigma = 2\Omega$

$x_1 = 98\Omega, \ x_2 = 102\Omega$

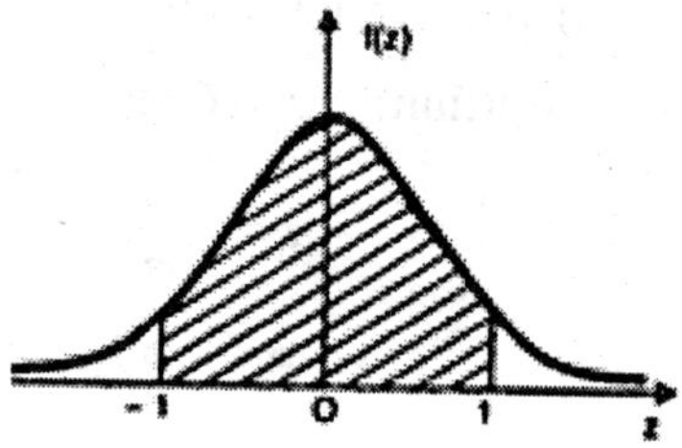

$\therefore \quad z_1 = \dfrac{x_1 - \mu}{\sigma} = \dfrac{98 - 100}{2} = -1$

and $\quad z_2 = \dfrac{x_2 - \mu}{\sigma} = \dfrac{102 - 100}{2} = 1.$

Now, $P(98 < x < 102) = P(-1 < z < 1)$

$$= P(-1 \le z \le 0) + P(0 \le z \le 1)$$

$$= P(0 \le z \le 1) + P(0 \le z \le 1)$$

$$= 0.3413 + 0.3413 = 0.6826.$$

$\therefore$ Percentage of resistors having resistance between 98 Ω and 102 Ω = 68.26%.

Example 6. *The mean yield per plot of a crop is 17 kg. and standard deviation is 3 kg. If distribution of yield per plot is normal, find the percentage of plots giving yields :*

(i) Between 15.5 kg. and 20 kg.; and

(ii) More than 20 kg.

(U.P.T.U. (MBA) 2005)

Solution: Mean $\mu = 17\,kg.$

S.D. $\sigma = 3\,kg.$

Standard Normal variable $z = \dfrac{x - \mu}{\sigma}$

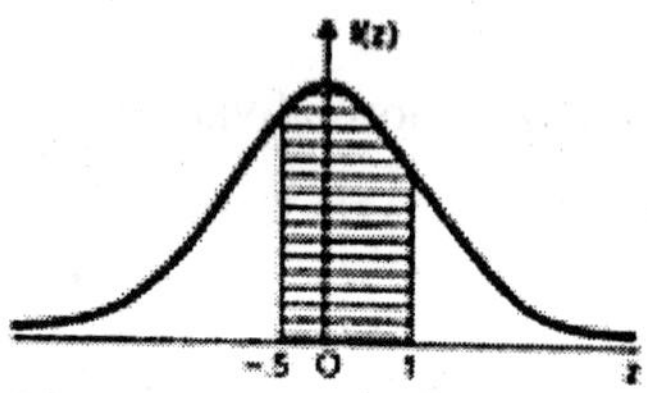

(i) When $x_1 = 15.5, \ z_1 = \dfrac{x_1 - \mu}{\sigma} = \dfrac{15.5 - 17}{3} = -0.5$

When $x_2 = 20, \ z_2 = \dfrac{x_2 - \mu}{\sigma} = \dfrac{20 - 17}{3} = 1$

$\therefore \quad P(15.5 < x < 20) = P(-0.5 < z < 1)$

$$= P(-0.5 < z < 0) + P(0 < z < 1)$$

$$= P(0 < z < .5) + P(0 < z < 1)$$

$$= 0.1915 + 0.3413$$

$$= 0.5328$$

$\therefore$ Required percentage of plots = 53.28

(ii) When $x = 20$, $\quad x = \dfrac{20-17}{3} = 1$

$$P(x > 20) = P(z > 1)$$
$$= 0.5 - P(0 < z < 1)$$
$$= 0.5 - 0.3413$$
$$= 0.1587$$

∴ Required percentage of plots = 15.87%.

Example 7. *The mean inside diameter of a sample of 200 washers produced by a machine is 0.502 cm and the standard deviation is 0.005 cm. The purpose for which these washers are intended allows a minimum tolerance in the diameter of 0.496 to 0.508 cm, otherwise the washers are considered defective. Determine the percentage of defective washers produced by the machine. Assume the diameters are normally distributed.*

(Q. Bank U.P.T.U. 2001)

Solution: Given : Mean $\mu = 0.502\ cm$.

S.D. $\sigma = 0.005\ cm$.

$x_1 = 0.496\ cm$.

$x_2 = 0.508\ cm$.

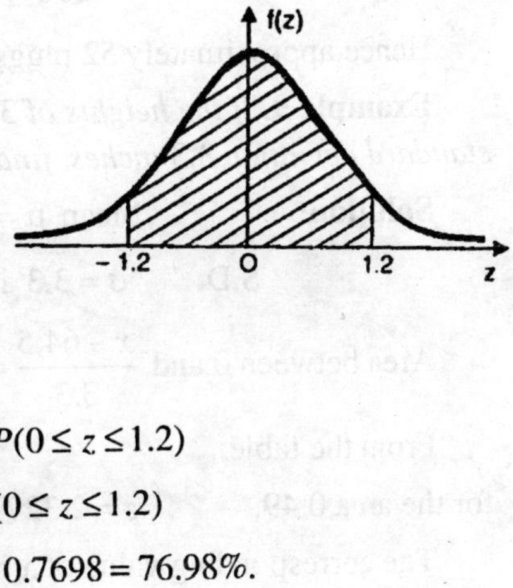

Now, $\quad z_1 = \dfrac{x_1 - \mu}{\sigma} = \dfrac{0.496 - 0.502}{0.005} = -1.2$

$$z_2 = \frac{x_2 - \mu}{\sigma} = \frac{0.508 - 0.502}{0.005} = 1.2$$

Area for non-defective washers $= P(-1.2 \le z \le 1.2)$

$$= P(-1.2 \le z \le 0) + P(0 \le z \le 1.2)$$
$$= P(0 \le z \le 1.2) + P(0 \le z \le 1.2)$$
$$= 0.3849 + 0.3849 = 0.7698 = 76.98\%.$$

∴ Percentage of defective washers = 100 − 76.98 = 23.02%.

Example 8. *Assuming that the diameters of 1000 brass plugs taken consecutively from a machine, form a normal distribution with mean 0.7515 cm. and standard deviation 0.002 cm., how many of the plugs are likely to be rejected if the approved diameter is* $0.752 \pm 0.004\,cm$.

(Q. Bank U.P.T.U. 2001)

Solution: Tolerance limits of the diameter of non-defective plugs are

$$0.752 - 0.004 = 0.748 \text{ cm. and}$$
$$0.752 + 0.004 = 0.756 \text{ cm.}$$

Standard normal variable, $z = \dfrac{x - \mu}{\sigma}$

If $x_1 = 0.748$, $z_1 = \dfrac{0.748 - 0.7515}{0.002} = -1.75$

If $x_2 = 0.756$, $z_2 = \dfrac{0.756 - 0.7515}{0.02} = 2.25$

Area from $(z_1 = +1.75)$ to $(z_2 = -2.25)$

$$= P(-1.75 \le z \le 2.25)$$
$$= P(-1.75 \le z \le 0) + P(0 \le z \le 2.25)$$
$$= P(0 \le z \le 1.75) + P(0 \le z \le 2.25)$$
$$= 0.4599 + 0.4878 = 0.9477$$

No. of plugs which are likely to be rejected

$$= 1000 \times (1 - 0.9477) = 1000 \times .0523 = 52.3$$

Hence approximately 52 plugs are likely to be rejected.

Example 9. *If the heights of* 300 *students are normally distributed with mean* 64.5 *inches and standard deviation* 3.3 *inches, find the height below which* 99% *of the students lie.*

Solution: Mean $\mu = 64.5$ inches

S.D. $\sigma = 3.3$ inches

Area between 0 and $\dfrac{x - 64.5}{3.3} = 0.99 - 0.5 = 0.49$

From the table,

for the area 0.49, $z = 2.327$

The corresponding value of x is given by

$$\frac{x - 64.5}{3.3} = 2.327$$

$\Rightarrow$ $x - 64.5 = 7.68$

$\Rightarrow$ $x = 7.68 + 64.5 = 72.18$ inches.

Hence 99% students are of height less than 6 ft. 0.18 inches.

Example 10. *The income of a group of* 10,000 *persons was found to be normally distributed with mean Rs.* 750 *p.m. and standard deviation of Rs.* 50. *Show that, of this group, about* 95%

had income exceeding Rs. 668 and only 5% had income exceeding Rs. 832. Also find the lowest income among the richest 100.

(U.P.T.U. 2005)

Solution: Given : $\mu = 750, \sigma = 50$

Standard normal variable, $z = \dfrac{x-\mu}{\sigma}$

(i) If $x_1 = 668$, $z_1 = \dfrac{x_1 - \mu}{\sigma} = \dfrac{668-750}{50} = -1.64$

$$P(x_1 > 668) = P(z_1 > -1.64)$$
$$= 0.5 + P(-1.64 \le z \le 0)$$
$$= 0.5 + P(0 \le z \le 1.64)$$
$$= 0.5 + 0.4495$$
$$= 0.9495$$

∴ Reqd. percentage of persons having income exceeding Rs. 668 = 94.95% = 95% (approx.)

(ii) If $x_2 = 832$, $z_2 = \dfrac{x_2 - \mu}{\sigma} = \dfrac{832-750}{50} = 1.64$

$$P(x_2 > 832) = P(z_2 > 1.64)$$
$$= 0.5 - P(0 \le z \le 1.64)$$
$$= 0.5 - 0.4495$$
$$= 0.0505$$

∴ Reqd. percentage of persons having income exceeding Rs. 832=5.05% = 5% (approx.)

(iii) Let x be the lowest income among the richest 100 persons *i.e.,* 1% of 10,000.

Thus, area between 0 and z =0.49 (see figure)

By Normal distribution table,

$$z = 2.33$$

thus, $\dfrac{x-\mu}{\sigma} = 2.33$

$\Rightarrow$ $\dfrac{x-750}{50} = 2.33$

$\Rightarrow$ $x = 866.5$

Hence Rs. 866.5 is the minimum income among the riches 100 persons.

Exercise 4.3

1. In a test on 2000 electric bulbs, it was found that the life of a particular make, was normally distributed with an average life of 2040 hours and S.D. of 60 hours, estimate the number of bulbs likely to burn for

   (i) more than 2150 hours *(ii)* less than 1950 hours

   (iii) more than 1920 hours but less than 2160 hours.

2. An aptitude test for selecting officers in a bank is conducted on 1000 candidates. The average score is 42 and the standard deviation of score is 24. Assuming normal distribution for the scores, find

   (i) the number of candidates whose scores exceed 60

   (ii) the number of candidates whose scores lie between 30 and 60.

3. In a normal distribution, 7% of the items are under 35 and 89% are under 63. What are the mean and standard deviation of the distribution?

4. Let X denote the number of scores on a test. If X is normally distributed with mean 100 and standard deviation 15, find the probability that X does not exceed 130.

5. It is known from the past experience that the number of telephone calls made daily in a certain community between 3 p.m. and 4 p.m. have a mean of 352 and a standard deviation 31. What percentage of the time will there be more than 400 telephone calls made in this community between 3 p.m. and 4 p.m.? (A.U.)

6. Students of a class were given a mechanical aptitude test. Their marks were fund to be normally distributed with mean 60 and standard deviation 5. What percent of students scored. (K.U.)

   (i) more than 60 marks? *(ii)* less than 56 marks?

   (iii) between 45 and 65 marks?

7. In an examination taken by 500 candidates, the average and the standard deviation of marks obtained (normally distributed) are 40% and 10%. Find approximately.

   (i) how many will pass, if 50% is fixed as a minimum?

   (ii) what should be the minimum if 350 candidates are to pass?

   (iii) how many have scored marks above 60%?

8. A manufacturer of envelopes knows that the weight of the envelopes is normally distributed with mean 1.9 gm. and variance .01 gm. Find how many envelopes weighing *(i)* 2 gm. or more *(ii)* 2.1 gm. or more can be expected in a given packet of 1000 envelopes.

   [Given : $P(0 \leq z \leq 1) = .3413$, $P(0 \leq z \leq 2) = 0.4772$]

9. East-East Airlines has the policy of employing only Indian woman whose height is between 62 inches and 69 inches. If the height of Indian women is approximately normally distributed with a mean of 64 inches and a standard deviation of 3 inches, Out of the 1000 applications received find the number of applicants that would be.

   (i) too tall *(ii)* too short *(iii)* of acceptable height.

10. Records kept by the goods inwards department of a large factory show that the average no. of lorries arriving each week is 248. It is known that the distribution approximates to be normal with a standard deviation of 26. (LU)

    If this pattern of arrival continues, what percentage of weeks can be expected to have number of arrivals of:

    (i) less than 229 per week?

    (ii) more than 280 per week?

11. The income distribution of workers in a certain factory was found to be normal with mean Rs. 500and standard deviation equal to Rs. 50. There were 228 persons getting above Rs. 600. How many workers were there in all?

12. In a certain examination, the percentage of passes and distinction were 46 and 9 respectively. Estimate the average marks obtained by the candidates, the minimum pass and distinction marks being 40 and 75 respectively. Assume the distribution of marks to be normal.

    [Hint. $\frac{40-\mu}{\sigma}=0.1$ and $\frac{75-\mu}{\sigma}=1.34$.]

Answers

1. *(i)* 67 *(ii)* 184 *(iii)* 1909.
2. *(i)* 227 *(ii)* 465
3. $\bar{x}=50.3,\ \sigma=10.33$
4. 0.9772
5. 6.06%
6. *(i)* 50% *(ii)* 21.2% *(iii)* 84%
7. *(i)* 79 *(ii)* 35% *(iii)* 11
8. *(i)* 159 *(ii)* 23
9. *(i)* 48 *(ii)* 251 *(iii)* 701
10. *(i)* 23% *(ii)* 11%
11. 10,000
12. 37.2.

Objective type Questions

1. Probability of a sure event is:
   (a) 1 (b) 0
   (c) 0.5 (d) none of these
2. If for two independent events A and B, P(A)= 0.8 and P(B) = 0.6 and, then the probability of their simultaneous occurrences:
   (a) 0.2 (b) 0.6
   (c) 0.8 (d) 0.48
3. If $P(A \cap B) = 0$,then the events A and B are:
   (a) Independent (b) Equally likely
   (c) Dependent (d) None of these
4. If P(AUB) =P(A) +P(B), then the two events A and B are:
   (a) Independent (b) Mutually exclusive
   (c) Dependent (d) None of these
5. If P(B/A)= P(B), then the two events A and B are:
   (a) Independent (b) Equally likely
   (c) Dependent (d) None of these
6. The conditional probability of B given A is:
   (a) $P\frac{(A \cap B)}{P(B)}$ (b) $P\frac{(A \cup B)}{P(A)}$
   (c) $P\frac{(A \cap B)}{P(A)}$ (d) P(A). P(B)
7. If $P(A \cap B) = 0.20$ and P(B) = 0.6, then P(A/B) is:
   (a) 0.40 (b) 0.12
   (c) 0.50 (d) 0.6
8. If P(A)= 0.8, P(B) =0.5, P(AUB)= 0.6,then $P(A \cap B)$ is:
   (a) 0.7 (b) 0.40
   (c) 0.8 (d) 0.6
9. If odds in favour of an events A are 5:6. then odds against the events are:
   (a) 6:5 (b) 5:11
   (c) 6:11 (d) None of these
10. If odds for an events are 5:1, the probability of non-happening of the event is:
    (a) 1/2 (b) 1/6
    (c) 1/5 (d) 1/6

11. If P(A) =0.4,P(B)= 0.2 and the events A and B are independent, then P(A∩B) is:
(a) 0.6 (b) 0.08
(c) 0.4 (d) 0.30
12. If, for two events A and B, P(A∩B) = 0.70 and P(AUB) = 0.60, then P(A)+P(B) is:
(a) 0.42 (b) 0.70
(c) 1.30 (d) 0.30
13. If P(A∩B) = 0.5,P(A) = 0.7,P(B) = 0.6, the value of P(B/A) is:
(a) 5/6 (b) 6/7
(c) 5/7 (d) None of these
14. If P(A)=0.7, P(B/A) =0.6, then P(A∩B) is
(a) 0.1 (b) 0.42
(c) 0.7 (d) 0.6
15. The mean of the binomial distribution is:
(a) p (b) np
(c) npq (d) p^2
16. The parameters of a binomial distribution with mean = 8 and variance= 4 are:
(a) n =2, p = 1/4 (b) n =16, p=1/2 **(UPTU-08)**
(c) n= 32, p=1/4 (d) None of these
17. The mean of the binomial distribution with probability function:
$P(X)={}^6C_x(1/2)^x (1/2)^{6-x}$; x= 0,1,2,...6,is
(a) 3 (b) 6
(c) 18 (d) 1.5
18. The variance of the binomial distribution with probability function:
$P(X)={}^9C_x(1/3)^x (2/3)^{9-x}$; x= 0,1,2,...9,is
(a) 9 (b) 3
(c) 2 (d) 27
19. For a Poisson distribution
$P(X)=\frac{e^{-2}2^x}{x!}$; x= 0,1,2, ...6,the mean value is:
(a) 2 (b) 4
(c) 0.5 (d) None of these
20. For a Poisson distribution:
$P(X)=\frac{e^{-4}4^x}{x!}$; x= 0,1,2, ...6,the standard deviation is:
(a) 4 (b) 8
(c) 2 (d) 16

21. For a Poisson distribution ,if P(0) =P(1), then the value of mean is: **(U.P.T.U. 2010)**
    (a) 1.0 (b) 2.0
    (c) 4.0 (d) None of these
22. For a Poisson distribution, P(1)=P(2), its variance is:
    (a) 3 (b) 4
    (c) 6 (d) 2
23. For a Poisson distribution, P(2) =P(3), then its probability function will be: **(UPTU-08)**
    (a) $\frac{e^{-2}2^x}{x!}$ (b) $\frac{e^{-6}6^x}{x!}$
    (c) $\frac{e^{-3}3^x}{x!}$ (d) None of these
24. For a Poisson distribution
    (a) Mean = variance (b) Mean = standard
    (c) Mean < variance (d) Mean > variance
25. For a binomial probability distribution, we observe that:
    (a) Mean < variance (b) Mean > variance
    (c) Mean = variance (d) None of these
26. The mean of a normal distribution is 50, its mode will be: **(UPTU-2010)**
    (a) 25 (b) 40
    (c) 50 (d) None of these
27. The mode of a normal distribution is 70 with S.D.25.Then its median will be: **(UPTU-08)**
    (a) 7 (b) 700
    (c) 70 (d) None of these
28. The following is the probability denisty function of a normal variable:

$$P(x) = \frac{1}{4\sqrt{2\pi}} e^{-1/2[x-30)/4]2}; \; -\infty \leq x \leq \infty$$

    The mean and variance of the distribution are
    (a) Mean = 30, variance=4 (b) Mean = 0, variance =16
    (c) Mean =30, variance=8 (d) Mean =30, variance=16
29. Within 2σ limits, the area under a normal curve is:
    (a) 0.6827 (b) 0.9545
    (c) 0.9973 (d) 0.5000
30. Within 3σ limits from mean, the area under the normal curve is:
    (a) 0.9973 (b) 0.9545
    (c) 0.6827 (d) 0.5000

31. If x is a normal variables with μ =50 and σ=10, then P(30<x<80) is the same as: **(UPTU-08)**

(a) P(3<Z<8) (b) P(-2<Z<3)

(c) P(-1<Z<3) (d) None of these

32. If X is a normal variable with μ = 100 and σ^2=25, then P(90<X<80) is the same as:

(a) P(-1<Z<1) (b) P(-2<Z<4)

(c) P(4<Z<4.1) (d) None of these

33. The standard deviation of the binomial distribution: **(UPTU-2010)**

(a) np (b) npq

(c) $\sqrt{(np)}$ (d) $\sqrt{(npq)}$

34. If n is large, neither p nor q is small, the limiting from of the binomial distribution is:

(a) Binomial (b) Poisson

(c) Normal (d) None of these

35. If n is large, p is small and np=m (a finite positive constant), the limiting from of the binomial distribution is:

(a) Binomial (b) Poisson

(c) Normal (d) None of these

36. Which of the following are true:

1. The probability derived from past experience is called emperical probability
2. Bayes theorem provides us with another formula for computing conditional probability, P(A/B)
3. The conditional probability of the given A is written as. P(A/B)

(a) 1,3 (b) 2,3

(c) 1,2 (d) Only 1

37. Probability range between :

(a) – 1 to 1 (b) – 1 to 0

(c) 0 to 1 (d) 1 to 0

38. If a card is drawn from a pack of cards, the probability of getting either a king or queen is:

(a) 1/52 (b) 2/13

(c) 1/26 (d) None of these

39. The probability of drawing a king from a pack of card is:

(a) $\frac{1}{26}$ (b) $\frac{1}{13}$

(c) $\frac{1}{52}$ (d) None of these

40. The classical school of thought on probability assumes that all possible outcomes of an experiment are:

(a) Equally likely (b) Mutually exclusive

(c) Independent (d) Equally likely and mutually exclusive

41. What is the probability of getting an even number when a die is tossed:

(a) $\frac{1}{3}$ (b) $\frac{1}{2}$

(c) $\frac{1}{6}$ (d) $\frac{1}{5}$

42. If the outcome of an event does not influence another event, then two events are:

(a) Mutually exclusive (b) Independent

(c) Dependent (d) Equally likely event

43. Probability that there will be 53 Sunday in a leap year is- **(AU)**

(a) $\frac{1}{7}$ (b) $\frac{3}{7}$

(c) $\frac{3}{7}$ (d) $\frac{4}{7}$

44. If the occurrence of one event stops the occurrence of others, then the event is called-

(a) Equally likely (b) Favourable

(c) Mutually exclusive (d) Simple

45. A and B are two mutually exclusive events, than P(A∩B) equally-

(a) 0 (b) 1/8

(c) 1 /4 (d) 1 /2

46. A Speakers the truth 3 out of 4 times. He throws a dice and claim it to be a six. The probability that it is a six is-

(a) $\frac{1}{8}$ (b) $\frac{3}{4}$

(c) $\frac{1}{5}$ (d) $\frac{3}{8}$

47. Baye's theorem helps the statistician to calculate-

(a) Classical Probability (b) Subjective Probability

(c) Posterior Probability (d) All of above

48. If $\frac{P(A)}{2} = 1, \frac{P(B)}{3} = 1, \frac{P(AB)}{12} = 1$, than the

Probability that at least on of A and B occurs is-

(a) $\frac{3}{4}$ (b) $\frac{2}{3}$

(c) $\frac{1}{3}$ (d) 0

49. If P(A or B) = P(B), then-

(a) A and B are mutually exclusive

(b) A and B must be independent

(c) P (A) = P (B)

(d) P (B/A) = 1

50. Which of the following is/are true-

(a) Normal distribution is a discrete distribution

(b) Normal distribution is a multimodal distribution

(c) Normal distribution is a symmetrical distribution

(d) Mean ≠ Median ≠ Mode

51. Probability that there will be 53 Tuesday in an ordinary year is- **(UPTU-08)**

(a) $\frac{1}{7}$ (b) $\frac{2}{7}$

(c) $\frac{3}{7}$ (d) $\frac{4}{7}$

Answers

1. a	9. a	17. a	25. b	33. d	41. b	49. d
2. d	10 .d	18. c	26. c	34. c	42. b	50. d
3. d	11. b	19. a	27. c	35. b	43. b	51. a
4. b	12. c	20. c	28. d	36. c	44. c	
5. a	13. c	21. a	29. b	37. c	45. a	
6. c	14. b	22. d	30. a	38. c	46. d	
7. c	15. b	23. c	31. b	39. b	47. c	
8. a	16. b	24. a	32. d	40. d	48. a	

Misc. Exercise 4.4

1. Define the following terms with example :-
   (a) Equally likely events
   (b) Mutually exclusive events
   (c) Independent and dependent events
   (d) Conditional probability
2. List the reasons for classical definition of probability not being very satisfactory. Give the modern definition of probability.
3. Distinguish between the following -
   (a) Mathematical and statistical probability
   (b) Mutually exclusive and independent events
4. Explain the addition and multiplication rule of probability with examples. **(UPTU-07)**
5. What is the probability of getting a total of more than 10 in a single throw with two dice.
6. One card is drawn from a back of 52, what is the probability that it is a king or queen.
7. The probability that a student passes mathematics is 2/3 and the probability that he passes English is 4/9. If the probability of passing at least one course is 4/5, what is the probability of his passing both the courses?
8. Two balls are drawn with replacement from a bag containing 3 red and 4 black balls. Find the probability that-
   (i) Both are red
   (ii) The first the red and second is black
   (iii) One is red and other is black.
9. A class consists of 10 boys and 8 girls. A committee of three students is constituted. What is the probability that the committee has –
   (i) All boys (ii) All girls
   (iii) 1 boy and 2 girls. (iv) At least one girl
10. A candidate is called for interview by the 3 companies. For the first there are 12 candidates, for the second 10 and for the third there are 15 candidates. What are the chances of the getting at least one of the companies.
11. A can hit a target 3 times in 5 shots, B 2 times in 5 shots, and C 3 times in 4 shots. They fire a volley what is the probability of hitting 2 shots.
12. A problem in business statistics is given to four students A, B, C and D. their respective chances of solving it are ½, 1/3, 1/5 and 1/6. What is the probability that:-
   (i) Problem will be solved
   (ii) problem will be solved by any two of them.

13. An electronic manufacturer has two lines A and B assembling identical electronic units. 5% of the units assembled on line A and 10% of those assembled on line B are defective, All defective units must be remarked at a significant increase in cost. During the last eight-hour shift, line A produced 200 units while the line B produced 300 units. One unit is selected at random from the 500 units produced and is found to be defective. What is the probability that it was assembled on line A?.

14. A husband and wife appear in an interview for two vacancies in the same post. The probability of husband's selection is 1/7 and of wife's selection is 1/5. What is the probability that :
    (a) both of them will be selected,
    (b) only one of them will be selected, and
    (c) None will be selected?

15. A machine will function successfully during the year only when all its three components X, Y and Z are working successfully. If the probability of X failing is 0.15, that of Y failing is 0.05 and that of Z failing is 0.10, then what is the probability that the machine will fail before the end of this year?

16. A University has to select an examiner from a list of 50 examiners : 20 of them being women and 30 the men, 10 of them knowing Hindi and 40 not, 15 of them being professors and 35 not. What is the probability of the University selecting a Hindi-knowing woman professor?

17. In a factory manufacturing electric razors, machines X, Y and Z manufacture 30%, 30% and 40 % of the total production of electric razors, respectively. Of their output, 4%, 5% and 10% of the electric razors respectively are defective. If one electric razor is selected at random and if it is found to be defective, what is the probability that it is manufactured by machine Z?

18. In a post office, three clerks are assigned to process incoming mail. The first clerk, B_1, processes 60%, the second clerk B_2 processes 15% and the third clerk B_3 processes 25% of the mail. The first clerk has an error rate of 0.04, the second has an error rate of 0.03 and the third has an error rate of 0.06. A mail selected at random from a day's output is found to have an error. The post master wishes to know the probability that the mail was processes by the first, second or third clerk, respectively.

19. Discuss the salient features of the binomial, normal and Poisson distribution. When does a Binomial Distribution tend to become a (i) Normal distribution and (ii) Poisson distribution?

20. An executive makes, on an average, 5 telephone calls per hour at a cost which may be taken as Rs. 2 per call. Determine the probability that in any hour the telephone calls cost exceed Rs. 6.

21. The values of the Mean and Standard Deviation for a Binomial Distribution are as Mean = 6 and Standard Deviation = 2. Find n, p and q of the distribution.

22. The incidence of a certain disease is such that on the average 20 of the workers suffer from it. If ten workers are selected at random, find the probability that :

(i) exactly 9 workers suffer from the disease.

(ii) not more than 2 persons suffer from the disease.

23. The mean yield per plot of a crop is 17 kg and standard deviation is 3 kg. If distribution of yield per plot is normal, find the percentage of plots giving yields :

    (i) Between 15.5 kg and 20 kg; and

    (ii) More than 20 kg.

24. The customer accounts at a certain departmental store have an average balance of Rs. 480 and a standard deviation of Rs. 160. Assuming that the account balances are normally distributed. Find

    (i) What proportion of the accounts is over Rs. 600?

    (ii) What proportion of the accounts is between Rs. 400 and Rs. 600?

    (iii) What proportion of the accounts is less then Rs. 360?

25. 2000 Students appeared in an examination. Distribution of marks is assumed to be normal with mean 30 and 6.25. How many students are expected to get marks.

    (i) Between 20 and 40

    (ii) Less then 35 and

    (iii) Above 50.

26. An Aptitude Test was conducted on 900 employees of the Metro Tyres Ltd., in which the Mean Score was found to be 50 with a Standard Deviation of 20. On the basis of this information, you are required to answer the following questions :-

    (i) What was the number of employees whose mean score was less than 30?

    (ii) What was the number of employees whose mean score exceeded 70?

    (iii) What was the number of employees whose mean scores were between 30 and 70?

27. The average monthly sales of 5000 firms in an industry in Bangalore are normally distributed with mean Rs. 36,000 and standard deviation Rs. 10,000. Find –

    (i) the number of firms with sales over Rs. 40,000

    (ii) the percentage of firms with sales between Rs. 38,500 and Rs. 41,000 and

    (iii) the number of firms with sales between Rs. 30,000 and Rs. 40,000

28. The Hyderabad Municipal Corporation had installed 10,000 electric tube lights in the different parts of the city. If these tube lights have an average life of 1,000 burning hours with a standard deviation of 200 hours, find the number of tube-lights that are expected (i) to fail in the first 800 burning hours, and those that are expected (ii) to burn between 800 and 1,300 burning hours. You may assume that the life data of the tube lights follows a normal distribution.

29. In probability theory P(AB) = P(A). P(B/A) always exists. **(UPTU-07)**

30. If a random variable X follows Poisson distribution such that P(X=1) = P(X=2), then find (i) the mean of the distribution and (ii) P(X=0).

    (Given $e^{-2} = 0.1353$) **(UPTU-07)**

31. Four persons in a group of 20 are graduates. If 4 persons are selected at random from 20, find the probability that (1) all are graduate (2) at least one is a graduate. (UPTU-07)

32. The average daily sales of 500 branch offices was Rs. 1,50,000 and the standard deviation Rs. 15, 000. Assuming the distribution to be normal, indicate how many branches have sales between

    (1) Rs.1,20,000 and Rs. 1,45,000

    (2) Rs. 1,40,000 and Rs. 1,65,000 **(UPTU-07)**

33. (a) Two dices are thrown. What is the probability that none of them show a "Six"?

    (b) An urn contains 4 white and 2 red balls. Two balls are drawn randomly with replacement. Find the probability that

    (i) both balls are white

    (ii) both balls will be of the same colour. **(UPTU-08)**

34. (a) The monthly mess bill of a student who is staying in the hostel follows a normal distribution with a mean of Rs.2000 and a standard deviation of Rs.185. What is the probabilities that in the next month his will go above Rs.2400?

    (b) In a normal distribution, 0.0107 of the items lie below 42 and 0.0446 of the items lie above 82. What is the mean and standard deviation of the normal distribution? **(UPTU-08)**

35. Define Probability Distribution. Explain the salient features of Binomial, Poisson and Normal distribution. **(UPTU-08)**

36. An aptitude test was conducted on 900 employees of the Metro Tyres Limited in which the mean score was found to be 50 units and standard deviation was 20 on the basis of this information, you are required to answer the following question :

    (i) What was the number of employees whose mean score Was less than 30 ?

    (ii) What was the number of employees whose mean score exceeded 70 ?

    (iii) What was the number of employees whose mean score were between 30 and 70 ? **(UPTU-08)**

List of Formulae

1. Mathematical Probability

   If a trial results in n exhaustive mutually exclusive and equally likely cases and m of them are favourable to the happening of an event A, then

$$P(A) = \frac{m}{n}, P(\bar{A}) = 1 - \frac{m}{n}$$

2. Statistical Probability

   If in n trails, an event A occurs m times, then

$$P(A) = \lim_{n \to \infty} \frac{m}{n}$$

3. Axiomatic Approach to Probability

   The probability P(A) of an even A with regard to a sample space S of an experiment satisfies the following axioms

   (i) $0 \leq P(A) \leq 1$ (ii) $P(S) = 1$

   (iii) $P(A) = P(1_1) + P(A_2) + ... + P(A_r)$

   where $A_1, A_2, ...A_r$ are the sample points comprising the event A.

4. Important Rules of Probability

   (a) Additive Rule

   $$P(A \cup B) = P(A) + P(B) - P(A \cap B))$$

   $$P(A \cup B) = P(A) + P(B) \quad \text{[if A and B are mutually exclusive]}$$

   (b) Conditional Probability :

   $$P(B / A) = \frac{P(A \cap B)}{P(A)} \qquad P(A / B) = \frac{P(A \cap B)}{P(B)}$$

5. Mathematical Expectation

   If X is a random variable with probability distribution

x	x_1 x_2 x_3 ....x_k
$f(x)$	$f(x_1)$ $f(x_2)$ $f(x_3)$ ....$f(x_k)$

   Then, the expected value of X is

   $$E(X) = \sum_{i=0} x_i fx_i) = x_1 f(x_1) + s_2 f(x_2) + ...x_k f(x_k)$$

6. Distribution

Characteristics	Binomial	Poisson	Normal
Probability functions	$P(r) = {}^n c_r p^r q^{n-r}$	$P(r) = \frac{e^{-\lambda} \cdot \lambda^r}{r!}$	$P(r) = \frac{1}{\sigma\sqrt{2\pi}} e^{1/2\left(\frac{(x-\mu)}{\sigma}\right)^2}$
Parameters	n and p	m	μ and σ
Mean	np	m	μ
Variance	npq	m	σ^2

5 SAMPLING THEORY

5.1 Introduction

Statistics which are collected and analysed are either descriptive or inductive in character. Descriptive statistics are those which describe some characteristics of a set of figures. Inductive statistics refer to drawing inference about a universe on the basis of the examination of a part of the universe only. In other words, inductive statistics refer to estimating values of the universe on the basis of sample study. In modern decision-making process in various fields of human activities, most of our decisions are based on the examination of a few objects only or in other words they are based on sample studies. This process of drawing inferences about a universe on the basis of sample studies naturally involves an element of risk, because one may draw wrong inferences about a universe by studying a sample. Modern statistical theory makes an attempt to evaluate this risk in terms of probability.

Types of Universe

Finite and Infinite Universe

By finite universe we mean such populations which contain a definite number of units. As against this, an infinite universe is one in which the number of units is infinite. For example, the number of leaves in a tree is an infinite universe. Even though it may be possible to count the number of leaves in a tree, since the number is quite large, it is considered an infinite universe. Infinite populations are better for sampling studies as the probabilities of various events can be better estimated of the universe is infinite.

Hypothetical and Existent Universe

Hypothetical universe is one which does not consist of concrete objects. Such universes consist of an infinite number of items. Existent universe, as the name suggests, refers to a population of concrete objects. In hypothetical universe the values of p and q remain constant in various trials. This is a very important property of such populations. It enables us to fit a particular curve to such data with a high degree of accuracy.

5.2 Objects of Sampling

The most important aim of sampling studies is to obtain maximum information about the phenomenon under study with the least sacrifice of money, time and energy. Another aim of sampling studies is to obtain the best possible values of the parameters.

Principles of Sampling

(*i*) *Law of Statistical Regularity.* A group of objects chosen at random from a particular group tends to possess the characteristics of that group (universe).

(*ii*) *Principle of Inertia of Large Numbers.* As sample size increases, results would be more reliable.

(*iii*) *Principle of Persistence.* If some items of the universe possess some specific characteristics, these characteristics would be found in the sample also and even if the sample size is increased or population is increased, these characteristics would be reflected.

(*iv*) *Principle of Optimisation.* Effort should be made to get the best possible or optimum results both in terms of cost as well as efficiency.

(*v*) *Principle of Validity.* A sample design is called valid only when the inferences drawn from it are valid for the universe from which the sample has been taken.

Census versus Sample Enumeration

Census Method. In census type of enquiry there is complete enumeration of all the items of the universe and the question of taking a sample does not arise. Normally, census method should give exact and accurate results, but it suffers from certain limitations:

(*i*) It is very expensive, particularly if the size of universe is large.

(*ii*) It requires more time fro completion.

(*iii*) It needs substantial manpower and administrative control.

The census method is however used in certain cases where

(*a*) Complete information is needed about the entire universe.

(*b*) The size of universe is not big and the need for accurate result is great.

(*c*) The occurrence of a defect (during the manufacture of an item) may cause damage to the machine itself or to the life of the person(s) operating it.

Sample Method. Sample method is one where we study some selected items from the entire universe for drawing general inferences. This method has many advantages over census such as speed, economy, adaptability and scientific approach. The merits of sampling method are:

(*i*) It takes less time.

(*ii*) It is less expensive.

(*iii*) It is more dependable. Even though the sampling method is not free from sampling and non-sampling errors, yet if it is properly designed, results would be more reliable and dependable than the results of census method. The reason is that in case of sampling it is possible to find out the degree of reliability of the result in terms of probability. Further, non-sampling errors due to wrong recording of observations or non-response or incomplete response or improper training of investigators, etc., which are substantial in case of census enquiry, can be easily controlled if the enquiry uses sampling where the numbers involved are less and one can have better trained personnel and can also use sophisticated statistical techniques of processing and analysis of data.

(*iv*) In some cases only sampling method is possible.

(*v*) This method has to be used in such cases also where the item itself is destroyed in the course of inspection.

Limitations of Sampling

Sampling studies can give better results only if the sample are drawn systematically, their size is adequate and an appropriate sample design is used. Other limitations are that if, for example, some selected units of the sample do not respond, or if the personnel conducting the survey are not qualified, the sample results may be highly misleading. Sometimes, if the sample size is large, sample surveys may need more time, money and labour also.

Precision in Sampling

Since the main aim of studies is to obtain information about the problem under study in the universe at large, and since sampling studies are made only from a few units collected out of a large number constituting the universe, the question of dependability often arises. It is clear that if a sample fails to reveal the main characteristics of the universe, it does not serve its purpose.

Theory of sampling makes an attempt to indicate the degree of reliability that can be placed on various estimates obtained from sampling studies. This is done by assigning limits within which the estimate is expected to vary. These limits vary with the degree of confidence which we wish to achieve in our assertions. Thus, if we want to assert a fact with a very high degree of confidence, the limits which can be placed, will be wide so that the chance of the estimate going beyond them is minimum. It means that the degree of confidence which can be put in any estimate is expressed in terms of probability.

The accuracy or precision of estimates depends on a variety of factors. The first is the manner in which the estimate is made from the sample data. This leads us to the theory of estimation. The second is the manner in which the sample was obtained. This leads us to the study of the technique of sampling. A third factor is the size of the sample. If the size of the sample is small, much reliance cannot be placed on the estimate.

5.3 Errors in Sampling

The word error is used in a specialized sense in statistics. It means the difference between the true value and the estimated value. Statistical errors may arise due to inappropriate definitions of statistical units, bias of the investigator or the inherent instability of the collected data. Such errors are called errors of origin. Errors may also arise on account of manipulation in counting, measurement, description or approximation. Such errors are known as errors of manipulation. Yet another cause of statistical errors may be the use of incomplete data, errors may also arise on account of inadequacy of the size of the sample and all such errors are called errors of inadequacy.

Sampling and Non-Sampling Errors

Errors in statistics are classified into two categories:

(1) **Sampling Errors:** Sampling errors have their origin in sampling and they arise on account of the fact that sample has been used to estimate parameters or population values. Sampling errors are attributed to fluctuations in sampling. These arise due to the following reasons:

(*i*) Improper selection of the sample.

(*ii*) Substitution.

(*iii*) Faulty demarcation of statistical units.

(*iv*) Errors due to variability of population and wrong method of estimation.

Measurement of Sampling Error. A measure of sampling error is provided by the standard of the estimate. Estimation of sampling error can reduce the element of uncertainty associated with interpretation of data. In most cases the degree of precision or the opposite of error, would depend on the size of the sample. The standard error of estimate is inversely proportional to the square root of the sample size. In other words, as the sample size increases, element of error is reduced.

(2) **Non-Sampling Errors :** Non-sampling errors generally arise when data are not properly observed, approximated and processed. These arise due to the following reasons:

(*i*) Improper or ambiguous definition of various terms.

(*ii*) Incomplete questionnaire and defective methods of interviewing.

(*iii*) Personal bias of the investigator.

(*iv*) Lack of trained and qualified investigators and failure of respondents to give correct answers.

(*v*) Improper coverage and inadequate or incomplete response.

(*vi*) Errors in compilation and tabulation.

Measurement of Errors

Statistical errors can be measured either:

(*a*) Absolutely or

(*b*) Relatively

Absolute and Relative Errors. If the error is measured absolutely it is called an absolute error and if it is measured relatively it is called relative error. Absolute error is the difference between the true value and the estimate. Relative error is the ratio of the absolute error to the estimate.

If U' stands for the actual value, U for the estimated value, U_e for the absolute error and e for the relative error, then

$$U_e = U' - U$$

$$e = \frac{U' - U}{U}$$

Positive and Negative Errors. Absolute and relative errors can be either positive or negative. If the true value exceeds the estimate, the error is said to be positive and, on the other hand, if the estimate exceeds the true value the error is called negative.

Classes of Errors

Broadly speaking, errors may be either

(*a*) Biased, or

(*b*) Unbiased.

Biased Errors. Biased errors are those which arise on account of some bias in the mind of the investigator or the informant or in the instruments of measurement. Biased errors are cumulative.

Unbiased Errors. Unbiased errors are those which arise just on account of chance. Unbiased errors are generally compensating.

5.4 Types of Sampling

Samples can be selected from a universe in any one of the following three manners:

(*i*) Purposive or subjective or judgement sampling.

(*ii*) Probability sampling.

(*iii*) Mixed sampling.

Some of the important sub-types of sampling schemes under probability and mixed sampling are:

(1) Simple random sampling.

(2) Stratified random sampling.

(3) Systematic sampling.

(4) Multi-stage sampling.

(5) Quasi-random sampling.

(6) Area sampling.

(7) Simple Cluster sampling.

(8) Multi-stage Cluster sampling.

(9) Quota sampling.

Choice of Sampling Techniques

It is very difficult to say that any one of the techniques listed above would always be better than the rest. Factors like nature of the problem, size of the universe, size of the sample, availability of resources and time affect the choice of an appropriate method. For example, in studies where the size of the sample is small in relation to the size of the universe, purposive sampling would be better than random sampling, but as the size of the sample increases, the importance of random sampling also goes up.

If level of significance (α)	
(*i*) $\alpha = 5\%$	reject H_0 if $\lvert Z \rvert > 1.96$
(*ii*) $\alpha = 1\%$	reject H_0 if $\lvert Z \rvert > 2.58$

Judging Reliability of a Sample

The reliability of a sample can be determined in the following ways:

(*i*) A number of samples may be taken from the same universe and the results of various samples compared. If there is not much variation in the results of the different samples, it is a measure of its reliability.

(*ii*) Sub-samples may be taken from the main sample and studied. If the results of the sub-samples are similar to those given by the main sample, it is a measure of its reliability.

(*iii*) If some mathematical properties are found in the distribution under study, the sample result can be compared with expected values obtained on the basis of mathematical relationship and if the difference between them is not significant, the sample has given dependable results.

In distributions where binomial, normal, Poisson or any other theoretical distribution is applicable, sample results can be compared with the expected values and they would give an idea about the reliability of the sample.

5.5 Estimation Theory and Hypothesis Testing

(U.P.T.U. 2005, 2006)

The aim of all sample studies is to obtain the best possible parameter values. Sample studies by themselves have no significance unless they enable us to have some idea about the universe from which the samples have been drawn. Therefore it is necessary that samples are representative of the universe and contain its main characteristics. We know that statistical data can be collected either through a census or through a sample. In case of a census study, the question of estimating parameter values does not arise as the study itself covers the entire universe. However, when sample studies are conducted, parameter values have to be estimated.

In this section we shall discuss the techniques which enable us to make generalizations on the basis of sample studies. We will also discuss the extent to which such generalizations are valid and, if they are valid, the degree of confidence with which such a statement can be made.

In sample studies, the following problems are encountered:

(*i*) How to estimate parameter values or how to generalize the result of the sample to the entire population?

(*ii*) How to find out whether the generalizations made are valid or not?

(*ii*) What is the level of confidence with which a particular generalization can be made?

The answers to these problems are provided by an important branch of statistics – statistical inference, which can be broadly divided into the following heads:

(*i*) Estimation Theory, and

(*ii*) Hypothesis Testing.

5.5.1 Estimation Theory

Estimation theory refers to the techniques and methods by which population parameters are estimated from sample studies. Estimation of parameter is absolutely essential whenever a sample study has been conducted as people are generally interested in parameter values only. The theory of estimation has been grouped in two classes:

(*i*) Point Estimation – a single statistic is used to estimate the parameter value.

(*ii*) Interval Estimation – a probable range is determined within which the real value of the parameter is expected to lie.

Point Estimation

A particular value of the sample (or statistic) which is used to estimate the parameter value is called the point estimate or estimator of the parameter. A good estimator would give us a parameter value which is as close to the real value as possible. It should possess the following characteristics:

(*i*) It should be unbiased.

(*ii*) It should be consistent.

(*iii*) It should be efficient.

(*iv*) It should be sufficient.

Interval Estimate

Even the best possible point estimate may differ from the population value and make the estimate unsatisfactory. In such a situation, the question arises that can we make some generalizations about the universe values if not precisely, then within a certain range? This is what we aim at in interval estimate. If sample size is large, we try and estimate the parameter values within certain limits. We can also determine the probability of our being wrong while making a particular statement about a parameter. The limits within which a parameter value is estimated is called the fiducially limits or confidence interval or confidence limits. These limits would vary on the basis of the degree of precision which is desired to be achieved.

We know that in a normal distribution mean ± 1.96σ includes 95% of the items of the distribution. It means that if our limits are within mean ± 1.96σ, the probability of our going wrong is 0.05.

5.5.2 Hypothesis Testing

A hypothesis in statistics is simply a quantitative statement about a population. It is an assumption that is made about parameter values and then its validity is tested by statistical techniques which ultimately tell us whether the hypothesis is correct and is sustained or whether it is false and is to be rejected.

To important concepts associated with hypothesis testing and theory of estimation are 'sampling distribution' and 'standard error.'

5.6 Sampling Distribution and Standard Error

(U.P.T.U.)

A sampling distribution is an array of sample studies relating to a universe. If we calculate the mean of the sampling distribution it could be deemed to be the mean of the universe. Similarly the standard deviation of the sampling distribution would be called the standard error.

If n samples are taken from a universe then the mean of their mean values would be close to the mean of the entire universe and the standard deviation of these mean values would be called the standard error. The concept of standard error is very useful in testing statistical hypothesis.

If all possible samples of a certain size are taken from the universe then the mean of the sampling distribution of means would be equal to the mean of the universe. That is

$E(X) = \mu$

where E(X) stands for the mean of sampling distribution and μ stands for the mean of the universe.

further, variance of X is nearly equal to $\frac{\sigma}{N}$. Variance of X depends on the sample size – the bigger the size of the sample, the smaller would be the variance. If the variance is small the standard error would also be small and the degree of precision would be greater.

According to Central Limit Theorem, if $X_1, X_2, X_3, \ldots, X_n$ is a random sample from a normal population with mean μ and variance σ^2, then the sample mean X is also normally distributed with mean μ and variance $\frac{\sigma^2}{N}$. This is true even if the universe from which the samples have been taken is not normal, provided the sample size is large (greater than 30).

Standard Error

Utility:

(*i*) It provides an idea about the degree of precision of a sample or in other words, it tells us about the extent to which a sample is reliable. The greater the standard error, the greater is the element of unreliability of the sample and lesser is the degree of precision. Precision is the reciprocal of standard error $\left(\frac{1}{SE}\right)$. The reliability of a sample would vary as the square root of the number of items in the sample. Therefore, if the degree precision has to be doubled or the degree of uncertainty has to be halved, the size of the sample would have to be increased fourfold $\because SE = \frac{\sigma}{\sqrt{N}}$.

(*ii*) The standard error helps in determining the limits within which a parameter value is expected to vary. This is so because, as we have already seen, the sampling distribution tends to be a normal distribution if the sample size is large. In a normal distribution we know that 95% of the items have a value within mean $\pm$ 1.96σ (where σ denotes standard error). This means that 95% of the sample means will range within the mean of the universe $\pm$ 1.96σ. similarly, in a normal distribution mean $\pm$ 3σ covers 99.73% of the items. The chance of sample mean going outside $\mu \pm 3$(standard error) is very small ($p = 0.0027$). it means that only 27 times out of 10,000 the sample mean can cross these limits.

(*iii*) The standard error helps in testing a hypothesis. Usually hypothesis is tested at 95% level of significance which means that we can afford to be wrong only in 5 cases out of 100. In a normal curve $\mu \pm 1.96\sigma$ covers 95% of the values. Therefore, if our sample has given us a result which falls outside the range of $\mu \pm 1.96\sigma$ it is outside the level of precision desired. On the other hand, if the difference between the observed and expected values is within this range, we can say that the difference is on account of fluctuations of sampling and can be ignored. We will be wrong in our assertion only 5 times out of 100 or the probability of our being wrong is 0.05. If we want greater caution, we can test the hypothesis at a higher level of precision. We can set the range at $\mu \pm 2.58\sigma$. this range covers 99% of the values. If the difference between observed and expected values falls within this range it means that the difference is not significant. We will be wrong in our assertion only once in a 100 cases ($p = 0.01$).

Difference between Standard Deviation and Standard Error

The difference between standard deviation and standard error is that the former concerns original values and the latter concerns the statistic computed from samples of original values. The standard deviation of the distribution of sample means is called the standard error of the mean. The standard deviation applies to the distribution of items around their average while the standard error of the mean applies to the distribution of averages of samples around the true average of the universe.

Hypothesis Testing

Hypothesis testing involves finding out whether the difference in the estimated value of the parameter and the true value, if known, is significant or it could have arisen due to fluctuations of sampling. Many times we may be interested in knowing whether the results given to us by two different samples drawn from the same universe are consistent with each other or whether the difference between their values is significant and could not have arisen due to fluctuations of sampling. In all such cases we formulate a hypothesis and then test its validity.

A hypothesis is a quantitative statement about a population. It may or may not be true. By testing the hypothesis we can find out whether it deserves acceptance or rejection.

Procedure for Hypothesis Testing

(*i*) ***Set up a hypothesis.*** Generally a single hypothesis is not set. Two complimentary hypotheses are set at the same time. If one hypothesis is accepted then the other is automatically rejected and vice versa. These hypotheses are known as

a. **Null hypothesis or hypothesis of no difference (denoted by H_0).**

b. **Alternative hypothesis (denoted by H_1).**

The concept of null hypothesis is very important in the theory of statistical inference and tests of significance. This hypothesis presumes that there is no difference between any two values which are being compared and any difference is on account of fluctuations of sampling. As against null hypothesis, the alternate hypothesis assumes that the differences are not due to fluctuations of sampling; they are real.

Definition:

a. **Null Hypothesis (H_0):** It is useful tool in testing the significance of difference. Hypothesis asserts that there is no real difference in the sample & population & the difference found is accidental unimportant arriving out of fluctuations.

b. **Alternative hypothesis (H_1):** This specific those value that researcher believe to hold true of course he hopes that the sample data lead to acceptance of this Hypothesis.

5% and 1% Level of significance (α) **(U.P.T.U.)**

The level of significance is the maximum probability of the including type I error. The commonly used level of significance are 5% (0.05) and 1% (0.01). If we adopt 5% level it implies that in 5 out of 100 we are likely to reject a correct number. In other words it implies that we are 95% confident that our decision to reject H_0 is correct. Level of significance desired is always fixed in advance before applying the test.

Degree of freedom **(U.P.T.U.)**

The degree of freedom play a very important role in χ^2 test of a Hypothesis. The χ^2 test depends on the number of degree of freedom. The data that are given in the form of a series of variables in a row or column or number of frequencies put in cells in a contingency table. Which can be calculated independently are known as the degree of freedom.

In case of data that are given in the form of a series of variable in a row or column one degree of freedom will be the number of items in the series is (r -1) (c - 1) where r = row, c = column

For example, it is there are two column and three rows d.f. will (2-1) (3-1) = 2

In case no. of frequencies are in the form of table then the formulae for d.f. will be (n – 1)

For example, there are 8 items d.f. = (n – 1) = (8 – 1) = 7

***An example*:**

H_0: $\mu = 120$kg

H_i: $\mu \neq 120$kg or

H_i: $\mu > 120$kg or $\mu < 120$kg

(*ii*) *Determine the level of significance*. It means that we have to determine the level of confidence with which a particular hypothesis is accepted or rejected.

(*iii*) *Decide the test statistic.* A test statistic is a statistic computed from a sample. Test statistics are generally based on some probability distribution. Some of the common probability distributions which are used in hypothesis testing are z, t, χ^2 and F, etc. The choice of the test statistic would depend upon the nature of the distribution and the size of the sample. In case of small samples the properties of a normal distribution are not applicable and z-test has to be replaced by t-test.

(*iv*) *Draw conclusions.* The last step in hypothesis is to draw conclusions about accepting or rejecting the hypothesis. A null hypothesis will be rejected if the sample statistic falls in the rejection region. For example, at 5% level of significance, the mean of a sample would not represent the mean of the universe if its value is not within 95% value enclosed in a normal distribution. The rejection area is 2.5% on either side of the normal curve. In such a case we reject the null hypothesis which means that we conclude that the difference between the sample mean and the population mean could not be due to chance. The alternative hypothesis is accepted. On the other hand, if the sample result is within the 95% level of acceptance, we conclude that the difference between sample mean and population mean could be due to chance and hence the sample mean can be used as a parameter value. The null hypothesis is accepted and the alternative hypothesis (of difference) stands rejected.

5.7 Errors in Hypothesis Testing (Type I & II Error)

(U.P.T.U. 2006, 2008)

Two types of errors are generally committed in hypothesis testing. They are Type I Error and Type II Error.

Type I error is committed when we reject a correct or true hypothesis. Type II error is committed when we accept a wrong or incorrect hypothesis. Type I error (of **rejecting a null hypothesis** when it is true) is denoted by α.

α = Probability of Type I Error = Probability of rejecting H_0 when it is true.

Type II error (of **accepting a null hypothesis** when it is not true) is denoted by β.

β = Probability of Type II Error = Probability of accepting H_0 when it is not true.

If the difference between two means is zero and if our test indicated rejection of the null hypothesis, we commit type I error. If the difference between the two means is not zero but our test suggests acceptance of null hypothesis, we commit type II error.

	Accept H_0	**Reject H_0**
H_0 is true	No error	*Type I Error*
H_0 is false	*Type II Error*	No error

Though efforts are made to reduce both type I and type II errors, it is not possible to reduce both at the same time. The value of α can be reduced only by increasing the value of β. A business executive will have to compare the payoff of α with the payoff of β and find out if it is worthwhile to have a larger probability of type I error or a larger probability of type II error. However, in general, it is more risky to accept a false hypothesis (type II error) than to reject a true hypothesis (type I error). The probability of committing a type I error is kept at 5% level, that is, the probability is generally fixed at 0.05. in other words, the critical region is 5% and acceptance region is 95%.

5.8 Two Tailed and One Tailed Test of Hypothesis

(U.P.T.U. 2008)

The critical region (or the region of rejection) which is generally 5%, is kept on both sides of the normal distribution in a two tailed test. It means that 2.5% of the critical region is on the extreme left of the normal curve and 2.5% is on the extreme right. The remaining 95% area would be the acceptance region.

Two tailed test is applied when, for example, the null hypothesis is that mean weight of the undergraduate male students is 120 pounds and the alternate hypothesis is that it is not 120 pounds. In such a situation the actual value of the population mean may be 120 pounds or more than 120 pounds or less than 120 pounds.

On the other hand, if the null hypothesis is that the mean weight of the male undergraduate students is 120 pounds and the alternate hypothesis is that it is more than 120 pounds then the one tailed test (right tailed test) would be applied. If the alternate hypothesis is that it is less than 120 pounds, then again we will use the one tailed test (left tailed test)

Sign of Alternative Hypothesis	Type of Test to be Used
>	Right Tailed Test
=	Two Tailed Test
<	Left Tailed Test

The Critical Value of z for Two Tailed and One Tailed Tests (taken from the Area Table of the Normal Curve)

	Critical Values of z		
Level of Significance	1%	5%	10%
z Critical Value for One Tailed Test	+2.33 or -2.33	+1.645 or -1.645	+1.28 or -1.28
z Critical Value for Two Tailed Test	+2.58 and -2.58	+1.96 and -1.96	+1645 and -1.645+

5.9 Techniques of Association of Attributes & Testing Association of Attributes

Introduction

(U.P.T.U. 2006, 2007, 2008)

Statistics deal with quantitative data. Quantitative data may arise in one of the following ways:

(*a*) An investigator may measure the actual magnitude of some variable. In such a situation a fairly accurate quantitative measurement is possible.

(*b*) However, at times the data might be such that it may not be possible for an investigator to measure their magnitude. In such cases the observer can only study the presence or absence of a particular quality in a group of individuals. He then has to take decision on the basis of some standard definition of the term in question. Such data in which the quantitative measurement of the magnitude is not possible and in which only the presence or absence of an attribute can be studied, are called the statistics of attributes.

Classification of Data

In the analysis of statistics relating to attributes, the first thing is the classification of data. Here data are classified on the basis of the presence or absence of a particular attribute. If only one attribute is being studied, the population would be classified into two groups – one comprising of those units in which this attribute is present and the other consisting of those in which it is not present. If more than one attributes are taken into account, the number of classes would be more than two.

The following points should be noted about the classification of data according to attributes:

(1) ***Classification is Arbitrary and Vague.*** It should be clearly understood that when the universe is divided in, say, two classes, there may not be any clear-cut line of demarcation between them. One attribute may gradually transform into the other attribute and there may be many cases on the borderline between the two attributes. In all types of analysis relating to statistics of attributes, this point should always be kept in mind.

(2) ***Classification by Dichotomy.*** If only one attribute is being studied the universe is divided in two parts – one in which the attribute is present and the other in which it is not present. These classes are mutually exclusive. Such a classification where the universe is divided in two parts is called classification by dichotomy. In actual analysis there are more than two classes in which the universe is divided and such classification is called manifold classification.

Notation and Terminology

Usually capital letters A, B, C, ... are used to denote the presence of attributes and the Greek lower case letters α, β, γ, ... are used to denote the absence of these attributes respectively. The number of units possessing a particular attribute represented by A would be termed as belonging to Class A. Similarly, those in which this attribute is absent would be termed as belonging to Class α.

If two attributes are being studied, their combination can be represented by the combination of the letters representing the two attributes. Thus, if blindness is represented by A and deafness by B then AB would represent blindness and deafness, Aβ would represent blindness and absence of deafness, αB would represent the absence of blindness and presence of deafness and αβ would represent the absence of both blindness as well as deafness.

Class Frequencies. The number of units in different classes are called class frequencies. Class frequencies are represented by enclosing the class symbols by braces. Thus (AB) would represent the frequency of the class AB.

Number of Classes. If there is one attribute represented by A, the total number of classes is 3, namely, A, α and N (if the total or N is also taken as a class). In general the number of classes is equal to 3^n, where n stands for the number of attributes.

Order of Classes. The various classes and their frequencies are demarcated on the basis of an order. Thus

N is a class of Zero Order.

$\left.\begin{matrix} A & B \\ \alpha & \beta \end{matrix}\right\}$ are classes of the First Order.

$\left.\begin{matrix} AB & \alpha\beta \\ A\beta & \alpha B \end{matrix}\right\}$ are classes of the Second Order.

Similarly the frequencies of these classes are also known as frequencies of the zero, first or second order. If there are only two attributes under study, then the second order classes and frequencies are called the classes or the frequencies of the ultimate order. Since these are the last set of classes and frequencies, the number of classes of the ultimate order is equal to 2^n, where n stands for the number of attributes.

Positive and Negative Classes. The classes which represent the presence of an attribute or attributes are called positive classes. The classes which represent the absence of an attribute or attributes are called negative classes. The classes in which one attribute is present and the other is absent are called pairs of contraries. Thus

N, A, B and AB are positive classes.

α and β are negative classes.

Aβ and αB are pairs of contraries.

Relationship between Classes of Various Order

In classifying statistical data according to attributes the following simple rule should be kept in mind. Any class frequencies can always be expressed in terms of class frequencies of higher order. On the basis of this rule we can set up various types of relationship[s between the frequencies of different orders. If there is one attribute only, represented by A, the frequency of the universe or N can be divided into two classes A and α. Thus

(N) = (A) + (α)

Now, if one more attribute B is taken into account, the first order classes, that is, A and α can each be divided into two classes – one in which attribute B is present and the other in which it is absent. Thus

(A) = (AB) + (Aβ)

(α) + (αB) + (αβ)

Similarly

(B) = (AB) + (αB)

(β) + (Aβ) + (αβ)

5.10 Consistency of Data

Meaning. It is obvious that in statistics of attributes no class frequency can be negative. If any class frequency is negative the data are said to be inconsistent. Such inconsistency may be due to wrong counting or inaccurate calculations. In order to test whether a set of figures is consistent or not, various class frequencies should be found and if no class frequency is negative, apparently the data are consistent. However, consistence of data is no proof of their accuracy. The easiest way to check for consistency is to find the ultimate class frequencies because if there is any inconsistency, one or more of these ultimate class frequencies would most probably be negative.

Some Rules for Testing the Consistency of Data

(*i*) In case of single attribute:

(1) (A) $\nless$ 0, otherwise (A) will be negative.

(2) (A) $\ngtr$ (N), otherwise (α) will be negative since (N) = (A) + (α).

(*ii*) Two attributes:

(1) (AB) $\nless$ 0, otherwise (AB) will be negative.

(2) (AB) $\nless$ (A) + (B) – (N), otherwise (αβ) will be negative.

(3) (AB) $\ngtr$ (A), otherwise (Aβ) will be negative since (A) = (AB) + (Aβ)

(4) (AB) $\ngtr$ (B), otherwise (αB) will be negative since (B) = (AB) + (αB)

Incomplete Data. The above rules are also used to fill the gaps if the data are incomplete. With the help of these rules it is possible to lay down the maximum and minimum limits of a particular class frequency.

5.11 Methods of Studying Association

Meaning of Association. Association of attributes refers to such techniques by which we can measure the relationship between two such phenomena whose size cannot be measured and where we can only find out the presence or absence of an attribute.

Just as in case of correlation analysis we study the relationship between two variables whose value can be measured, similarly in case of association we study the relationship between two attributes which are not capable of quantitative measurement.

The study of association can be done by any of the following methods:

(*i*) Comparison of Actual and Observed Frequencies.

(*ii*) Comparison of Various Proportions and Products.

(*iii*) Calculation of Yule's Coefficient of Association.

(*iv*) Calculation of Coefficient of Colligation.

(*v*) Calculation of Coefficient of Contingency.

6.1.1 Comparison of Actual and Observed Frequencies

Whenever we want to study association between two attributes A and B we try to find out whether attribute A is more commonly found with attribute B than is ordinarily expected. Thus, in a study of association, the first thing to be calculated is the expected value of (AB). This value is calculated on the basis of simple rules of probability. Thus, if in a population of 100 students, 20 are married, the probability of coming across a married student is $\frac{20}{100}$.

If two attributes A and B are studied in a universe and if the frequency of A is represented by (A) and of B by (B), then

$$\textit{The probability of } A = \frac{(A)}{(N)}$$

$$\textit{and the probability of } B = \frac{(B)}{(N)}$$

The combine probability of two independent events is equal to the product of their individual probabilities.

$$\therefore \textit{the combined probability of A and B} = \frac{(A)}{(N)} \times \frac{(B)}{(N)}$$

$$\textit{and the expectation of A and B combined} = \frac{(A)}{(N)} \times \frac{(B)}{(N)} \times (N) = \frac{(A) \times (B)}{(N)}$$

Therefore, if attributes A and B are independent,

$$\textit{the expected frequency of } (AB) = \frac{(A) \times (B)}{(N)}$$

Criterion of Independence. If there is no kind of relationship between the attributes A and B we may expect to find the same proportion of A's in B's as in β's. If this is not the case, it indicates an association between the attributes A and B.

Two attributes A and B are said to be independent if the observed frequency of (AB) is equal to its expected frequency, i.e., $\frac{(A) \times (B)}{(N)}$.

Complete Association and Dissociation. There is complete association (perfect positive association) between two attributes A and B if all A's are B's or all B's are A's. This would be possible in any one of the following three cases.

(*i*) (A) = (B) =(AB).

(*ii*) (A) = (AB).

(*iii*) (B) = (AB).

There would be complete dissociation (perfect negative association) between A and B if none of the A's is B. Alternatively, if N contains no such unit which possesses neither of the two attributes, it is also taken to be a case of complete dissociation. Therefore, there is complete dissociation between attributes A and B if

(*i*) (AB) = 0 or

(*ii*) (αβ) = 0

Limitation. The main limitation is that this method only determines the nature of association between A and B, that is, whether the association is positive or negative. It does not tell us about the degree of association.

While studying association using this method, it must be kept in mind that if the value of (AB) is found to be greater than the value of $\frac{(A) \times (B)}{(N)}$, it should not be at once concluded that there is positive association between the two attributes. It is quite possible, particularly when the difference between observed and the expected values is not much, that the association may be the result of sampling fluctuations and the true association may be zero. As such, unless the difference the observed and the expected values is very significant, we should not conclude that there is any association or dissociation between the two attributes.

6.1.2 Comparison of Various Proportions and Products

This method is slightly better than the previous method as it compares the proportion between the various classes.

Thus attributes A and B are

(*i*) Independent if

$$\frac{(AB)}{(B)} = \frac{(A\beta)}{(\beta)}$$

(*ii*) Positively associated if

$$\frac{(AB)}{(B)} > \frac{(A\beta)}{(\beta)}$$

(*iii*) Negatively associated if

$$\frac{(AB)}{(B)} < \frac{(A\beta)}{(\beta)}$$

If the first relation holds good, the corresponding relationships

$$\frac{(\alpha B)}{(B)} < \frac{(\alpha\beta)}{(\beta)}; \frac{(AB)}{(A)} = \frac{(\alpha\beta)}{(A)} \text{ and } \frac{(\alpha\beta)}{(A)} = \frac{(\alpha\beta)}{(\alpha)}$$

would also hold good

further it can also be concluded that A and B would be independent if

$$\frac{(AB)}{(A)} = \frac{(B)}{(N)}; \frac{(AB)}{(B)} \text{ and } \frac{(AB)}{(N)} = \frac{(A)}{(N)} \times \frac{(B)}{(N)}$$

It can also be found out easily that A and B would be independent if

$$(AB)(\alpha\beta) = (A\beta)(\alpha B)$$

6.1.3 Yule's Coefficient of Association (U.P.T.U. 2005)

Yule's coefficient aims at finding out the extent of association between two attributes. It is given by

$$Q = \frac{(AB)(\alpha\beta) - (A\beta)(\alpha B)}{(B)(\alpha\beta) + (A\beta)(\alpha\beta)}$$

If Q = 0, the two attributes are independent.

If Q = +1, there is perfect association between the two attributes.

If Q = -1, there is perfect dissociation between the two attributes.

The chief characteristic of this coefficient is that it is independent of the relative proportions of A's, B's, α's and β's in the data. That is, if all terms containing A are multiplied by a constant, the value of Q would not be affected. The same would hold good for all values containing B, α and β.

5.12 Significance Tests In Variables (Large Samples)

Introduction

(U.P.T.U. 2007)

The aims of sampling studies in statistics of variables are the same as in case of statistics of attributes. Here also we *compare the actual or observed frequencies with those expected under certain assumptions* and try to find out whether the difference can be attributed to chance. As in sampling of attributes here too we try *to obtain one or two constants for the universe* – mean or standard deviation because these can give an idea about the parent distribution. In sampling studies relating to variables, as in sampling studies of attributes, our third aim is *to assess the reliability of our estimates.*

Difference between Large and Small Samples

Though no hard and fast line can be drawn between large and small samples, yet, conventionally if a sample consists of more than 30 items, it is considered to be large. A sample consisting of up to 30 items is deemed to be a small sample.

The tests of significance used in large samples are different from those used in small samples because small samples fail to satisfy the assumptions under which large sample analysis is done. The assumptions under which significance tests are applied in case of large samples are:

(*i*) The random sampling distribution of statistic has the properties of the normal curve. In case of small samples it may not be so.

(*ii*) Sample values are close to parameter values and can be used for analysis in the absence of parameter values. For example, for calculating the standard error, if the standard deviation of the universe is not known, it can be substituted by the standard deviation of the sample. This is not possible in case of small samples unless necessary adjustments are made.

Significance Tests

The significance tests used in statistics of variables are based on the calculation of standard error. The method of calculating standard error of various measures associated with variables are given below:

1.	SE of Mean (when population σ is known)	$\frac{\sigma_p}{\sqrt{n}}$
2.	SE of Mean (when population σ is not known)	$\frac{\sigma(sample)}{\sqrt{n}} = \frac{S}{\sqrt{n}}$
3.	SE of Median	$1.25331 \frac{\sigma}{\sqrt{n}}$
4.	SE of Quartiles	$1.36263 \frac{\sigma}{\sqrt{n}}$

5.	SE of Quartile Deviation	$0.78672 \frac{\sigma}{\sqrt{n}}$
6.	SE of Mean Deviation	$0.6028 \frac{\sigma}{\sqrt{n}}$
7.	SE of Standard Deviation	$\frac{\sigma}{\sqrt{2n}}$
8.	SE of Variance	$\sigma^2 \sqrt{\frac{2}{n}}$
9.	SE of Coefficient of Variation	$\frac{V}{\sqrt{2n}} \sqrt{1 + \frac{2V^2}{10^4}}$
10.	SE of Coefficient of Skewness	$\sqrt{\frac{3}{2n}}$
11.	SE of Pearsonian Coefficient of Correlation	$\frac{1 - r^2}{\sqrt{n}}$
12.	SE of Spearman's Rank Correlation	$\frac{1}{\sqrt{n-1}}$
13.	SE of Regression Coefficient of Y on X (b_{yx})	$\frac{\sigma_y \sqrt{1-r^2}}{\sigma_x \sqrt{n}}$
14.	SE of Regression Coefficient of X on Y (b_{xy})	$\frac{\sigma_x \sqrt{1-r^2}}{\sigma_y \sqrt{n}}$
15.	SE of Regression Estimate of Y on X	$\sigma_y \sqrt{1-r^2}$
16.	SE of Regression Estimate of X on Y	$\sigma_x \sqrt{1-r^2}$
17.	SE of Coefficient of Association	$\frac{1-Q^2}{2} \sqrt{\frac{1}{(AB)} + \frac{1}{(A\beta)} + \frac{1}{(\alpha B)} + \frac{1}{(\alpha\beta)}}$

Standard Error of the Difference of Sample Means

Suppose two samples have given us two mean values and we have to find out whether there is a significant difference between the two values, or whether they could have come from one universe or universes having the same mean and standard deviation. Here we shall calculate the standard error of the difference of the two sample means and then we shall find out whether the difference between them is more than, say, three times the standard error of the difference. If the actual difference between the two means is more than thrice the standard error of the difference, it is said to be significant, otherwise the difference can be due to fluctuations of sampling.

There is no hard and fast rule of taking the criterion of three standard errors only. We know that mean ± 3 standard error would cover 99.73% of the cases and the probability of a difference equal to or more than three standard errors arising out of chance would only be 1–0.9973 or 0.0027. we can test the results at 1.96 standard error in which case the probability of getting a difference equal to or more than 1.96 standard error due to sampling fluctuations would be 0.05.

The formulae for the standard error of the difference of two sample means are as follows:

1.	Difference of two Sample Means (If σp is known)	$SE_{(\bar{X}_1-\bar{X}_2)} = \sqrt{\frac{\sigma_p^2}{n_1}+\frac{\sigma_p^2}{n_2}} = \sqrt{\sigma_p^2\left(\frac{1}{n_1}+\frac{1}{n_2}\right)}$
2.	Difference of two Sample Means (If σp is not known) ($\sigma_1 = S_1$, $\sigma_2 = S_2$)	$SE_{(\bar{X}_1-\bar{X}_2)} = \sqrt{\frac{S_1^2}{n_1}+\frac{S_2^2}{n_2}}$
3.	Difference of two Sample Means (when correlation exists)	$SE_{(\bar{X}_1-\bar{X}_2)} = \sqrt{\frac{\sigma_1^2}{n_1}+\frac{\sigma_2^2}{n_2} - 2r\left(\frac{\sigma_1}{n_1}+\frac{\sigma_2}{n_2}\right)}$
4.	Difference between first Sample Mean and Combined Mean $\sigma p = \sigma_{12}$ (Combined)	$SE_{(\bar{X}_1-\bar{X}_2)} = \sqrt{\frac{\sigma_p^2}{(n_1+n_2)} x \frac{n_2}{n_1}}$
5.	Difference between second Sample Mean and Combined Mean $\sigma p = \sigma_{12}$ (Combined)	$SE_{(\bar{X}_1-\bar{X}_2)} = \sqrt{\frac{\sigma_p^2}{(n_1+n_2)} x \frac{n_1}{n_2}}$

Comparing Mean of a Sample with the Pooled Mean of two Samples

Sometimes the mean of a sample is compared with the combined mean of the two samples taken together. In such cases the standard error of the difference of first sample and the combined sample is calculated as

$$SE_{(\bar{X}_1-\bar{X}_{12})} = \sqrt{\sigma^2\left(\frac{n^2}{n(n_1+n_2)}\right)}$$

Comparing Means of Correlated Samples

If the two samples whose mean values are being compared are not independent but are correlated the formula for the calculation of standard error of the difference between two such means is modified as follows

$$SE_{(\bar{X}_1-\bar{X}_{12})} = \sqrt{\frac{\sigma_1^{\ 2}}{n_1}+\frac{\sigma_2^{\ 2}}{n_2}-2r\left(\frac{\sigma_1}{n_1}x\frac{\sigma_2}{n_2}\right)}$$

Standard Error of the Difference between two Sample Medians

The standard error of the difference of two sample medians

$$SE_{(M_1-M_2)} = \sqrt{SE_{M_1}^{\ 2}+SE_{M_2}^{\ \ 2}}$$

Standard Error of the difference between two Sample Standard Deviations

1.	Difference of two sample standard deviations (when σ_p is known)	$SE_{\sigma_1-\sigma_2} = \sqrt{\frac{\sigma_p^{\ 2}}{2n_1}+\frac{\sigma_p^{\ 2}}{2n_2}} = \sqrt{\sigma_p^{\ 2}\left(\frac{1}{2n_1}+\frac{1}{2n_2}\right)}$
2.	Difference of two sample standard deviations (when σ_p is not known) ($\sigma_1 = S_1^2, \sigma_2^2 = S_2^2$)	$SE_{\sigma_1-\sigma_2} = \sqrt{\frac{\sigma_1^{\ 2}}{2n_1}+\frac{\sigma_2^{\ 2}}{2n_2}} = \sqrt{\frac{S_1^{\ 2}}{2n_1}+\frac{S_2^{\ 2}}{2n_2}}$
3.	Difference of σ_1 and combined standard deviation ($\sigma_p = \sigma_{12}$)	$SE_{\sigma_1-\sigma_{12}} = \sqrt{\frac{\sigma_p^{\ 2}}{2(n_1+n_2)}x\frac{n_2}{n_1}}$
4.	Difference of σ_2 and combined standard deviation ($\sigma_p = \sigma_{12}$)	$SE_{\sigma_2-\sigma_{12}} = \sqrt{\frac{\sigma_p^{\ 2}}{2(n_1+n_2)}x\frac{n_1}{n_2}}$

5.13 Significance Tests in Small Samples

The analysis of small samples has to be done by techniques which are different from those applicable in case of large samples.

Size of Samples and Standard Measures. Some effects of the smallness of the sample size on various standard measures:

(1) The smaller the sample the greater would be the variation in the value of mean of different samples.

(2) The standard deviation of the smaller samples tends to be smaller than true standard deviation of the universe; the smaller the sample, the smaller would be the standard deviation.

(3) Since the standard deviation of small samples tends to be smaller than the standard deviation of the universe, all errors base on these smaller standard deviations also tend to be small. As such, unless corrections are made for the errors of small samples, they would tend to underestimate the actual error.

5.14 Student's t-Distribution

(U.P.T.U. 2005, 2007)

The sampling distribution of any statistic in the standardised form is *N(0, 1)* asymptotically that is the sampling distribution of any statistic t is normally distributed with mean 0 and variance 1 and given by

$$Z = \frac{t - E(t)}{S.E.(t)} - N(0,1) \text{ as } n \to \infty$$

The theory of large sample $(n > 30)$ depends on the above property of the sampling distribution. But if the sample is small, then the distribution of the standardised variable Z of the statistic t will be far from normally and as a result the normal test cannot be applied. So far the small samples (when n; < 30) new method and tests of significance known as EXACT SAMPLE TECHNIQUES have been developed. Exact sample technique can be applied even for large samples but the large sample theory cannot be applied for small samples. This theory was developed by Irish statistician William S. Cossect gave his statistic name as

Students t-distribution or t-test. The quantity t is defined as

$$t = \frac{\text{Difference of population parameter and the corresponding statistic}}{\text{Standard error of the statistic}}$$

with $(n - 1)$ degrees of freedom if the sample size is n. (The degree of freedom for t = size of sample - 1).

Student's Distribution

If $x_1, x_2, \ldots\ldots\ldots x_n$ is a random sample size of n drawn from a normal population with mean μ and variance σ^2 then the student's statistic is defined as

$$t = \frac{\overline{x} - \mu}{S.E.(\overline{x})} = \frac{\overline{x} - \mu}{\sqrt{s^2 / n - 1}}$$

These are the following assumptions for t-test :

(1) Samples are drawn from normal population and are random.

(2) For testing the equality of two population means, the population variances are regarded as equal.

(3) The population standard deviation may not be known.

(4) In case of the two samples same adjustment in degree of freedom for t are made.

Properties of t-Distribution

1. t-distribution is asymptotic to n-axis and it is extended to infinity on either side.
2. The shape of the curve or form of t-distribution varies with the degrees of freedom. The degree of freedom is defined as $(n - 1)$.
3. t-distribution is a symmetrical distribution with mean zero.
4. Graphical representation of the t-distribution curve is similar to the manual distribution.
5. t-distribution curve is flater than the manual distribution. This means that the area near the tail is larger for the t-distribution than for the normal distribution.
6. The values of t for different values of $(n - 1)$ and different levels of significance are tabulated in the t-tables. The significant values of t at a specified level of the significance say α for a single tailed test is the same as the value at the level of significance 2α for two tailed test.
7. Sampling distribution of t does not depend on population parameter but it depends only on degree of freedom that is on the sample size.

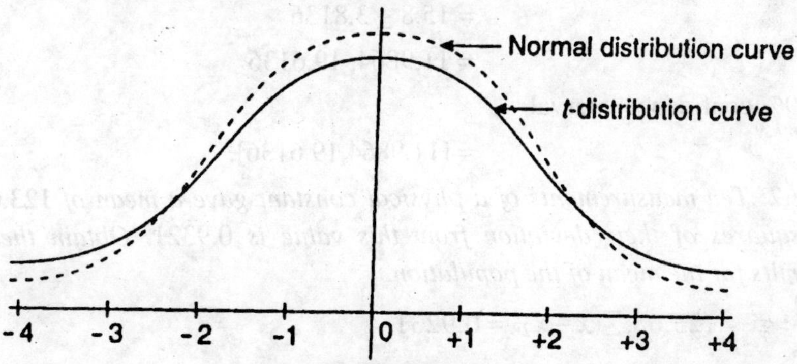

Fig. 6.

Application of t-Distribution

(U.P.T.U. 2007)

The t-distribution is useful to test :

1. Whether the sample mean (x) differs significantly from the hypothetical value μ for the population mean.
2. Whether the two sample means differ significantly.
3. Whether an observed correlation or regression co-officient is significant.

Confidence interval for μ.

It $t_{0.5}$, and $t_{,01}$ denote the values of t at 5% and 1% level of significance interval for μ at these level of significance are given by

$$x \pm t_{.05} SE(\overline{x}) \;\; and \;\; x \pm t_{.01} SE(\overline{x})$$

where $SE(\overline{x})$ is standard error of mean and is defined as

$$\frac{S}{\sqrt{n-1}}, S^2 = \frac{\Sigma(x-\bar{x})^2}{n}$$

Illustrative Examples

Example 1. *A sample of size* 9 *from a normal population gave* $\bar{x}$ =15.8 *and* S_x^2 = 10.3. *Find a* 99% *interval for population mean.*

Solution: $\bar{x}$ = 15.8; S_x^2 = 10.3 and n = 9

Degree of freedom = n - 1 = 9 - 1 = 8.

Also tool for 8 degree of freedom = 3.36.

99% confidence limits for the population mean $\bar{x}$ are

$$\bar{x} \pm t_{.01}\frac{S}{\sqrt{n-1}} = 15.8 \pm 3.36 \times \sqrt{\frac{10.3}{8}}$$

$$= 15.8 \pm 3.36 \times 1.135$$

$$= 15.8 \pm 3.8136$$

$$= 11.9864, 19.6136$$

Hence, 99% confidence interval

$$= [11.9864, 19.6136].$$ **Ans.**

Example 2. *Ten measurements of a physical constant gave a mean of* 123.69 *units and the sum of the squares of their deviation from this value is* 0.9321. *Obtain the* 95% *and* 99% *confidence limits for the mean of the population.*

Solution : $\bar{x} = 123.68, \Sigma(x-\bar{x})^2 = 0.9231$

$$S = \sqrt{\frac{\Sigma(x-\bar{x})^2}{n-1}} = \sqrt{\frac{0.9321}{9}} = 0.3218$$

95% confidence limits are

$$\bar{x} \pm t_{.05} SE(\bar{x}) = 123.68 \pm (2.26) \times \frac{(0.3218)}{\sqrt{10}}$$

$$= 123.45, 123.909$$ **Ans.**

95% confidence limits are

$$\bar{x} \pm t_{.01} SE(\bar{x}) = 123.68 \pm \frac{(3.25)(0.3218)}{\sqrt{10}}$$

$$= 123.349, 124.001$$ **Ans.**

Determination of Sample Size

The determination of the size of a sample is the most important of the value of the population parameters.

(i) Sample size for estimating a mean : To determine the sample size for estimating a population mean, the following factors must be required :

(a) The desired confidence level.

(b) The permissible sampling error

$$E = \overline{x} - \mu$$

(c) The standard deviation σ

Sample size

$$\boxed{n = \left(\frac{\sigma Z}{E}\right)^2}$$

(ii) Sampling size for estimating a proportion : To determine the sample for estimating a proportion we required three factors :

(a) The desired confidence level.

(b) The permissible sampling error E- difference between the estimate from the sample p and the parameter P to be estimated = P - p.

(c) The estimated true proportion of success.

$$\boxed{n = \left(\frac{Z^2 pq}{E^2}\right)}$$

where q - 1 - p.

Example 3. *It is known that the population standard deviation in waiting time for L.P.G. gas cylinder in Bareilly is 15 days. How large a sample should be chosen to be 95% confident, the waiting time is within 7 days of true average?*

Solution:

$$n = \left(\frac{\sigma Z}{E}\right)^2$$

$$= \left(\frac{15 \times 1.96}{7}\right)^2 = \left(\frac{29.4}{2}\right)^2 = (4.2)^2 = 17.64 \approx 18$$

Hence, the size of the sample is 18. **Ans.**

Example 4: *Rama wants to determine on the basis of sample study the mean time required to complete a definite job so that he may be 95% confident that the mean may remain within ± 2* *days of the true mean. As per the available records the population variance is 64 days. How large should the sample be for his study?*

Solution: Here $\sigma = \sqrt{64} = 8$

Also Z is $N(0,1)$

Ii is given that

$$P[|\bar{x} - \mu| < 2] = 0.95 \quad ...(1)$$

But

$$P\left[(\bar{x} - \mu) \leq 1.96 \frac{\sigma}{\sqrt{n}}\right] = 0.95 \quad ...(2)$$

From Eqs. (1) and (2), we get

$$\frac{1.96 \times \sigma}{\sqrt{n}} = 2$$

$$n = \left(\frac{1.96 \times 8}{2}\right)^2$$

$$= (7.84)^2 = 61.42 = 62$$

Hence, the sample size should be 62. **Ans.**

Example 5: The mean weekly sales of soap bars in department store was 146.3 bars per store. After an advertising companies the mean weekly sales in 22 stores for a typical week increased to 153.7 and showed a standard deviation of 17.2 was the advertising companies successful (Given tabulated value of t for 21 d.f. at 5% Level of significance = 1.72) **(U.P.T.U. 2009)**

Ans. $\bar{x}$ = sample mean = 153.7

μ = universal or population mean = 146.3

S.D. = 17.2

then

$$t = \frac{\bar{x} - \mu}{\frac{\sigma}{\sqrt{n-1}}} = \frac{153.7 - 146.3}{\frac{17.2}{\sqrt{22-1}}}$$

$$= \frac{7.4}{\frac{17.2}{\sqrt{21}}} = 1.97$$

No. of degree of freedom = 22-1 = 21

Level of significance - 5%

Tabulated value = 1.72

So, $t_{cal}(1.97) > t_{table}(1.72)$

So, Calculated value Higher than tabulated value

→ null Hypothesis (H_0) is rejected.

Large Sample Theory (Z-Test)

- **Test of significance in case of Attributes**
  - **for one sample**

    $$z=\frac{x-np}{\sqrt{npq}}$$

    where,
    n = number of trials
    p = probability of success
    q = 1 − p = prob. of failure
    $\sqrt{npq}$ = standard error
  - **for two sample**

    $$z=\frac{p_1 \sim p_2}{\sqrt{p_0 q_0\left(\frac{1}{n_1}+\frac{1}{n_1}\right)}}$$

    where,
    P_1, P_2 are the proportions of attributes

    $$P_0=\frac{P_1n_1+P_2n_2}{n_1+n_2}$$

    $$q_0=1-p_0$$
- **Test of significance for Variables**
  - **Test of significance for mean**

    $$z=\frac{\overline{x}\sim\mu}{\sigma/\sqrt{n}}$$

    where,
    $\overline{x}$ = sample mean
    μ = population mean
    σ = standard deviation of population
    n = sample size
  - **Test of significance of the difference between mean of two samples**

    $$z=\frac{\overline{x}_1\sim\overline{x}_2}{\sqrt{\frac{\sigma_1^2}{n_1}+\frac{\sigma_2^2}{n_2}}}$$

    where,
    $\overline{x}_1, \overline{x}_2$ are the sample mean and σ_1 and σ_2 their standard deviations with sample size n_1 and n_2.

5.15 Z-Transformation

Z-Test of Significance of Correlation Coefficient

According to this method of testing the significance of the coefficient of correlation in small samples, given by Fisher, the coefficient of correlation in the sample, r is transformed into Z, where

$$Z=\frac{1}{2}\log_e\frac{1+r}{1-r}=\log_{10}\frac{1+r}{1-r}\times 1.513$$

The standard error of Z

$$SE_Z=\frac{1}{n-3}$$

Similarly, the coefficient of correlation in the universe, P can be transformed into ξ (the Greek small letter xi). The value of ξ is calculated in exactly the same manner as the value of Z. If the coefficient of correlation of the universe is not known, it is supposed to be 0 and then the value of ξ also becomes 0.

To test the significance of a coefficient of correlation the difference between Z and ξ is calculated and the relationship of the difference and the standard error of Z is then found out. If this difference is more than twice (or thrice, depending upon the level of significance), the standard error is supposed to be significant.

This test is used to test the significance of the correlation co-efficient in small samples. If r is the correlation co-efficient of the sample and p, the of the population, calculate the value of

$$\frac{z-\xi}{\frac{1}{\sqrt{n-3}}}, \text{ where } z=\frac{1}{2}\tan h^{-1} r=\frac{1}{2}\log\left(\frac{1+r}{1-r}\right) \text{ or } 1.1513 \log_{10}\left(\frac{1+r}{1-r}\right)$$

$$\xi=\frac{1}{2}\tanh^{-1}\rho=\frac{1}{2}\log,\left(\frac{1+\rho}{1-\rho}\right) \text{ or } 1.1513 \log_{10}\left(\frac{1+\rho}{1-\rho}\right)$$

$$\frac{1}{\sqrt{n-3}}=S.E.$$

If the absolute value of this $\frac{\text{difference}}{\text{S.E.}}$ exceeds 1.96, the difference is significant at 5% level.

Illustrative examples

Example 1. *Test the significance of the correlation* $r = 0.5$ *from a sample of size* 18 *against hypothetical correlation* $\rho = 0.7$

Solution: Null Hypothesis H_0: Correlation in the population is 0.7.

$$z=\frac{1}{2}\log_e\left(\frac{1+r}{1-r}\right)=1.1513\log_{10}\left(\frac{1+0.5}{1-0.5}\right)$$

$$= 1.1513 \log 3 = 1.1513 \times 0.4771 = 0.549$$

$$\xi=\frac{1}{2}\log_e\left(\frac{1+\rho}{1-\rho}\right)=1.1513\log_{10}\left(\frac{1+0.7}{1-0.7}\right)$$

$$= 1.1513 \log 5.67 = 0.868$$

$$z-\xi=0.549-0.868=-0.319$$

$$\text{S.E.} = \frac{1}{\sqrt{n-3}} - \frac{1}{\sqrt{18-3}} = \frac{1}{\sqrt{15}} = 0.26$$

Absolute value of $\dfrac{z-\xi}{\text{S.E.}} = \dfrac{0.319}{0.26} = 1.23$ which is less than 1.96

(5% level of significance) = 0.7, H_0 is Accepted

Example 2. *From a sample of 19 pairs of observations, the correlation is 0.5 and the corresponding population value is 0.3. Is the difference significant?*

Solution: H_0: There is no significant difference between the two correlation i.e., r = P

Here $n = 19, r = 0.5, p = 0.3$

$$z = \frac{1}{2}\log_e\left(\frac{1+r}{1-r}\right) = 1.1513\log_{10}\left(\frac{1+0.5}{1-0.5}\right)$$

$$= 1.1513\log 3 = 1.1513 \times 0.4771 = 0.55 \text{ and } \xi = \frac{1}{2}\log_e\left(\frac{1+\rho}{1-\rho}\right) = 0.3$$

$$Z - \xi = 0.55 - 0.31 = 0.24;\ \text{S.E.}_r = \frac{1}{\sqrt{n-3}} = \frac{1}{\sqrt{19-3}} = \frac{1}{3} = 0.25$$

$$\therefore \quad \frac{Z-\xi}{\text{S.E.}} = \frac{0.24}{0.25} = 0.96$$

which is less than 1.96 (5% level of significance) and is, therefore not significant. Hence the sample may be regarded as coming from population with p = 0.3.

To Test the significant difference between two independent correlation co-efficient.

To test the significance of two correlation co-efficient derived from two separate samples, the

test statistic is $z = \dfrac{z_1 - z_2}{\sqrt{\dfrac{1}{n_1-3} + \dfrac{1}{n_1-3}}}$

where $z_1 = 1.1513\log_{10}\left(\dfrac{1+r_1}{1-r_1}\right), z_2 = 1.1513\log_{10}\left(\dfrac{1+r_2}{1-r_2}\right)$

If $|z| > 1.96$, the difference will be significant at 5% level.

Example 3. *The following data gives sample sizes and correlation co-efficient. Test the significant of the difference between two values using z-test.*

Sample size	*r*
5	*0.870*
12	*0.560*

Solution: Let H_0 : The sample are drawn from same population.

Under H_0,
$$z = \frac{z_1 - z_2}{\sqrt{\frac{1}{n_1 - 3} + \frac{1}{n_1 - 3}}}$$

where
$$z_1 = 1.1513 \log\left(\frac{1+0.87}{1-0.87}\right)$$
$$= 1.1513\log\left(\frac{187}{013}\right) = 1.1513\log 14.385$$
$$= 1.1513 \times 1.1579 = 1.333$$
$$z_2 = 1.1513\log\left(\frac{1+0.560}{1-0.560}\right) = 1.1513\log\left(\frac{1.560}{0.44}\right)$$
$$= 1.1513\log 2.545 = 1.1513 \times 0.5496 = 0.633$$

Also
$$n_1 = 5, n_2 = 12$$

$\therefore$
$$z = \frac{1333 - 0.633}{\sqrt{\frac{1}{2} + \frac{1}{2}}} = \frac{0.7}{0.782} = 0.895$$

$\Rightarrow$
$$|z| = 0.895 < 1.96$$

$\therefore$ The difference is not significant *i.e.,* the samples are not drawn from same population.

Example 4: An automatic machine was designed to pack 2.0 kg. of vanaspati. A sample of 100 tins examined to test the machine. The average weight was found to be 1.94 gg. with standard deviation 0.10 kg. Is the machine working properly. **(U.P.T.U. 2006)**

Solution: Sample size n = 100, standard deviation = 0.10 kg. sample mean = 1.94 kg.

Let us suppose the null Hypothesis that there is no difference in the average machine is working properly.

$$Z = \frac{\text{Difference in mean}}{\text{Standard error}} = \frac{2 - 1.94}{\sigma / \sqrt{n}} = \frac{0.06.\sqrt{100}}{0.10} = 6$$

Since the calculated value of z is greater than the standard value (2.58) at 5% level of significance. Hence the null Hypothesis is rejected. So machine is not working properly.

Example 5: A company produce two marks of bulks A and B. 200 bulks of each make were tested and it was found that make A has mean life of 2560 hrs. and S.D. of 90 hrs. whereas make B has 2650 hrs. of mean life with S.D. of 75 hrs. Is there a significant difference between the mean life of the two makes. **(U.P.T.U. 2005)**

Solution: Let for make A, $\bar{x}_1 = 2560$ hrs., $\sigma_1 = 90$ hrs., $n_1 = 200$

for make B, $\bar{x}_2 = 2650$ hrs., $\sigma_2 = 75$ hrs., $n_2 = 200$

Let us suppose the null Hypothesis that there is no significant difference between the mean life of two makes.

Standard error of difference of $\bar{x}_1$ and $\bar{x}_2$

$$\text{S.E. } (\bar{x}_1 - \bar{x}_2) = \sqrt{\frac{\sigma_1^2}{n_1} + \frac{\sigma_2^2}{n_2}} = \sqrt{\frac{(90)^2 + (75)^2}{200}}$$

$$= 8.22$$

$$\text{The value of z} = \frac{\bar{x}_1 \sim \bar{x}_2}{\text{S.E.}} = \frac{2650 - 2560}{8.22} = 10.9$$

The critical value of z at 5% level of significance is 1.96 and the calculated value being more than this critical value.

The difference significant .

Thus null Hypothesis (H_0) is rejected.

Example 6: Two types of batteries x and y are tested for their length of life and the following results are obtained.

Battery	Sample size	Mean (hr)	Std. deviation (hr)
X	100	1000	10
Y	120	1020	11

Can you conclude that the two types of batteries are having the same mean life.

(U.P.T.U. 2004)

Solution: Given that $n_1 = 100$, $n_2 = 120$

$\bar{x}_1 = 1000$, $\bar{x}_2 = 1020$

$\sigma_1 = 100$, $\sigma_2 = 11$

$$\text{Applying the test, for large sampling theory } z = \frac{\text{difference in mean}}{\text{S.E.}}$$

$$\text{where, S.E.} = \sqrt{\frac{\sigma_1^2}{n_1} + \frac{\sigma_2^2}{n_2}} = \sqrt{\frac{(10)^2}{100} + \frac{(11)^2}{120}}$$

$$= 1.417$$

$$\text{then, } z = \frac{\bar{x}_1 \sim \bar{x}_2}{\text{S.E.}}$$

$$= \frac{1000 \sim 1020}{1.417} = \frac{20}{1.417}$$

$$= 14.1143$$

Since the calculated value is greater than the standard value (1.96 S.E.) at 5% level of significance. So our hypothesis is rejected. Thus there is difference between the mean life of two types of batteries. Thus two types of batteries cannot have the same mean.

5.16 F-Test or Snedecor's Variance Ratio Test

(U.P.T.U. 2005)

The *F*-test was first developed by the statistician R.A. Fisher. The test is also known as Fisher's F-test or simply *F*-test. F-test is based on *F*-distribution, which is defined as the ratio of the two independent chi-square variates with degree of freedom v_1 and v_2 respectively, then *F* statistic is defined by

$$F = \frac{\sigma_1^2}{\sigma_2^2}$$

where,
$$\sigma_1^2 = \frac{n_1 S_1^2}{n_1 - 1}$$

and
$$\sigma_2^2 = \frac{n_2 S_2^2}{n_2 - 1}$$

The *F*-test refers to a test of hypothesis concerning two variances derived from two samples. The sampling distribution of F statistic does not involve any population parameter and depends only on the degree of freedom v_1 and v_2.

ASSUMPTIONS IN *F*-TEST

The *F*-test is based on the following assumptions :

(*a*) Normality: Values in each group should be normally distributed.

(*b*) Independence of error: The variation of each value around its own group mean that is error should be independent of each values.

(*c*) Homogeneity: The variances within each group should be equal for all group that is $\sigma_1^2 = \sigma_2^2 = \sigma_3^2 = \ldots \sigma_n^2$.

APPLICATIONS OF F-DISTRIBUTION

F-test for the equality of population variances.

Suppose we want to find :

(*a*) whether the two samples $(x_1, x_2, \ldots\ldots x_n)$ $(y_1, y_2, \ldots\ldots x_m)$ have been drawn from the normal populations having the same variances, (or)

(b) the two independent estimates of the population variances based on the two samples are homogeneous.

If the calculated value of F exceeds the table value (which depends on the degree of freedom $v_1 = n_1 - 1$ and $v_2 = n_2 - 1$) then we reject the null hypothesis.

$H_0 = \sigma_x^2 = \sigma_y^2$.. If the calculated value of F is less than the table value, then we accept H_0 and conclude that the two normal population have same variance.

i.e.

$F_{cal} > F_{table} \rightarrow$	H_0 Reject
$F_{cal} < F_{table} \rightarrow$	H_0 Accept

TESTS OF HYPOTHESIS ABOUT THE VARIANCE OF TWO POPULATIONS

(1) Null Hypothesis $H_0 = \sigma_1^2 = \sigma_2^2$.

Alternate Hypothesis $H_1 = \sigma_1^2 \neq \sigma_2^2$

(2) Calculation of test statistic (Two tailed test)

$$F = \frac{\sigma_1^2}{\sigma_2^2}.\text{if } \sigma_1^2 \geq \sigma_2^2$$

or

$$F = \frac{\sigma_2^2}{\sigma_1^2}.\text{if } \sigma_2^2 \geq \sigma_1^2$$

(3) Level of significance: Take the level of significance $\alpha = 0.05$ if α is not known.

(4) Decision: Accept H_0 if computed $F \leq$ Tabled $F\alpha$

Reject H_0 if computed $F >$ Tabled $F\alpha$.

ILLUSTRATIVE EXAMPLES

Example 1. *The standard deviations calculated from two random samples of sizes* 9 *and* 13 *are* 2.1 *and* 1.8 *respectively. May the samples be regarded as drawn from the normal populations with the same standard deviation? The value of F from the table with degrees of freedom* 8 *and* 12 *is* 2.85.

Solution: $n_1 = 9, S_1 = 2.1, n_2 = 13, S_2 = 1.8$

$$\sigma_1^2 = \frac{n_1 S_1^2}{n_1 - 1} = \frac{9 \times (2.1)^2}{8} = 4.96$$

$$\sigma_2^2 = \frac{n_2 S_2^2}{n_2 - 1} = \frac{13 \times (1.8)^2}{12} = 3.51$$

Null Hypothesis $H_0 : \sigma_1^2 = \sigma_2^2$

Alternative Hypothesis $H_1 : \sigma_1^2 \neq \sigma_2^2$

$$\therefore \qquad F = \frac{\sigma_1^2}{\sigma_2^2} = \frac{4.96}{3.51} = 1.41$$

Decision: The calculated value of F is less than the tabulated value of F at the degree of freedom 8 and 12 so we accept the null hypothesis H_0.

⇒The samples may be regarded as drawn from the normal population with same standard deviation.

Example 2: *Random samples are drawn from two populations and the following results were obtained :*

Sample X	16	17	18	19	20	21	24	23	26	27		
Sample Y	19	22	23	25	26	28	29	30	31	32	35	36

Find the variance of two populations and test whether the two samples have the variance.

Solution: Null Hypothesis $H_0 : \sigma_x^2 = \sigma_y^2$ that is the two samples have the sample variance.

Alternative Hypothesis $H_0 : \sigma_x^2 \neq \sigma_y^2$ (two tailed test).

Calculation of σ_x^2 and σ_y^2 by using the table.

X	$X-\bar{X}$	$(X-\bar{X})^2$	Y	$Y-\bar{Y}$	$(Y-\bar{Y})^2$
16	-5	25	19	-9	81
17	-4	16	22	-6	36
18	-3	09	23	-5	25
19	-2	04	25	-3	09
20	-1	01	26	-2	04
21	0	00	28	0	0
22	1	01	29	1	1
24	3	09	30	2	04
26	5	25	31	3	09
27	6	36	32	4	16
			35	7	49
			36	8	64
$\Sigma X = 210$	$\Sigma(X-\bar{X})^2 = 126$		$\Sigma Y = 336$		$\Sigma(Y-\bar{Y})^2 = 298$

$$\bar{X} = \frac{210}{10} = 21$$

$$\bar{Y} = \frac{336}{12} = 28$$

$$\sigma_1^2 = \frac{\Sigma(X - \bar{X})^2}{n_1 - 1} = \frac{126}{9} = 14$$

$$\sigma_2^2 = \frac{\Sigma(Y - \bar{Y})^2}{n_2 - 1} = \frac{298}{11} = 27.09$$

Test statistic

$$F = \frac{\sigma_2^2}{\sigma_1^2} = \frac{27.09}{14} = 1.94$$

Critical value: The tube tabulated value of F at $\alpha = 0.05$ for degrees of freedom 14 and 9 is 2.6458.

Decision: The calculated value of *F* is less than the tabulated value so the null hypothesis H_o is accepted.

$\Rightarrow$ The two samples have the same variance.

Example 3: *In a laboratory experiment, two samples gave the following results.*

Sample	Size	Sample mean	Sum of squares of deviation from the mean
1	10	15	90
2	12	14	108

Test the equality of sample variance at 5% level of significance.

Solution: Null hypothesis $H_0 : \sigma_1^2 = \sigma_2^2$

Alternative hypothesis $H_1 : \sigma_1^2 \neq \sigma_2^2$ (Two tailed test)

An unbiased estimate of the variance for sample I

$$\sigma_1^2 = \frac{\Sigma(x_i - \bar{x})^2}{n = 1} = \frac{90}{9} = 10$$

An unbiased estimate of the variance for sample II

$$= \frac{\Sigma(y_i - \bar{y})^2}{n - 1} = \frac{108}{11} = 9.82 = \sigma_2^2$$

Test statistic $$F = \frac{\sigma_1^2}{\sigma_2^2} = \frac{10}{9.82} = 1.018$$

Critical value: The tabulated value of F at $\alpha = 5\%$ for 9 and 11 degrees of freedom is = 2.90

Decision : The computed value of F is less than the tabulated value of F, so the null hypothesis H_0 is accepted $\Rightarrow$ so the population have the same variance.

5.17 χ^2 TEST, Chi-Square Test

In Z-test, t-test and F-test we make assumptions about the population values or parameters. Therefore these tests are called parametric tests. However, in many situations it is not possible to make dependable assumptions about the form of the parent distribution (that is, whether it is normal or not) from which the samples have been drawn. Z-, t- and F-tests are not applicable in such cases. To study the problem connected with such situations various tests have been evolved which do not need any assumptions about the parameters. Such tests are distribution-free tests and are called non-parametric tests.

χ^2 (chi-square) test is a non-parametric test: Such non-parametric tests have assumed great importance in statistical analysis and statistical inference because they are easy to compute and can be used without making assumptions about parameters as they are distribution-free tests. These tests are not as reliable as parametric tests but where parameters cannot be rigidly assumed, such tests have to be used.

χ^2-test is a test which describes the magnitude of difference between observed frequencies and the frequencies expected under certain assumptions. With the help of χ^2-test, it is possible to find out whether such differences are significant or are insignificant and could have arisen due to fluctuations of sampling. In χ^2-test the only problem is to decide how the expected frequencies have to be arrived. Once the expected values have been arrived at the calculation of χ^2 and its interpretation are very easy and involve the following steps:

(*i*) Calculate the expected frequencies (denoted by E).

(*ii*) Find out the difference between observed frequencies (denoted by O) and expected frequencies (O–E).

(*iii*) Square up the various values of (O–E) [that is, find out $(O-E)^2$] and divide each value of $(O-E)^2$ by the respective value of $\sum[\frac{(O-E)^2}{E}]$.

(*iv*) Total all values of $\frac{(O-E)^2}{E}$ and this gives the value of χ^2. That is

$$\chi^2 = \Sigma \frac{(O-E)^2}{E}$$

(*v*) Compare the calculated value of χ^2 with the independent value of χ^2 (from tables) for the given degrees of freedom and at the desired level of significance.

(*vi*) If the calculated value of χ^2 is more than the relevant table value, the difference between observed and expected values is significant. If the observed value of χ^2 is less than the table value, the differences between the observed and expected frequencies is not significant and could have arisen due to fluctuations of sampling.

Certain Terms used in χ^2-Test

Degrees of Freedom

The term refers to the number of "independent constraints" in a set of data. Suppose there is a 2×2 association table and the actual frequencies of the various classes are as follows:

	A	**α**	
B	AB 22	αB 38	60
β	Aβ 8	αβ 32	40
	30	70	100

Suppose that we presume that the two attributes A and B are independent then the expected frequency of the class AB would be $\frac{30\times 60}{100}$ or 18. Now, once we decide the expected frequency of the class AB, the expected frequencies of the remaining three classes are automatically fixed. Thus, for the class αB, expected frequency must be 60–18 or 42. Similarly, for Aβ the frequency will be 30–18 or 12. For αβ it will be 70–42 or 28. It means that so far as this table is concerned, we have only one choice of our own and in the remaining three classes we have no freedom to fill in the frequencies as we like. It means that we have only one degree of freedom in this case. There is one independent constraint and three constraints are dependent.

In such tables, the degrees of freedom are calculated by the formula

$$\nu = (c-1)(r-1)$$

Where v stands for the degrees of freedom, c for the number of columns and r for the number of rows.

Thus in a 2x2 table, there will be (2–1)x(2–1) or 1 degree of freedom. Similarly, in a 2x3 table there will be (2–1)x(3–1), that is 2 degrees of freedom.

If the data are not given in the shape of a contingency table as above but are given in the shape of a series of individual observations or discrete or continuous series, then the degrees of freedom are calculated in a different way. Take the following illustration relating to 1024 throws of ten coins each, which gives the following distribution:

Number of Heads	Actual Frequencies
0	2
1	10

Number of Heads	Actual Frequencies
2	38
3	106
4	188
5	257
6	226
7	128
8	59
9	7
10	3
Total	1024

In this illustration, if we write down the expected frequencies we have the freedom to write any ten figures we may choose, but the eleventh figure must be equal to the difference between 1024 and the total of the ten figures that we have written. Thus, there are 10 degrees of freedom in this case. In such cases, therefore, the degrees of freedom would be equal to n–1, where n is the number of frequencies (or values in case of a series of independent observations.

Thus, in the above illustration where the binomial distribution was applicable, we lost one degree of freedom, when a poison distribution is fit, two degrees of freedom are lost, as in its calculation there are two constraints (total frequency and arithmetic average). In case of a normal distribution, three degrees of freedom are lost as there are three constraints, viz., total frequency, mean and standard deviation.

Form of χ^2 Distribution

The χ^2-distribution has only one parameter and it is v or the degree of freedom. Like t-distribution, the χ^2-distribution also varies as the degrees of freedom change. If the degrees of freedom are low, the χ^2-distribution is highly skewed to the right. As the degrees of freedom increase the degree of skewness decreases, and if the degrees of freedom are substantial, $\sqrt{2\chi^2}$ assumes the shape of a normal distribution with a mean $\sqrt{2v-1}$ and standard deviation equal to unity.

Constants of χ^2 Distribution

The constants of a χ^2-distributionwith v degrees of freedom are

(*i*) Mean = v; Mode = v–2; Variance = 2v

(*ii*) Moments:

$\mu_1 = 0; \mu_2 = 2v; \mu_3 = 8v; \mu_4 = 48v + 12v^2$

(iii) $\beta_1 = \frac{\mu_3^2}{\mu_2^3} = \frac{64v^2}{8v^3} = \frac{8}{v}$

hence

$$\gamma_1 = \sqrt{\frac{8}{v}}$$

$$\beta_2 = \frac{\mu_4}{\mu_2^2} = \frac{48 + 12v^2}{4v^2} = 3 + \frac{12}{v}$$

hence

$$\gamma_2 = \beta_2 - 3 = \frac{12}{v}$$

5.18 Application of χ2 Distribution

(i) χ^2-test for goodness of fit.

(ii) χ^2-test for association of attributes or for independence of attributes.

(iii) χ^2-test to determine if the universe has a specified value of variance.

Conditions for Validity of χ^2 Test

The χ^2-test should be used only when

(i) The total frequency is fairly large. Conventionally this test is not used if $n < 50$.

(ii) No expected frequency should be small (say, less than 5). If an expected frequency is less than 5, it should be pooled with the frequency of the neighbouring class. However, this reduces the degree of freedom.

(iii) The distribution should not be of proportions or percentages, etc. It should be of original units.

Note: If an expected frequency is less than 5 in case of a 2x2 table, it cannot be pooled with the frequency of the adjoining class. In such cases Yate's Correction is used. In Yate's correction, 0.5 is added to the observed frequency which is less than 5. The remaining frequencies are adjusted so as to keep the sub-totals and the grand total unchanged. For example

	A	α	
B	2	10	**12**
β	6	6	**12**
	8	**16**	**24**

would become

	A	α	
B	2.5	9.5	**12**
β	5.5	6.5	**12**
	8	**16**	**24**

6.8.1 χ^2 Test for Goodness of Fit

If we have a set of observations through an experiment and we are interested in knowing whether these values are consistent with the values which may be obtained under some hypothesis, then the test is said to be test for goodness of fit. If the observed values are close to the hypothesized or expected values, the fit is said to be good. If however, the difference between the two set of figures are found to be significant, the fit is not good.

χ^2 can also be calculated by the formula

$$\chi^2 = \Sigma\left[\frac{(O)^2}{E}\right] - N$$

This formula is helpful if there are fractions in the deviations, and the application of the earlier formula becomes tedious.

6.8.2 χ^2 Test for Independence of Attributes

In testing association of attributes or their independence the expected values are calculated on the criterion of independence. Thus, the independence values of class $AB = \frac{A \times B}{N}$. Similarly, other expected values are calculated. The same principle which applies in a 2x2 table is applied for n x n and other forms of contingency table also. The rest of the procedure of calculating the value of χ^2 is the same as in case of testing the goodness of fit. The interpretation is also done in the same way.

Alternate Method

In 2x2 tables it is not necessary to calculate the expected values and the value of χ^2 can be obtained directly. This method was first used by Brandt and Snedecar.

b_1	B_2	T_b
c_1	c_2	T_c
T_1	T_2	T

$$\chi^2 = \frac{(b_1c_2 - c_1b_2)^2 \times T}{T_1 \times T_2 \times T_b \times T_c}$$

Where b_1, b_2, c_1, c_2 are observed values.

6.8.3 χ^2 for Population Variance

χ^2 may also be used to ascertain whether the variance in the universe could be a specified figure. For this we find the value of χ^2 by the following rule:

$$\chi^2 = \frac{ns^2}{\sigma^2} = \frac{\Sigma(X - \bar{X})^2}{\sigma^2}$$

Where n denoted the size of sample, s^2 denotes the variance of the sample and σ^2 denotes the variance of the universe.

The Additive Property of χ^2

χ^2 has a very useful property of addition. If a number of sample studies have been conducted in the same field then the results can be pooled together for obtaining an accurate idea about the real position. Suppose ten experiments have been conducted to test whether a particular vaccine is effective against a particular disease. Now here we shall have ten different values of χ^2 and ten different values of ν. We can add the ten values of χ^2 to obtain one value and similarly the ten values of ν can also be added together. Now we can test the results of all these ten experiments combined together.

Precautions in the Use of χ^2 Test

(*i*) Frequencies should not be small. Normally no frequency should be less than 10 but generally χ^2 test can be used if no frequency is less than 5.

(*ii*) Frequency of non-occurrence should never be omitted. For example, if we know the number of cases which have been cured by, say, 4 different medicines, we should not use χ^2 test unless we also know the number of cases not cured by these medicines.

(*iii*) χ^2 test should not be used if we do not have the original data. It is not used on proportions, percentages, or rates.

(*iv*) If repeated measurements are made on the same units, χ^2 test should not be used. For example, if we have obtained the marks of 10 students before and after coaching, we should not use χ^2 test to find out if coaching has done any good. In such cases the difference of means should be tested. χ^2 test cannot be used because the table we will get in such cases would not be a contingency tables as the same persons would be counted twice.

(*v*) Care should be taken that

a. The degrees of freedom are correctly found out;

b. The critical values of χ^2 are correctly used;

c. The hypothesis is properly set and tested;

d. The sum of observed and expected frequencies in various sub-totals and in the grand total are the same; and

e. The expected values have been calculated on a rational basis.

$\chi^2_{\text{claculated}}$	>	$\chi^2_{\text{table}} \rightarrow H_0$ Rejected
$\chi^2_{\text{claculated}}$	<	$\chi^2_{\text{table}} \rightarrow H_0$ Accepted

Test of Goodness of Fit

Illustrative examples

Example 1. *The following table gives the number of accidents that take place in an industry during various days of the week. Test if accidents are uniformly distributed over the week.*

Day	Mon	Tue	Wed	Thu	Fri	Sat
No. of accidents	14	18	12	11	15	14

Solution: Null hypothesis H_0. The accidents are uniformly distributed over the week.

Under this H_0 the expected frequencies of the accidents on each of these days = $\frac{84}{6} = 14$

Observed frequency O_i	14	18	12	11	15	14
Expected frequency E_i	14	14	14	14	14	14
$(O_i - E_i)^2$	0	16	4	9	1	0

$$\chi^2 = \Sigma\left(\frac{(O_i - E_i)^2}{E_i}\right) = \frac{30}{14} = 2.1428.$$

Conclusion. Table value of x^2 at 5% level for (6 - 1 = 5 d.f.) is 11.09. (see x^2-table) Since the calculated value of x^2 is less than the tabulated value, H_0 is accepted *i.e.*, the accidents are uniformly distributed over the week.

Example 2. *A die is thrown* 270 *times and the results of these throws are given below :*

No. appeared on the die	1	2	3	4	5	6
Frequency	40	32	29	59	57	59

The Whether the die is biased or not.

Solution: Null hypothesis H_0. Die is unbiased.

Under this H_0, the expected frequencies for each digit is $\frac{276}{6} = 46$

Table of x^2, consider the following table.

0_i	40	32	29	59	57	59
E_i	46	46	46	46	46	46
$(0_i - E_i)^2$	36	196	289	169	121	169

$$x^2 = \frac{\Sigma(0_i - E_i)^2}{E_i} = 21.30.$$

Conclusion. Tabulated value of x^2 at 5% level of significance for (6- 1=5) d.f. is 11.09. (see x^2-table) Since the calculated value of $x^2 = 21.30 > 11.07$ (the tabulated value), H_0 is rejected i.e., Die is not unbiased or Die is biased.

Example 3. *The following table shows the distribution of digits in numbers chosen at random from a telephone directory :*

Digits	0	1	2	3	4	5	6	7	8	9
Frequency	1026	1107	997	966	1075	933	1107	972	964	853

Test whether the digits may be taken to occur equally frequently in the directory.

Solution: Null hypothesis H_0 : The digits taken in the directory occur equally frequency i.e., there is no significant difference between the observed and expected frequency.

Under H_0, the expected frequency is given by

$$E_i = \frac{1026+1107+997+966+1075+933+1107+972+964+853}{10}$$

$$= \frac{10,000}{10} = 1000$$

To find the value of x^2

O_i	1026	1107	997	996	1075	953	1107	972	964	853
E_i	1000	1000	1000	1000	1000	1000	1000	1000	1000	1000
$(O_i - E_i)^2$	676	11449	9	16	5625	4489	11449	784	1296	21609

$$\chi^2 = \Sigma\frac{(O_i - E_i)^2}{E_i} = \frac{57402}{1000} = 57.402$$

Conclusion. The tabulated value of χ^2 at 5% level of significance for 9 d.f. is 16.919 as χ^2-table). Since the calculated value of χ^2 is greater than the tabulated value, H_0, is rejected *i.e.,* there is significant difference between the observed and theoretical frequency. *i.e.* the digits taken in the directory do not occur equally frequently.

Example 4. 200 *digits are chosen at random from a set of table. The frequencies of the digits are as follows :*

Digit	0	1	2	3	4	5	6	7	8	9
Frequencies	18	19	23	21	16	25	22	20	21	18

Use chi-square test to assess the correctness of the hypothesis that the digits were distributed in equal numbers in the tables from where they are chosen. **(P.T.U., M.B.A. May 2008)**

Solution: Null hypothesis H_0 : The digits were distributed in equal numbers.

The expected frequencies of each digits = $\frac{200}{10} = 20$. To apply χ^2, consider the following table :

O_i	18	19	23	21	16	25	22	20	21	15
E_i	20	20	20	20	20	20	20	20	20	20
$(O_i - E_i)^2$	4	1	9	1	16	25	4	0	1	25
$\frac{(O_i - E_i)^2}{E_i}$	0.20	0.05	0.45	0.05	0.80	1.25	0.20	0	0.05	1.25

Under H_0, $\chi^2 = \sum_{i=1}^{10} \frac{(O_i - E_i)^2}{E_i}$

= 0.20 + 0.05 + 0.45 + 0.05 + 0.80 + 1.25 + 0.20 + 0.05 + 1.25 = 4.3 Also χ^2 0 05 = The tabulated value of χ^2 at 5% level of significance for y in - 1 = 9 d.f.) = 16.22 (see χ^2-table)

Conclusion. The calculated value of χ^2 < the tabulated value of χ^2 at 5% level of significance for 9 d.f. ∴ H_0 is accepted *i.e.*, the digits were distributed in equal numbers.

Example 5. *Records taken of the number of male and female births in 800 families having four children are as follows:*

No. of male births	0	1	2	3	4
No. of female births	4	3	2	1	0
No. of families	32	178	290	236	94

Test whether the data are consistent with the hypothesis that the Binomial law holds and the chance of male birth is equal to that of female birth, namely p = q = 1/2.

Solution: Null Hypothesis H_0 : The data are consistent with the hypothesis of equal probability for male and female births, *i.e.*, $p = q = 1/2$.

We use Binomial distribution to calculate theoretical frequency given by :

$$N(r) = N \times P(X = r)$$

where N is the total frequency, $N(r)$ is the number of families with r male children and

$$P(X = r) = {}^nC_r p^r q^{n-r},$$

where p and q are probability of male and female birth, n is the number of children.

∴ N(0) = No. of families with 0 male children $= 800 \times {}^4C_0 \left(\frac{1}{2}\right)^4 = 800 \times 1 \times \frac{1}{2^4} = 50$

∴ $N(1) = 800 \times {}^4C_1 \left(\frac{1}{2}\right)^1 \left(\frac{1}{2}\right)^3 = 200; N(2) = 800\,{}^4C_2 \left(\frac{1}{2}\right)^2 \left(\frac{1}{2}\right)^2 = 300$

∴ $N(3) = 800 \times {}^4C_3 \left(\frac{1}{2}\right)^1 \left(\frac{1}{2}\right)^3 = 200; N(4) = 800 \times {}^4C_4 \left(\frac{1}{2}\right)^0 \left(\frac{1}{2}\right)^4 = 50$

Observed frequency O_i	32	178	290	236	94
Expected frequency E_i	50	200	300	200	50
$(O_i - E_i)^2$	324	484	100	1296	1936
$\frac{(O_i - E_i)^2}{E_i}$	6.48	2.42	0.333	6.48	38.72

$$\chi^2 = \Sigma \frac{(O_i - E_i)^2}{E_i} = 54.433$$

Conclusion. Table value of χ^2 at 5% level of significance for 5 - 1 = 4 d.f. is 9.49 (see χ^2-table). Since the calculated value of χ^2 is greater than the tabulated value, H_0 is rejected. *i.e.,* the data are not consistent with the hypothesis that the Binomial law holds and that the chance of a male birth is not equal to that of a female birth.

Note. Since the fitting is Binomial, the degrees of freedom $v = n - 1$ *i.e.,* V = 5 - 1 = 4.

Example 6. *Verify whether Poisson distribution can be assumed from the data given below:*

No. of defects	0	1	2	3	4	5
Frequency	6	13	13	8	4	3

Solution: Null Hypothesis H_0 : Poisson fit is a good fit to the data.

Mean of the given distribution $\frac{\Sigma f_i x_i}{\Sigma f_i} = \frac{94}{47} = 2$

To fit a Poisson distribution we, require *m*. Parameter $m = \bar{x} = 2$.

By Poisson distribution, the frequency of *r* success is

$N(r) = N \times e^{-m} . \frac{m^r}{r!}$, N is the total frequency, *i.e.,*

$$N(0) = 47 \times e^{-2} . \frac{(2)^0}{r!} = 6.36; N(1) = 47 \times e^{-2} . \frac{(2)^1}{1!} = 12.72$$

$$N(2) = 47 \times e^{-2} . \frac{(2)^2}{2!} = 12.72; N(3) = 47 \times e^{-2} . \frac{(2)^3}{3!} = 8.48$$

$$N(4) = 47 \times e^{-2} . \frac{(2)^4}{4!} = 4.24; N(5) = 47 \times e^{-2} . \frac{(2)^3}{5!} = 1.696$$

X	0	1	2	3	4	5
O_i	6	13	13	8	4	3
E_i	6.36	12.72	12.72	8.48	4.24	1.969
$\frac{(O_i - E_i)^2}{E_i}$	0.2037	0.00616	0.00616	0.02716	0.0136	1.0026

$$x^2 = \frac{\Sigma(O_i - E_i)^2}{E_i} = 1.2864.$$

. I(6,-E,)» E,

Conclusion. The calculated value of χ^2 is 1.2864. Tabulated value of χ^2 at 5% level of significance for $y = 6 - 2 = 4$ d.f. is 9.49 (see χ^2-table). Since the calculated value of %^{2} is less than that of tabulated value. H_0 is accepted *i.e.,* Poisson distribution provides a good fit to the data.

Example 7. *The theory predicts the proportion of beans in the four groups* G_1, G_2, G_3, G_4 *should be in the ratio 9:3:3:1. In an experiment with 1600 beans, the numbers in the four groups were 882, 313, 287 and 118. Does the experimental result support the theory.*

(U.P.T.U. 2008)

Solution: Null Hypothesis H_0: The experimental result support the theory, *i.e.,* there is no significant difference between the observed and theoretical frequency under H_0, the theoretical frequency can be calculated as follows .

$$E(G_1) = \frac{1600 \times 9}{16} = 900; E(G_2) = \frac{1600 \times 3}{16} = 300;$$

$$E(G_2) = \frac{16000 \times 3}{16} = 300; E(G_4) = \frac{1600 \times 1}{16} = 100$$

To calculate the value of x^2.

Observed frequency O_i	882	313	287	118
Expected frequency E_i	900	300	300	100
$\frac{(O_i - E_i)^2}{E_i}$	0.36	0.5633	0.5633	3.24

$$\chi^2 = \Sigma \frac{(O_i - E_i)^2}{E_i} = 4.7266$$

Conclusion. Table value of χ^2 at 5% level of significance for 3 d.f. is 7.815 (see χ^2-table). Since the calculated value of χ^2 is less than that of the tabulated value. Hence H_0 is accepted. *i.e.,* the experimental result supports the theory.

Example 8. *Fit a Poisson distribution to the following :*

x:	0	1	2	3	4
f:	46	38	22	9	1

Solution: Null Hypothesis H_0: Poisson fit is a good fit to the data.

Here mean of the given distribution = $\frac{\Sigma f_i x_i}{\Sigma f_i} = \frac{113}{116} = 0.97$

To fit a Poisson distribution, we require *m*

Here $\quad m = \bar{x} = 0.97$

By Poisson distribution, the frequency of *r* success is

$$N(r) = N \times e^{-m}, \frac{m^r}{r!} N \text{ is the total frequency}$$

$$N(0) = 116 \times e^{-0.97} = 116 \times 0.37 = 43.97;$$

$$N(2) = 116 \times e^{-0.97} \times \frac{(0.97)^2}{2} = 116 \times 0.17 = 19.72$$

$$N(3) = 116 \times e^{-0.97} \times \frac{(0.97)^3}{3!} = 6.688$$

$$N(4) = 116 \times e^{-0.97} \times \frac{(0.97)^4}{4!} = 1.62$$

x	0	1	2	3	4
O_i	46	38	22	9	1
E_i	43.97	41.78	19.72	6.68	1.62
$\frac{(O_i - E_i)^2}{E_i}$	0.093	0.338	0.263	0.805	0.23

$$\therefore \qquad \chi^2 = \Sigma \frac{(O_i - E_i)^2}{E_i} = 1.729$$

Conclusion. The calculated value of χ^2 is 1.729. Also the tabulated value of χ^2 at 5% level of significance for v = 5 - 2 = 3 *d.f.* is 7.815 (see χ^2-table). Since the calculated value of χ^2 at 5% level of significance is less than the tabulated value. Hence H_0 is accepted i.e., Poisson distribution is a best fit to the given data.

Example 9. *Fit a Binomial distribution to the following frequency distribution.*

x	0	1	2	3	4	5	6
f	13	25	52	58	32	16	4

Solution: Null Hypothesis H_0 : Binomial distribution is a good fit to the given data. We first find mean of the given distribution.

x_i	f_i	$f_i x_i$
0	13	0
1	25	25

Here mean $= \frac{\Sigma f_i x_i}{\Sigma f_i}$

2	52	104
3	58	174
4	32	128
5	16	80
6	4	24
	$N=\sum f_i=200$	$\sum f_i x_i=535$

$\Rightarrow \quad np=\frac{535}{200}=2.675$

$\Rightarrow \quad p=\frac{2.675}{7}\doteq 0.38 \quad (n=7)$

$\therefore \quad q=1-p=0.62$

When $r=0$, $P(X=0)=200\times{}^7C_0(0.62)^7=7.043$

When $r=1$, $P(X=1)=200\times{}^7C_1(0.38)(0.62)^6$

$=200\times 7\times 0.38\times 0.0568=30.2176$

When $r=2$. $P(X=2)=200\times{}^7C_2(0.38)^2(0.62)^5$

$=200\times 21\times 0.1444\times 0.0916=55.55$

When $r=3$, $P(X=3)=200\times{}^7C_3(0.38)^3(0.62)^4$

$=200\times 35\times 0.054\times 0.1477=55.83$

When $r=4$, $P(X=4)=200\times{}^7C_4(0.38)^4(0.62)^3$

$=200\times 35\times 0.020.\times 0.23=33.32$

When $r==5$, $P(X=5)=200\times{}^7C_5(0.38)^5(0.62)^2$

$=200\times 21\times 0.0079\times 0.3344=12.75$

When $r=6$, $P(X=6)=200\times{}^7C_6\times(0.38)^6(0.62)^1$

$=200\times 7\times 0.0030)\times(0.62)=2.64$

E_i	O_i	$(O_i-E_i)^2$	$\frac{(O_i-E_i)^2}{E_i}$
7.043	13	35.48	178.73
30.21	25	27.144	24.38
55.55	52	12.60	2.85
55.83	58	4.70	0.39
33.32	32	1.74	0.09
12.75	16	10.56	8.74
2.64	4	1.84	1.28
	Total = 200		

(adjust the observed frequencies such that their total sum = 200)

$$\chi^2=\sum\frac{(O_i-E_i)^2}{E_i}=207.72$$

Conclusion: The tabulated value of χ^2 at 5% level of significance for 7 - 1 = 6 d.f 12.592 (see-chi-square table). Since the calculated value of χ^2 is the tabulated value of χ^2 at 5% level significance.

Therefore H_0 is rejected *i.e.,* The Binomial law does not hold good according to the given data.

Example 10. A *survey of* 320 *families with* 5 *children each revealed the following distribution.*

No. of Boys	*No. of Girls*	*No. of Families*
5	0	14
4	1	56
3	2	110
2	3	88
1	4	40
0	5	12

Is this result consistent that the males and females births are equally probable ? (x^2 at 5% level for 5 d.f. = 11.05).

(P.T.U., M.B.A Dec. 2004)

Solution: Null Hypothesis H_0 : The males and females births are equally probable.

As the males and females births are equally probable $\therefore$ $p = \frac{1}{2}, q\frac{1}{2}$

The expected frequencies are the successive terms of the Binomial distribution

$$N(q+p)^n = 320\left(\frac{1}{2}+\frac{1}{2}\right)^5$$

The successive terms are :

$$320 \times {}^5C_0 \times \left(\frac{1}{2}\right)^5, 320 \times {}^5C_1 \times \left(\frac{1}{2}\right)^5;$$

$$320 \times {}^5C_2 \times \left(\frac{1}{2}\right)^5, 320 \times {}^5C_2 \times \left(\frac{1}{2}\right)^5;$$

$$320 \times {}^5C_4 \times \left(\frac{1}{2}\right)^5, 320 \times {}^5C_5 \times \left(\frac{1}{2}\right)^5$$

or

10, 50,100, 100, 50,10.

To apply x^2-test, consider the following table :

O_i	14	56	110	88	40	12
E_i	10	50	100	100	50	10
$(O_i - E_i)^2$	16	36	100	144	100	4
$\frac{(O_i - E_i)^2}{E_i}$	1.6	0.72	1	1.44	2	0.4

$$\chi^2 = \sum_{i=1}^{6} \frac{(O_i - E_i)^2}{E_i} = 1.6 + 0.72 + 1 + 1.44 + 2 + 0.4 = 7.16$$

Also $\chi^2{}_{0}$ 05 = The tabulated value of χ^2 at 5% level of significance for u = /i-l = 6- 1 = 5d.f. = 11T05 (see χ^2-table)

Conclusion. The calculated value of χ^2 is less than the tabulated value of χ^2 at 5% level of significance for 5 d.f. H_0 is accepted *i.e.,* the males and females births are equally probable.

Exercise 5.1

1. The following table gives the frequency of occupancies of the digits 0, 1, ..., 9 in the last place is four logarithm of numbers 10-99, Examine if there is any peculiarity.

Digit :	0	1	2	3	4	5	6	7	8	9
Frequency :	6	16	15	10	12	12	3	2	9	5

2. The sales in a supermarket during a week are given below. Test the hypothesis that the sales do not depend on the day of the week, using a significant level of 0.05.

Days	:	Mon	Tue	Wed	Thurs	Fri	Sat
Sales (in 1000 Rs.)	:	65	54	60	56	71	84

3. Four 4 coins were tossed at a time and this operation s repeated 160 times. It is found that 4 heads occur 6 times, 3 heads occur 43 times, 2 heads occur 69 times, one head occur 34 times. Discuss whether the coin may be regarded as unbiased?

4. A survey of 800 families with 4 children each revealed the following distribution :

No of boys	0	1	2	3	4
No. of girls	4	3	2	1	0
No. of families	32	178	290	236	64

Is this result consistent with the hypothesis that the male and female births are equally probable?

5. Fit a poison distribution to the following data and best the goodness of fit :

x	:	0	1	2	3	4
f	:	109	65	22	3	1

6. Four coins were tossed 160 times and the following results were obtained. (U.P.T.U. 2006)

No. of heads observe	:	0	1	2	3	4
Frequencies	:	17	52	54	31	6

Under the assumption that coins are balanced, find the expected frequencies of getting 0, 1, 2, 3 or 4 heads and test the goodness of fit. :

7. A set of 5 coins is tossed 3200 times and the number of heads appearing each time is noted. The results are given below :

No. of heads	:	0	1	2	3	4	5
Frequencies	:	80	570	1100	900	50	50

Test the hypothesis that the coins are unbiased.

8. The number of scooter accidents per month in a certain town was as follows :

12	8	20	2	14	10	15	6	9	4

Use chi-square test to determine if these frequencies are in agreement with the belief that accident conditions were the same during 10 month period.

9. In the accounting department of bank, 100 accounts are selected at random and estimated for errors. The following results were obtained :

No. of errors	:	0	1	2	3	4	5	6
No of accounts	:	35	40	19	2	0	2	2

Does this information verify that the errors are distributed according to the Poisson probability law?

10. A sample analysis of examination results of 500 students, it was found that 220 students have failed, 170 have secured a third class, 90 have secured a second class and 20 got a first class. Do these figures support the general belief that above categories are in the ratio 4 : 3 : 2 : 1 respectively? (U.P.T.U. 2008)

Answers

1. There is no peculiarity in the occupancy of the digits.
2. The sales do not depend on the day of the week.
3. Unbaised
4. **The meal and female birth are not equally probable**
5. Poisson law fits the data.

6. The coins are a not balanced and the fit is not good (χ^2 = 12.725)

7. The coins are biased (χ^2 = 58.80)

8. The frequencies were not in agreement with the given belief (χ^2 = 26.60)

9. The errors are distributed according to the Normal distribution (χ^2 = 1.40)

10. The observed results are not commensurate with the general examination result (χ^2 = 23.667)

χ^2 - Test as a Test of Independence

With the help of χ^2 test, we can find whether or not two attributes are associated. We take the null hypothesis that there is no association between the attributes under study, *i.e.,* we assume that the two attributes are independent. If the calculated value of χ^2 is less than the table value at a specified level (generally 5%) of significance, the hypothesis holds good, *i.e.,* the attributes are independent and do not bear any association. On the other hand, if the calculated value of χ^2 is greater than the table value at a specified level of significance, we say that the results of the experiment do not support the hypothesis. Thus a very useful application of χ^2 test is to investigate the relationship between trials or attributes which can be classified into two or more categories.

The sample data set out into two-way table, called contingency table.

Let us consider two attributes A and B divided into r classes A_1, A_2, A_3, A_r and B divided into *s* classes B_1, B_2, B_3, B_s. If (A_i), (B_j) represents the number of persons possessing the attributes A_i, B_j respectively, (i = 1, 2 ....*r,j* = 1,2......, s) and (A_i B_j) represent the number of persons possessing attributes A_i; and B_j. respectively, $(i = 1,2,.....,r, j = 1,2,.....,s)$ and (A_i B_j) represent the number of persons possessing attributes A_i, B_j Also we have $\sum_{i=1}^{r} A_i = \sum_{j=1}^{s} B_j = N$, where N is the total frequency. The contingency table for r × s is given below :

A / B	A_1	A_2	A_3	...A_r	Total
B_1	(A_1 B_1)	(A_2 B_1)	(A_3 B_1)	(A_r B_1)	B_1
B_2	(A_1 B_2)	(A_2 B_2)	(A_3 B_2)	(A_r B_2)	B_1
B_3	(A_1 B_3)	(A_2 B_3)	(A_3 B_3)	(A_r B_3)	B_1
...	...	...	...	...	...

...	...	...	...	...	...
B_s	$(A_1 B_s)$	$(A_2 B_s)$	$(A_3 B_s)$	$(A_r B_s)$	(B_1)
Total	(A_1)	(A_2)	(A_3)	(A_r)	N

H_0 : Both the attributes are independent i.e., A and B are independent under the null hypothesis, we calculate the expected frequency as follows :

$P(A_i)$ = Probability that a person possesses the attributed $A_i = \frac{(A_i)}{N} i = 1, 2, ...$

$P(B_j)$ = Probability that a person possesses the attributed $B_i = \frac{(B_i)}{N}$

$P(A_iB_j)$ = Probability that a person possesses both attributes A_i and $B_j = \frac{(A_iB_j)}{N}$

If $(A_i B_j)_0$ is the expected number of person possessing both the attributes A_i and B_j

$$= N \frac{(A_i)}{N} \frac{(B_j)}{N} = \frac{(A_i)(B_j)}{N}$$ ($\because$ A and B are independent)

Hence $$\chi^2 = \sum_{i=1}^{r} \sum_{j=1}^{s} \left[\frac{[(A_iB_j)_0 - (A_iB_j)]^2}{(A_iB_j)_0} \right]$$

Note 1: For a 2 × 2 contingency table where the frequencies are $\frac{a/b}{c/d}$ χ^2 can be calculated from

independent frequencies as $$\boxed{\chi^2 = \frac{(a+b+c+d)(ad-bc)^2}{(a+b)(c+d)(b+d)(a+c)}}$$

Note 2: If the contingency table is not 2 × 2, then the formula for calculating x^2 as given in note 1. can't be used. Hence, we have another formula for calculating the expected frequency $(A_iB_j)_0 = \frac{(A_i)(B_j)}{N}$ *i.e.,* expected frequency in each cell is

$$= \frac{\text{Product of column total and row total}}{\text{whole total}}$$

Note 3. If $\frac{a/b}{c/d}$ is the 2 × 2 contingency table with two attributes, $Q = \frac{ad-bc}{ad+bc}$ is called the coefficient of association.

If the attributes are independent then $\frac{a}{b}=\frac{c}{d}$.

Note 4. Yate's Correction. In a 2 × 2 table, if the frequencies of a cell is small, we make Yate's correction to make χ^2 continuous.

Decrease by $\frac{1}{2}$ those cell frequencies which are greater than expected frequencies, and increase by $\frac{1}{2}$ those which are less than expectation. This will not affect the marginal columns. This correction is known as Yate's correction to continuity.

After Yate's correction $\chi^2 = \dfrac{N\left(bc-ad-\frac{1}{2}N\right)^2}{(a+c)(b+d)(a+b)(c+d)}$ when $ad-bc<0$

$$\chi^2 = \frac{N\left(ad-bc-\frac{1}{2}N\right)^2}{(a+c)(b+d)(c+d)(a+b)} \text{ when } ad-bc>0.$$

Illustration Examples

Example 1. *What are the expected frequencies of* 2 × 2 *contingency tables given below :*

(i)

a	*b*
c	*d*

(ii)

2	10
6	6

Solution:

(i) Observed frequencies

a	*b*	*a* + *b*
c	*d*	*c* + *d*
a + *c*	*b* + *d*	*a* + *b* + *c* + *d* = *N*

→ Expected frequencies

$\frac{(a+c)(a+b)}{a+b+c+d}$	$\frac{(b+d)(a+b)}{a+b+c+d}$
$\frac{(a+c)(c+d)}{a+b+c+d}$	$\frac{(b+d)(c+d)}{a+b+c+d}$

(i) Observed frequencies

2	10	12
6	6	12
8	16	24

→ Expected frequencies

$\frac{8\times12}{24}=4$	$\frac{16\times12}{24}=2$
$\frac{8\times12}{24}=4$	$\frac{16\times12}{24}=8$

Example 2. *From the following table regarding the colour of eyes of fathers and sons test if the colour of son's eye is associated with that of the father.*

Eye Colour of Son

Eye colour of father		*Light*	*Not light*
	Light	471	51
	Not Light	148	230

Solution: Null hypothesis H_0. The colour of son's eye is not associated with that of father *i.e.,* they are independent.

Degree of freedom $v = (r-1)(s-1) = (2-1)(2-1) = 1$

Under H_0, we calculate the expected frequency in each cell as

$$= \frac{\text{Product of column total and row total}}{\text{Whole total}}$$

Eye colour of son / Eye colour of father	Light	Not light	Total
Light	$\frac{619 \times 522}{900} = 359.02$	$\frac{289 \times 522}{900} = 167.62$	522
Not Light	$\frac{619 \times 378}{900} = 259.98$	$\frac{289 \times 378}{900} = 121.38$	378
Total	619	289	900

$$\chi^2 = \sum_{i=1}^{4} \frac{(O_i - E_j)^2}{E_i}$$

$$= \frac{(471-359.02)^2}{359.02} + \frac{(51-167.62)^2}{167.62} + \frac{(148-259.98)^2}{259.98} + \frac{(230-121.38)^2}{121.38}$$

Also $\chi^2_{.05}$ = Tabulated value of χ^2 at 5% level for 1 d.f. is 3.841.

Conclusion. Since the calculated value of χ^2 > tabulated value of χ^2, H_0 is rejected. They are dependent *i.e.,* he colour of son's eye is associated with that of the father.

Example 3. *The following table gives the number of good and bad parts produced by each of the three shifts in a factors :*

	Good parts	Bad parts	Total
Day shift	960	40	1000
Evening shift	940	50	990
Night shift	950	45	995
Total	2850	135	2985

Test whether or not the production of bad parts in independent of the shift on which they were produced.

Solution: Null hypothesis H_0. The production of bad parts is independent of the shift on which they were produced.

Degree of freedom $=(r-1)(s-1)=(2-1)(3-1)=2$

i.e., the two attributes, production and shifts are independent.

$$\text{Under } H_0, \quad \chi^2 = \sum_{i=1}^{2} \sum_{j=1}^{3} \left[\frac{[(A_iB_j)_0 - (A_iB_j)]^2}{(A_iB_j)_0} \right]$$

Calculation of Expected frequencies.

Let A and B be the two attributes namely production and shifts. A is divided into two classes A_1, A_2 and B is divided into three classes B_1, B_2, B_3.

$$(A_1B_1)_0 = \frac{(A_1)(B_1)}{N} = \frac{(2850)\times(1000)}{2985} = 954.77$$

$$(A_1B_2)_0 = \frac{(A_1)(B_2)}{N} = \frac{(2850)\times(990)}{2985} = 945.226$$

$$(A_1B_3)_0 = \frac{(A_1)(B_3)}{N} = \frac{(2850)\times(995)}{2985} = 950$$

$$(A_2B_1)_0 = \frac{(A_2)(B_1)}{N} = \frac{(135)\times(1000)}{2985} = 45.27$$

$$(A_2B_2)_0 = \frac{(A_2)(B_2)}{N} = \frac{(135)\times(990)}{2985} = 44.773$$

$$(A_2B_3)_0 = \frac{(A_2)(B_3)}{N} = \frac{(135)\times(995)}{2985} = 45$$

To calculate the value of χ^2

Class	O_i	E_i	$(O_i - E_i)^2$	$(O_i - E_i)^2 / E_i$
$(A_1 B_1)$	960	954.77	27.3529	0.02864
$(A_1 B_2)$	940	945.226	27.3110	0.02889
$(A_1 B_3)$	950	950	0	0
$(A_2 B_1)$	40	45.27	27.7729	0.61349
$(A_2 B_2)$	50	44.773	27.3215	0.61022
$(A_2 B_3)$	45	45	0	0
Total				1.28126

$$\therefore \quad \chi^2 = \sum_{i=1}^{6} \frac{(O_i - E_i)^2}{E_i} = 1.28126$$

Also $\chi^2_{0.05}$ = The tabulated value of χ^2 at 5% level of significance for 2 degrees of freedom is 5.991. Since the calculated value of χ^2 is less than the tabulated value, we accept *i.e.*, the production of bad parts is independent of the shift on which they were produced.

Example 4. *A cigarette company interested in the effect of sex on the type of cigarettes smoked and has collected the following data from a random sample of 150 persons,*

Cigarette size	*Number of people smoked*		*Total*
	male	*female*	
Small	25	30	55
Medium	40	15	55
King size	30	10	40
Total	95	55	150

Test whether the type of cigarette smoked and sex are independent at level of significance α = 5%:

(P.T.U., M.B.A. Dec. 2006)

Solution: Let H_0 : The type of cigarette smoked and sex are independent

$\therefore$ Degree of freedom $= (r-1)(s-1) = (2-1)(3-1) = 2$

Observed Frequencies

	Male	*Female*	*Total*
Small	25	30	55
Medium	40	15	55
King size	30	10	40
Total	95	55	150

Expected Frequencies

$\frac{95\times55}{150}=34.83$	$\frac{55\times55}{150}=20.16$
$\frac{95\times55}{150}=34.83$	$\frac{55\times55}{150}=20.16$
$\frac{95\times40}{150}=38$	$\frac{55\times40}{150}=14.66$

Calculate χ^2, we have the following table :

O_i	25	30	40	15	30	10
E_i	34.83	20.16	34.83	20.16	38	14.66
$\frac{(O_i-E_i)^2}{E_i}$	2.774	4.80	0.76	1.32	1.684	1.481

$$\therefore \quad \chi^2=\sum_{i=1}^{6}\frac{(O_i-E_i)^2}{E_i}=2.774+4.80+0.76+1.32+1.684+1.48 = 12.819$$

Also $\chi^2_{0.05}$ = The tabulated value of χ^2 at 5% level of significance for 2 d.f. = 5.991

Conclusion. The tabulated value of χ^2 is greater than the tabulated value of χ^2 at 5% level of significance. Hence H_0 is rejected, *i.e.,* the type of cigarette smoked and sex depends on such other.

Example 5. *From the following data, find whether hair colour and sex are associated.*

Colour / Sex	Fair	Red	Medium	Dark	Black	Total
Boys	592	849	504	119	36	2100
Girls	544	677	451	97	14	1783
Total	1136	1526	955	216	50	3883

Solution: Null hypothesis H_0. The two attributes hair colour and sex are not associated, i.e., they are independent.

Let A and B be the attributes hair colour and se respectively. A is divides into 5 classes $(r = 5)$. B is divided into 2 classes (s = 2).

$\therefore$ Degrees of freedom $= (r-1)(s-1) = (5-1)(2-1) = 4$

Under H_0, we calculate $x^2 = \sum_{i=1}^{5} \sum_{j=1}^{2} \frac{[(A_i B_j)_0 - (A_i B_i)]^2]}{(A_i B_j)_0}$

To calculate the expected frequency $(A_1B_1)_0$ as follows :

$$(A_1 B_1)_0 = \frac{(A_1)(B_1)}{N} = \frac{1136 \times 2100}{3883} = 614.37$$

$$(A_1 B_2)_0 = \frac{(A_1)(B_2)}{N} = \frac{1136 \times 1783}{3883} = 521.629$$

$$(A_2 B_1)_0 = \frac{(A_2)(B_1)}{N} = \frac{1526 \times 2100}{3883} = 852.289$$

$$(A_2 B_2)_0 = \frac{(A_2)(B_2)}{N} = \frac{1526 \times 1783}{3883} = 700.71$$

$$(A_3 B_1)_0 = \frac{(A_3)(B_1)}{N} = \frac{955 \times 2100}{3883} = 516.482$$

$$(A_3 B_2)_0 = \frac{(A_3)(B_2)}{N} = \frac{955 \times 1783}{3883} = 483.517$$

$$(A_4 B_1)_0 = \frac{(A_4)(B_1)}{N} = \frac{216 \times 2100}{3883} = 116.816$$

$$(A_4 B_2)_0 = \frac{(A_4)(B_2)}{N} = \frac{216 \times 1783}{3883} = 99.183$$

$$(A_5 B_1)_0 = \frac{(A_5)(B_1)}{N} = \frac{50 \times 2100}{3883} = 27.04$$

$$(A_5 B_2)_0 = \frac{(A_5)(B_2)}{N} = \frac{50 \times 1783}{3883} = 22.959$$

Class	O_i	E_i	$(O_i - E_i)^2$	$\frac{(O_i - E_i)^2}{E_i}$
$A_1 B_1$	592	614.37	500.416	0.8145
$A_1 B_2$	544	521.629	500.462	0.959

$A_2 B_1$	849	852.289	10.8175	0.0127
$A_2 B_2$	677	700.71	562.1641	0.8023
$A_3 B_1$	504	516.482	155.800	0.3016
$A_3 B_2$	451	438.517	155.825	0.3553
$A_4 B_1$	119	116.816	4.7698	0.0408
$A_4 B_2$	97	99.183	4.7654	0.0480
$A_5 B_1$	36	27.04	80.2816	2.9689
$A_5 B_2$	14	22.959	80.2636	3.495
Total				**9.79975**

$$\therefore \quad \chi^2 = \sum_{i-1}^{10} \frac{(O_i - E_i)^2}{E_i} = 9.799$$

Conclusion. Tabulated value of χ^2 at 5% level of significance for 4 d.f. is 9.488. (see χ^2-table) Since the calculated value of $\chi^2 <$ tabulated value H_0 is rejected *i.e.,* the two attributes are not independent. *i.e.,* the two attributes are not independent, *i.e,* the hair colour and sex are associated.

Example 6. *Can vaccination be regarded as preventive measure of small-pox as evidenced by the following data of 1482 persons exposed to small pox in a locality 368 in all were attach of those 1482 persons and 343 were vaccinated and of these only 35 were attacked.*

Solution: For the given data, we from the contingency table. Let the two attributes be vaccination and exposed to small-pox. Each attributes is divided into two classes.

Vaccination A / Disease small pox B	Vaccinated	Not	Total
Attacked	35	333	368
Not	308	806	1114
Total	343	1139	1482

Null hypothesis H_0. The two attributes are independent *i.e.,* vaccination can't be regarded as preventive measure of small pox.

Degrees of freedom $v = (r-1)(s-1) = (2-1)(2-1) = 1$

Under H_0, $$\chi^2 = \sum_{i=1}^{2} \sum_{j=1}^{2} \frac{[(A_i B_i)_0 - (A_i B_j)]^2]}{(A_i B_j)_0}$$

Calculation of expected frequency

$$(A_1B_1)_0 = \frac{(A_1)(B_1)}{N} = \frac{343 \times 368}{1482} = 85.1713$$

$$(A_1B_2)_0 = \frac{(A_1)(B_2)}{N} = \frac{343 \times 1114}{1482} = 257.828$$

$$(A_2B_1)_0 = \frac{(A_2)(B_1)}{N} = \frac{1139 \times 368}{1482} = 282.828$$

$$(A_2B_2)_0 = \frac{(A_2)(B_2)}{N} = \frac{1139 \times 1114}{1482} = 856.171$$

Calculation of χ^2

Class	O_i	E_i	$(O_i - E_i)^2$	$\frac{(O_i - E_i)^2}{E_i}$
$(A_1 B_1)$	35	85.1713	2517.159	29.554
$(A_1 B_2)$	308	257.828	2517.229	8.1728
$(A_2 B_1)$	333	282.828	2517.2295	7.5592
$(A_2 B_2)$	806	856.171	2517.1292	2.93999
Total				48.2261

Calculated value of $\chi^2 = \sum_{i=1}^{6} \sum_{j=1}^{3} \left[\frac{[(A_iB_j)_0 - (A_iB_j)]^2}{(A_iB_j)_0} \right]$

Conclusion. Tabulated value of χ^2 > tabulated value H_0 is rejected, *i.e.*, he two attributes are not independent. *i.e.*, the vaccination can be regarded as preventive measure of small pox.

Example 7. *Three sales persons account for the following amount of sales (in thousands of rupees) over a period of 4 months. Test for the significant difference in their performance of α = 5% level of significance :*

Sales person	Monthly sales in '000 Rs.				Total
C	48	49	50	49	196
Y	47	49	48	48	192
Z	49	51	50	50	200
Total	144	149	148	147	588

(P.T.U., M.B.A. May 2006)

Solution: Null Hypothesis H_0. There is no significant difference between the sales Degree of freedom $= (r-1)(s-1) = (4-1)(3-1) = 6$

Under H_0.
$$\chi^2 = \sum_{i=1}^{6} \sum_{j=1}^{3} \left[\frac{[(A_iB_j)_0 - (A_iB_j)]^2}{(A_iB_j)_0} \right]$$

Calculation of Expected Frequencies

Let A and B be the two attributes namely sales and persons. A is divided into Four classes (r = 4) A_1, A_2, A_3 and A_4 and B is divided into three classes B_1, B_2, B_3, (R = 3).

$$\therefore \quad (A_1B_1)_0 = \frac{(A_1B_1)}{N} = \frac{144 \times 196}{588} = 48$$

$$(A_1B_2)_0 = \frac{(A_1)(B_2)}{N} = \frac{144 \times 192}{588} = 47.02$$

$$(A_1B_3)_0 = \frac{(A_1)(B_3)}{N} = \frac{144 \times 200}{588} = 48.97$$

$$(A_2B_1)_0 = \frac{(A_2)(B_1)}{N} = \frac{149 \times 196}{588} = 49.66$$

$$(A_2B_2) = \frac{(A_2)(B_2)}{N} = \frac{149 \times 192}{588} = 48.65$$

$$(A_2B_3)_0 = \frac{(A_2)(B_3)}{N} = \frac{149 \times 200}{588} = 50.68$$

$$(A_3B_1)_0 = \frac{(A_3)(B_1)}{N} = \frac{148 \times 196}{588} = 49.33$$

$$(A_3B_2)_0 = \frac{(A_3)(B_2)}{N} = \frac{148 \times 192}{588} = 48.32$$

$$(A_3B_3)_0 = \frac{(A_3)(B_3)}{N} = \frac{148 \times 200}{588} = 50.34$$

$$(A_4B_1)_0 = \frac{(A_4)(B_1)}{N} = \frac{147 \times 196}{588} = 49$$

$$(A_4B_2)_0 = \frac{(A_4)(B_2)}{N} = \frac{147 \times 192}{588} = 48$$

$$(A_4B_3)_0 = \frac{(A_4)(B_3)}{N} = \frac{147 \times 200}{588} = 50$$

To calculate the value of x^2, consider the following table :

Class	O_i	E_i	$(O_i - E_i)^2$	$\frac{(O_i - E_i)^2}{E_i}$
$A_1 B_1$	48	48	0	0
$A_1 B_2$	47	47.02	0.0002	0.00004
$A_1 B_3$	49	48.97	0.0009	0.0001
$A_2 B_1$	49	49.6	0.4356	0.087
$A_2 B_2$	49	48.65	0.1225	0.025
$A_2 B_3$	51	50.68	0.1024	0.020
$A_3 B_1$	50	49.33	0.4489	0.09
$A_3 B_2$	48	48.32	0.1024	0.021
$A_3 B_3$	50	50.34	0.1156	0.022
$A_4 B_1$	49	49	0	0
$A_4 B_2$	48	48	0	0
$A_4 B_3$	50	50	0	0
		Total		**0.26514**

$$\chi^2 = \sum_{i=1}^{11} \frac{(O_i - E_i)^2}{E_i}$$

Also $\chi^2_{0.05}$ = the tabulated value of χ^2 is less than the tabulated value of χ^2 at 5% level of significance for 6 d.f.

∴ H_o is accepted *i.e.,* there is no significant difference between the sales.

Example 8. *In an experiment on immunization of cattle from tuberculosis, the following results were obtained.*

	Affected	Not affected
Inoculated	12	26
Not inoculated	16	8

Calculate x^2 and discuss the effect of vaccine in controlling the disease (given $x^2_{0.05}$ = 3.84).

Solution: Null Hypothesis H_0: There is no effect of vaccine in controlling the disease.

Since one of the frequency (observed) b, is less than 10, Apply Yate's correction, adding 0.5 in 6 and adjusting others, so that the total remains same.

Take the contingency table for observed frequencies as under :

Observed Frequencies

	Affected	Not-affected	Total
Inoculated	12.5	25.5	38
Not inoculated	15.5	6.5	22
Total	28	32	60

Expected Frequencies

$\frac{28\times38}{60}=17.7$	$\frac{32\times38}{60}=2.3$
$\frac{28\times22}{60}=10.3$	$\frac{32\times22}{60}=11.7$

To calculate x^2, we have the following table.

Q_i	12.5	25.5	15.5	6.5
E_i	17.7	20.3	10.3	11.7
$\frac{(O_i-E_i)^2}{E_i}$	1.528	2.625	1.332	2.3111

$$\therefore \quad \chi^2=\sum_{i=1}^{4}\frac{(O_i-E_i)^2}{E_i}=1.528+2.625+1.332+2.3111=7.796$$

Also, $\chi^2_{0.05}$ = The tabulated value of χ^2 at 5% level of significance = 3.84. i.e., the calculated value of x^2 is greater than the tabulated value of χ^2 at 5% level of significance. Therefore H_0 is rejected. Hence the vaccine is effected in controlling the disease.

Example 9. *From the following data, use χ^2 test and conclude whether inoculation is effective in preventing tuberculosis.*

	Attached	Not-attached	Total
Inoculated	31	469	500
Not inoculated	185	1315	1500
Total	216	1784	2000

(P.T.U., M.B.A. May 2004)

Solution: Null Hypothesis H_0. The inoculation is not effective in presenting tuberculosis

Degree of freedom = $(r-1)(s-1) = (2-1)(2-1) = 1$

The given data can be shown in the form of 2 × 2 contingency table.

Observed Frequencies

	Attached	Not-attached	Total
Inoculated	31	469	500
Not inoculated	185	1315	1500
Total	216	1784	2000

Expected Frequencies

$\frac{216 \times 500}{2000} = 54$	$\frac{1784 \times 500}{2000} = 446$
$\frac{216 \times 1500}{2000} = 162$	$\frac{1784 \times 1500}{2000} = 1338$

To calculate χ^2, we have the following table:

Q_i	31	185	469	1315
E_i	54	162	446	1338
$(Q_i - E_i)^2$	529	529	529	529
$\frac{(O_i - E_i)^2}{E_i}$	9.79	3.26	1.186	0.395

$$\therefore \quad \chi^2 = \sum_{i=1}^{4} \frac{(O_i - E_i)^2}{E_i} = 9.79 + 3.26 + 1.186 + 0.395 = 14.631$$

Also, $\chi^2_{0.05}$ = The tabulated value of χ^2 at 5% level of significance = 3.841.

Conclusion. The calculated value of χ^2 is greater than the tabulated value of χ^2 at 5% level of significance. for 1 d.f.

∴ H_0 is rejected *i.e.*, the inoculation is effective in preventing tuberculosis.

Example 10. *A certain drug was administered to 500 people out of a total of 800. Out of these, 480 had an attack of typhoid and among them 200 were administered the drug. Test if the drug is effective in preventing the attack of typhoid* ($\chi^2_{0.05}$ for 1 d.f. = 3.841).

Sol Null Hypothesis H_0: There is no effect of drug in preventing the attack of typhoid. The given data can be shown in the form of 2 × 2 contingency table.

Observed Frequencies

	Affected	Not-Affected	Total
Administered	200	300	500
Not administered	280	20	300
Total	480	320	800

↓

Expected Frequencies

$\frac{480 \times 500}{800} = 300$	$\frac{480 \times 300}{800} = 180$
$\frac{320 \times 500}{800} = 200$	$\frac{320 \times 300}{800} = 120$

To calculate χ^2, we have the following table:

O_i	200	300	280	20
E_i	300	180	200	120
$\frac{(O_i - E_i)^2}{E_i}$	33.33	80	32	83.33

$$\therefore \quad \chi^2 = \sum_{i=1}^{4} \frac{(O_i - E_i)^2}{E_i} = 33.33 + 80 + 32 + 83.33 = 228.66$$

Also, $\chi^2_{0.05}$ = The tabulated value of χ^2 at 5% level of significance at 1 d.f. = 3.841. The calculated value of χ^2 is greater than the tabulated value at 5% level of significance. Hence H_0 is rejected, *i.e.*, the drug is effective in controlling the attack of typhoid.

Example 11. *In a locality,* 100 *persons were randomly selected and asked about their educational achievements. The results are given below.*

Education

		Middle	High School	College
Sex	Male	10	15	25
	Female	25	10	15

Based on this information, can you say that the education depends on sex.

($\chi^2_{0.05}$ for 2 d.f. = 5.991)

Solution: Null Hypothesis H_0: The education and sex are not associated.

Degree of freedom $v = (r-1)(s-1) = (3-1)(2-1) = 2$

Under H_0, we calculate

$$\chi^2 = \sum_{i=1}^{3} \sum_{i=1}^{2} \frac{[(A_iB_j)_0 (A_iB_j)]^2}{(A_iB_j)_0}$$

Observed Frequencies

	Middle	High School	College	
Male	10	15	25	50
Female	25	10	15	50
Total	35	25	40	100

To calculate the expected frequencies $(A_1)(B_1)_0$, we have

$$(A_1)(B_1)_0 = \frac{(A_1)(B_1)}{N} = \frac{35 \times 50}{100} = 17.5$$

$$(A_1)(B_2)_0 = \frac{(A_1)(B_2)}{N} = \frac{35 \times 50}{100} = 17.5$$

$$(A_2)(B_1)_0 = \frac{(A_2)(B_1)}{N} = \frac{25 \times 50}{100} = 12.5$$

$$(A_2)(B_2)_0 = \frac{(A_2)(B_2)}{N} = \frac{25 \times 50}{100} = 12.5$$

$$(A_3)(B_1)_0 = \frac{(A_3)(B_1)}{N} = \frac{40 \times 50}{100} = 20$$

$$(A_3)(B_1)_0 = \frac{(A_3)(B_1)}{N} = \frac{40.50}{100} = 20$$

Calculation of χ^2

Class	O_i	E_i	$(O_i - E_i)^2$	$\frac{(O_i - E_i)^2}{E_i}$
$A_1 B_1$	10	17.5	56.25	3.26
$A_1 B_2$	25	17.5	56.25	3.26

$A_2 B_1$	15	12.5	6.25	0.5
$A_2 B_2$	10	12.5	6.25	0.5
$A_3 B_1$	25	20	25	2.5
$A_3 B_2$	15	20	25	2.5

$$\therefore \quad \chi^2 = \Sigma \frac{(O_i - E_i)^2}{E_i} = 3.26 + 3.26 + 0.5 + 0.5 + 2.5 + 2.5 = 12.52$$

Also $\chi^2_{0.05}$ = The tabulated value of χ^2 at 5% level of significance for 2 d.f. = 5.991.

Thus the calculated value of x^2 is greater than the tabulated value of x^2 of 5% level of significance. Hence H_0 is rejected *i.e.,* the education depends on sex.

Example 12. *A sample of* 200 *people with a particular disease was selected. Out of these,* 100 *were given a drug and others were not given any drug. The results are as given :*

	With drug	Without drug	Total
Cured	65	55	120
Not cured	35	45	80
Total	100	100	200

Test whether the drug is effective or not at α = 5% level of significance.

(P.T.U., M.B.A. May 2006)

Solution: Null Hypothesis H_0. The drug is not effective. Degree of freedom

$$= (r-1)(s-1) = (2-1)(2-1) = 1$$

The given data can be shown in the form of 2 × 2 contingency table :

Observed Frequencies

	With drug	Without drug	Total
Cured	65	55	120
Not cured	35	45	80
Total	100	100	200

Expected Frequencies

$\frac{100 \times 120}{200} = 60$	$\frac{100 \times 120}{200} = 60$
$\frac{100 \times 80}{200} = 40$	$\frac{100 \times 80}{200} = 40$

To calculate χ^2, we have the following table:

O_i	65	35	55	45
E_i	60	40	60	40
$(O_i - E_i)^2$	25	25	25	25
$\frac{(O_i - E_i)^2}{E_i}$	0.4166	0.625	0.4166	0.625

$$\therefore \quad \chi^2 = \sum_{i=1}^{4} \frac{(O_i - E_i)^2}{E_i} = 0.4166 + 0.625 + 0.4166 + 0.625 = 2.0832$$

Also, $\chi^2_{0.05}$ = The tabulated value of x^2 at 5% level of significance at 1 d.f.
= 3.841 (see x^2-table).

Conclusion. The calculated value of χ^2 < the tabulated value of χ^2 at 5% level of significance for 1 d. f.

∴ H_0 is accepted, *i.e.,* the drug is effective.

Exercise 5.2

1. In a locality 100 persons were randomly selected and asked about their educational achievements. The results are given below :

		Education		
		Middle	High School	College
Sex	Male	10	15	25
	Female	25	10	15

Based on this information can you say the education depends on sex.

2. The following data is collected on two characters :

	Smokers	Non smokers
Literate	83	57
Illiterate	45	68

Base on this information can you say that there is no relation between habit of smoking and literacy.

3. 500 students at school were graded according to their intelligences and economic conditions of their homes. Examine whether there is any association between economic condition and intelligence, from the following data :

Economic conditions	Intelligence	
	Good	Bad
Rich	85	75
Poor	165	175

4. In an experiment on the immunisation of goats from anthrox, the following results were obtained. Derive your inferences on the efficiency of the vaccine.

	Died anthrox	Survived
Inoculated with vaccine	2	10
Not inoculated	6	6

5. From the adult male population of seven large cities, random samples of married and unmarried men as given below were taken. Can it be said that there is a significant variation among the people of different cities in the tendency to marry?

City	A	B	C	D	E	F	G	Total
Married	170	285	165	106	153	125	146	1150
Unmarried	40	125	35	37	55	35	33	360
Total	210	410	200	143	208	160	179	1510

6. From the following data, find out whether there is any relationship between sex and preference of colour.

Colour	Sex.	
	Males	Females
Red	10	40
White	70	30
Green	30	20

7. A survey among women was conducted to study the family life. The observation were as follows :

	Family Life	
	Happy	Not happy
Educated	70	30
Non Educated	60	40

Test whether there is any association between family life and education.

8. A sample of 300 students of under-graduate and 300 students of post-graduate classes of university were asked to give their opinion towards the autonomous colleges 190 of the undergraduate and 210 of the post graduate students favoured the autonomous status. Present the above fact in the form of a frequency table and test that opinions of undergraduate and postgraduate students on autonomous status of colleges are independent.
9. A drug a said to be useful for treatment of cold. In an experiment carried out on 160 person suffering from cold, half of the person were treated with the drug and rest of the half with sugar pills. The effect of treatment of this described in the following table (for 2 d.f. the value of $\chi^2 = 5.99$ at 5% level)

	Helped	Harmful	No. of Effect
Drug	52	10	18
Sugar pills	44	10	26

(U.P.T.U. 2010)

Answers

1. Yes 2. No 3. No 4. No effective
5. There is a difference in the tendency of people to marry in different cities. ($x^2 = 21.381$)
6. There is a relationship between sex and preference of colour ($x^2 = 34.35$)
7. there is no association between family life and education. ($x^2 = 2.198$)
8. The opinions of the undergraduate and post graduate students on autonomous status of colleges is independent. ($x^2 = 30$)

5.19 Analysis of Variance (ANOVA)

(U.P.T.U.)

It was R. A. Fisher who introduced the term '*Variance*' in the analysis of statistical data. Fisher developed an elaborate technique of analysing the variance of two or more series for the purpose of studying their characteristic. Variance is a measure of the variability of the values of various items of a series from the mean. The technique of the analysis of variance (ANOVA) as developed by Fisher is capable of fruitful application in a variety of problems.

$$F = \frac{S_1^2}{S_2^2} = \frac{\dfrac{n_1 S_1^2}{n_1 - 1}}{\dfrac{n_2 S_2^2}{n_2 - 1}}$$

F-ratio is therefore the ratio of two independent χ^2 variates divided by their respective degrees of freedom. The F-test tells us whether the variances of the two universes from which the samples have been taken are equal. We set up a null hypothesis $H_0: \sigma_1^2 = \sigma_2^2$, that is, the population variances are the same. In other words, the assumption we make is that the two independent estimates of the population variances do not differ significantly and we test this hypothesis by calculating F-ratio and comparing the calculated value of F with the critical value of F from the table. If the calculated value of F is more than the critical value for the given degrees of freedom and the given significance level, the null hypothesis is rejected and the inference is that the difference is significant. The samples in such cases do not come from the same universe or if they have come from two universes, the variance of these two universes are not the same.

In ANOVA, an attempt is made to find out whether the means given by a number of samples are significantly different from one another. In case of just two samples, Z-test or t-test may be used for the purpose, but these tests cannot be used if the number of samples is more than two. The technique of ANOVA is very useful in such cases and with its help it is possible to study the significance of the difference of mean values of a large number of samples at the same time. For example, it can be used in a research where the effects of one or two variables has to be determined on the basis of a number of experiments conducted simultaneously. Variance analysis can tell us whether different sample data classified on the basis of one or two variables are meaningful or not. *ANOVA studies the significance of the difference in means by analysing variance.* The variances would differ only when the means are significantly different.

Assumptions in F-Test

(*i*) The universe from which the samples are drawn follows the properties of the standard normal curve.

(*ii*) The samples drawn from the universe are random and independent of each other.

(*iii*) The variances of the populations from which the samples have been taken do not significantly differ from each other. We start with the null hypothesis, $H_0 = \sigma_1^2 = \sigma_2^2 = \sigma_3^2 = \cdots = \sigma_n^2$

In real life problems, these assumptions may or may not hold good. However, unless the universes are highly skewed, minor variations in the assumptions do not affect the validity of the F-test. If the means of the samples are not significantly different from the mean of all the samples taken together, then it can be safely assumed that they have come from the same or similar population.

Technique of Analysing Variance

The technique of ANOVA in case of single variable and in case of two variables is similar. In both cases a comparison is made between the variance of sample means with the *residual variance*. However, in case of a single variable (**one-way classification**), the total variance is divided into two parts:

(*i*) Variance between the samples; and

(*ii*) Variance within the samples.

The latter variance is the residual variance. In case of two variables (**two-way classification**) the total variance is divided into three parts:

(*i*) Variance due to the first variable;

(*ii*) Variance due to the second variable; and

(*iii*) Residual variance.

Variance Analysis in One-Way Classification

If there are, say, four samples, the null hypothesis would be that their means are not different, that is $H_0: \mu_1 = \mu_2 = \mu_3 = \mu_4$. The alternate hypothesis shall be $H_1: \mu_1 \neq \mu_2 \neq \mu_3 \neq \mu_4$. With these hypotheses, we perform the following steps for ANOVA in one-way classification:

(*i*) Calculate the sum of the squares of variation between samples.

(*ii*) Calculate the sum of the squares of variation within the samples.

(*iii*) Calculate the total sum of the squares of variation. This will be the sum of (i) and (ii) and should be calculated directly also for verification of calculations.

(*iv*) Calculate the F-ratio.

(*v*) Compare the calculated F-ratio with the critical value of F-ratio from the table.

(*vi*) Draw inference whether the null hypothesis is accepted or rejected.

These steps are discussed below:

(*i*) ***Variation between Samples.*** The variation between sample means can be either on account of difference in variable or due to chance. On the other hand, the difference between the values of items in any single sample can be on account of chance only as the variable remains uniform throughout the sample. The results of different samples are shown in columns. The sum of squares of variation between the samples is called SSC (sum of squares in column). If the number of items is equal in all samples, it is calculated as follows:

a. Find out the mean of each sample ($\bar{X}_1, \bar{X}_2, \bar{X}_3, ..., \bar{X}_n$).

b. Find the mean of the sample means or the grand mean $\left(\frac{\bar{X}_1+\bar{X}_2+\bar{X}_3+\cdots+\bar{X}_n}{N_1+N_2+N_3+\cdots+N_n}\right)$.

c. Find the deviation of sample means from the grand mean; square these deviations and multiply by the number of items in samples; find the sum of these figures. This is SSC.

d. Divide the sum of squares of deviations from previous step by the degrees of freedom, given by (c–1), where c denotes the number of samples. This is denoted as MSC (mean square of columns).

(*ii*) ***Variation within the Samples.*** Any variation within a sample could be on account of chance only. The difference in the values of various items within a sample, which is due to chance, is called an estimate of the error. It is denoted by SSE (sum of the squares of the deviations from the mean of the series). It is calculated as follows:

a. Find the mean of the sample.

b. Find the deviation of various items of the sample from the mean value (of the sample). Square these deviations and obtain their total.

c. Repeat this process for all samples, and total the sum of the squares of the deviation of the various samples from their respective means. This would give the value of SSE.

d. Divide SSE by the degrees of freedom which would be $(n_1 - 1) + (n_2 - 1) + (n_3 - 1) + \cdots$ or $N - K$, where N is the total number of items in all samples and K is the number of samples. It could be also calculated as $N - C$, as the number of columns would be equal to the number of samples. This would be the variance within the sample (or variance due to chance). This is denoted by MSE (means square of the error).

(iii) ***Total sum of Squares.*** This is the total of SSR and SSE. In other words, it is found by adding the sum of squares of deviations between the samples and the sum of squares of deviations within the samples. However, for the sake of verification of calculations, it should be calculated as follows:

a. Find the grand mean.

b. Find the deviations of all the items of all the samples from the grand mean. Square these deviations and obtain the total of these squares (SST, that is the total sum of squares).

c. Divide SST by the degrees of freedom ($N - 1$). This is the total variance.

(iv) ***Calculation of Variance Ratio (F-Ratio), comparison with tabulated value and inference.*** F-ratio (variance ratio) is the ratio between greater variance and smaller variance. Generally variance between the samples is more than the variance within the samples and

$$F = \frac{\text{variance between samples}}{\text{variance within samples}} = \frac{MSC}{MSE}$$

If, however, the variance within the samples is more than the variance between the samples, the numerator and denominator should be interchanged and the degrees of freedom adjusted accordingly.

The calculated F-ratio is compared with the critical value of F to draw inferences. If the calculated value of F is more than the critical value, the null hypothesis is rejected and the differences between means is said to be significant. It means that we accept the alternate hypothesis that $\mu_1 \neq \mu_2 \neq \mu_3 \neq \mu_4$.

The above points for analysing variance in one-way classification can be analysed in the following ANOVA table:

Analysis of Variance (ANOVA) Table (One-Way Classification)

Source of Variation	Sum of Squares	Degrees of Freedom	Mean Squares	F-Ratio
Between Samples	SSC	C–1	$MSC = \frac{SSC}{C-1}$	
Within Samples	SSE	N–C	$MSE = \frac{SSE}{N-C}$	$\frac{MSC}{MSE}$
Total	SST	n–1		

Where

SSC = Sum of squares between samples

SSE = Sum of squares within samples

SST = Total sum of squares

MSC = Mean square between samples

MSE = Mean square within samples

F = Ratio of MSE to MSC.

Coding of Data (Change of Scale or Origin)

The F ratio has a very important property that its value remains unchanged if all the figures are multiplied or divided by a common factor or if a common factor is added to or subtracted from each figure.

The above property is of very great help in calculating the F ratio when the figures are large, and the calculations become tedious. In such cases the figures may be divided or multiplied to get a convenient set of figures. This property may also be used in case of fractional figures. When such simplification is done, it is said that the data have been coded to simplify calculations. The value of F remains unchanged when coded data are used for calculations.

Variance Analysis in Two-Way Classification

Here we study the effect of two variables. The procedure of analysis in two-way classification is: total columns as well as rows. The effect of one factor is studied through the column-wise figures and totals and the effect of the other factor is studied through the row-wise figures and totals. The variances are calculated for both the columns and rows and they are compared with the residual variance or error. The table of variance analysis in a two-way classification takes the following form:

ANOVA Table (Two-Way Classification)

Source of Variation	Sum of Squares	Degrees of Freedom	Mean Square	Variance Ratio
(i)	(ii)	(iii)	(iv)	(v)
Between Columns	SSC	(c–1)	$MSC = \frac{SSC}{c-1}$	$\frac{MSC}{MSE}$
Between Rows	SSR	(r–1)	$MSR = \frac{SSR}{r-1}$	$\frac{MSR}{MSE}$
Residual or Error	SSE	(c–1)(r–1)	$MSE = \frac{SSE}{c-1}$	
Total	SST	n–1	(r–1)	

Where

SSC = Sum of squares between columns

SSR = Sum of squares between rows

SSE = Sum of squares due to errors

SST = Total sum of squares.

The SSE or residual sum of squares is found out by subtracting the total of SSC and SSR from the total sum of squares.

In a two-way classification one should be careful in finding out the degrees of freedom. For column figures it is (c–1), for row it is (r–-1) and for the residual it is (c–1)(r–1). Therefore, while calculating F-ratio for columns and for rows the degrees of freedom for the numerator may not be the same. In the first case it is (c–1) and in the second case it is (r–1). However, the degrees of freedom for the denominator in both cases would be the same, that is, (c–1)(r–1).

Assumption in Analysis of Variance of Two Variables

When we analyse the variance in a two-way classification, we assume that the factor effects are *additive* so that the values are affected by a constant amount on account of each variable. But this may not necessarily be true. There may be interaction between the two factors. One factor might be affecting the other in some way. However, in the analysis of variance in a two-way classification, this effect is ignored, and the inference drawn by variance analysis is subject to this limitation.

Exercise 5.3

1. What is the major purpose of hypothesis is testing. Explain the various steps involved in hypothesis testing. **(UPTU-07)**
2. Define sampling. Explain the different methods of sampling.
3. What is standard error of mean? How it is calculated.
4. "Chi-square test is used for testing of goodness of fit, homogeneity of data and independence", discuss.
5. How will you distinguish between 'large samples' and 'small samples'? Is the stand and error of mean of large sample different from the standard error of mean of a small sample?.
6. What is meant by Association of Attributes? How does it differ from correlation.
7. Two types of batteries X and Y are tested for their length of life and the following results are obtained:

Battery	Sample size	Mean (hr)	Std. Deviation (hr)
X	100	1000	10
Y	120	1020	11

Can you conclude that the two types of batteries are having the same mean life?

8. The following information is obtained concerning an investigation of 50 ordinary shops of small size :

Organisation Run by	Shops located in	
	Urban area	Rural area
Men	17	18
Women	3	12

Can it be inferred that shops run by women are relatively more in rural areas than in urban areas? Use Chi-Square –test. **(U.P.T.U. 2004)**

9. The following data pertain in two types of tube-bulbs tested for their length of life:

Type	Sample Size	Mean life (in hours)	S.D. of life (in hours)
I	50	550	10
II	70	500	9

Test whether there is a significant difference between the two means (test at 5% level)

10. A company produces two makes of bulks A and B. 200 bulks of each make were tested and it was found that make A has mean life of 2,560 hours and S.D. of 90 hours, whereas make B has 2,650 hours of mean life with S.D of 75 hours. Is there a significant difference between the mean life of the two makes?

11. Examine by any suitable method, whether the nature of area is related to voting preference in the election for which the data are tabulated below :

Votes for Area	A	B	Total
Rural	620	480	1100
Urban	380	520	900
Total	1000	1000	2000

12. Two salesmen A and B are working in a district from a sample survey conducted by the office the following results were obtained. State whether there is any significant difference in the average sale of two salesmen.

	A	B
No. of sales	20	18
Av. Sales (in Rs.)	170	205
S. D. (in Rs.)	20	25

13. Strength test carried out on samples of two yarn spun to the same count gave the following results :

	Sample Size	Mean	Variance
Yarn A	4	50	42
Yarn B	9	42	56

14. The Strengths are expressed in pounds. Is the difference in mean strengths significant?

15. The employees of 4 different firms are distributed in three skill categories as shown in the following table. Test the hypothesis that there is no relationship between the firm and the type of labour. Let the level of significance be 5%.

Firm Type of Labour	A	B	C	D
Skilled	24	24	23	49
Semi-skilled	32	60	37	51
Manual	24	56	40	80

16. A sample of 400 is drawn from a normal population whose mean is 5 and variance is 4. If the sample mean is 4,45, can the sample be reasonably regarded as a truly random sample? Also obtain the 95% and 98% confidence limits for the population mean.

17. A coin is tossed, 400 times and it turns up head 216 times. Discuss whether the coin may be an unbiased one.

18. Ten soldiers visit the rifle range two weeks running. The first week their scores were :

67, 24, 57, 55, 63, 54, 56, 68, 33, 43

19. The second week scores :

70, 38, 58, 58, 56, 67, 68, 75, 42, 38

It there any significant improvement?

20. In a random sample of 1000 persons form town A, 400 are found to be consumers of rice. In a sample of 800 from town B, 400 are found to be consumers of rice. Whether the data reveal a significance between A and B so far as the proportion of rice consumers is conceded.

A random sample of 200 villages was taken from Jaipur and the average population per village was found to be 485 with a standard deviation of 50. Another random sample of 200 villages was taken from Udaipur and the average population per village was found to be 510 with standard deviation of 40. Examine if the difference between the two means is statistically significant at 5% level.

1,600 families were selected at random in Chandigarh to test the belief that high-income families usually send their children to Public Schools and low-level families often send their children to Government Schools. The survey so conducted for the purpose revealed the following results :

Family income	Type of School		Total
	Public	Government	
Low	494	506	1,000
High	162	438	600
Total	656	944	1,600

Applying Chi square – test, examine the proposition that family income and type of school are independent.

21. A soap manufacturing company was selling a particular type of brand through a large number of retail shops. Before a heave advertising campaign, the average sales per week per shop was 140 dozens. After the campaign, a sample of 26 shops was taken and the average sales per week per shop was found to be 147 dozens with a standard deviation of 16 dozens. Do you consider that the advertising campaign was effective? Use students' t-test, either at 5% or 1% level, to answer this question.

22. 100 Students of a management institute obtained the following grades in the Statistics paper :

Grade	A	B	C	D	E	Total
Frequency	15	17	30	22	16	100

Using Chi Square – test, examine the hypothesis that the distribution of grades is uniform.

23. A sample of 400 managers is found to have a mean height of 171.38 cm. Can it be reasonably regarded as a sample from a large population of mean height 171.17 cm and standard deviation of 3.3 cm. (Test at 5% level of significance.)

24. A sample of 300 units was taken out from a population, the mean of which was 25 and S.D. 6 Another sample of 200 units was also taken out form the same population, the mean of which was 28 and S.D. 7. Does the S.D. of first sample differ significantly from the combined S.D. of the two samples.

25. The table given below shows the data obtained during an epidemic of cholera:

	Attacked	Not Attacked	Total
Inoculated	31	469	500
Not inoculated	185	1315	1500
Total	216	1784	2000

Test the effectiveness of inoculation of preventing of cholera by chi square-test.

26. The particulars of two kinds of shop A and B in the same city are given as such:

	Mean Sale	S.D.	No. of Shop
A	28	1.5	25
B	26	1.0	25

Is there significant difference in the mean sale of two kinds of shop?
(Test at 5% level of significance).

27. Two types of drugs were used on 5 and 7 patients for reducing weight. Drug A was imported and drug B indigenous. The decrease in weight after using the drug for 6 months was as follows :

Drug 'A'	:	10	12	13	11	14		
Drug 'B'	:	8	9	12	14	15	10	9

Is there a significant difference in the efficacy of the two drugs? If not which drug should you buy.

28. 1000 students at college level are graded according to their I.Q. and their economic conditions. Use chi square test to find out whether there is any association between economic conditions and the level of I.Q.

Economic		I.Q.		
Conditions	High	Medium	Low	Total
Rich	160	300	140	600
Poor	140	100	160	400
Total	300	400	300	1000

29. Write short notes on the following -
    (*i*) Sampling and Non-sampling errors.
    (*ii*) Type I and II errors **(UPTU-CO-08) (UPTU-08)**
    (iii) One tailed and two tailed test. **(UPTU-08)**
    (*iv*) F-lest.
    (*v*) Rules coefficient of association.
    (*vi*) Degree of freedom and level of significance.
    (*vii*) χ^2-test
    (*viii*) Null and alternative hypothesis
    (*ix*) Consistency of data
    (*x*) Techniques of association of attributes and testing **(UPTU-08)**
    (*xi*) Level of significance **(UPTU-08)**
30. What is test of significance? Discuss its role in large sample theory. Test the significance of the difference between the means of the sample from the following data:

Sample	Size	Mean	SD
A	100	50	4
B	150	51	5

(UPTU-07)

31. What is 't' test? Explain its applications. **(UPTU-07)**
32. By using chi-square test, find out whether there is any association between income level and type of schooling :

Income	Public School	Govt. School
Low	200	400
High	1000	400

(Given for degree of freedom 1, $\chi^2_{0.05} = 3.84$) **(UPTU-07)**

33. A sample analysis of examination results of 500 students was made. It was found that 220 had failed, 170 had secured a third class, 90 were placed in second class and 20 got a first class. Are these figures commensurate with the general examination result which is in the ratio of 4:3:2:1 for the various categories respectively.

    (The tabular value of chi-square for three degrees of free at 5% level of significance is 7.81)

Objective type Questions

1. The test-statistics for testing $H_0:\mu= \mu_0$, when sample size is small:

(a) $t = \dfrac{x-\mu_0}{S/\sqrt{n}}$ (b) $z = \dfrac{x-\mu_0}{\sigma/\sqrt{n}}$

(c) $t = \dfrac{x-\mu_0}{\sigma/\sqrt{(n-1)}}$ (d) None of these

2. The number of degrees of freedom for the

t-statistic, $t= \dfrac{x-y}{S\sqrt{[1 + 1]}}$.
$n_1 \; n_3$

(a) (n-1) (b) (n_1+n_2-2)
(c) (n-2) (d) None of these

3. Non-sampling error are:

(a) Error in response (b) Faculty planning
(c) Error of compilation (d) All of these

4. The test statistic $\dfrac{F= S_1^2}{S_2^2}$ is used for testing:

(a) $H_0: \mu_1 = \mu_0$ (b) $H_0: \sigma_1^2 = \sigma^2_2$
(c) $H_0: \sigma^2 = \sigma_0^2$ (d) none of these

5. The number of the degrees of freedom for a contingency table of order 5×4 is: **(UPTU-08)**

(a) 20 (b) 15
(c) 12 (d) 16

6. A sample of size n=9 is down from a normal population to test H_0: $\mu =\mu_0$, the test statistic has

(a) 9 d.f. (b) 8 d.f.
(c) 7 d.f. (d) none of these

7. The test statistic $F =S_1^2/S_2^2$ is used when:

(a) $S_1^2>S_2^2$ (b) $S_1^2<S_2^2$
(c) $S_1^2=S_2^2$ (d) None of these

8. The statistic $x^2 = \frac{\Sigma(0-E)^2}{E}$ is used for testing:

(a) $H_0: \mu^2 = \mu_0^2$ (b) $H_0: \mu_1^2 = \mu_2^2$

(c) $H_0: \mu = \mu_0$ (d) None of these

9. Paired t-test is used when: **(UPTU-08)**

(a) Observation in the two sample are paired

(b) Observation in the two sample are independent

(c) Observation in the two sample are the same

(d) None of these

10. A significant difference between the statistic and parametric value means:

(a) The difference is real

(b) The difference is due to sampling instability

(c) The sample is a representative of the population

(d) None of these

11. The test statistic for testing $H_0: \sigma_1^2 = \sigma_2^2$ is :

(a) $F = \frac{S_1^2}{S_2^2}$ (b) $t = \frac{\overline{x}-\overline{y}}{S\sqrt{[\frac{1}{n_1}+\frac{1}{n_2}]}}$

(c) $Z = \frac{\overline{x}-\overline{y}}{\sqrt{[\frac{\sigma_1^2}{n_1}+\frac{\sigma_2^2}{n_2}]}}$ (d) None of these

12. Non- sampling errors can arise only in:

(a) Census survey (b) Sample survey

(c) Both census & sample survey (d) None of these

13. Sampling errors are presents in :

(a) Only samples survey

(b) Only census enumeration

(c) Both census enumeration and sample survey

(d) Neither sample nor census enumeration

14. The term standard error in statistics refers:

(a) Biases

(b) Mistakes

(c) Both biases and mistakes

(d) Difference between the value of a statistics and that of the corresponding parameter

15. A random sample of size 100 has mean 15,the population variance being 25. then the 95% confidence interval for the mean is:

(a) 13.71, 16.29 (b) 14.02, 15.98

(c) 13.71, 14.09 (d) 14.02, 16.29

(e) 13.71, 15.98

16. If the population standard deviation is 20 and the sample size is 16 then the standard error of mean will be:

(a) 1.12 (b) 1.25 (c) 5.00

(d) 6.75 (e) 9.23

17. Which of the following is a case of type II error.

(a) The null hypothesis is true and rejected.

(b) The null hypothesis is false and accepted.

(c) The null hypothesis is true and accepted.

(d) The null hypothesis is false and rejected.

(e) None of the above.

18. Which of the following distribution can be identified by a pair of degrees of freedom?

(a) t-distribution (b) Binomial distribution

(c) Normal distribution (d) F-distribution

(e) Chi-square distribution

19. A Type error occurs in hypothesis testing when the:

(a) Null hypothesis

(b) Alternate hypothesis is false

(c) Null hypothesis is false and accepted.

(d) Null hypothesis is false is rejected.

(e) Null hypothesis is true is rejected.

20. In a right tailed test of hypothesis the:

(a) Acceptance region lies under the right tail.

(b) Rejection region lies under the right tail.

(c) Acceptance region lies under the right and left tails.

(d) Rejection region lies at the center of the distribution.

(e) Entire region lying on the right of the mean of the distribution is the rejection region.

21. Calculated value of x^2 is:
(a) Always position (b) Always negative
(c) Positive and negative (d) None of the above

22. When observed and expected frequencies completely coincide, then the value of x^2 will be:
(a) +1 (b) -1
(c) More than 1 (d) zero

23. Type – I error is also known as-
(a) Sampling error (b) non-sampling error
(c) Producers risk (d) Customer risk

24. Type- II error is also known as-
(a) Sampling error (b) non-sampling error
(c) Producers risk (d) Customer risk

25. Sampling errors can be reduced by-
(a) Reducing sample size (b) Increasing sample size
(c) By both (d) None of these

26. The basis of dichotomous classification is:
(a) One attribute (b) Two attribute
(c) Three attribute (d) More than three attribute

27. Out of the following, contrary class is:
(a) (AB) (b) (BC)
(c) (Aγ) (d) (AC)

28. The formula for finding out number of ultimate classes is:
(a) 1^n (b) 2^n (c) 3^n (d) 4^n

29. The total number of classes in case of classification on the basis of three attributes is:
(a) 8 (b) 9 (c) 27 (d) 30

30. In case of classification on the basis of two attributes:
(a) (AB) = (A) –(Aß) (b) (AB) =(B) –(aB)
(c) (AB) = N-(a) –(Aß) (d) All the above

31. The meaning of $(AB) > \frac{(A)\times(B)}{N}$ is :
(a) Positive association (b) Negative association
(c) Mutually independent (d) None of the above

32. The formula of coefficient of association is :

(a) $Q = \dfrac{(AB)\ (a\beta) - (A\beta)\ (aB)}{(AB)\ (a\beta) + (A\beta)\ (aB)}$

(b) $Q = \dfrac{(AB)\ (a\beta) + (A\beta)\ (aB)}{(AB)\ (a\beta) - (A\beta)\ (aB)}$

(c) $Q = \dfrac{(AB)\ (aB) - (A\beta)\ (a\beta)}{(AB)\ (aB) + (A\beta)\ (a\beta)}$

(d) $Q = \dfrac{(AB)\ (aB) - (A\beta)\ (a\beta)}{(AB)\ (aB) + (A\beta)\ (a\beta)}$

33. Under association of attributes, any class frequency cannot be:

(a) Zero (b) Negative

(c) Zero or negative (d) None of these

34. Chi-square distribution is completely known if its --------- is known.**(UPTU – 08)**

35. The standard error of sample mean, when the population is finite, is **(UPTU – 08)**

(a) $\dfrac{\sigma}{\sqrt{\bar{a}}}$ (b) $\dfrac{\sqrt{n}}{\bar{a}}$

(c) $\sqrt[n]{\dfrac{\sigma}{\sqrt{n}}}$ (d) None of these.

True of False

36. Any population constant is called a parameter.
37. The sampling error increases with an increase in sample size.
38. The standard error decreases with an increase in sample size.
39. The standard deviation of a sampling distribution is called the standard error.
40. A large sample size means n > 30.
41. Sampling distribution in approximately normal, if the Sample size is large.
42. The sample theory is based on exact sampling distributions if the sample size is small.
43. For large samples, the standard error of mean is $\sigma/\sqrt{n}$.
44. For testing the independence of two attributes in contingency table we use χ^2– statistic.
45. χ^2– statistic is used for testing the goodness of fit.
46. F-statistic used for testing $H_0 : \mu_1 = \mu_2$.
47. In paired t-test, the observations in the two samples are independent.

48. t-distribution has only one parameter which is its degrees of freedom.

49. χ^2–distribution is completely determined by its only parameter, the degrees of freedom.

Answers

1. a	11. a	21. a	31. a	41. T
2. b	12. c	22. d	32. a	42. T
3. d	13. a	23. c	33. b	43. T
4. b	14. d	24. d	34. d.	44. T
5. c	15. b	25. b	35. c	45. T
6. b	16. c	26. a	36. T	46. F
7. a	17. b	27. c	37. F	47. F
8. d	18. d	28. d	38. T	48. T
9. a	19. d	29. c	39. T	49. T
10.a	20. b	30. d	40. T	

(UPTU-08)

List of Formulae

1. Point Estimators of some parameters

(i) Sample mean $\bar{x}$ is an unbiased estimator of population mean μ.

(ii) $S^2 = \dfrac{\Sigma(x-\bar{x})^2}{n-1}$ is an unbiased estimator of population variance σ^2.

(iii) Sample proportion P is an unbiased estimator of population proportion p.

2. Standard Error of some statistics

$$\text{S.E. } (\hat{p}) = \sqrt{\left[\frac{pq}{n}\right]} \quad ; \quad \text{when } p \text{ is known}$$

$$\text{S.E. } (\hat{p}) = \sqrt{\left[\frac{\hat{p}\hat{q}}{n}\right]} \quad ; \quad \text{when } p \text{ is unknown}$$

$$\text{S.E. } (\hat{x}) = \frac{\sigma}{\sqrt{n}} \quad ; \quad \text{when population is large.}$$

$$\text{S.E. } (\hat{x}) = \sqrt{\left[\frac{N-n}{N-1}\right]}\frac{\sigma}{\sqrt{n}} \quad ; \quad \text{when the population is finite.}$$

Here $\sqrt{\left[\dfrac{N-n}{N-1}\right]}$ is known as finite population multiplier.

$$S.E.\ (\bar{x}-\bar{y}) = \sqrt{\left[\frac{\sigma_1^2}{n_1}+\frac{\sigma_2^2}{n_2}\right]}$$

3. Large Sample Tests

H_0	Test Statistic	H_1	Critical or Rejection Region (For α level of sig)
$\mu = \mu_0$	$Z = \frac{\bar{x}-\mu_0}{\sigma/\sqrt{n}}$	$\mu > \mu_0$ $\mu < \mu_0$ $\mu \neq \mu_0$	$Z > Z_a$ $Z < -Z_a$ $\lvert Z \rvert > Z_{a/2}$
$\mu_1 = \mu_2$	$Z = \frac{\bar{x}-\bar{y}}{\sqrt{\left[\frac{\sigma_1^2}{n_1}+\frac{\sigma_2^2}{n_2}\right]}}$	$\mu_1 > \mu_2$ $\mu_1 < \mu_2$ $\mu_1 \neq \mu_2$	$Z > Z_a$ $Z < -Z_a$ $\lvert Z \rvert > Z_{a/2}$
$p = p_0$	$Z = \frac{\hat{p}-p_0}{\sqrt{\left[\frac{p_0 q_0}{n}\right]}}$ $= \frac{x-nP_0}{\sqrt{(np_0q_0)}}$	$p > p_0$ $p < p_0$ $p \neq p_0$	$Z > Z_a$ $Z < -Z_a$ $\lvert Z \rvert > Z_{a/2}$
$p_1 = p_2$	$z = \frac{\hat{p}_1-\hat{p}_2}{\sqrt{\left[\hat{p}\hat{q}\left(\frac{1}{n_1}+\frac{1}{n_2}\right)\right]}}$ where $\hat{p} = \frac{n_1\hat{p}_1+n_2\hat{p}_2}{n_1+n_2}$	$p_1 > p_2$ $p_1 < p_2$ $p_1 \neq p_2$	$Z > Z_a$ $Z < -Z_a$ $\lvert Z \rvert > Z_{a/2}$

4. Confidence Internals (Large Samples)

(i) (1 – a) 100% confidence limits for μ are :

$$\bar{x} \pm Z_{a/2}\frac{\sigma}{\sqrt{n}}$$

(ii) Most probable limits for μ are :

$$\bar{x} \pm 3\frac{\sigma}{\sqrt{n}}$$

(iii) (1 – *a*) 100% confidence limits for p are

$$\hat{p} \pm Z_{a/2}\sqrt{\left[\frac{\hat{p}\hat{q}}{n}\right]}$$

(iv) Most probable limits for p are

$$\hat{p} \pm 3\sqrt{\left[\frac{\hat{p}\hat{q}}{n}\right]}$$

5. One-way analysis of variance

In usual notations, the steps involved are:

1. Set up the null hyothesis $H_0 : \mu_1 = \mu_2 = ... = \mu_k$ against H_1 : At least two of μ_i;*s* are not equal.
2. Find C.F. $= \frac{T^2}{N}$, where $N = \sum_{i=1}^{k} n_i$
3. Then, $TSS = \sum_{i=1}^{k}\sum_{j=1}^{n_1} x_{ij}^2 - C.F.,$ $BSS = \sum_{i=1}^{k}\frac{T_i^2}{n_i} - C.F.$

   $ESS = TSS - BSS.$
4. Decide
   (*i*) the number of *d.f.*: for *TSS* = $N - 1$.
   (*ii*) the number of *d.f.*: for *BSS* = $k - 1$.
   (*iii*) the number of *d.f.*: for *ESS* = $N - k$.

The results so obtained are shown in ANOVA Table

ANOVA Table (one-way classification)

Source of Variation	Sum of Squares	Degrees of freedom	Mean sum of squares	Calculated F	Tabulated F
Between Class With in Class	BSS BSS	$k - 1$ $N - k$	$\frac{BSS}{k-1} = V_1$ $\frac{ESS}{N-k} = V_2$	$F = \frac{V_i}{V_2}$	$F(k-1),(N-k)(a)$
Total	TSS	$N - 1$			

Conclusion : If (i) $F \le F_{(k-1),}(N-k)(\alpha)$; Accept H_0

(ii) $F > F_{(k-1),}(N-k)(\alpha)$; Reject H_0

5. Small Sample Tests or Exact Tests (Based on t-distribution)

H_0	Test Statistic	H_1	Critical or Rejection Region (For α level of sig)
$\mu = \mu_0$	$t = \frac{\bar{x} - \mu_0}{S/\sqrt{n}} \sim t_{(n-1)}$ where $S^2 = \frac{1}{n-1}\Sigma(x-\bar{x})^2$	$\mu > \mu_0$ $\mu < \mu_0$ $\mu \neq \mu_0$	$t > t_v(a); v = (n-1)$ $t < -t_v(a)$ $\vert t\vert > t_v(a/2)$
$\mu_1 = \mu_2$	$t = \frac{\bar{x} - \bar{y}}{s\sqrt{\left[\frac{1}{n_1} + \frac{1}{n_2}\right]}} \sim t_{(n_1+n_2)}$ where $S^2 = \frac{\Sigma(x-\bar{x})^2 + \Sigma(y-\bar{y})^2}{n_1+n_2-2}$	$\mu_1 > \mu_2$ $\mu_1 < \mu_2$ $\mu_1 \neq \mu_2$	$t > t_v(a); v = (n_1+n_2-2)$ $t < -t_v(a)$ $\vert t\vert > t_v(a/2)$
Paired t-test $\mu_1 = \mu_2$	$t = \frac{\bar{d}}{S_d/\sqrt{n}} \sim t(n-1)$ $S_d^2 = \frac{1}{n-1}\Sigma(d-\bar{d})^2$	$\mu_1 > \mu_2$ $\mu_1 < \mu_2$ $\mu_1 \neq \mu_2$	$t > t_v(a); v = (n-1)$ $t < -t_v(a)$ $\vert t\vert > t_v(a/2)$

6. Confidence Interval (Small Sample)

(1 – a) 100% confidence limits for population mean are :

$$\bar{x} \pm t,(a/2)\frac{S}{\sqrt{n}}; \text{ Where } v = (n-1)$$

7. Test based on χ^2 -distribution

H_0	Test Statistic	H_1	Critical or Rejection Region (For α level of significance)
$\sigma^2 = \sigma_0^2$	$\chi^2 = \frac{\Sigma(x-\bar{x})^2}{\sigma_0 2}$ $= \frac{(n-1)S^2}{\sigma_0^2} \sim x_{n-1}^2$	$\sigma^2 > \sigma_0^2$ $\sigma^2 < \sigma_0^2$ $\sigma^2 \neq \sigma_0^2$	$\chi^2 > \chi^2(\alpha); v = (n-1)$ $\chi^2 < \chi^2(1-\alpha)$ $\chi^2 < \chi^2(1-\alpha/2)$ or $\chi^2 > \chi^2(\alpha/2)$

Fit is good	$\chi^2 = \sum_{i=1}^{k} \frac{(o_i - e_i)^2}{e_i} \sim x^2_{k-1}$	Fit is not good	$\chi^2 > \chi^2(\alpha); v = (k-1)$
The two attributes are independent.	$\chi^2 = \sum_i \sum_j \frac{(o_i - e_i)^2}{e_{ij}} \sim \chi^2_{r-1)(s-1)}$	Two attributes are not independent.	$x^2 > x^2_v(\alpha); v = (r-1)(s-1)$

8. Two-way Analysis of variance

In usual notations, the steps involved in the analysis are :

1. Set up (i) $H'_0 : \mu_{1,} = \mu - ... = \mu_k$

   $H'_1 =$ The μ'_{is} are not all equal.

   (ii) $H''_0 : \mu_{1,} = \mu_2 = ... = \mu_n$

   $H''_1 :$ The μ'_{js} are not all equal.

2. Find C.F. = $\frac{T^2}{nk}; TSS = \sum\sum x^2_{ij} - C.F.$

$$RSS = \sum_{j=1}^{k} \frac{T_i^2}{n} - C.F.; \qquad CSS = \sum_{j=1}^{k} \frac{T_j^2}{k} - C.F.$$

$$ESS = TSS - (RSS + (CSS)$$

3. Decide (i) the number of *d.f.* for *TSS* = *nk* – 1

   (ii) the number of *d.f.* for *RSS* = *k* - 1

   (iii) the number of *d.f.* for *CSS* = *n* - 1

   (iv) the number of *d.f.* for *ESS* = (*k* – 1) (*n* - 1

4. Form the ANOVA Table as shown below :

ANOVA Table (Two-way classification)

Source of variation	Sum of Squares	Degrees of freedom	Mean sum of Squares	Calculated F-Ratio	Tabulated F
Row	RSS	$k-1$	$\frac{RSS}{k-1} = V_1$	$F_1 = \frac{V_1}{V_3}$	$F_{v_1,v_3}(\alpha)$
Column	CSS	$n-1$	$\frac{CSS}{n-1} = V_2$	$F_2 = \frac{V_2}{V_3}$	$F_{v_2,v_3}(\alpha)$
Error	ESS	$(k-1)(n-1)$	$\frac{ESS}{k-1(n-1)} = V_2$		
Total	TSS				

Here $v_1 = (k-1), v_2 = (n-1)$ and $v_3 = (k-1)(n-1)$

5. Conclusion:

If (i) $F_1 \le F_{v_1, v_3,}(\alpha)$; Accept H'_0

$F_1 > F_{v_1, v_3,}(\alpha)$; Reject H'_0

(ii) $F_1 \le F_{v_1, v_3,}(\alpha)$; Accept H'_0

$F_1 > F_{v_1, v_3,}(\alpha)$; Reject H'_0

9. Test Based on F-distribution

H_0	Test Statistic	H_1	Critical or Rejection Region (For α level of significance)
$\sigma_1^2 = \sigma_2^2$	$F = \dfrac{S_1^2}{S_2^2} \sim F_{v1,v2}$ where, $S_1^2 = \dfrac{\Sigma(x-\bar{x})^2}{n_1 - 1}$ $S_2^2 = \dfrac{\Sigma(y-\bar{y})^2}{n_2 - 1}$ $v_1 = (n_1 - 1), v_2 = (n_2 - 1)$ and $(S_1^2 > S_2^2)$	$\sigma_1^2 > \sigma_2^2$	$F > F_{v_1, v_2}(\alpha)$

10. Estimation of sample size

(i) Determination of sample size when estimating the population mean.

$$n = \left[\frac{Z\sigma}{E}\right]^2$$

(ii) Determination of sample size when estimating the population proportion.

$$n = \frac{z^2 pq}{E^2}.$$

11. χ^2-test

$\chi^2 cal < \chi^2 table \Rightarrow$ H_0 Accepted (Dependent)

$\chi^2 cal > \chi^2 table \Rightarrow$ H_0 Rejected (Not independent)

$$\text{Expected frequency} = \frac{\text{Total Row} \times \text{Total Column}}{\text{Grand Total}}$$

Appendix I : Case Studies

Appendix II : Question Paper (U.P.T.U. 2010, 06, 05)

Appendix III : Statistical Tables

Table A: Area under the Standard Normal Curve

Table B: Ordinates of the Standard of Normal Curve

Table C: Critical values of the t-distribution

Table D: Critical values of the χ^2-distribution

Table E: Critical value of F-distribution ($\alpha = 0.05$)

Table F: Critical value of F-distribution ($\alpha = 0.01$)

Table G: Value of e^{-m}

Table H: Factors in control charts

Table I: Logarithms

Table J: Antilogarithms

Case Study 1

A fundamental concept of quality management is that the process providing good or service should be efficient enough to meet the expectations of the organization's customer. The management should not promise error-free products unless the process is capable of producing error-free products.

In this regard, consider the case of local fire department that has been assigned the work of responding to all fires in less than 3 minutes from the time the call is received. Data are collected for the last 100 calls indicating the time from when the call is received until the first unit arrives at the fire place. The Data are shown in the following table.

Table showing response times

Time Range	Frequency
Under 1 minute	6
1 00-1-49 minutes	10
1-50-1-99 minutes	15
2-00-2-49 minutes	20
2-50-2-99 minutes	18
3-00-3-49 minutes	11
3-50-3-99 minutes	8
over 4 minutes.	12
Total	**100**

In the light of given data and the fundamental concept of quality management, write your conclusion regarding management's promise to the customer.

Solution : The given frequency distribution shows that the fire-department is not able to meet 3-minutes standard in all the cases. For the present data, the standard is not met in (11 + 8 + 12) = 31% of the cases Thus, from the view point of quality standard, the alternatives are either to make some change in the system to allow the response distribution to be lowered, or admit that the present system cannot always meet the standard.

Case Study 2

A company is producing Tennis balls. The company has two manufacturing plants say *A* and *B* The plant *A* has an average daily production of34,000 Tennis balls. The output varies, with a S.D. of 4,500 tennis balls per day. The other plant 5 is a bit smaller and averages 12, 000 balls per day with a S.D of 3,000

In a near future, the production manager was giving a speech to the Association of Sports goods manufactures. In that speech he says that the company is having real problems with its plant *A* in maintaining consistency in production output and the problem is not so great with plant *B*.

Based on the production data, was the manager justified in drawing the conclusions he made in the speed. Discuss and support your discussion with appropriate statistical method.

Solutions : The production manager seems to have justified his claim speech if he compares the two S.D.'s as measure of consistency. However, since the average output of the two plants differ significantly, the coefficient of variation *(C. V.)* be used to measure consistency of the two plants. In the present case, the coefficient of variation for the data regarding plant *A* is

$$C.V.A) = \frac{\sigma_A}{X_A} \times 100 = \frac{4,500}{34,000} \times 100 = 13.24\%$$

Similarly, for plant $B, C.V.(B) = \frac{\sigma_B}{X_B} \times 100 = \frac{3,000}{12,000} \times 100 = 25.00\%$

A comparison of the two coefficients of variations clearly shows that plant *A* is more consistent in maintaining the production output, as such the manager is not justified in his claim.

Case Study 3

An industrial chemical company sells 100 different products. The distribution of annual sales amounts last year was as under.

Annual Sales (Rs. 000)	No. of Products.
0-10	19
10- 50	44
50 – 100	17
100-200	14
200-500	6
Total	100

Answer the following

(*a*) A executive of the company, upon studying the distribution, says that products with annual sales between Rs. 10-50 thousand are the most common. Do you agree or disagree ? Explain.

(*b*) Construct a histogram for the distribution and locate mode by graphical method. Does your graph support your answer in (a) ?

Solution : Do yourself.

Case Study 4

The distribution of a company's stock according to the number of shares held is as under-

No. of Shares held	% of Stock holders
0-25	41
25-50	25
50 - 100	19
100 - 500	12
500 and over	03
Total	100

(*a*) Construct a less-than cumulative percent distribution.

(*b*) What percentage of the stock holders held fewer than 75 shares each ? The 50 percent of the share holders with the most shares each held what number of shares or more ?

Solution : Do yourself

Case Study 5

A survey of college students engaged in summer work last year obtained the following information for hours worked and total earnings :

Statistic.	Hours Worked	Earnings ($)
Mean	490	2900 260
Standard Deviation	53	

(*a*) Calculate coefficients of variation for hours worked and for earnings. In what units is each coefficient expressed ?

(*b*) Which shows greater variability, hours worked or earnings ? Be specific and explain your choice of the measure of variability used in the comparison.

Solution : Do yourself.

Case Study 6

Determine whether each of the following random variables is quantitative or qualitative If quantitative, determine whether the phenomenon of interest is discrete or continuous.

(*a*) Number of telephones per households.

(*b*) Type of telephone.

(*c*) Number of long-distance calls made per month.

(*d*) Length (in minutes) of the longest long-distance calls made per month.

(*e*) Colour of telephone

(*f*) Monthly charges for long-distance calls made.

(*g*) Ownership of a cordless phone.

(*h*) Number of local calls made per month.

(*i*) Length (in minutes) of local calls per month.

(*j*) Whether there is a telephone line connection to a Computer in the household, (k) Whether there is a FAX machine in the household

Case Study 7

Suppose that the following information in obtained from students upon exiting from the campus book store during the first week of classes :

(*a*) Amount of money spent on books,

(*b*) Number of text books purchased.

(*c*) Amount of time spent shopping in the book store.

(*d*) Academic subjects.

(*e*) Gender

(*f*) Ownership of a personal computer.

(*g*) Ownership of a video-cassette recorder.

(*h*) Mode of payment

Classify each of these variables as qualitative or quantitative. If it is quantitative, determine whether the variable is discrete or continuous.

Case Study 8

Mr. X has been asked by the director of marketing to make a presentation at next month's annual meeting of tyre manufacturing company. The presentation relates to the company's advertising budget for the past year and also the projected budget for the next year. In preparing for the meeting, Mr. X collected the following data :

Medium of Advertisement	Past year's expenses (Rs.)	Next year's expenses (Rs.)
Newspaper	50,000	60, 000
Television	90, 000	100, 000
Trade Publications	25,000	30, 000
Miscellaneous.	15, 000	10, 000

Use these data to develop a bar chart that effectively shows the advertising expenses for both the years.

Solution : Do yourself.

Case Study 9

Suppose a business man is willing to run the T-shirt shop in summer. This is the first summer the shop will be open. The businessman has to determine the inventory mix. T-shirts for adults come in five sizes : small (*S*), medium *(M)*, Large (*L*) extra large *(XL.)* and very extra large *(VXL)*. For knowing the inventory level for each size, the businessman has selected a sample of fifty customers and recorded their shirt sizes, as shown in the following table :

Table : Adult T-shirt Sizes.

L	*S*	*L*	*M*	*S*	*L*	*S*	*M*	*L*	*S*
L	*VXL*	*XL*	*M*	*M*	*XL*	*XL*	*M*	*XL*	*M*
M	*M*	*XL*	*S*	*M*	*XL*	*XL*	*XL*	*M*	*M*
M	*M*	*M*	*VXL*	*M*	*XL*	*L*	*XL*	*VXL*	*L*
M	*L*	*M*	*XL*	*L*	*S*	*M*	*VXL*	*XL*	*XL*

Using these data, help the businessman to estimate the inventory mix and also estimate T-shirt size that will be demanded most often.

Solution : For estimating the inventory mix, we prepare the following frequency distribution :

T-shirt size	Frequency	Estimates of inventory mix
5	06	0.12 or 12%
M	18	0.36 or 36%
L	09	0.18 or 18%
XL	13	0.26 or 26%
VXL	04	0.08 or 8%
Total	50	

Here mode is the medium T-shirt size since this was observed eighteen times in the sample, more than any other size. So the medium T-shirt size will be demanded most often.

Case Study 10

An Agricultural company operates in west. The company owns a farmland of 40, 000 acres. Most of the crops are grain. After the first test year the company is willing to determine which seed types produce greatest yields. The following data were recorded :

	Seed Type A	Seed Type B.	Seed Type C
Mean yield/acre :	90	57	100
Standard deviation :	16	15	25

Answer the Following :

(*a*) Based on the results, which seed seems to produce the greatest average yield per acre ? Use the correct statistical tool that should have been used to make this study.

(*b*) Suppose the company is interested in consistency in yield. Which seed type shows the least relative variability in yield.

Solution :

(*a*) On comparing mean yield/acre for different seed types, we observe that the mean yield for seed type *C* is highest. So type *C* produce the greatest average yield per acre.

(*b*) Here, the average yield for the three seed types differ widely, as such, for comparing consistency in yields, a relative measure of dispersion has to be used in the light of given data. Thus, in the light of data, we first calculate coefficients of variations for yields of all types of seeds.

Thus,

$$C.V. \text{ (For yields using seed types } A) = C.V._{(A)} = \frac{\sigma_1}{X_1} \times 100 = \frac{16}{90} \times 100 = 17.78\%$$

$$C.V. \text{ (For yields using seed types } B) = C.V._{(B)} = \frac{\sigma_2}{X_2} \times 100 = \frac{15}{57} \times 100 = 36.63\%$$

$$C.V. \text{ (For yields using seed types } C) = C.V._{(C)} = \frac{\sigma_3}{X_3} \times 100 = \frac{25}{100} \times 100 = 25\%$$

On comparing, we can say that seed type *A* shows the least relative variability.

Case Study 11

Mr. *X* is thinking about opening a restaurant and recently performed a resident survey as a part of s decision making process. Probabilities are often used in the analysis process. One question of particular interest to Mr. *X* how often the respondent dines out. Table below shows the results of the survey for this question of interest:

Table : Respondent Responses.

How often dines out:	Frequency	Relative Frequency
10 or more times a week	500	0.10
3 to 9 times a week	1800	0.36
1 or 2 times a week	1600	0.32
Less than once a week	1100	0.22
Total	5000	1.00

Using the table, Find the probability that a randomly selected respondent (*i*) dines out 10 or more times a week (*ii*) dines out 3 to 9 times a week (*iii*) dines out 1 to 9 times a week.

Solution : The sample space for the experiment for each respondent is $S = (e_1, e_2, e_3, e_4)$

Here, e_1= dines out 10 or more times in a week.

e_2= dines out 3 to 9 times in a week.

e_3= dines out 1 to 2 times in a week.

e_4= dines out less than once in a week.

Using the relative frequencies,

(i) $P(e_1) = \frac{500}{5000} = 0.10.$

(ii) $P(e_2) = \frac{1800}{5000} = 0.36.$

(iii) $P(e_2 \text{ or } e_3) = P(e_2) + P(e_3) = \frac{1800}{5000} + \frac{1600}{5000} = 0.36 + 0.32 = 0.68.$

Case Study 12

Suppose in the restaurant survey in case study also contained questions about the respondent's age. Mr, ,*Y* considers age as another factor in making decision about the location of the restaurant as its restaurant do better in areas with older population base. Table below shows the classification of the respondents by age group and by the number of times he dines out per week.

Table : Classification of respondents by age group.

How often dines out	Age group			Total
	(E_5) (Less than 30	(E_6) 30 to 50	(E_7) over 50	
(E_1)10 or more times	200	200	100	500
(E_2) 3 to 9 times	600	800	400	1800
(E_3) 1 to 2 times	500	600	500	1600
(E_4) Less than once a week.	600	500	0	1100
Total	1900	2100	1000	5, 000

The table clearly illustrates two concepts of data analysis, namely joint frequencies and marginal frequencies. Marginal frequencies are the row and column totals while the joint frequencies are given in various cells of the table. For example, 2100 people in the survey are in the age group (30 50) Using the information, find the probabilities that:

(i) a randomly selected respondent is less than 30 years of age.

(ii) a randomly selected respondent is in over 50 age group.

(*iii*) a randomly selected respondent is dining out less than once a week or being in the age group 30-50.

(*iv*) a randomly selected respondent will either be in the 30 to 50 age group or eat out 3 to 9 times a week.

Solution : Symbolically we need,

(*i*) $P(E_5)=\dfrac{1900}{5000}=0.38$

(*ii*) $P(E_7)=\dfrac{1000}{5000}=0.20$

(*iii*) $P(E_4 \text{ or } E_6)-P(E_4)+P(E_6)-P(E_4 \text{ and } E_6)=\dfrac{1100}{5000}+\dfrac{2100}{5000}=\dfrac{500}{5000}$

$=0.22+0.42-0.10=0.54$

(*iv*) $P(E_2 \text{ or } E_6)=P(E_2)+P(E_6)-P(E_2 \text{ and } E_6)=\dfrac{1800}{5000}+\dfrac{2100}{5000}=\dfrac{800}{5000}$

$=0.36+0.42-0.16=0.62$

Case Study 13

A small town has two ambulances. Records show that the first ambulance is in service 65% of the cases and the second one is in service 45% of the times Then find the probability that when an ambulance is needed, one will not be available.

Solution: The sample space in consists of the following events :

A, A = both available

A ,B = one available

B, A = one available

B, B = both busy

Assuming that the availabilities of the ambulances are independent events, the probability of both ambulant being busy is

P(*B* and *B*) = *P* (*B*) ×*P* (*B*) - (0.65) (0.45) = 0.2925.

Case Study 14

Assume that you are working for an automobile manufacturing company. Based on engineering reports, .3% of the cars the company produces will receive a below standard rating from the Environmental Protection Agency (EPA). If 20 cars are selected at random from the inventory, what is the probability for each to the following events ?

(*a*) Finding no 'below standard cars.

(*b*) Finding two or three below standard cars.

(c) Finding more than three below-standard cars.

Solution : Assuming that the binomial distribution is applicable we have, $n = 20$, $p = 0.03$, $q = 1 - 0.03 = 0.97$. Now if x is the number of below standard' cars in a sample of size n then the probabilities of observing exactly x 'below standard' cars is

$$P(x) = \left(\frac{n}{x}\right) p^x q^{n-x}; x = 0, 1, 2 \ldots\ldots, n.$$

$$= \left(\frac{20}{x}\right)(0.03)^x (0.97)^{20-x}; x = 01, 2, \ldots\ldots, n. \qquad \ldots\text{(i)}$$

(a) Thus, the probability of finding no 'below standard' car can be obtained by putting $x = 0$ in (i)

$$\therefore \quad P(x=0) = \left(\frac{20}{0}\right)(0.03)^0 (0.97)^{20} = 0.5438.$$

(b) P (two or three below standard cars)

$$P(x=2) + P(x=3) = \left(\frac{20}{0}\right)(0.03)^{18} + \left(\frac{20}{3}\right)(0.03)^3 = (0.97)^{17}$$

$$= 0.0988 + 0.0183 = 0.1126$$

(c) P (more than three below standard cars) $= P(x > 3)$

$$= 1 - P(x \le 2) = 1 - [P(x=0) + P(x=1) + P(x=2)]$$

$$= 1 - \left[\left(\frac{20}{0}\right)(0.03)^0 (0.97)^{20} + \left(\frac{20}{2}\right)(0.03)^2 (0.97)^{18}\right]$$

$$= 1 - [0.5438 + 0.3364 + 0.0988] = 0.021$$

Further Applications:

Suppose a particular state with strict pollution control standard has decided to base its enforcement policy on the EPA 3% standard. Since the state government cannot test every car sold, it samples randomly 20 cars of each make and model. If it finds one car in the sample with a substandard pollution rating, the manufacturer receives a fine and is ordered to recall all cars of that make. The state rule says that if more than one substandard car is found, the conclusion is that the automobile company is exceeding the 3% limit. On the other hand, the car manufacturers are concerned about the chance (probability) of being unjustly accused. That is, the manufacturing company many in fact be producing 3% or fewer cars with substandard pollution control devices, but the state could find more than one such car in its sample of 20. The probability of being unjustly accused will be

$$P(x > 1) = 1 - P(x \le 1) = 1 - P(0) + P(1)]$$

$$= 1 - [0.5438 + 0.364] = 0.1198$$

This means that, under this sampling procedure, there is about 0.1198 or 12% chance with which the car manufacturing company may be unjustly accused of making too many substandard cars according to the pollution standards.

Because of this high chance of being unjustly accused, the car manufacturing company would like to challenge the sampling plan. The arguments may be

1, That more car (more than 20) be sampled

2. The cutoff point (more than one car) for recalling should be changed to reduce the probabilities of being unjustly accused

Case Study 15

Consider a problem which a mill manager is facing. Logs arrive by truck are scaled before they are dumped into the log room. The mill manager is willing to open a reasonable number of scale stations during various times of the day. If he has too many stations open, the scalers will have excessive idle time and the cost of scaling will be unnecessarily high. On the other hand, if too few scale stations are open, some trucks will have to wait.

To win over the problems, the manager has studied the truck arrival patterns. During the first open hour (8 A.M - 9 A.M.), the trucks arrive randomly at six per hour. He also notices that if eight or fewer arrive, during an hour, two scale stations are enough to bear the load. However, if more than eight trucks arrive, three scale stations are required. He has also noticed that the distributions of log truck arrivals during an Hour is representable by poison distribution with mean $\lambda = 6.0$ truck per hour.

With this knowledge, the manager calculates the probability that more than eight trucks will arrive luring (8 9 A.M.). Now, since that fitted poison distribution to the problem is

$$P(x) = \frac{e^{-\lambda}\lambda^x}{x!} = \frac{e^{-60}(60)^x}{x!}, x = 0,1,2,\ldots\ldots \quad \ldots(i)$$

Here x is the number of trucks that arrive during (89 A.M.)

$\therefore$ P (that more than 8 trucks arrive) $= P(x > 8)$

$= p(9) + p(10) + \ldots\ldots\ldots p(17)$

$$= \sum_{x=9}^{\infty} \frac{e^{-6.0}(6.0)^x}{x!} = (0.0688) + 0.0413 + 0.0225 + \ldots + 0.0001) = 0.1526$$

Probability of more than 17 trucks arriving is small enough to be ignored The probability of having three scale stations is therefore 0.1526 and that for two stations will be (I -0.1526) or 0.8474. The manager has to make a tradeoff between the cost of having an additional scale station and the dissatisfaction of both log truck drivers and the companies they represent.

Further Application :

Suppose, in the above example, the manager observes that the average number of trucks arriving during some one hour span in 3.5. Assuming truck arrivals lo be distributed as poison, the probability of eight or fewer trucks arriving will be

P (8 or fewer trucks) = $p(0) + p(1) + \ldots\ldots\ldots + P(8)$

$$= \sum_{x=0}^{8} \frac{c^{-35}(3.5)^x}{x!}$$

$$= 0.0302 + 0.1057 + \ldots\ldots\ldots\ldots + 0.0169 = 0.9902$$

Since misindicates a very high chance (99%) of 8 or fewer trucks arriving and, as such, the manager can decide to have only two scale stations during that one hour duration.

Case Study 16

Let there be a company producing electronic goods. One of its goods is electronic calculators. These calculators are sent to ware houses division in lost of 1000. You, as the warehouse manager, will not accepts a lot of calculators if it contains more than 5% defective. You sample 20 calculators and test to see how many ire defective and how many are good. Then answer the following :

(*a*) the probability of observing exactly one defective .

(*b*) the probability of finding more than one defective.

(*c*) the probability of finding one to three defectives.

(*d*) Suppose you observe three defectives in the sample. Would you recommend to keep the lot of 1000 calculators or return them ?

(*e*) How many defective would you expect to find in a sample of $n = 20$ if there is actually 5% defectives in a lot ?

Solution : (*a*) Here, the number of repeated trials is n 20, p, the proportion of a calculator being defective is 0.05 $\therefore$ $q = (1 - p) = 1 - 0.05 = 0.95$. Let x be the number of defective calculators. Then the probability of x defectives in a sample $n = 20$ can be obtained by using the binomial distribution

$$P(x) = \left(\frac{n}{x}\right) p^x q^{n-x}$$

$$= \left(\frac{20}{x}\right)(0.05)^x (0.95)^{20-x}; \quad x = 0,1,2,\ldots,20 \qquad \ldots\text{(i)}$$

(*b*) P (more than one defective) = $P(x > 1)$

$= 1 - P(x \leq Z\ 1) = 1 - [P(x = 0) + P(.x = 1)$

$= 1 - [0.3585 + 0.3774] = 0.26411$

(*c*) *P* (finding one to three defectives) $= P(x = 1) + P(x = 2) + P(x = 3)$

$= 0.3774\ 10.1887 + 0.0596 = 0.6257$

(*d*) Your recommendation would depend on the probability of observing three or more defective calculators. If this probability is small very small, we would conclude that the lost must actually contain more than 5% defective. However, if it is large, the recommendation should be to keep the calculators. In the present case, *P* (3 or more defectives) $= P(x \geq 3)$

$= 1\text{-}[P(x = 0) + P(x = 1) + P(.x = 2)]$

$= 1\text{-}[0.3585 + 0.3774 + 0.1887] = 0.0754.$

So this probability shows 7.5% defective while the population (lot) contains, at the most, 5% defectives. So one has to make a decision. However, such decision making process has to be completed through tests of significance that we study under sampling theory.

QUESTION PAPER (U.P.T.U.)

M.B.A

(SEM. I) ODD SEMESTER THEORY EXAMINATION 2010-11

BUSINESS STATISTICS

Time : 3 hrs. ***Total Marks : 100***

Note: 1. *The question paper contains three parts.*

2. *All question are compulsory.*

3. *Figures given at the right margin indicate marks.*

PART-I

1. Choose the correct answer and write its serial order :— **(1 × 20 = 20)**

(*a*) Which of the following is the most uncertain average ?

(*i*) Mode (*ii*) Medium

(*iii*) Geometric Mean (*iv*) Harmonic Mean

(*b*) The father of Statistics is :

(*i*) Marshal (*ii*) Gottfried Achenwall

(*iii*) Galton (*iv*) None of these

(*c*) For Calculation of Arithmetic Mean, the class intervals shall be:

(*i*) Middle Value (*ii*) Middle most value

(*iii*) Most frequent value (*iv*) None of these

(*d*) If arithmetic mean is 25 and S.D. is 6-25, then co-efficient of variation will be:

(*i*) 50% (*ii*) 20% (*iii*) 25% (*iv*) 30%

(*e*) For a symmetric distribution Q, = 25 and Q_3 = 45, the medium is:

(*i*) 20 (*ii*) 25 (*iii*) 30 (*iv*) 35

(*f*) In a mesokurtic distribution the fourth central moment is 1,875, the value of Standard Deviation will be :

(*i*) $\sqrt{1875}$ (*ii*) 625 (*iii*) 5 (*iv*) 25

(*g*) The method of minimum least squares is connected with the analysis of time series for measuring :

(*i*) Seasonal Variation (*ii*) Log-period Variation

(*iii*) Cyclical Variation (*iv*) For all the above

(*h*) The suitable index number for the comparison of changes in price level every year is :

(*i*) Fixed base index number based on Average prices

(*ii*) Chain base index numbers

(*iii*) Single year fixed base index numbers

(*iv*) None of these

(*i*) Co-efficient of correlation is significant, if:

(*i*) r > 5 RE. (*ii*) r < 6 RE.

(*iii*) r > 6 RE. (*iv*) r = 6 RE.

(*j*) The co-efficient of correlation between two varieties X and Y is 0-8 and then covariance is 20. If the variance of X-series is 16, find the Standard Deviation of Y-series.

(*i*) 7-25 (*ii*) 6-25 (*iii*) 5-25 (*iv*) 390625

(*k*) Calculate two regression coefficients from the following information:

$$\sigma_x = 14, \sigma_y = 20, r_{xy} = +0.8$$

(*i*) bxy = 0-56, byx= 1143

(*ii*) bxy = 0-46, byx = 1 043

(*iii*) bxy = 0-67, byx = 1246

(*iv*) bxy = 0-32, byx = 1013

(*l*) In multiple regression analysis there are at least variables.

(*i*) 2 (*ii*) 3 (*iii*) 4 (*iv*) 5

(*m*) A dice is tossed twice. Find the probability of having a number greater than 3 on each toss.

(*i*) 1/4 (*ii*) 3/4 (*iii*) 1/3 (*iv*) 1/2

(*n*) The Total number of permutations of letters in REGRESSION is :

(*i*) 2,53,600 (*ii*) 4,53,800

(*iii*) 4,53,600 (*iv*) 5,63,600

(*o*) The standard deviation of Binomial Distribution is:

(*i*) np (*ii*) npq

(*iii*) -Jnpq (*iv*) None of these

(*p*) For a Poisson distribution, if P(o) = P(1), then the value of $m(\lambda)$ is:

(*i*) 10 (*ii*) 20

(*iii*) 40 (*iv*) None of these

(*q*) When the null hypothesis is H_0: p = 50 the alternative hypothesis can be:

(*i*) $H_1 : \mu \geq 50$ (*ii*) $H_1 : \mu \leq 50$

(*iii*) $H_1 : \mu \neq 45$ (*iv*) None of these

(*r*) 99% fiducial limits of population means are:

(*i*) $\overline{X} \pm 3$ S.E. (*ii*) $\overline{X} \pm 2.58$ S.E.

(*iii*) $\overline{X} \pm 1.96$ S.E. (*iv*) None of these

(*s*) While testing significance of difference of two sample means in case of small samples, the degree of freedom is calculated by:

(*i*) $n_1 + n_2$ (*ii*) $n_1 + n_2 - 1$

(*iii*) $n_1 + n_2 - 2$ (*iv*) None of these

(*t*) Mean Square between row or MSR is equal to :

(*i*) $\dfrac{\text{SSR}}{r-1}$ (*ii*) $\dfrac{\text{SSR}}{c-1}$

(*iii*) $\dfrac{\text{SSE}}{n}$ (*iv*) None of these

PART-II

2. Attempt any two :— **(15 × 2 = 30)**

(*a*) Calculate the co-efficient of correlation between the age of husbands and wives from the under noted data and comment upon the result obtained :

Age of Husbands	Age of Wives					Total
	10-20	20-30	30-40	40-50	50-60	
10-20	6	3	-	-	-	9
20-30	3	16	10	. -	-	29
30-40	-	10	15	7	-	32
40-50	-	-	7	10	4	21
50-60	-	-	-	4	5	9
Total	9	29	32	21	9	100

(*b*) A drug is said to be useful for treatment of cold. In an experiment carried out on 160 persons suffering from cold, half of the persons were treated with the drug and rest of the half with sugar pills. The effect of treatment is described in the following table:

	Helped	**Harmful**	**No. Effect**
Drug	52	10	18
Sugar Pills	44	10	26

[for 2 d.f. the value of x^2 is 5.99 at 5% level]

(*c*) 8 coins are tossed at a time, 256 times. The actual results of getting the numbers of heads are as follows :

No. of getting heads	:	0	1	2	3	4
Frequencies	:	2	6	30	52	67
No. of getting heads	:	5	6	7	8	Total
Frequencies	:	56	32	10	1	256

Find out expected frequencies. Also calculate the mean and standard deviation.

PART-III

(12½×4=50)

3. "Statistics are numerical statements of facts in any department of inquiry and placed in relation to each other." Comment and discuss the characteristics of Statistics.

OR

Find the measure of Skewness and Kurtosis on the basis of moments for the following distribution :

Marks	:	5-15	15-25	25-35	35-45	45-55
No. of Students	:	1	3	5	7	4

4. Fit a straight line trend by the method of least squares to the following data, tabulate the trend value and estimate the value for 2011 from the same :

Year :	2001	2002	2003	2004	2005	2006	2007	2008
Value :	380	400	650	720	690	695	600	850

OR

The equation of two regression lines in a correlation analysis are as follows :

$$3X + 2Y = 26$$

$$6X + Y = 31.$$

A student obtains the mean value $\overline{X}=7, \overline{Y}=4$ and the value of correlation co-efficient r = 0.5, you agree with him ? If not, suggest your results.

5. Five cards are drawn from a pack of 52 cards. Find the probability that

(i) 4 are aces,

(ii) 4 are aces and 1 is a king,

(iii) 3 are kings and 2 are queens,

(iv) a king, queen, jack, 10 and 9 are obtained,

(v) 3 are of any one suit and 2 are of another.

OR

(a) The experience shows that 4 industrial accidents occur in a plant on an average per month. Calculate the probabilities of less than 3 accidents in a certain month. Use Poisson distribution. (Given :$e^{-4} = 0.01832$)

(b) If the mean height of soldiers is 68.22" with a variance of 10.8". How many soldiers in a regiment of 1000 can be expected to be over a 6 ft. tall ?

6. The following table gives the yields of four plots each of four varieties of rice. Find out that the variety differences are significant or not:

Variety of Rice (Yield in k.g.)

A	B	C	D
8	10	16	14
10	11	12	10
10	8	14	12
8	11	6	16

[Given : $F_{.05}(v_1 = 3, v_2 = 12) = 5.95$]

OR

The following table gives the distribution of students and also regular players among them according to age in complete years. Calculate the co-efficient of association between majority and playing habit, on the assumption that majority is attained on completion of 17 years.

Age :	15	16	17	18	19	20
No. of Students :	250	200	150	120	100	80
Regular Players :	200	150	90	48	30	12

M.B.A.

FIRST SEMESTER EXAMINATION, 2005-06

BUSINESS STATISTICS

Time : 3 Hours *Total Marks : 100*

Note : *(i) Answer ALL questions.*

(ii) The figures in the right hand margin indicate marks.

(iii) Statistical table will he supplied on demand.

(iv) Be precise in your answer.

1. Answer *any four* of the following in about 250 words **(5 × 4 = 20)**

(*a*) Statistics affects everybody and touches life at many points. It is both a science and an art." Comment.

(*b*) What do you mean by dispersion ? Enlist the important measures of dispersion.

(*c*) Describe the addition and multiplication rules of probability with an example for each.

(*d*) Define normal distribution and list its properties.

(*e*) Distinguish between Laspeyre's and Paasche's Index Number formulae.

(*f*) Steps in a test of significance problem.

2. 'Measure of central tendency, dispersion and skewness are complementary to one another in understanding a frequency distribution'. Elucidate. Find the coefficient of variation, if the sum of squares of the deviations of 10 observations taken from mean 50 is 250.

OR

(*a*) What is a time series ? Explain its methods for isolating trends. (10)

(*b*) The number of units of a product exported during 1997-2004 is given below. Fit straight line trend by the method of least square. Estimate the export for 2005. (10)

Year	No. of units (in '000)
1997	15
1998	20
1999	24
2000	29
2001	35
2002	45
2003	60
2004	85

(*a*) Discuss the meaning of correlation and distinguish between positive and negative correlation. (10)

(*b*) Regression equation of two valuables X and Y are as follow: (10)

3X + 2Y = 26 and bX + Y = 31

Find (*i*) The mean of X and Y series.

(*ii*) The coefficient of correlation and

(*iii*) The most probable value of Y when X = 5.

OR

(*a*) A problem in Business Statistics is given to four students A, B, C and D. Their respective chances of solving it are 1/2, 1/3, 1/5 and 1/6. What is the probability that the problem will be solved by any two of them ? (10)

(*b*) 2000 Students appeared in an examination. Distribution of marks is assumed to be normal with mean $\mu = 30$ and $\sigma = 6.25$. How many students are expected to get marks (10)

(*i*) Between 20 and 40

(*ii*) Less then 35 and

(*iii*) Above 50.

(*iv*) 't'- test.

4. (a) Explain the following terms (10)

(*i*) Null hypothesis

(*ii*) 5% and 1% level of significance

(*iii*) degrees of freedom

(*iv*) *'if* - test.

(b) A company produces two makes of bulks A and B. 200 bulks of each make were tested and it was found that make A has mean life of 2,560 hours and S.D. of 90 hours, whereas make B has 2,650 hours of mean life with S.D of 75 hours. Is there a significant difference between the mean life of the two makes ? (10)

OR

(a) Chi-square test is used for testing of goodness of fit, homogenity of data and Independence, Discuss. (10)

(b) Examine by any suitable method, whether the nature of area is related to voting preference in the election for which the data are tabulated below : (10)

Votes for Area	A	B	Total
Rural	620	480	1100
Urban	380	520	900
Total	1000	1000	2000

5. Write short notes on *any two* of the following :
   (a) Binomial distribution
   (b) F - test
   (c) Yules coefficient of Association
   (d) Cost of living Index Number

M.B.A.

FIRST SEMESTER EXAMINATION, 2006-07

BUSINESS STATISTICS

Time : 3 Hours *Total Marks : 100*

Note : *(i) Answer ALL questions.*

(ii) All questions carry equal marks.

(iii) In case of numerical problems assume data wherever not provided.

(iv) Be precise in your answer. Attempt any four parts of the following

1. Attempt any four parts of the following **(5 × 4 = 20)**
   (a) Explain briefly what you understand by the science of statistics.
   (b) What do you understand by dispersion ? What is the need of studying dispersion ?
   (c) Define Probability. What is the probability of getting more then 10 in a single throw of 2 dice ?

(*d*) Distinguish between Binomial and Poisson distribution.

(*e*) Distinguish between Time Reversal and Factor Reversal tests.

(*f*) Distinguish between :

(*i*) Type I error and Type II error

(*ii*) Parameter and statistic

(*iii*) Sample and population

2. (*a*) Distinguish between measure of central tendency and dispersion. Illustrate with the help of examples. (10)

(*b*) Find arithmetic mean and standard deviation from the following data. Also find coefficient of variation.

Age (less than)	:	10	20	30	40	50	60	70	80
No. of persons	:	15	30	50	75	100	110	115	125

(10)

(*a*) What is a Time Series ? Explain the objectives of the analysis of a time series. (10)

(*b*) Fit a straight line trend to the following data. (10)

Year	**Sales (in lakh tonnes)**
1998	100
1999	120
2000	135
2001	170
2002	200
2003	250
2004	290

and estimate sales for 2005.

(*a*) Distinguish between Correlation and Regression. Why there are two regression lines ? (10)

(*b*) In the following table X is advertising cost (in thousand rupees) and Y is sales (in lakh rupees). (10)

X:	12	18	24	30	36	42	48
Y:	5.7	6.9	7.1	8.3	10.1	12.2	13.6

Find Karl Pearson Correlation Coefficient between X and Y.

OR

(*a*) State and prove addition theorem of probability. (10)

(*b*) As a result of tests on 20,000 electric bulbs manufactured by a company it was found that life time of the bulbs was normally distributed with an average life of 2040 hours and standard deviation of 60 hours. Estimate the number of bulbs that is expected to burn for : (10)

(*i*) more than 2150 hours and

(*ii*) less than 1960 hours.

(*a*) Describe the various steps involved in testing a statistical hypothesis. (10)

(*b*) An automatic machine was designed to pack 2.0 kg of Vanaspati. A sample of 100 tins was examined to test the machine. The average weight was found to be 1.94 kg with standard deviation 0.10 kg. Is the machine working properly ? (10)

OR

(*a*) What is a Chi-square test ? Give an example. (10)

(*b*) What is analysis of variance ? Explain its testing procedure when data is classified according to two ways. (10)

5. Write short notes on any two of the following : (20)

(*a*) Association of Attributes

(*b*) Skewness

(*c*) Fisher Index Numbers

(*d*) Property of Normal Distribution

Statistical Table

Top of Form

Standard Normal (Z) Table

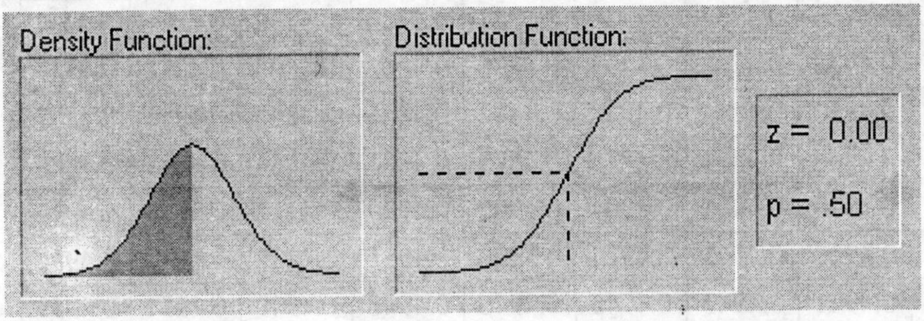

Area between 0 and z

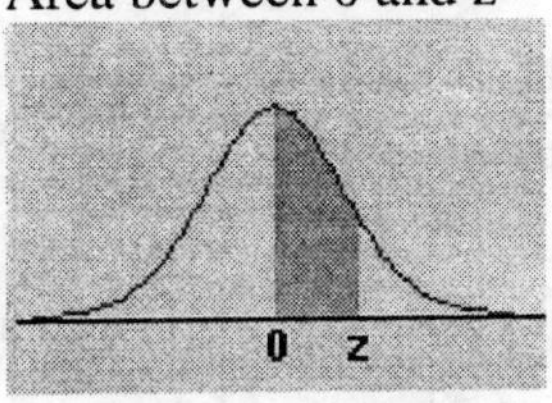

	0.00	0.01	0.02	0.03	0.04	0.05	0.06	0.07	0.08	0.09
0.0	0.0000	0.0040	0.0080	0.0120	0.0160	0.0199	0.0239	0.0279	0.0319	0.0359
0.1	0.0398	0.0438	0.0478	0.0517	0.0557	0.0596	0.0636	0.0675	0.0714	0.0753
0.2	0.0793	0.0832	0.0871	0.0910	0.0948	0.0987	0.1026	0.1064	0.1103	0.1141
0.3	0.1179	0.1217	0.1255	0.1293	0.1331	0.1368	0.1406	0.1443	0.1480	0.1517
0.4	0.1554	0.1591	0.1628	0.1664	0.1700	0.1736	0.1772	0.1808	0.1844	0.1879
0.5	0.1915	0.1950	0.1985	0.2019	0.2054	0.2088	0.2123	0.2157	0.2190	0.2224
0.6	0.2257	0.2291	0.2324	0.2357	0.2389	0.2422	0.2454	0.2486	0.2517	0.2549
0.7	0.2580	0.2611	0.2642	0.2673	0.2704	0.2734	0.2764	0.2794	0.2823	0.2852
0.8	0.2881	0.2910	0.2939	0.2967	0.2995	0.3023	0.3051	0.3078	0.3106	0.3133
0.9	0.3159	0.3186	0.3212	0.3238	0.3264	0.3289	0.3315	0.3340	0.3365	0.3389
1.0	0.3413	0.3438	0.3461	0.3485	0.3508	0.3531	0.3554	0.3577	0.3599	0.3621
1.1	0.3643	0.3665	0.3686	0.3708	0.3729	0.3749	0.3770	0.3790	0.3810	0.3830
1.2	0.3849	0.3869	0.3888	0.3907	0.3925	0.3944	0.3962	0.3980	0.3997	0.4015
1.3	0.4032	0.4049	0.4066	0.4082	0.4099	0.4115	0.4131	0.4147	0.4162	0.4177
1.4	0.4192	0.4207	0.4222	0.4236	0.4251	0.4265	0.4279	0.4292	0.4306	0.4319
1.5	0.4332	0.4345	0.4357	0.4370	0.4382	0.4394	0.4406	0.4418	0.4429	0.4441

1.6	0.4452	0.4463	0.4474	0.4484	0.4495	0.4505	0.4515	0.4525	0.4535	0.4545
1.7	0.4554	0.4564	0.4573	0.4582	0.4591	0.4599	0.4608	0.4616	0.4625	0.4633
1.8	0.4641	0.4649	0.4656	0.4664	0.4671	0.4678	0.4686	0.4693	0.4699	0.4706
1.9	0.4713	0.4719	0.4726	0.4732	0.4738	0.4744	0.4750	0.4756	0.4761	0.4767
2.0	0.4772	0.4778	0.4783	0.4788	0.4793	0.4798	0.4803	0.4808	0.4812	0.4817
2.1	0.4821	0.4826	0.4830	0.4834	0.4838	0.4842	0.4846	0.4850	0.4854	0.4857
2.2	0.4861	0.4864	0.4868	0.4871	0.4875	0.4878	0.4881	0.4884	0.4887	0.4890
2.3	0.4893	0.4896	0.4898	0.4901	0.4904	0.4906	0.4909	0.4911	0.4913	0.4916
2.4	0.4918	0.4920	0.4922	0.4925	0.4927	0.4929	0.4931	0.4932	0.4934	0.4936
2.5	0.4938	0.4940	0.4941	0.4943	0.4945	0.4946	0.4948	0.4949	0.4951	0.4952
2.6	0.4953	0.4955	0.4956	0.4957	0.4959	0.4960	0.4961	0.4962	0.4963	0.4964
2.7	0.4965	0.4966	0.4967	0.4968	0.4969	0.4970	0.4971	0.4972	0.4973	0.4974
2.8	0.4974	0.4975	0.4976	0.4977	0.4977	0.4978	0.4979	0.4979	0.4980	0.4981
2.9	0.4981	0.4982	0.4982	0.4983	0.4984	0.4984	0.4985	0.4985	0.4986	0.4986
3.0	0.4987	0.4987	0.4987	0.4988	0.4988	0.4989	0.4989	0.4989	0.4990	0.4990

Student's t Table

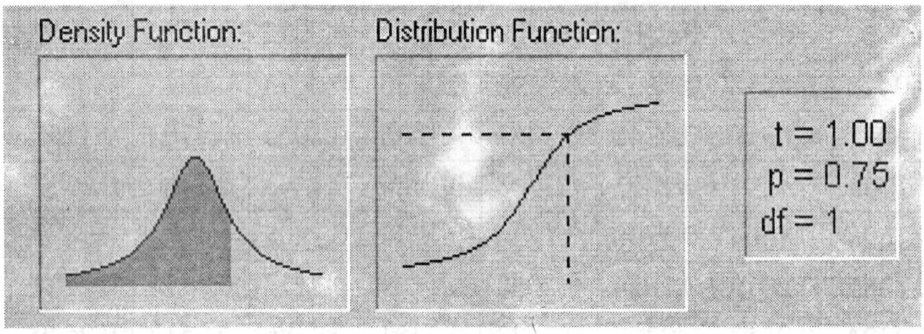

The Shape of the Student's t distribution is determined by the degrees of freedom. As shown in the animation above, its shape changes as the degrees of freedom increases. For more information on how this distribution is used in hypothesis testing, see t-test for independent samples and t-test for dependent samples in Basic Statistics and Tables. See also, Student's t Distribution. As indicated by the chart below, the areas given at the top of this table are the right tail areas for the t-value inside the table. To determine the 0.05 critical value from the t-distribution with 6 degrees of freedom, look in the 0.05 column at the 6 row: t(.05,6) = 1.943180.

Table with right tail probabilities

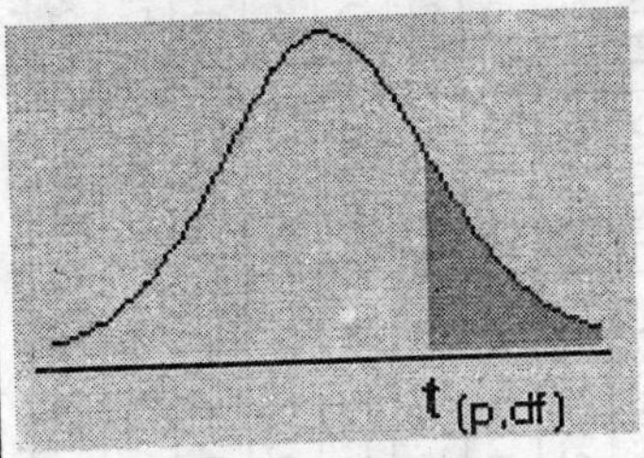

df\p	0.40	0.25	0.10	0.05	0.025	0.01	0.005	0.0005
1	0.324920	1.000000	3.077684	6.313752	12.70620	31.82052	63.65674	636.6192
2	0.288675	0.816497	1.885618	2.919986	4.30265	6.96456	9.92484	31.5991
3	0.276671	0.764892	1.637744	2.353363	3.18245	4.54070	5.84091	12.9240
4	0.270722	0.740697	1.533206	2.131847	2.77645	3.74695	4.60409	8.6103
5	0.267181	0.726687	1.475884	2.015048	2.57058	3.36493	4.03214	6.8688
6	0.264835	0.717558	1.439756	1.943180	2.44691	3.14267	3.70743	5.9588
7	0.263167	0.711142	1.414924	1.894579	2.36462	2.99795	3.49948	5.4079
8	0.261921	0.706387	1.396815	1.859548	2.30600	2.89646	3.35539	5.0413
9	0.260955	0.702722	1.383029	1.833113	2.26216	2.82144	3.24984	4.7809
10	0.260185	0.699812	1.372184	1.812461	2.22814	2.76377	3.16927	4.5869
11	0.259556	0.697445	1.363430	1.795885	2.20099	2.71808	3.10581	4.4370
12	0.259033	0.695483	1.356217	1.782288	2.17881	2.68100	3.05454	4.3178
13	0.258591	0.693829	1.350171	1.770933	2.16037	2.65031	3.01228	4.2208
14	0.258213	0.692417	1.345030	1.761310	2.14479	2.62449	2.97684	4.1405
15	0.257885	0.691197	1.340606	1.753050	2.13145	2.60248	2.94671	4.0728
16	0.257599	0.690132	1.336757	1.745884	2.11991	2.58349	2.92078	4.0150
17	0.257347	0.689195	1.333379	1.739607	2.10982	2.56693	2.89823	3.9651
18	0.257123	0.688364	1.330391	1.734064	2.10092	2.55238	2.87844	3.9216
19	0.256923	0.687621	1.327728	1.729133	2.09302	2.53948	2.86093	3.8834
20	0.256743	0.686954	1.325341	1.724718	2.08596	2.52798	2.84534	3.8495

Chi-Square Table

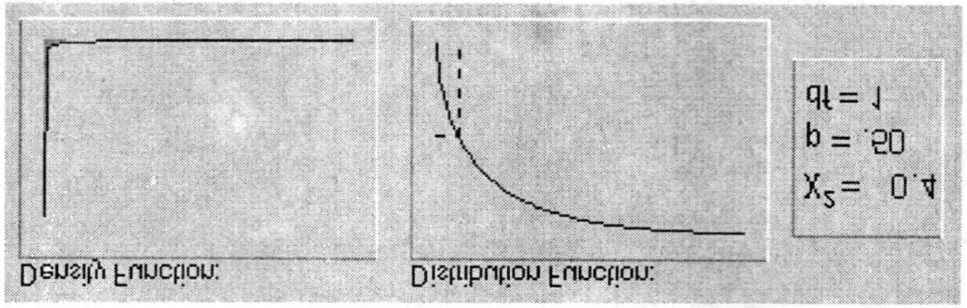

Right tail areas for the Chi-square Distribution

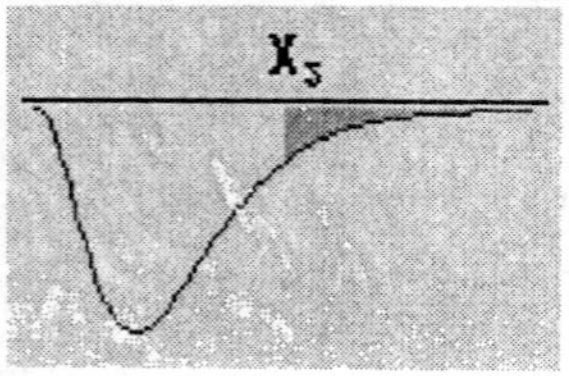

df\area	.995	.990	.975	.950	.900	.750	.500	.250	.100	.050	.025	.010	.005
1	0.00004	0.00016	0.00098	0.00393	0.01579	0.10153	0.45494	1.32330	2.70554	3.84146	5.02389	6.63490	7.87944
2	0.01003	0.02010	0.05064	0.10259	0.21072	0.57536	1.38629	2.77259	4.60517	5.99146	7.37776	9.21034	10.59663
3	0.07172	0.11483	0.21580	0.35185	0.58437	1.21253	2.36597	4.10834	6.25139	7.81473	9.34840	11.34487	12.83816
4	0.20699	0.29711	0.48442	0.71072	1.06362	1.92256	3.35669	5.38527	7.77944	9.48773	11.14329	13.27670	14.86026
5	0.41174	0.55430	0.83121	1.14548	1.61031	2.67460	4.35146	6.62568	9.23636	11.07050	12.83250	15.08627	16.74960
6	0.67573	0.87209	1.23734	1.63538	2.20413	3.45460	5.34812	7.84080	10.64464	12.59159	14.44938	16.81189	18.54758
7	0.98926	1.23904	1.68987	2.16735	2.83311	4.25485	6.34581	9.03715	12.01704	14.06714	16.01276	18.47531	20.27774
8	1.34441	1.64650	2.17973	2.73264	3.48954	5.07064	7.34412	10.21885	13.36157	15.50731	17.53455	20.09024	21.95495
9	1.73493	2.08790	2.70039	3.32511	4.16816	5.89883	8.34283	11.38875	14.68366	16.91898	19.02277	21.66599	23.58935
10	2.15586	2.55821	3.24697	3.94030	4.86518	6.73720	9.34182	12.54886	15.98718	18.30704	20.48318	23.20925	25.18818
11	2.60322	3.05348	3.81575	4.57481	5.57778	7.58414	10.34100	13.70069	17.27501	19.67514	21.92005	24.72497	26.75685
12	3.07382	3.57057	4.40379	5.22603	6.30380	8.43842	11.34032	14.84540	18.54935	21.02607	23.33666	26.21697	28.29952

13	3.56503	4.10692	5.00875	5.89186	7.04150	9.29907	12.33976	15.98391	19.81193	22.36203	24.73560	27.68825	29.81947
14	4.07467	4.66043	5.62873	6.57063	7.78953	10.16531	13.33927	17.11693	21.06414	23.68479	26.11895	29.14124	31.31935
15	4.60092	5.22935	6.26214	7.26094	8.54676	11.03654	14.33886	18.24509	22.30713	24.99579	27.48839	30.57791	32.80132
16	5.14221	5.81221	6.90766	7.96165	9.31224	11.91222	15.33850	19.36886	23.54183	26.29623	28.84535	31.99993	34.26719
17	5.69722	6.40776	7.56419	8.67176	10.08519	12.79193	16.33818	20.48868	24.76904	27.58711	30.19101	33.40866	35.71847
18	6.26480	7.01491	8.23075	9.39046	10.86494	13.67529	17.33790	21.60489	25.98942	28.86930	31.52638	34.80531	37.15645
19	6.84397	7.63273	8.90652	10.11701	11.65091	14.56200	18.33765	22.71781	27.20357	30.14353	32.85233	36.19087	38.58226
20	7.43384	8.26040	9.59078	10.85081	12.44261	15.45177	19.33743	23.82769	28.41198	31.41043	34.16961	37.56623	39.99685
21	8.03365	8.89720	10.28290	11.59131	13.23960	16.34438	20.33723	24.93478	29.61509	32.67057	35.47888	38.93217	41.40106
22	8.64272	9.54249	10.98232	12.33801	14.04149	17.23962	21.33704	26.03927	30.81328	33.92444	36.78071	40.28936	42.79565
23	9.26042	10.19572	11.68855	13.09051	14.84796	18.13730	22.33688	27.14134	32.00690	35.17246	38.07563	41.63840	44.18128
24	9.88623	10.85636	12.40115	13.84843	15.65868	19.03725	23.33673	28.24115	33.19624	36.41503	39.36408	42.97982	45.55851
25	10.51965	11.52398	13.11972	14.61141	16.47341	19.93934	24.33659	29.33885	34.38159	37.65248	40.64647	44.31410	46.92789
26	11.16024	12.19815	13.84390	15.37916	17.29188	20.84343	25.33646	30.43457	35.56317	38.88514	41.92317	45.64168	48.28988
27	11.80759	12.87850	14.57338	16.15140	18.11390	21.74940	26.33634	31.52841	36.74122	40.11327	43.19451	46.96294	49.64492
28	12.46134	13.56471	15.30786	16.92788	18.93924	22.65716	27.33623	32.62049	37.91592	41.33714	44.46079	48.27824	50.99338
29	13.12115	14.25645	16.04707	17.70837	19.76774	23.56659	28.33613	33.71091	39.08747	42.55697	45.72229	49.58788	52.33562
30	13.78672	14.95346	16.79077	18.49266	20.59923	24.47761	29.33603	34.79974	40.25602	43.77297	46.97924	50.89218	53.67196

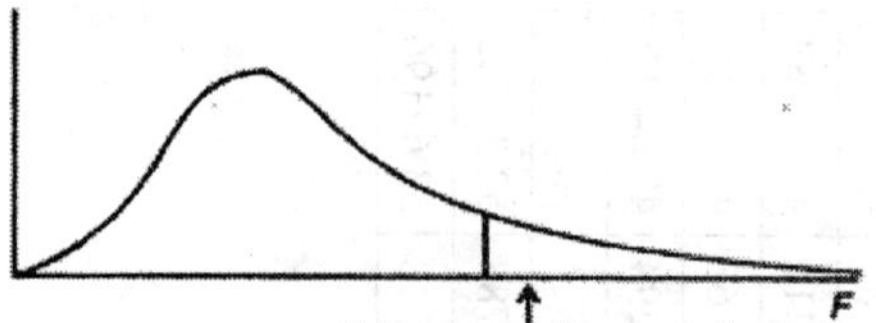

Critical point For example $F_{.05}$ leaves 5% probability in the tail

F-Critical Points

DEGREES OF FREEDOM FOR NUMERATOR

		1	2	3	4	5	6	8	10	20	40	
1	$F_{.25}$	5.83	7.50	8.20	8.58	8.82	8.98	9.19	9.32	9.58	9.71	9.85
	$F_{.10}$	39.9	49.5	53.6	55.8	57.2	58.2	59.4	60.2	61.7	62.5	63.3
	$F_{.05}$	161	200	216	225	230	234	239	242	248	251	254
2	$F_{.25}$	2.57	3.00	3.15	3.23	3.28	3.31	3.35	3.38	3.43	3.45	3.48
	$F_{.10}$	8.53	9.00	9.16	9.24	9.29	9.33	9.37	9.39	9.44	9.47	9.49
	$F_{.05}$	18.5	19.0	19.2	19.2	19.3	19.3	19.4	19.4	19.4	19.5	19.5
	$F_{.01}$	98.5	99.0	99.2	99.2	99.3	99.3	99.4	99.4	99.4	99.5	99.5
	$F_{.001}$	998	999	999	999	999	999	999	999	999	999	999
3	$F_{.25}$	2.02	2.28	2.36	2.39	2.41	2.42	2.44	2.44	2.46	2.47	2.47
	$F_{.10}$	5.54	5.46	5.39	5.34	5.31	5.28	5.25	5.23	5.18	5.16	5.13
	$F_{.05}$	10.1	9.55	9.28	9.12	9.10	8.94	8.85	8.79	8.66	8.59	8.53
	$F_{.01}$	34.1	30.8	29.5	28.7	28.2	27.9	27.5	27.2	26.7	26.4	26.1
	$F_{.001}$	167	149	141	137	135	133	131	129	126	125	124
4	$F_{.25}$	1.81	2.00	2.05	2.06	2.07	2.08	2.08	2.08	2.08	2.08	2.08
	$F_{.10}$	4.54	4.32	4.19	4.11	4.05	4.01	3.95	3.92	3.84	3.80	3.76
	$F_{.05}$	7.71	6.94	6.59	6.39	6.26	6.16	6.04	5.96	5.80	5.72	5.63
	$F_{.01}$	21.2	18.0	16.7	16.0	15.5	15.2	14.8	14.5	14.0	13.7	13.5
	$F_{.001}$	74.1	61.3	56.2	53.4	51.7	50.5	49.0	48.1	46.1	45.1	44.1
5	$F_{.25}$	1.69	1.85	1.88	1.89	1.89	1.89	1.89	1.89	1.88	1.88	1.87
	$F_{.10}$	4.06	3.78	3.62	3.52	3.45	3.40	3.34	3.30	3.21	3.16	3.10
	$F_{.05}$	6.61	5.79	5.41	5.19	5.05	4.95	4.82	4.74	4.56	4.46	4.36
	$F_{.01}$	16.3	13.3	12.1	11.4	11.0	10.7	10.3	10.1	9.55	9.29	9.02
	$F_{.001}$	47.2	37.1	33.2	31.1	29.8	28.8	27.6	26.9	25.4	24.6	23.8
6	$F_{.25}$	1.62	1.76	1.78	1.79	1.79	1.78	1.77	1.77	1.76	1.75	1.74
	$F_{.10}$	3.78	3.46	3.29	3.18	3.11	3.05	2.98	2.94	2.84	278	2.72
	$F_{.05}$	5.99	5.14	4.76	4.53	4.39	4.28	4.15	4.06	3.87	3.77	3.67
	$F_{.01}$	13.7	10.9	9.78	9.15	8.75	8.47	8.10	7.87	7.40	7.14	6.88
	$F_{.001}$	35.5	27.0	23.7	21.9	20.8	20.0	19.0	18.4	17.1	16.4	15.8
7	$F_{.25}$	1.57	1.70	1.72	1.72	1.71	1.71	1.70	1.69	1.67	1.66	.165
	$F_{.10}$	3.59	3.26	3.07	2.96	2.88	2.83	2.75	2.70	2.59	2.54	2.47
	$F_{.05}$	5.59	4.74	4.35	4.12	3.97	3.87	3.73	3.64	3.44	3.34	3.23
	$F_{.01}$	12.2	9.55	8.45	7.85	7.46	7.19	6.84	6.62	6.16	5.91	5.65
	$F_{.001}$	29.3	21.7	18.8	17.2	16.2	15.5	14.6	14.1	12.9	12.3	11.7
8	$F_{.25}$	1.54	1.66	1.67	1.66	1.66	1.65	1.64	1.63	1.61	1.59	1.58
	$F_{.10}$	3.46	8.11	2.92	2.81	2.73	2.67	2.59	2.54	2.42	2.36	2.29
	$F_{.05}$	5.32	4.46	4.07	3.84	3.69	3.58	3.44	3.35	3.15	3.04	2.93
	$F_{.01}$	11.3	8.65	7.59	7.01	6.63	6.37	6.03	5.81	5.36	5.12	4.66
	$F_{.001}$	25.4	18.5	15.8	14.4	13.5	12.9	12.0	11.5	10.5	9.92	9.33
9	$F_{.25}$	1.51	1.62	1.63	1.63	1.62	1.61	1.60	1.59	1.56	1.55	1.53
	$F_{.10}$	3.36	3.01	2.81	2.69	2.61	2.55	2.47	2.42	2.30	2.23	2.16
	$F_{.05}$	5.12	4.26	3.86	3.63	3.48	3.37	3.23	3.14	2.94	2.83	2.71
	$F_{.01}$	10.6	8.02	6.99	6.42	6.06	5.80	5.47	5.26	4.81	4.57	4.31
	$F_{.001}$	22.9	16.4	13.9	12.6	11.7	11.1	10.4	9.89	8.90	8.37	7.81

		DEGREES OF FREEDOM FOR NUMERATOR										
		1	2	3	4	5	6	8	10	20	40	
10	$F_{.25}$	1.49	1.60	1.60	1.59	1.59	1.58	1.56	1.55	1.52	1.51	1.48
	$F_{.10}$	3.28	2.92	2.73	2.61	2.52	2.46	2.38	2.32	2.20	2.13	2.06
	$F_{.05}$	4.96	4.10	3.71	3.48	3.33	3.22	3.07	2.98	2.77	2.66	2.54
	$F_{.01}$	10.0	7.56	6.55	5.99	5.64	5.39	5.06	4.85	4.41	4.17	3.91
	$F_{.001}$	21.0	14.9	12.6	11.3	10.5	9.92	9.20	8.75	7.80	7.30	6.76
12	$F_{.25}$	1.56	1.56	1.56	1.55	.154	1.53	1.51	1.50	1.47	1.45	1.42
	$F_{.10}$	3.18	2.81	2.61	2.48	2.39	2.33	2.24	2.19	2.06	1.99	1.90
	$F_{.05}$	4.75	3.89	3.49	3.26	3.11	3.00	2.85	2.75	2.54	2.43	2.30
	$F_{.01}$	9.33	6.93	5.95	5.41	5.06	4.82	4.50	4.30	3.86	3.62	3.36
	$F_{.001}$	18.6	13.0	10.8	9.63	8.89	8.38	7.71	7.29	6.40	5.93	5.42
14	$F_{.25}$	1.44	1.53	1.53	1.52	1.51	1.50	1.48	1.46	1.43	1.41	1.38
	$F_{.10}$	3.10	2.73	2.52	2.39	2.31	2.24	2.15	2.10	1.96	1.89	1.80
	$F_{.05}$	4.60	3.74	3.34	3.11	2.96	2.85	2.70	2.60	2.39	2.27	2.13
	$F_{.01}$	8.86	5.51	5.56	5.04	4.69	4.46	4.14	3.94	3.51	3.27	3.00
	$F_{.001}$	17.1	11.8	9.73	8.62	7.92	7.13	6.80	6.40	5.56	5.10	4.60
16	$F_{.25}$	1.42	1.51	1.51	1.50	1.48	1.48	1.46	1.45	1.40	1.37	1.34
	$F_{.10}$	3.05	2.67	2.46	2.33	2.24	2.18	2.09	2.03	1.89	1.81	1.72
	$F_{.05}$	4.49	3.63	3.24	3.01	2.85	2.74	2.59	2.49	2.28	2.15	2.01
	$F_{.01}$	8.53	6.23	5.29	4.77	4.44	4.20	3.89	3.69	3.26	3.02	2.75
	$F_{.001}$	16.1	11.0	9.00	7.94	7.27	6.81	6.19	5.81	4.99	4.54	4.06
20	$F_{.25}$	1.40	1.49	1.48	1.46	1.45	1.44	1.42	1.40	1.36	1.33	1.29
	$F_{.10}$	2.97	2.59	2.38	2.25	2.16	2.09	2.00	1.94	1.79	1.71	1.61
	$F_{.05}$	4.35	3.49	3.10	2.87	2.71	2.60	2.45	2.35	2.12	1.99	1.84
	$F_{.01}$	8.10	5.85	4.94	4.43	4.10	3.87	3.56	3.37	2.94	2.69	2:42
	$F_{.001}$	14.8	9.95	8.10	7.10	6.46	6.02	5.44	5.08	4.29	3.86	3.38
30	$F_{.25}$	1.38	1.45	1.44	1.42	1.41	1.39	1.37	1.35	1.30	1.27	1.23
	$F_{.10}$	2.88	2.49	2.28	2.14	2.05	1.98	1.88	1.82	1.67	1.57	1.46
	$F_{.05}$	4.17	3.32	2.92	2.69	2.53	2.42	2.27	2.16	1.93	1.79	1.62
	$F_{.01}$	7.56	5.39	4.51	4.02	3.70	3.47	3.17	2.98	2.55	2.30	2.01
	$F_{.001}$	13.3	8.77	7.05	6.12	5.53	5.12	4.58	4.24	3.49	3.07	2.59
40	$F_{.25}$	1.36	1.44	1.42	1.40	1.39	1.37	1.35	1.33	1.28	1.24	1.19
	$F_{.10}$	2.84	2.44	2.23	2.09	2.00	1.93	1.83	1.76	1.61	1.51	1.38
	$F_{.05}$	4.08	3.23	2.84	2.61	2.45	2.34	2.18	2.08	1.84	1.69	1.51
	$F_{.01}$	7.31	5.18	4.31	3.83	3.51	3.29	2.99	2.80	2.37	2.11	1.80
	$F_{.001}$	12.6	8.25	6.60	5.70	5.13	4.73	4.21	3.87	3.15	2.73	2.23
60	$F_{.25}$	1.35	1.42	1.41	1.38	1.37	1.35	1.32	1.30	1.25	1.21	1.15
	$F_{.10}$	2.79	2.39	2.18	2.04	1.95	1.87	1.77	1.71	1.54	1.44	1.29
	$F_{.05}$	4.00	3.15	2.76	2.53	2.37	2.25	2.10	1.99	1.75	1.59	1.39
	$F_{.01}$	7.08	4.98	4.13	3.65	3.34	3.12	2.82	2.63	2.20	1.94	1.60
	$F_{.001}$	12.0	7.76	6.17	5.31	4.76	4.37	3.87	3.54	3.83	2.41	1.89
120	$F_{.25}$	1.34	1.40	1.39	1.37	1.35	1.33	1.30	1.28	1.22	1.18	1.10
	$F_{.10}$	2.75	2.35	2.13	1.99	1.90	1.82	1.72	1.65	1.48	1.37	1.19
	$F_{.05}$	3.92	3.07	2.68	2.45	2.29	2.17	2.02	1.91	1.66	1.50	1.25
	$F_{.01}$	6.85	4.79	3.95	3.48	3.17	2.96	2.66	2.47	2.03	1.76	1.38
	$F_{.001}$	11.4	7.32	5.79	4.95	4.42	4.04	3.55	3.24	2.53	2.11	1.54
x	$F_{.25}$	1.32	1.39	1.37	1.35	1.33	1.31	1.28	1.25	1.19	1.14	1.00
	$F_{.10}$	2.71	2.30	2.08	1.94	1.85	1.77	1.67	1.60	1.42	1.30	1.00
	$F_{.05}$	3.84	3.00	3.60	2.37	2.21	2.10	1.94	1.83	1.57	1.39	1.00
	$F_{.01}$	6.63	4.61	3.78	3.32	3.02	2.80	2.51	2.32	1.88	1.59	1.00
	$F_{.001}$	10.8	6.91	5.42	4.62	4.10	3.74	3.27	2.96	2.27	1.84	1.00

BINOMIAL COEFFICIENTS

n	$\binom{n}{0}$	$\binom{n}{1}$	$\binom{n}{2}$	$\binom{n}{3}$	$\binom{n}{4}$	$\binom{n}{5}$	$\binom{n}{6}$	$\binom{n}{7}$	$\binom{n}{8}$	$\binom{n}{9}$	$\binom{n}{10}$
0	1										
1	1	2									
2	1	3	1								
3	1	4	6	4	1						
4											
5	1	5	10	10	5	1					
6	1	6	15	20	15	6	1				
7	1	7	21	35	35	21	7	1			
8	1	8	28	56	70	56	28	8	1		
9	1	9	36	84	126	126	84	36	9	1	
10	1	10	45	120	210	252	210	120	45	10	1
11	1	11	55	165	330	462	462	330	165	55	11
12	1	12	66	220	495	792	924	792	495	220	66
13	1	13	78	286	715	1287	1716	1716	1287	715	286
14	1	14	91	364	1001	2002	3003	3432	3003	2002	1001
15	1	15	105	455	1365	3003	5005	6435	6435	5005	3003
16	1	16	120	560	1820	4368	8008	11440	12870	11440	8008
17	1	17	136	683	2380	6188	12376	19448	24310	24310	19448
18	1	18	153	816	3060	8568	18564	31824	43758	48620	43758
19	1	19	171	969	3876	11628	27132	50388	75582	92378	92378
20	1	20	190	1140	4845	15504	38760	77520	125970	167960	184756

VALUES OF e^{-m}
(O<M<1)

m	0	1	2	3	4	5	6	7	8	9
0.0	1.0000	.9900	.9802	.9704	.9608	.9512	.9418	.9324	.9231	.9139
0.1	.9048	.8958	.8869	.8781	.8694	.8607	.8521	.8437	.8353	.8270
0.2	.8187	.8106	.8025	.7945	.7866	.7788	.7711	.7634	.7558	.7483
0.3	.7408	.7334	.7261	.7189	.7118	.7047	.6977	.6907	.6839	.6771
0.4	.6703	.6636	.6570	.6505	.6440	.6376	.6313	.6250	.6188	.6126
0.5	.6065	.6005	.5945	.5886	.5827	.5770	.5712	.5655	.5599	.5543
0.6	.5488	.5434	.5379	.5326	.5273	.5220	.5169	.5117	.5066	.5016
0.7	.4966	.4916	.4868	.4819	.4771	.4724	.4677	.4630	.4584	.4538
0.8	.4493	.4449	.4404	.4360	.4317	.4274	.4232	.4190	.4148	.4107
0.9	.4066	.4025	.3985	.3946	.3906	.3867	.3829	.3791	.3753	.3716

(M=1,2,3, ...10)

m	1	2	3	4	5	6	7	8	9	10
e^{-m}	.36788	.13534	.04979	.01832	.00638	.002479	.00091	.000335	.000153	.000045

Note : To obtain values of e^{-m} for other values of m, use the laws of exponents.

Example. $e^{-2.35}=(e^{-2.00}).(e^{-0.35})=$ (.13534) (.7047)= .095374

LOGARITHMS

	0	1	2	3	4	5	6	7	8	9	1	2	3	4	5	6	7	8	9
10	0000	0043	0086	0128	0170	0212	0253	0294	0334	0374	4	8	12	17	21	25	29	33	37
11	0414	0453	0492	0531	0569	0607	0645	0682	0719	0755	4	8	11	15	19	23	26	30	34
12	0792	0328	0864	0899	0934	0969	1004	1038	1072	1106	3	7	10	14	17	21	24	28	31
13	1139	1173	1206	1239	1271	1303	1335	1367	1399	1430	3	6	10	13	16	19	23	26	29
14	1461	1492	1523	1553	1584	1614	1644	1673	1703	1732	3	6	9	12	15	18	21	24	27
15	1761	1790	1818	1847	1875	1903	1931	1959	1987	2014	3	6	8	11	14	17	20	22	25
16	2041	2068	2095	2122	2148	2175	2201	2227	2253	2279	3	5	8	11	13	16	18	21	24
17	2304	2330	2355	2380	2405	2430	2455	2480	2504	2529	2	5	7	10	12	15	17	20	22
18	2553	2577	2601	2625	2648	2672	2695	2718	2742	2765	2	5	7	9	12	14	16	19	21
19	2788	2810	2633	2856	2878	2900	2923	2945	2967	2989	2	4	7	9	11	13	16	18	20
20	3010	3032	3054	3075	3096	3118	3139	3160	3181	3201	2	4	6	8	11	13	15	17	19
21	3222	3243	3263	3284	3304	3324	3345	3365	3385	3404	2	4	6	8	10	12	14	16	18
22	3424	3444	3464	3483	3502	3522	3541	3560	3579	3598	2	4	6	8	10	12	14	15	17
23	3617	3636	3655	3674	3692	3711	3729	3747	3766	3784	2	4	6	7	9	11	13	15	17
24	3802	3820	3838	3856	3874	3892	3909	3927	3945	3962	2	4	5	7	9	11	12	14	16
25	3979	3997	4014	4031	4048	4065	4082	4099	4116	4133	2	3	5	7	9	10	12	14	15
26	4150	4166	4183	4200	4216	4232	4249	4265	4281	4298	2	3	5	7	8	10	11	13	15
27	4314	4330	4346	4362	4378	4393	4409	4425	4440	4456	2	3	5	6	8	9	11	13	14
28	4472	4487	4502	4518	4533	4548	4564	4579	4594	4609	2	3	5	6	8	9	11	12	14
29	4624	4639	4654	4669	4683	4698	4713	4728	4742	4757	1	3	4	6	7	9	10	12	13
30	4771	4786	4800	4814	4829	4843	4857	4871	4886	4900	1	3	4	6	7	9	10	11	13
31	4914	4928	4942	4955	4969	4983	4997	5011	5024	5038	1	3	4	6	7	8	10	11	12
32	5051	5065	5079	5092	5105	5119	5132	5145	5159	5172	1	3	4	5	7	8	9	11	12
33	5185	5198	5211	5224	5237	5250	5263	5276	5289	5302	1	3	4	5	6	8	9	10	11
34	5315	5328	5340	5353	5366	5378	5391	5403	5416	5428	1	3	4	5	6	8	9	10	11
35	5441	5453	5465	5478	5490	5502	5514	5527	5539	5551	1	2	4	5	6	7	9	10	11
36	5563	5575	5587	5599	5611	5623	5635	5647	5658	5670	1	2	4	5	6	7	8	10	11
37	5682	5694	5705	5717	5729	5740	5752	5763	5775	5786	1	2	3	5	6	7	8	9	10
38	5798	5809	5821	5832	5843	5855	5866	5877	5888	5899	1	2	3	5	6	7	8	9	10
39	5911	5922	5933	5944	5955	5966	5977	5988	5999	6010	1	2	3	4	5	7	8	9	10
40	6021	6031	6042	6053	6064	6075	6085	6096	6107	6117	1	2	3	4	5	6	8	9	10
41	6128	6138	6149	6160	6170	6180	6191	6201	6212	6222	1	2	3	4	5	6	7	8	9
42	6232	6243	6253	6263	6274	6284	6294	6304	6314	6325	1	2	3	4	5	6	7	8	9
43	6335	6345	6355	6365	6375	6385	6395	6405	6415	6425	1	2	3	4	5	6	7	8	9
44	6435	6444	6454	6464	6474	6484	6493	6503	6513	6522	1	2	3	4	5	6	7	8	9
45	6532	6542	6551	6561	6571	6580	6590	6599	6609	6618	1	2	3	4	5	6	7	8	9
46	6628	6637	6646	6656	6665	6675	6684	6693	6702	6712	1	2	3	4	5	6	7	7	8
47	6721	6730	6739	6749	6758	6767	6776	6785	6794	6803	1	2	3	4	5	5	6	7	8
48	6812	6821	6830	6839	6848	6857	6866	6875	6884	6893	1	2	3	4	4	5	6	7	8
49	6902	6911	6920	6928	6937	6946	6955	6964	6972	6981	1	2	3	4	4	5	6	7	8
50	6990	6998	7007	7016	7024	7033	7042	7050	7059	7067	1	2	3	3	4	5	6	7	8
51	7076	7084	7093	7101	7110	7118	7126	7135	7143	7152	1	2	3	3	4	5	6	7	8
52	7160	7168	7177	7185	7193	7202	7210	7218	7226	7235	1	2	2	3	4	5	6	7	8
53	7243	7251	7259	7267	7275	7284	7292	7300	7308	7316	1	2	2	3	4	5	6	6	7
54	7324	7332	7340	7348	7356	7364	7372	7380	7388	7396	1	2	2	3	4	5	6	6	7
	0	1	2	3	4	5	6	7	8	9	1	2	3	4	5	6	7	8	9

LOGARITHMS

	0	1	2	3	4	5	6	7	8	9	1	2	3	4	5	6	7	8	9
55	7404	7412	7419	7427	7435	7443	7451	7459	7466	7474	1	2	2	3	4	5	5	6	7
56	7482	7490	7497	7505	7513	7520	7528	7536	7543	7551	1	2	2	3	4	5	5	6	7
57	7559	7566	7574	7582	7589	7597	7604	7612	7619	7627	1	2	2	3	4	5	5	6	7
58	7634	7642	7649	7657	7664	7672	7679	7686	7694	7701	1	1	2	3	4	4	5	6	7
59	7709	7716	7723	7731	7738	7745	7752	7760	7767	7774	1	1	2	3	4	4	5	6	7
60	7782	7789	7796	7803	7810	7818	7825	7832	7839	7846	1	1	2	3	4	4	5	6	6
61	7853	7860	7868	7875	7882	7889	7896	7903	7910	7917	1	1	2	3	4	4	5	6	6
62	7924	7931	7938	7945	7952	7959	7966	7973	7980	7987	1	1	2	3	3	4	5	6	6
63	7993	8000	8007	8014	8021	8028	8035	8041	8048	8055	1	1	2	3	3	4	5	5	6
64	8062	8069	8075	8082	8089	8096	8102	8109	8116	8122	1	1	2	3	3	4	5	5	6
65	8129	8136	8142	8149	8156	8162	8169	8176	8182	8189	1	1	2	3	3	4	5	5	6
66	8195	8202	8209	8215	8222	8228	8235	8241	8248	8254	1	1	2	3	3	4	5	5	6
67	8261	8267	8274	8280	8287	8293	8299	8306	8312	8319	1	1	2	3	3	4	5	5	6
68	8325	8331	8338	8344	8351	8357	8363	8370	8376	8382	1	1	2	3	3	4	4	5	6
69	8388	8395	8404	8407	8414	8420	8426	8432	8439	8445	1	1	2	2	3	4	4	5	6
70	8451	8457	8463	8470	8476	8482	8488	8494	8500	8506	1	1	2	2	3	4	4	5	6
71	5513	8519	8525	8531	8537	8543	8549	8555	8561	8567	1	1	2	2	3	4	4	5	5
72	8573	8579	8585	8591	8597	8603	8609	8615	8621	8627	1	1	2	2	3	4	4	5	5
73	8633	8639	8645	8651	8657	8663	8669	8675	8681	8686	1	1	2	2	3	4	4	5	5
74	8692	8698	8704	8710	8716	8722	8727	8733	8739	8745	1	1	2	2	3	4	4	5	5
75	8751	8756	8762	8768	8774	8779	8785	8791	8797	8802	1	1	2	2	3	3	4	5	5
76	8808	8814	8820	8825	8831	8837	8842	8848	8854	8859	1	1	2	2	3	3	4	5	5
77	8865	8871	8876	8882	8887	8803	8899	8904	8910	8915	1	1	2	2	3	3	4	4	5
78	8921	8927	8932	8938	8943	8949	8954	8960	8965	8971	1	1	2	2	3	3	4	4	5
79	8976	8982	8987	8993	8998	9004	9009	9015	9020	9025	1	1	2	2	3	3	4	4	5
80	9031	9036	9042	9047	9053	9058	9063	9069	9074	9079	1	1	2	2	3	3	4	4	5
81	9085	9090	9096	9101	9106	9112	9117	9122	9128	9133	1	1	2	2	3	3	4	4	5
82	9138	9143	9149	9154	9159	9165	9170	9175	9180	9186	1	1	2	2	3	3	4	4	5
83	9191	9196	9201	9206	9212	9217	9222	9227	9232	9238	1	1	2	2	3	3	4	4	5
84	9243	9248	9253	9258	9263	9269	9274	9279	9284	9289	1	1	2	2	3	3	4	4	5
85	9294	9299	9304	9309	9315	9320	9325	9330	9335	9340	1	1	2	2	3	3	4	4	5
86	9345	9350	9355	9360	9365	9370	9375	9380	9385	9390	1	1	2	2	3	3	4	4	5
87	9395	9400	9405	9410	9415	9420	9425	9430	9435	9440	0	1	1	2	2	3	3	4	4
88	9445	9450	9455	9460	9465	9469	9474	9479	9484	9489	0	1	1	2	2	3	3	4	4
89	9491	9499	9504	9509	9513	9518	9523	9523	9533	9538	0	1	1	2	2	3	3	4	4
90	9542	9547	9552	9557	9562	9566	9571	9576	9581	9586	0	1	1	2	2	3	3	4	4
91	9590	9595	9600	9605	9609	9614	9619	9624	9628	9633	0	1	1	2	2	3	3	4	4
92	9638	9643	9647	9652	9657	9661	9666	9671	9675	9680	0	1	1	2	2	3	3	4	4
93	9685	9689	9694	9699	9703	9708	9713	9717	9722	9727	0	1	1	2	2	3	3	4	4
94	9731	9736	9741	9745	9750	9754	9759	9763	9768	9773	0	1	1	2	2	3	3	4	4
95	9777	9782	9786	9791	9795	9800	9805	9809	9814	9818	0	1	1	2	2	3	3	4	4
96	9823	9827	9832	9835	9841	9845	9850	9854	9859	9868	0	1	1	2	2	3	3	4	4
97	9868	9872	9877	9881	9886	9890	9894	9899	9903	9908	0	1	1	2	2	3	3	4	4
98	9912	9917	9921	9926	9930	9934	9939	9942	9948	9952	0	1	1	2	2	3	3	4	4
99	9956	9961	9965	9969	9974	9978	9983	9987	9991	9936	0	1	1	2	2	3	3	4	4
	0	1	2	3	4	5	6	7	8	9	1	2	3	4	5	6	7	8	9

ANTI-LOGARITHMS

	0	1	2	3	4	5	6	7	8	9	1	2	3	4	5	6	7	8	9
.00	1000	1002	1005	1007	1009	1012	1014	1016	1019	1021	0	0	1	1	1	1	2	2	2
.01	1023	1026	1028	1030	1033	1035	1038	1040	1042	1045	0	0	1	1	1	1	2	2	2
.02	1047	1050	1052	1054	1057	1059	1062	1064	1067	1069	0	0	1	1	1	1	2	2	2
.03	1072	1074	1076	1079	1081	1084	1086	1089	1091	1094	0	0	1	1	1	1	2	2	2
.04	1096	1099	1102	1104	1107	1109	1112	1114	1117	1119	0	1	1	1	1	2	2	2	2
.05	1122	1125	1127	1130	1132	1135	1138	1140	1143	1146	0	1	1	1	1	2	2	2	2
.06	1148	1151	1153	1156	1159	1161	1164	1167	1169	1172	0	1	1	1	1	2	2	2	2
.07	1175	1178	1180	1183	1186	1189	1191	1194	1197	1199	0	1	1	1	1	2	2	2	2
.08	1202	1205	1208	1211	1213	1216	1219	1222	1225	1227	0	1	1	1	1	2	2	2	3
.09	1230	1233	1236	1239	1242	1245	1247	1250	1253	1256	0	1	1	1	1	2	2	2	3
.10	1259	1262	1265	1268	1271	1274	1276	1279	1282	1285	0	1	1	1	1	2	2	2	3
.11	1288	1291	1294	1297	1300	1303	1306	1309	1312	1315	0	1	1	1	2	2	2	2	3
.12	1318	1321	1324	1327	1330	1334	1337	1340	1343	1346	0	1	1	1	2	2	2	2	3
.13	1349	1352	1355	1358	1361	1365	1368	1371	1374	1377	0	1	1	1	2	2	2	3	3
.14	1380	1384	1387	1390	1393	1396	1400	1403	1406	1409	0	1	1	1	2	2	2	3	3
.15	1413	1416	1419	1422	1426	1429	1432	1435	1439	1442	0	1	1	1	2	2	2	3	3
.16	1445	1449	1452	1455	1459	1462	1466	1469	1472	1476	0	1	1	1	2	2	2	3	3
.17	1479	1483	1486	1489	1493	1496	1500	1503	1507	1510	0	1	1	1	2	2	2	3	3
.18	1514	1517	1521	1524	1528	1531	1535	1538	1542	1545	0	1	1	1	2	2	2	3	3
.19	1549	1552	1556	1560	1563	1567	1570	1574	1578	1581	0	1	1	1	2	2	3	3	3
.20	1585	1589	1592	1596	1600	1603	1607	1611	1614	1618	0	1	1	1	2	2	3	3	3
.21	1622	1626	1629	1633	1637	1641	1644	1648	1652	1656	0	1	1	2	2	2	3	3	3
.22	1660	1663	1667	1671	1675	1679	1683	1687	1690	1694	0	1	1	2	2	2	3	3	3
.23	1698	1702	1706	1710	1714	1718	1772	1726	1730	1734	0	1	1	2	2	2	3	3	4
.24	1738	1742	1746	1750	1754	1758	1762	1766	1770	1774	0	1	1	2	2	2	3	3	4
.25	1778	1782	1786	1791	1795	1799	1803	1807	1811	1816	0	1	1	2	2	2	3	3	4
.26	1820	1824	1828	1832	1837	1841	1845	1849	1854	1858	0	1	1	2	2	3	3	3	4
.27	1862	1866	1871	1875	1879	1884	1888	1892	1897	1901	0	1	1	2	2	3	3	3	4
.28	1905	1910	1914	1919	1923	1928	1932	1936	1941	1945	0	1	1	2	2	3	3	4	4
.29	1950	1954	1959	1963	1968	1972	1977	1982	1986	1991	0	1	1	2	2	3	3	4	4
.30	1995	2000	2004	2009	2014	2018	2023	2028	2032	2037	0	1	1	2	2	3	3	4	4
.31	2042	2046	2051	2056	2061	2065	2070	2075	2080	2084	0	1	1	2	2	3	3	4	4
.32	2089	2094	2099	2104	2109	2113	2118	2123	2128	2133	0	1	1	2	2	3	3	4	4
.33	2138	2143	2148	2153	2158	2163	2168	2173	2178	2183	0	1	1	2	2	3	3	4	4
.34	2188	2193	2198	2203	2208	2213	2218	2223	2228	2234	1	1	2	2	3	3	4	4	5
.35	2239	2244	2249	2254	2259	2265	2270	2275	2280	2286	1	1	2	2	3	3	4	4	5
.36	2291	2296	2301	2307	2312	2317	2323	2328	2333	2339	1	1	2	2	3	3	4	4	5
.37	2344	2350	2355	2360	2366	2371	2377	2382	2388	2393	1	1	2	2	3	3	4	4	5
.38	2399	2404	2410	2415	2421	2427	2432	2438	2443	2449	1	1	2	2	3	3	4	4	5
.39	2455	2460	2466	2472	2477	2483	2489	2495	2500	2506	1	1	2	2	3	3	4	5	5
.40	2512	2518	2523	2529	2535	2541	2547	2553	2559	2564	1	1	2	2	3	4	4	5	5
.41	2570	2576	2582	2588	2594	2600	2606	2612	2618	2624	1	1	2	2	3	4	4	4	5
.42	2630	2636	2642	2649	2655	2661	2667	2673	2679	2685	1	1	2	2	3	4	4	5	6
.43	2692	2698	2704	2710	2716	2723	2729	2735	2742	2748	1	1	2	3	3	4	4	5	6
.44	2754	2761	2767	2773	2780	2786	2793	2799	2805	2812	1	1	2	3	3	4	4	5	6
.45	2818	2825	2831	2838	2844	2851	2858	2864	2871	2877	1	1	2	3	3	4	5	5	6
.46	2884	2891	2897	2904	2911	2917	2924	2931	2938	2944	1	1	2	3	3	4	5	5	6
.47	2951	2958	2965	2972	2979	2985	2992	2999	3006	3013	1	1	2	3	3	4	5	5	6
.48	3020	3027	3034	3041	3048	3055	3062	3069	3076	3083	1	1	2	3	4	4	5	6	6
.49	3090	3097	3105	3112	3119	3126	3133	3141	3148	3155	1	1	2	3	4	4	5	6	6
	0	1	2	3	4	5	6	7	8	9	1	2	3	4	5	6	7	8	9

ANTI-LOGARITHMS

	0	1	2	3	4	5	6	7	8	9	1	2	3	4	5	6	7	8	9
.50	3162	3170	3177	3181	3192	3199	3206	3214	3221	3228	1	1	2	3	4	4	5	6	7
.51	3235	3243	3251	3258	3266	3273	3281	3289	3296	3304	1	2	2	3	4	5	5	6	7
.52	3311	3319	3327	3334	3342	3350	3357	3365	3373	3381	1	2	2	3	4	5	5	6	7
.53	3388	3396	3404	3412	3420	3428	3436	3443	3451	3459	1	2	2	3	4	5	5	6	7
.54	3467	3475	3483	3491	3499	3508	3516	3524	3532	3540	1	2	2	3	4	5	6	6	7
.55	3548	3556	3565	3573	3581	3589	3597	3606	3614	3622	1	2	2	3	4	5	6	6	7
.56	3631	3639	3648	3656	3664	3673	3681	3690	3698	3707	1	2	3	3	4	5	6	7	8
.57	3715	3724	3733	3741	3750	3758	3767	3776	3784	3793	1	2	3	3	4	5	6	7	8
.58	3802	3811	3819	3828	3837	3846	3855	3864	3873	3882	1	2	3	4	4	5	6	7	8
.59	3890	3899	3908	3917	3926	3936	3945	3954	3963	3972	1	2	3	4	5	5	6	7	8
.60	3981	3990	3999	4009	4018	4027	4036	4046	4055	4064	1	2	3	4	5	6	6	7	8
.61	4074	4083	4093	4102	4111	4121	4130	4140	4150	4159	1	2	3	4	5	6	7	8	9
.62	4169	4178	4188	4198	4207	4217	4227	4236	4246	4256	1	2	3	4	5	6	7	8	9
.63	4266	4276	4285	4295	4305	4315	4325	4335	4345	4355	1	2	3	4	5	6	7	8	9
.64	4365	4375	4385	4395	4406	4416	4426	4436	4446	4457	1	2	3	4	5	6	7	8	9
.65	4467	4477	4487	4498	4508	4519	4529	4539	4550	4560	1	2	3	4	5	6	7	8	9
.66	4571	4581	4592	4603	4613	4624	4634	4645	4656	4667	1	2	3	4	5	6	7	9	10
.67	4677	4688	4699	4710	4721	4732	4742	4753	4764	4775	1	2	3	4	5	7	8	9	10
.68	4786	4797	4808	4819	4831	4842	4853	4864	4875	4887	1	2	3	5	6	7	8	9	10
.69	4898	4909	4920	4932	4943	4955	4966	4977	4989	5000	1	2	3	5	6	7	8	9	10
.70	5012	5023	5035	5047	5058	5070	5082	5093	5105	5117	1	2	4	5	6	7	8	9	11
.71	5129	5140	5152	5164	5176	5188	5200	5212	5224	5236	1	2	4	5	6	7	8	10	11
.72	5248	5260	5272	5284	5297	5309	5321	5333	5346	5358	1	2	4	5	6	7	9	10	11
.73	5370	5383	5395	5408	5420	5433	5445	5458	5470	5483	1	3	4	5	6	8	9	10	11
.74	5495	5508	5521	5534	5546	5559	5572	5585	5598	5610	1	3	4	5	6	8	9	10	12
.75	5623	5636	5649	5662	5675	5689	5702	5715	5728	5741	1	3	4	5	7	8	9	10	12
.76	5754	5768	5781	5794	5808	5821	5834	5848	5861	5875	1	3	4	5	7	8	9	11	12
.77	5888	5902	5916	5929	5943	5957	5970	5984	5998	6012	1	3	4	5	7	8	10	11	12
.78	6026	6039	6053	6067	6081	6095	6109	6124	6138	6152	1	3	4	6	7	8	10	11	13
.79	6166	6180	6194	6209	6223	6237	6252	6266	6281	6295	1	3	4	6	7	9	10	11	13
.80	6310	6324	6339	6353	6368	6383	6397	6412	6427	6442	1	3	4	6	7	9	10	12	13
.81	6457	6471	6486	6501	6516	6531	6546	6561	6577	6592	2	3	5	6	8	9	11	12	14
.82	6607	6622	6637	6653	6668	6683	6699	6714	6730	6745	2	3	5	6	8	9	11	12	14
.83	6761	6776	6792	6808	6823	6839	6855	6871	6887	6902	2	3	5	6	8	9	11	13	14
.84	6918	6934	6950	6966	6982	6998	7015	7031	7047	7063	2	3	5	6	8	10	11	13	15
.85	7019	7096	7112	7129	7145	7161	7178	7194	7211	7228	2	3	5	7	8	10	12	13	15
.86	7244	7261	7278	7295	7311	7328	7345	7362	7379	7396	2	3	5	7	8	10	12	13	15
.87	7413	7430	7447	7464	7482	7499	7516	7534	7551	7568	2	3	5	7	9	10	12	14	16
.88	7586	7603	7621	7638	7656	7674	7691	7709	7727	7745	2	4	5	7	9	11	12	14	16
.89	7762	7780	7798	7816	7834	7852	7870	7889	7907	7925	2	4	5	7	9	11	13	14	16
.90	7943	7962	7980	7998	8017	8035	8054	8072	8091	8110	2	4	6	7	9	11	13	15	17
.91	8128	8147	8166	8185	8204	8222	8241	8260	8279	8299	2	4	6	8	9	11	13	15	17
.92	8318	8337	8356	8375	8395	8414	8433	8453	8472	8492	2	4	6	8	10	12	14	15	17
.93	8511	8531	8551	8570	8590	8610	8630	8650	8670	8690	2	4	6	8	10	12	14	16	18
.94	8710	8730	8750	8770	8790	8810	8831	8851	8872	8892	2	4	6	8	10	12	14	16	18
.95	8913	8933	8954	8974	8995	9016	9036	9057	9078	9099	2	4	6	8	10	12	15	17	19
.96	9120	9141	9162	9183	9204	9226	9247	9268	9290	9311	2	4	6	8	11	13	15	17	19
.97	9333	9354	9376	9397	9419	9441	9462	9484	9506	9528	2	5	7	9	11	13	15	17	20
.98	9550	9572	9594	9616	9638	9661	9683	9705	9727	9750	2	5	7	9	11	13	16	18	20
.99	9772	9795	9817	9840	9863	9886	9908	9931	9954	9977	2	5	7	9	11	14	16	18	20
	0	1	2	3	4	5	6	7	8	9	1	2	3	4	5	6	7	8	9